I0834849

The Consummation.

THE FREEMASON'S MANUAL

OR

ILLUSTRATIONS OF MASONRY

CONTAINING, IN ADDITION TO THE RITES SANCTIONED

BY THE

UNITED GRAND LODGE AND GRAND CHAPTER OF ENGLAND AND WALES,

THE MARK AND MARK MASTER

A FULL ACCOUNT OF ALL THE DEGREES INCLUDED

IN THE ANCIENT AND ACCEPTED RITE

AND THE

KNIGHTS TEMPLAR DEGREE

WITH BRIEF NOTICES OF ALL THE RITES PROFESSING TO BE

CONNECTED WITH FREEMASONRY

BY

JEREMIAH HOW

Past Master of Lodge Nos. 82 and 661; P.Z. of Chapters 593 and 661;
Prov. Grand Director of Ceremonies of Hertfordshire;
P.E.C. of the Royal and Exalted Order of Masonic Knights Templar;
Sov. Prince of Rose-Croix Heredom, and Grand Elected Knight Kadosh.

STONE GUILD PUBLISHING
PLANO, TEXAS
HTTP://WWW.STONEGUILDPUBLISHING.COM/

2009

Originally Published By:
Simpkin, Marshall, and Co.
Stationers' Hall Court, London
1862

Plano, Texas
http://www.stoneguildpublishing.com/

First Paperback Edition 2009

ISBN-13 978-1-60532-052-6
ISBN-10 1-60532-052-8

10 9 8 7 6 5 4 3 2

PREFACE.

ON commencing his undertaking, the Editor intended to have adopted the title of Brother Preston's work, with such additions as English Masonry demands; but as the "Illustrations of Masonry" has, since the volume was put to press, been reproduced, it was but just to abandon the title originally proposed.

To comprehend the entire system of the Institution, a thorough acquaintance with the Volume of the Sacred Law, or Holy Scriptures, and a full appreciation of the Book which contains the treasures of God's revealed will, are essential.

Its aim and end throughout all time has been to incite men to acts of kindness to their fellows; it recognizes no sect or creed in Craft Masonry, which is universal, but it requires an acknowledgment of the true and living God Most High.

The first great doctrines held in sacred veneration by the Order are the existence of God and the immortality of the soul, pointing its votaries to that clouded canopy where all good Masons trust eventually to arrive, by Faith in God, Hope in immortality, and Charity towards man.

The next prominent doctrine is unity of mankind; it levels all those distinctions which wealth has created, making no difference but personal merit. In a Masons' Lodge the noblest peer of the realm, and the poorest peasant that tills the soil, the minister who serves at God's altar, the father of venerable age, and the young man in the prime of life, all meet on equal ground, hailing each other as "Brother!" At his first step, the Mason has impressed upon his mind the practice of moral and social duties—his duty to his God, his neighbours, and himself; and to be, in whatever land he may dwell, a quiet and peaceable citizen. These precepts of Craft Masonry are more strongly enforced in the Ineffable Degrees, which are but an extension of the former.

A considerable portion of the illustrations of Craft Masonry is derived from Preston's work, but all beyond the three degrees is for the first time presented in a consecutive form. The importance attached to the degrees under the Ancient and Accepted Rite, as well as the Templar Degree, and the vast annual increase of their recipients, equally required illustration.

Two of the degrees, now a part of the Ancient and Accepted Rite—viz., the Eighteenth and Thirtieth—are of long standing, and for a considerable period have been practised in England; and by the good management of the Supreme Council are now firmly established. The support which the Rite receives from the highly educated Brethren of the learned professions has unquestionably been a means of retaining many as active members of the Fraternity who might otherwise—as their predecessors aforetime—have ceased Membership of Lodges.

It is not to be overlooked that the teaching of the Degrees in this Rite—that are practised—is but an expansion of that of the Symbolic Degrees; and that the great principles upon which our Order is founded—BROTHERLY LOVE, RELIEF, and TRUTH—obtain their Consummation in the Cardinal Virtues of FAITH, HOPE, and CHARITY.

With reference to the Degrees referred to and their origin, it may be observed that the transmission of the Institution, by whatever names it has borne, as a secret Society, is by many, and with some reason, traced from the Egyptian mysteries, through Persia and Greece, thence by the Manichæans, Paulicians, Albigenses, and Troubadours, to the poets of the middle ages, as Dante, Boccaccio, and men of science, as Porta; and in one of the earliest printed books of the Continent, dated 1495, any one who has a key to the cyphers it contains will readily see the Rose-Croix is referred to. Rosetti's work on the Antipapal Spirit which produced the Reformation, throws considerable light on the Secret Societies of the middle ages.

During the middle ages, when the light of learning was confined to the ecclesiastics, the papal power, following the system adopted by Gregory VII., of keeping the human mind in darkness, prevented as far as possible the spread of knowledge, except theology and medicine: many of these learned priests united in the study of what was termed *occult philosophy,* which was a search after some secret hitherto unknown, and, as Rosicrucians, professed to be engaged in discovering the art of transmuting metals, when in fact it was *the Truth* of which they were in search. That they succeeded in concealing their real object is proved by their printed books, which, without a key, are unintelligible even now, and must have been equally so at the time of their production, when the darkness of ignorance covered the earth. The ceremonies of the secret schools were derived from the ancient mysteries of Egypt, Persia, and Greece. "Dante's grand poem can only be understood by those initiated in the history of the time. It is a disguised paraphrase of the Revelation, written in the same allegorical language, but applied to a political design. To the generality of readers, of course, this language is an enigma; but the very small number who can read it in its double sense, and enter into the spirit of a volume which is written *within and without,* in imitation of Ezekiel and St. John, have thereby entered into the *realm of spirits,* and can comprehend works without number, which differ from each other in nothing but the title. Allegorically speaking;—he who once breaks the seven seals of this fast-closed volume, may afterwards open every seal imposed by the jealous Order who forged them, and enter into the knowledge of things which the wise man is not permitted to manifest openly." "*Apuleius,* describing his initiation into the Egyptian mysteries, narrates that, after *he had touched the gates of death,* and *the interior courts of the queen of eternal woe* (exactly Dante's case), he returned to life, and then celebrated the happy day of his birth." *Rosetti.*

Darwin (Botanic Garden, note xxii.) affirms that the Eleusinian mysteries consisted of scenical exhibitions, representing and inculcating the expectation of a future life after death.

"Among our ancient brethren the initiated were supposed to be born again, and put on a new life. The fables which describe Bacchus, Orpheus, Hercules, Theseus, Ulysses, and Æneas, descending into hell, and then returning to earth again, appear to signify those persons were *regenerate,* according to the Roman system. This new life is the *Vita Nuova* of Dante." *Rosetti.*

In a note on a character introduced in one of the mystical Italian poems called a *Widow,* Rosetti says that the sect of the Knights of St. John, founded by Gerard, called themselves *the Sons of the Widow.*

The Templar Degree, which for a long period has been in practice with the Fraternity in England, and been considered a step beyond the Royal Arch, also retains its members even when they may have relinquished attendance on Craft Masonry. The Encampments which are scattered wide throughout the realm, prove the encouragement given to the Degrees which have a bearing on Christianity. So also the Mark Master has its illustrations drawn from the Book of the New Covenant: altogether showing that Freemasonry, like every other institution, necessarily has its colouring from age to age.

The end and object of the Editor is to make Freemasonry more fully understood by those who have been admitted into its temples; and should any of the outer world take it up to while away an hour, a better appreciation of the truths it promulgates may be obtained, and Freemasonry be acknowledged to be something more than a name.

Rose Cottage, Blackstock Lane,
Seven Sisters' Road, London, N.

CONTENTS.

ILLUSTRATIONS.

ILLUSTRATIONS OF MASONRY.

CHAPTER I.

ON THE ANCIENT MYSTERIES OR ASSOCIATIONS ANALOGOUS TO FREEMASONRY, FROM THE EARLIEST AGES TO THE SUBVERSION OF THE ROMAN EMPIRE BY THE GOTHS.

"Although the origin of our fraternity is clouded with darkness, and its history is, to a great extent, obscure, yet we can confidently say that it is the most ancient society in the world; and we are equally certain that its principles are based on pure morality—that its ethics are the ethics of Christianity—its doctrines, the doctrines of patriotism and brotherly love—and its sentiments, the sentiments of exalted benevolence. Upon these points there can be no doubt. All that is good, and kind, and charitable it encourages—all that is vicious, and cruel, and oppressive it reprobates." —DE WITT CLINTON, *Governor of the State of New York,* 1824.

IN entering upon the task of endeavouring to illustrate and explain the ceremonies and symbols of Freemasonry, the author does not profess to present any novelties, but only to bring together the results of the labours of others in a clear and readable form,—as a text-book for the Brethren to dilate upon in their various Lodges, for the instruction of the younger members of the Craft. In writing upon our ceremonies and mysteries great caution must, of course, be at all times used, lest we should go too far, and lay bare to those who are not members of the Order, secrets only to be divulged to the Brethren, and then only under circumstances well understood by Masons.

The object being to illustrate the different degrees of Freemasonry, it may naturally be expected that some conjectures should be offered as to its origin. None of the ancient historians furnish us with actual testimony on this point; oral tradition of the Fraternity refers us to the East, and traces its rise to King Solomon; but there are traces of some such institutions long before that time.

The institution of Freemasonry undoubtedly must have been framed by a people who had made considerable advance in science. The Egyptians, in the time of Moses, were proficient in all the arts and sciences, as the gigantic works constructed in those early ages, still existing, prove. Their language was mystical, and their priests secured the mysteries of their religion from the knowledge of the vulgar or uninitiated by symbols and hieroglyphics comprehensible alone to those of their order. We are told that the fraternity of ancient Egypt was denominated the Hiero-Laotomi, or sacred builders. They were a selected first caste, and connected with the government and priesthood, being, in fact, Masons of the priestly order; whilst the ordinary Masons or artificers were of an inferior caste. Champollion says: "A theocracy or government of priests was the first known to the Egyptians, and it is necessary to give the word *priests* the acceptation that it bore in ancient times, when the ministers of religion were also the ministers of science and learning; so that they united in their own persons two of the noblest missions with which men could be invested—the worship of the Deity, and the cultivation of science." The intent and purpose of those stupendous fabrics, the pyramids, was a great mystery, and a mystery they still remain. All authorities who have investigated the subject concur in fixing the age of these piles at 4000 years. Many of the works of this ancient nation now in the British Museum, are of equal, if not greater age, and their execution is marvellous.

Moses was initiated into the secrets and mysteries of the

priestly order when in Egypt, and some have imagined that the Hebrews assisted in the construction of the pyramids; but in all probability these wondrous efforts of Masonic skill were hoary with age when the children of Israel settled in the land of Goshen, and were emblems of sublime truths to a civilized nation when Abraham was a wanderer in the wilderness.

By Egyptian colonists, according to our biblical chronology, the arts were carried to Greece two or three centuries before the age of Moses.

By the Israelites the arts of building were conveyed to the promised land; and when they became a settled people, the remembrance of the beautiful fabrics they had seen in Egypt led them to attempt constructions suited to their future home. But it is evident that by the death of their great master, Moses, the Israelites were not in full possession of the knowledge requisite to complete the glorious fabric which the G.A.O.T.U. had in a vision to King David directed his son Solomon to erect; as we find by Holy Writ, that "the wisest man" needed the assistance of the King of Tyre. Tyre and Sidon were the chief cities of the Phoenicians: the latter boasts an antiquity anterior to any other whose site can be determined. It was a place of considerable importance in the time of Joshua, who speaks of it as "great Sidon." Hence it is evident that the Phoenicians were far advanced in the arts of life when the Israelites reached the promised land. *Homer* frequently mentions the Sidonians. All superior articles of dress, all good workmanship, and all ingenious trinkets and toys are ascribed by him to the skill and industry of the Sidonians. These people were great adepts in the sciences of their time, particularly astronomy and arithmetical calculation. The Phoenicians were an industrious people, and their cities were the emporia of commerce,—commercial communities having ever been the best promoters of the arts and sciences. They have the reputation of being the inventors of scarlet and purple dyes; and the buildings of Tyre were very magnificent, the walls being 150 feet high. From this city, with materials to assist King Solomon in eructing his temple, came, by order of his sovereign master, *Hiram,* the widow's son. The Israelites also formed among the Chaldeans, in after intercourse, a more extensive acquaintance with one science—astronomy—than they themselves were possessed of; and this science, we all know, can only be approached by a long study of mathematical formulas.

Among the most remarkable men of the early ages of the world, ZOROASTER, in science and knowledge—and Bacon says, "Knowledge is power"—must have foremost rank. Of Zoroaster, so called by the Greeks, or Zerdusht, as the Persians render his name, the Orientalists have the most extravagant statements. His history, when divested of all extraneous matter, can be reduced to this account. He appeared in Persia or Iran about 550 B.C., and with remarkable rapidity established a new faith. The ancient religion which Djamshid had established in Persia had lost its influence over the people, and new sects sprung up in every direction when Zoroaster appeared. He taught that God existed from all eternity, and was alike infinity of time or space. There were, he affirmed, two principles in the universe—good and evil: the one termed Ormuzd, or the good principle (God himself), the presiding agent of all good; the other, Ariman (the devil), the lord of evil. God, the creator of all things, has produced light and darkness; and from the composition of these two—of generation and corruption—the composition and decomposition of the parts of the world are affected. There is an admixture of good and evil in every thing created. The angels of Ormuzd sought to preserve the elements, the seasons, and the human race, which the spirits of Ariman wished to destroy; but the power of good was eternal, and therefore must prevail. Light was the type of the good spirit; darkness of the evil spirit. Hence the Magian or Guebre, the disciple of Zoroaster, when he performs his devotions, turns to the sacred fire upon the altar, or towards the sun when in the open air, as the light by which God sheds his Divine influence over the whole, and perpetuates the works of creation.

The principles of the ancient Magi, and the adherents to fireworship, are handed down to us in the Zend-Avesta, which is attributed to Zoroaster; and the chief doctrine inculcated and to be noticed is the eternity and self-existence of the Supreme Deity, whose ineffable attributes are emphatically celebrated. Prayer is to be made to Light, or Fire,—not as being themselves deities, but as conveying the sacrifice to Divine Intelligence.

The original purity of the religion of Zoroaster soon became corrupted, and it gradually sank into a mere idolatrous worship of the sun and fire; and driven out of Persia by the Mohammedans, fled to the mountains, and at last left the country. They finally settled in Guzerat, in Hindostan, where they are to this day.

Zoroaster's fame has been transmitted to us as an astrologer and magician, and we are told that he communicated his knowledge by slow degrees. Porphyrius states that Darius was so proud of having been initiated into the mysteries of the art by Zoroaster himself, that he ordered the fact to be engraven on his tomb. We are also told that Pythagoras derived his system from the Persian philosopher.

There is considerable disagreement as to the era in which this philosopher flourished. *Huet* (Demonstratio Evangelica) identifies him with Moses; *Abulfaraj,* the celebrated Arabian historian, says he was the servant of the prophet Elijah; *Abu-Mohammed* says he was servant to Ezra, and that he foretold to his Magians the coming of the Messiah, and that at the time of his birth there should appear a wonderful star, and left a command that when that star should appear, they should follow the direction of it, and go to the place and offer gifts and adoration to the Child. *Hyde* (Veterum Persarum et Magorum Religionis Historia) refers to his being a native of Palestine, and supposes him to have been Esdras; and *Prideaux,* who bestows considerable space to Zoroaster's history, says he is convinced he was a Jew by birth as well as religion, and that he served one of the disciples of the prophet Jeremiah, and is led to conclude it was Daniel he served. Now, as all the authorities of any value coincide in the Persian reformer being well skilled in all the learning of the East, and that he was thoroughly versed in the Jewish religion and in all the sacred writings of the Israelitish people then extant, he could have been no common man to have been possessed of all this knowledge, which must have been confined to the priests and scribes. He was, doubtless, either carried to Babylon when an infant, among other captives to the Medes, or born in their land. Daniel was taken there when very young, and was early chosen to reside at the court of the sovereign. Inspiration enabled him to interpret the remarkable dream of Nebuchadnezzar, and as a reward, he was made governor of Babylon, and chief of the Magi. His explanation of Belshazzar's vision established his fame, and Darius, the Mede, promoted him above all the other governors. The envy and jealousy of persons in authority being excited by his advancement, he was thrust into a den of lions; but being found unhurt, Darius ordered him to be released and restored to his favour.

Daniel remained in Persia, and is supposed to have died at Susa (*Ulai,* c. viii.), the capital. *Benjamin of Tudela* says his monument was shown to him at that place, A.D. 1160.

The ancient Persians were fire-worshippers, and Zoroaster, in reforming their religion, accomplished his object without disturbing their prejudices. The fire he preserved, and derived authority for it from the law of Moses (*Levit.* ix. 24). His doctrine for its use was not on the same grounds as the Persians previously held. Fire is often used in the Holy Scriptures as a symbol of the Deity: "For the Lord thy God is a consuming fire" (*Deut.* iv. 24). And God appeared to Moses in the burning bush, and led the Israelites through the wilderness by a pillar of fire. The sacred fire on the altar was kept perpetually burning, by God's command; and therefore it would be just as reasonable to charge the ancient Hebrews as being worshippers of fire as the ancient Persians, because they kept it burning in their temples.

With reference to the next point in the religious system propounded to the Persians, we may remark, that when the prophet Isaiah (chap. xi. 6, 7), in speaking of Cyrus, and God's charge to that monarch, says, "I am the Lord, and there is none else: I form the light and create darkness; I make peace and create evil," this is quite consistent with what Zoroaster taught: we have no right to make any observations on what fire-worship was before his time, or how it has become corrupted since. We think there is the strongest evidence that this great philosopher taught only that which the law of Moses sanctioned, and that he was possessed of some authority to enable him to propagate his faith. He did not urge his religion by the sword, as Mohammed did, and hence we may ask, what was his position? A mean man he could not be, and we venture to suggest he could be no other than the prophet Daniel.

We have been thus discursive, as many writers on Freemasonry point to Persia and the Magian religion for its origin, and numerous illustrations are brought forward in proof. All difficulty, we think, is cleared away, and its derivation from the Israelites is established, and this was part of the mysteries of the Magians, and which they dispersed throughout the world.

Mohammedanism being the state religion of Persia, there are but few followers of the ancient religion in that country. At Bombay, the Parsees, as they are designated in India, are a rich and powerful class, and they are proprietors of the greater part of the island. They are generous and splendid in the higher orders, and in the lower ranks of life industrious and intelligent; in both surpassing Hindoos or Mohammedans. It is also worthy of remark that their private conduct in all relations of life is such as to cause a blush on the Englishman's face when the immoral and irreligious habits of his own countrymen are contrasted with those of the Parsees. It is some testimony for the simple faith taught by Zoroaster, that after twenty-four centuries his followers are the most peaceable, most orderly, and most humane among the subjects of the British Crown in India; the truly Masonic virtues of charity and beneficence are their constant practice: many Parsees are numbered among the Fraternity.

Rosetti, in his "Disquisitions on the Anti-papal Spirit of the Secret Societies that produced the Reformation," traces the Institution of Freemasonry to the ancient mysteries of Persia. *Mani,* who was a native of that country, and well acquainted with the doctrines and secret practices of the Magi, attempted to amalgamate the Persian religion with Christianity. For this he was put to death by the King. It is not certain at what date he lived, but his doctrines were introduced into Europe in the third century.

The Manichæans believed, like the Magi, in two eternal principles, from which all things proceed, namely, light and darkness, which are respectively subject to the dominion of two beings, one the God of good, and the other the god of evil. They also believed that the first parents of the human race were created by the god of darkness, with corrupt and mortal bodies, but that their souls formed part of that eternal light which was subject to the God of light. They maintained that it was the great object of the government of the God of light to deliver the captive souls of men from their corporeal prisons; and that with this view he created two sublime beings, Christ and the Holy Spirit, and sent Christ into the world, clothed with the shadowy form of a human body, and not with the real substance, to teach mortals how to deliver the rational soul from the corrupt body, and to overcome the power of malignant matter. They believed that Mani was the Comforter whom Jesus promises "should lead them into all truth." They denied the doctrine of the resurrection, and rejected the authority of the Old Testament; and Mani asserted that the books of the New Testament were interpolated and falsified.

The disciples of Mani were divided into two classes, one of which was called the Elect, and the other Hearers. The former were bound to abstain from animal food, wine, and all sensual enjoyments: the latter were not bound to these severities. The ecclesiastical constitution consisted of twelve apostles and a president who represented Christ, seventy-two bishops, who represented the seventy-two disciples of Christ; they had also presbyters and deacons.

The Paulicians, a branch of the Manichæans, appeared in the seventh century in Armenia, and derived their name from Paul their teacher. They were protected by the Emperor Constantine, and in the eleventh and twelfth centuries spread their doctrines over France and Italy.

Among the eminent Greek Philosophers who were impressed with the advanced state of knowledge to which the Egyptians and others had arrived, we may especially notice PYTHAGORAS, who flourished some 500 years B.C.; for we find that he visited those countries, gained the confidence of the priests, and learned from them the symbolic language by which their proceedings were guarded, which, at the same time, concealed the artful policy by which they governed princes as well as people. On his way to Egypt he visited Phoenicia, and was initiated by the priests into their mysteries. He also visited the noted cities of Greece; and, after an absence of many years, settled at Crotona, and taught his doctrines. According to Aristotle, the "Pythagoreans were the first who determined any thing in moral philosophy. Their ethics were of the loftiest and most spiritual description: virtue was with them a harmony, unity, and an endeavour to resemble the Deity: the whole life of man should be an attempt to represent on earth the beauty and harmony displayed in the order of the universe: the mind should have the body and passions under perfect control: the gods should be worshipped by simple purifications, offerings, and, above all, by sincerity and purity of heart." From Diogenes Laertius we learn that the society was at once philosophical, a religious brotherhood, and a political association, whose proceedings were transacted in the greatest secrecy—perhaps more on account of the religious doctrines inculcated than of its political principles. Religion, indeed, seems to have been the foundation of the society. Pythagoras instituted among his disciples secret worship, or mysteries, and they were also taught the science of numbers, geometry, and music. The various discoveries in mathematics, music, and astronomy, that are ascribed to Pythagoras, are proofs of the mighty impression which he made on his contemporaries, as well as on after ages. From the great respect which he paid to geometry, all Masons have ever hailed him as an ancient Brother; and certainly his system is a close approximation to the science of Freemasonry. He is said to have been instructed in the sacred things of the Hebrews by either Daniel or Ezekiel during the Babylonish captivity. The symbols adopted by Pythagoras, in his secret instruction, are said to have been principally derived from Geometry; among them may be noticed what are sometimes termed the five Platonic bodies,—viz., the *right angle,* an emblem of morality and justice; the *equilateral triangle,* a symbol of God, the essence of light and truth; the *square,* an emblem of the divine mind; the *cube,* the symbol of the mind of man; and the *dodecahedron,* a symbol of the universe.

The institutions of this great philosopher resembled the Masonic system in many respects. His assemblies were arranged due east and west, because, he said, motion began in the east and proceeded to the west. He adopted a system of signs whereby his disciples, dispersed through various countries, made themselves known to each other at first sight, and became as familiar at their first interview as if they had been acquainted from their birth; and so closely, says Iamblicus, were their interests united, that many of them passed over seas and risked their fortune to re-establish that of one of their brethren who had fallen into distress.

Various aphorisms and pointed replies are ascribed to Pythagoras, as we learn from *Diogenes Laertius,* such as the following:—

What is the most ancient of beings?—God, for he is uncreated. What the most beautiful?—The Universe, for it is the work of God. What the most extensive?—Space, for it contains all things. What the most rapid?—Wind, for it traverses all things. What the most powerful?—Necessity, for it prevails over all things. How shall we live most virtuously and justly?—If we refuse to do ourselves what we reprehend in others. Who is happy?—He who possesses a sound body, competence of fortune, and a mind disposed to receive instruction.

Toland says, "The Pythagorean philosophers concealed their sentiments of the nature of things under the veil of Divine allegories; lest, being accused of impiety by the priests (which often happened), they might be exposed in their turn to the hatred, if not the fury, of the vulgar."

We do not deem it necessary in this place to institute an inquiry into the Eleusinian mysteries, or, to any extent, the Dionysia. We find that a colony of Greeks from Attica settled in Asia Minor, and united the district under the name of Ionia, where they introduced the mysteries of Dionysia, as they existed before they were corrupted by the Athenians. We are indebted to these Dionysian artificers—an association which possessed the exclusive privilege of erecting temples, theatres, &c.—for many splendid buildings, including the magnificent temple at Teos. This Ionic fraternity had words and signs by which they could recognize each other, and, like Freemasons, they were divided into Lodges, which were distinguished by different appellations.

As the Dionysia were instituted four hundred years before Solomon's time, we have every right to maintain the tradition of our Order, that it flourished at the building of the temple. *Josephus* tells us that the Grecian style of architecture was that adopted in building the temple; and it may be inferred that these Dionysiac Masons assisted in raising that magnificent fabric.

In the disastrous wars of the Jews, before and during the captivity, all social order must have been destroyed, and hence we have no distinct account of either the origin or organization of the community of the Essenes, whose life and practice present many similarities to Freemasonry. The Essenes, in spite of continued persecution, sustained an existence until the fifth century of the present era, in which age they fell, with other ancient institutions, on the subversion of the Roman empire by the Goths. *Josephus* in his youth passed some time among the Essenes, and he tells us they lived in perfect union; they do not marry, but bring up other men's children as if they were their own, and infuse into them very early their own spirit and maxims. All who desired admittance into the sect were subjected to a year's probation, and then, after two or more years of trial, were allowed to make a profession to observe the laws of the Society, and by solemn oaths preserve the secrets: besides the laws of piety, justice, and modesty, they vowed fidelity to God and loyalty to their sovereign. *Philo* informs us that they sent gifts to the Temple, but never offered sacrifices; they held the Scriptures in the greatest reverence, but considered them as mystic writings, and explained them allegorically; they possessed sacred books which explained their peculiar doctrines and practices; they had all things in common, ate at a common table, and were exceedingly abstemious; they were divided into four classes, according to the time of their initiation; they admitted no one to their society till after a probation of three years; those who were admitted had to take solemn oaths that they would worship God, and be just to their fellow-creatures, to speak the truth, and never disclose the secrets and mysteries of their order. Their studies were the laws of Moses, whom next to God they held in the greatest reverence. They very much used symbols, allegories, and parables after the manner of the ancients.

Mr. Charles Taylor, in his edition of Calmet's Dictionary of the Bible, remarks that it is surprising commentators and divines make no reference to these peculiarities in the character, manner, and principles of the Jewish sect of the Essenes, and by inference expresses an opinion that John the Baptist belonged to the Community.

Suidas and some others are of opinion that the Essenes were a branch of the Rechabites, while others take them to be the Chasdim of the Psalms, and Assidæans of the Maccabees.

The charitable and peaceful disposition of this Community, as well as the three fundamental maxims of their morality, being the love of God, of virtue, and of their neighbour, and in addition that they were a secret society, leads to the belief that it was a fraternity of a like character to Freemasonry.

CHAPTER II.

ON MASONIC INSTITUTIONS OF THE PRESENT ERA.

"Remember, O my friends, the law delivered down,
From age to age, by your renowned forefathers;
O never let it perish in your hands!
But piously transmit it to your children."

ADDISON.

IN the dark ages of history, and amidst the rapid transitions of society, we have little to guide us, save what we can gather from a few isolated cases in our own land, and which would make it appear that the Druidical system was a Masonic institution. But we trace the use of Masonic language in the time of Charlemagne; and at the close of the eighth century the Popes conceded to the Masons of Como the exclusive monopoly of erecting churches. This body of artificers, who then, and for ages afterwards, when the title "Magistri Comacini" had long been absorbed in that of "Free and Accepted Masons," associated as a Craft or Brotherhood in Art and Friendship. From Lombardy, which they soon filled with religious edifices, they passed into other countries where churches were required. The Popes, by bulls, conferred upon them most extensive privileges: they were to be independent of the sovereigns in whose dominions they might temporarily reside, being subject only to their own laws, and were exempted from all kinds of taxation; and in one of these papal decrees it was declared that "these regulations have been made after the example of Hiram, King of Tyre, when he sent artisans to King Solomon for the purpose of building the Temple of Jerusalem."

During the period when the incursions of the barbarian hordes desolated the fair fields of Greece in Italy and overthrew those glorious fabrics, the ruined fragments of which alone remain to tell of their beauty and grandeur, the operations of so peaceful a society were buried in the dust with those monuments. But with the Crusades arose several communities, who united with the chivalrous duty of protecting the feeble, clothing the naked, and feeding the hungry, a holy vow to wrest from the hands of the Moslem the Holy City of the Hebrew and the Christian, and also the Masonic practice of building temples, towers, and hospitals. These societies were, to serve their own purposes, fostered and protected by the Church of Rome and the sovereigns of Europe, until their accumulated possessions tempted their holy and regal patrons to undertake their overthrow.

Mr. Hope, in his History of Architecture, when treating of that of the Middle Ages, says: "A new style of Gothic appeared, unlike its predecessors, of one undivided people, but of the Teutonic mind in general, as represented in those parliaments of genius—*the Lodges of the North*—an architecture peculiarly ecclesiastical, and equally susceptible of adaptation to any civil purposes as Gothic cathedrals."

Of these "Lodges of the North" we have this narrative, which we extract from *Essai sur les Illuminés,* published in 1786. The author of the letter was the Abbé Grandidier, a learned Frenchman:—

"The cathedral church of Strasbourg, begun in 1277, a masterpiece of Gothic architecture, was erected by the Society of Freemasons; and from it emanated other Lodges, which spread over Germany and Lombardy; and several splendid structures arose under their guidance. Although each *Hutten,* or Lodge, had self-government, yet they all recognized the authority of the original Mother Lodge at Strasbourg, which was named *Haupte-Hutte,* or Grand Lodge, In 1459 the several Masters of the different Lodges assembled at Ratisbon, and drew up the Act of Fraternity, which established the chief Master Mason of Strasbourg and his successors as sole and perpetual Grand Masters of the Fraternity of Freemasons of Germany. This Act was confirmed by the Emperor Maximilian in 1498, and renewed by Charles V. and his successors.

"The cathedral of Cologne is a proud monument to Gerhard, Master of the Cologne Lodge of Freemasons; and resisting, as this huge mass does, the attacks of nature and the labour of man, is a testimony of the skill and perseverance of its builders. It is recorded that during the interval between 1248 and 1323 there were not only fifty Masters and three times as many fellow-craft daily employed, but a large number of entered apprentices from all parts of Christendom, who had come to study both the operative and speculative branches of the art, and carried home with them the principles which directed the erection of almost every Gothic monument of the age." After the secession of the fraternity from the Church, the works were suspended, leaving only the splendid choir and side aisles, with the chapels, completed. This pile, which, if completed, would be the most magnificent specimen of Gothic architecture in Europe, was for five centuries untouched, save by the iron hand of Time. The government of Prussia, however, has undertaken the work; and although it may be the work of some years, there is now a probability of its completion.

We are assured that the original plans belonging to the Lodge, which had been preserved in the church, were taken away by the French in 1794, had been recovered, and were delivered over to the architect entrusted with the direction of the work: he has scrupulously adhered to the original designs, and even adopted the ancient and accepted division of the workmen into three classes—the second and third receiving promotion when their industry and ability merit it.

Throughout Europe (in England especially) the fraternity continued for a considerable period to pursue their labours, and constructed many edifices which still remain as stable monuments of their skill as workmen, and refined memorials of their taste as architects. Kings, we know, were their patrons, and their labours were superintended by nobles and eminent prelates, who for this purpose were admitted as members of the fraternity. Being in the first instance an ecclesiastical community, and the popes, bishops, and abbots protecting them, their chief employment was the construction of churches. There is no doubt originally all were operatives; but learning in those ages was almost entirely confined to the clergy, and consequently the fraternity was compelled to seek among those men of learning for those whose wisdom might contrive, and whose cultivated taste might adorn, the plans which they, by their practical skill, were to carry into effect. Hence the germ of that speculative Masonry which, once dividing the character of the fraternity with the operative, now completely occupies it, to the exclusion of the latter.

If we look to the Druses—a sect of Syrian Christians established from time immemorial—we find that there still exists amongst them a society which has a secret doctrine, the members of which are divided into three classes—the first being admitted, the second *partly* initiated, and the third *completely* initiated. Those admitted into the second class may return to the first, but may not communicate what they have learned in the *second*. The *third* suffer death if they reveal their knowledge, or become Mohammedans, or members of any other sect than the Druses. *Jowett* says, the members of this society, if they have been ever so loose in their morals, leave off their licentions life and become altered men; they are the best ordered people in the East. They produce silk in considerable quantity, and corn in their valleys. They are industrious, brave, and hospitable, and their land is a refuge from Turkish oppression. They do not attempt to make proselytes. All travellers agree in having noticed that the Druses have great esteem for Englishmen, and show them marked attention.

Sir Christopher Wren, in corroboration, tells us "that the Holy Wars gave the Christians who had been there an idea of the Saracens' works, which were afterwards imitated by them in their churches, and they refined upon it every day as they proceeded in building. The Italians (among whom were yet some Greek refugees), and with them French, Germans, and Flemings, joined into a fraternity of architects, procuring Papal bulls for their encouragement and particular privileges. They styled themselves Freemasons, and ranged from one country to another as they found churches to be built. Their government was regular, and when they fixed upon the site of the building, they made near it a camp of huts. A surveyor governed in chief: every tenth man was called a warden, and overlooked each nine. The gentlemen of the neighbourhood, either out of charity or commutation of penance, gave the materials and carriages. Those who have seen the exact accounts in records of the charge of the fabrics of some of our cathedrals near four hundred years old, cannot but have a great esteem for their economy, and admire how soon they erected such lofty structures." It has been maintained, that until the statute of 3rd Henry VI., c. 1, which, by prohibiting them from meeting in Chapter, greatly impaired their organization and prosperity, they enjoyed a kind of building monopoly in this country. In an indenture of covenants made in the reign of Henry VI., between the churchwardens of a parish in Suffolk and a company of Freemasons, the latter stipulated that each man should be provided with a pair of white leather gloves and a white apron, and that a Lodge fitted to be properly tiled, in which they were to carry on their works, should be erected at the expense of the parish.

Herder (Theological Professor at Göttingen) asserts, but without stating his authority, that modern European Freemasonry had its origin, during the erection of St. Paul's Cathedral of London, in Sir Christopher Wren. His story is, that on the stated days on which Wren was accustomed to inspect the progress of the building, he and his friends, (we suppose the overseer workmen,) were accustomed to dine at a house in the neighbourhood, and a club was there formed, which by degrees introduced a formula of initiation, and rules for the conduct of the members expressed in symbolical language, derived from the Masonic practice.

In a "History of Freemasonry in France," by George Kloss, Darmstadt, 1852, a similar statement appears. After a few words of introduction, which are intended to show that the institution of Freemasonry, although very ancient, has rather gradually grown up as circumstances led to it, than originated all of a sudden, or started into life without any preparation or foreshadowing, he remarks:—

"When Wren had completed the building of the Cathedral of St. Paul in London, in 1708, and thus the work-people had no common centre remaining, their corporate customs, like the customs of many other bodies, would, in course of time, have been lost and been wiped away, if the brotherhood had not been sustained, as such, by the power of that addition,—the nonprofessional members of the various grades of society. The religious contentions, which had been dominant for 200 years, were at last compelled to recede before the spirit of toleration. The necessity for some place of rest, where political discussion might not enter, was the cause and reason for the adoption, about the year 1716, of an organized system, then first appearing as Freemasonry."

There may be some truth in this statement, as there is no doubt that Freemasonry, which had been dormant for some time, was revived, or at any rate was brought into more vigorous action, by Wren. Freemasonry in Europe was doubtless operative, as is shown both in England and on the continent, and Wren's learning and genius enabled him to unite the speculative with the operative, and thus to draw all orders of men into the Institution.

The Lodge of which Wren was so long the master met at the "Goose and Gridiron" in St. Paul's Churchyard, and was there located until a recent period; and from this Lodge, now known by the name of the Lodge of Antiquity, we have reason to believe all others in England have emanated. This Lodge is in possession of the maul used by Wren in his capacity of architect of the glorious structure he raised.

The system organized or revived by Wren was speedily transplanted into other lands,—into France about 1720; in which country it made rapid progress, and all from warrants of the Grand Master of England; the Loge l'Anglaise at Bourdeaux has been working from that authority, granted 1722. In a Paris Lodge ten persons were initiated at one time, and of these, we are told, six were Knights of the Holy Ghost. The rapid strides that the Order was making caused the Papal Court to make a stir about it, and a learned civilian of Florence was by the Inquisitor arrested in May, 1739. The Grand Lodge in London took the matter up, and by means of the Grand Duke, (afterwards Francis I. of Austria,) who had been initiated a few years before, he was set at liberty in the December following.

In taking a retrospect of other institutions, whether founded for the purposes of government, science, mutual security, or any other purpose, we find they have all been unstable in their duration, and generally failing in the accomplishment of the design for which they were framed. Kingdoms, with their mighty founders, have had their rise, their meridian, and their decline. In vain we ask who were the founders of Palmyra's boasted temples, of Baalbec's gorgeous domes, or the gigantic works of Egypt—the wrecks of their mouldering grandeur only seeming to frown contempt on their founders' schemes.

Masonry has witnessed the rise, revolutions, and wane of empires, withstood the inroads of war, and the still more desolating ravages of barbarous ignorance and the gloomy superstition of ancient and modern times. Through the dark ages, from the sixth to the sixteenth century, Masonry was the chief lamp of knowledge that illumined the gloom of the then degraded human mind; it was the nurse that fostered, the guardian that watched over, and the ark that preserved, amidst the deluge of Gothic gloom that overspread the earth, all the science that had survived the wrecks of the Grecian and Roman empires.

> "Hence, 'midst the ruin of three thousand years,
> Unhurt, unchanged, Freemasonry appears:
> Her towers and monuments may fade away,
> Her truth and social love shall ne'er decay."

CHAPTER III.

FREEMASONRY IN ITS GENERAL APPLICATION.

THE EXCELLENCY OF MASONRY DISPLAYED.

"Like every other blessing,
Derives its value from its use alone:
Not for itself, but for a nobler end
The Eternal gave it, and that end is virtue."
JOHNSON.

GENERAL PRINCIPLES.

WHOEVER attentively observes the objects which surround him, will find abundant reason to admire the works of nature, and to adore the Being who directs such astonishing operations; he will be convinced that Infinite Wisdom could alone design, and Infinite Power complete, such amazing works.

Were a man placed in a beautiful garden, would not his mind be affected with exquisite delight on a calm survey of its rich collections? Would not the groves, the grottoes, the artful wilds, the flowery parterres, the opening vistas, the lofty cascades, the winding streams, the whole variegated scene awaken his sensibility, and inspire his soul with the most exalted ideas? When he observed the delicate order, the nice symmetry, and beautiful disposition of every part, seemingly complete in itself, yet reflecting new beauties on the other, and all contributing to make one perfect whole,—would not his mind be agitated with the most agreeable sensations; and would not the view of the delightful scene naturally lead him to admire and venerate the happy genius who contrived it?

If the productions of Art so forcibly impress the mind with admiration, with how much greater astonishment and reverence must we behold the operations of Nature, which present to view unbounded scenes of utility and delight, in which Divine Wisdom is most strikingly conspicuous? These scenes are, indeed, too expanded for the narrow capacity of man to comprehend. Yet, whoever contemplates the general system must naturally, from the uniformity of the plan, be directed to the original source, the Supreme Governor of the world, the one perfect and unsullied beauty!

Beside all the pleasing prospects that every where surround us, and with which our senses are every moment gratified; beside the symmetry, good order, and proportion which appear in all the works of creation; something farther attracts the reflecting mind, and draws its attention nearer to the Divinity; that is, the universal harmony and affection among the different species of beings of every rank and denomination. These are the cements of the rational world, and by these alone it subsists. When they cease, Nature must be dissolved, and man, the image of his Maker, and the chief of his works, be overwhelmed in the general chaos.

In the whole order of beings, from the seraph which adores and burns, down to the meanest insect,—all, according to their rank in the scale of existence, have, more or less, implanted in them the principle of association with others of the same species. Even the most inconsiderable animals are formed into different ranks and societies for mutual benefit and protection. Need we name the careful ant or the industrious bee—insects which the wisest of all mankind has recommended as patterns of unwearied industry and prudent foresight? When we extend our ideas, we shall find that the innate principle of friendship increases in proportion to the extension of our intellectual faculties; and the only criterion by which a judgment can be formed respecting the superiority of one part of the animal creation above the other is, by observing the degrees of kindness and good-nature in which it excels.

Such are the general principles which pervade the whole system of creation; how forcibly, then, must such lessons predominate in our assemblies, where civilization and virtue are most zealously cherished under the sanction of science and the arts!

THE ADVANTAGES RESULTING FROM FRIENDSHIP.

No subject can more properly engage the attention than the benevolent dispositions which indulgent Nature has bestowed upon the rational species. These are replete with the happiest effects, and afford to the mind the most agreeable reflections. The breast which is inspired with tender feelings is naturally prompted to a reciprocal intercourse of kind and generous actions. As human nature rises in the scale of beings, the social affections likewise arise. Where friendship is unknown, jealousy and suspicion prevail; but where that virtue is the cement, true happiness subsists. In every breast there is a propensity to friendly acts, which, being exerted to effect, sweetens every temporal enjoyment; and, although it does not remove the disquietudes, it tends at least to allay the calamities of life.

Friendship is traced through the circle of private connexions to the grand system of universal benevolence, which no limits can circumscribe, as its influence extends to every branch of the human race. Actuated by this sentiment, each individual connects his happiness with the happiness of his neighbour, and a fixed and permanent union is established among men.

But though friendship, considered as the source of universal benevolence, be unlimited, it exerts its influence more or less powerfully, as the objects it favours are nearer or more remote.

Hence the love of friends and of country takes the lead in our affections, and gives rise to that true patriotism which fires the soul with the most generous flame, creates the best and most disinterested virtue, and inspires that public spirit and that heroic ardour which enable us to support a good cause, and risk our lives in its defence.

This commendable virtue crowns the lover of his country with unfading laurels, gives a lustre to his actions, and consecrates his name to latest ages. The warrior's glory may consist in murder, and the rude ravage of the desolating sword; but the blood of thousands will not stain the hands of his country's friend. His virtues are open, and of the noblest kind. Conscious integrity supports him against the arm of power; and should he bleed by tyrant hands, he gloriously dies a martyr in the cause of liberty, and leaves to posterity an everlasting monument of the greatness of his soul.

Though friendship appears divine when employed in preserving the liberties of our country, it shines with equal splendour in more tranquil scenes. Before it rises into the noble flame of patriotism, aiming destruction at the heads of tyrants, thundering for liberty, and courting danger in defence of rights,—we behold it calm and moderate, burning with an even glow, improving the soft hours of peace, and heightening the relish for virtue. In those happy moments contracts are formed, societies are instituted, and the vacant hours of life are employed in the cultivation of social and polished manners.

On this general plan the universality of the system of Masonry is established. Were friendship confined to the spot of our nativity, its operation would be partial, and imply a kind of enmity to other nations. Where the interests of one country interfere with those of another, Nature dictates an adherence to the welfare of our own immediate connexions; but such interference apart, the true Mason is a citizen of the world, and his philanthropy extends to all the human race. Uninfluenced by local prejudices, he knows no preference in virtue but according to its degree, from whatever country or clime it may spring.

GENERAL ADVANTAGES OF MASONRY.

Abstracted from the pure pleasures which arise from friendship so wisely constituted as that which subsists among Masons, and which it is scarcely possible that any circumstance or occurrence can erase, Masonry is a science confined to no particular country, but extends over the whole terrestrial globe. Wherever arts flourish, there it flourishes too: add to this, that by secret and inviolable signs, carefully preserved among the Fraternity, it becomes an universal language: hence many advantages are gained. The distant Chinese, the wild Arab, and the American savage, will embrace a brother Briton, and know, that besides the common ties of humanity, there is still a stronger obligation to induce him to kind and friendly offices. The spirit of the fulminating priest will be tamed, and a moral brother, though of a different persuasion, engage his esteem; for mutual toleration in religious opinions is one of the most distinguishing and valuable characteristics of the Craft. As all religions teach morality, if a brother be found to act the part of a truly honest man, his private speculative opinions are left to God and himself. Thus, through the influence of Masonry, which is reconcileable to the best policy, all those disputes which embitter life, and sour the tempers of men, are avoided, while the common good, the general object, is zealously pursued.

From this view of our system, its utility must be sufficiently obvious. The universal principles of the art unite, in one indissoluble bond of affection, men of the most opposite tenets, of the most distant countries, and of the most contradictory opinions; so that in every nation a Mason may find a friend, and in every climate a home.

Such is the nature of our institution, that in the Lodge,

which is confined to no particular spot, union is cemented by sincere attachment, and pleasure reciprocally communicated in the cheerful observance of every obliging office. Virtue, the grand object in view, luminous as the meridian sun, shines refulgent on the mind, enlivens the heart, and heightens cool approbation into warm sympathy and cordial attention.

Freemasonry in its general and universal application, as comprehending the two divisions of human and moral science—operative and speculative—is wisely planned and adapted for the welfare of man; for as man is a compound of body and soul, so Masonry, as a compound of human and moral science, is admirably calculated for the promotion of man's highest interests in his present as well as future state, and to make him what his Creator intended him to be—useful, wise, happy; and not only to be happy in himself, but, as far as humanity will admit, to make all around him equally happy.

The teachings of Masonry in its *operative* and *speculative* departments will be treated upon in their proper divisions: but in a general view of the institution it is necessary to state, that by the former we allude to a proper application of the useful rules of architecture, whence a structure derives figure, strength, and beauty, and whence result a due proportion and a just correspondence in all its parts; by the latter we learn to rule and direct our passions, act upon the square, keep the tongue of good report, maintain secrecy, practise charity and every other virtue that can adorn the man.

Speculative Masonry is so far interwoven with religion as to lay us under the strongest obligations to pay that rational homage to the Deity, which at once constitutes our duty and our happiness. It leads the contemplative to view with reverence and admiration the glorious works of creation, and inspires them with the most exalted ideas of the perfections of the Divine Creator. Operative Masonry furnishes us with dwellings, and convenient shelter from the inclemencies of seasons; and whilst it displays the effects of human wisdom, as well in the choice as in the arrangement of the materials of which an edifice is composed, it demonstrates, that a fund of science and industry is implanted in man, for the best, most salutary, and beneficent purposes.

The attentive ear receives the sound from the instructive tongue, and the sacred mysteries are safely lodged in the repository of faithful breasts. Tools and implements of architecture (symbols the most expressive!) are selected by the Fraternity, to imprint on the memory serious and solemn truths; and thus the excellent tenets of the institution are transmitted, unimpaired, under circumstances precarious, and even adverse, through a succession of ages.

Thus speculative Masonry is a science, which, borrowing from the operative art its working tools and implements, sanctifies them, by symbolic instruction, to the holiest of purposes—the veneration of God, and the purity of the soul.

The operative Mason constructs his edifice of material substances; the speculative Mason is taught to erect a spiritual building, pure and spotless, and fit for the residence of Him who dwelleth only with the good. The operative Mason works according to the designs laid down for him on the trestle board by the architect; the speculative is guided by the great trestle board, on which is inscribed the revealed will of God, the supreme architect of heaven and earth. The operative Mason tries each stone and part of the building by the square, level, and plumb; the speculative Mason examines every action of his life by the square of morality, seeing that no presumption nor vain-glory has caused him to transcend the level of his allotted destiny, and no vicious propensity has led him to swerve from the plumb-line of rectitude. And, lastly, as it is the business of the operative Mason, when his work is done, to prove every thing "true and trusty," so it is the object of the speculative Mason, by a uniform tenor of virtuous conduct, to receive, when his allotted course has passed, the inappreciable reward, from his celestial Grand Master, of "Well done, thou good and faithful servant."

The good Mason might justly say with Job, that "the blessing of him that was ready to perish came upon me; and I caused the widow's heart to sing for joy. I was eyes to the blind, and feet to the lame. I was a father to the poor; and the cause which I knew not I searched out. The stranger did not lodge in the street, but I opened my doors to the traveller. When the ear heard me, then it blessed me; and when the eye saw me it beamed with delight; because I delivered the poor that cried, and the fatherless, and him that had none to help him."

The law as promulgated by Moses has a clause to a like effect. "And if thy brother be waxen poor and fallen in decay with thee, then thou shalt relieve him; yea, though he be a stranger or a sojourner, that he may live with thee."—Levit. xxv. 35.

Masonry is a progressive science, and not to be attained in any degree of perfection excepting by time, patience, and a considerable degree of application and industry; for no one should be admitted to the profoundest secrets or highest honours of the Fraternity till by time he has learned secrecy and morality.

In our own times, the vast progress and general diffusion of Masonry throughout the habitable globe cannot but be satisfactory to every one interested in the cause of humanity and the happiness of his species. At present, as in every former age over which it hath spread its principles, Masonry constitutes the affectionate and indissoluble alliance which unites in warm cordiality man to man. It forms the most liberal and extensive connexions. No private prepossession, nor national predilection; no civil policy, nor ecclesiastical tyranny; no party spirit, nor dissocial passion, is suffered to prevent the engagement, or interfere with the free exercise of that *brotherly love, relief*, and *fidelity*, which it never fails to produce. It has for ages been lamented that petty distinctions and partial considerations, irrational prejudices and contracted sentiments, should so much obstruct the free intercourse of mankind. Masonry breaks down these barriers. In its solemn assembly, around its social altar, meet the inhabitants of different countries with benignant looks of esteem, and sentiments of unfeigned friendship. Around distant lands it casts philanthropy's connecting zone, and binds together in the same sympathies the whole family on earth.

Blending their resources in a common stock, and forming a community of interests, Freemasonry makes the prosperity of each individual the object of the whole; the prosperity of the whole the object of each. How nearly does this approach the patriarchal life, and the state of the primitive Christians, who were "of one heart and soul; neither said any of them that aught of the things which he possessed was his own, but they had all things in common." Were such the unanimity, love, equality, generosity, and disinterestedness of professing Christians *now*, Freemasonry would be less necessary than it is for the welfare of man.

CHAPTER IV.

REASONS WHY THE SECRETS OF FREEMASONRY OUGHT NOT TO BE PUBLICLY EXPOSED; AND THE IMPORTANCE OF THOSE SECRETS DEMONSTRATED.

"Damnant quod non intelligunt."—OVID.

ONE of the most frequent objections raised against Freemasonry is the profound secrecy observed upon certain parts of the institution. To have secrets is not peculiar to Freemasonry: every trade, every art, and every occupation has its secrets, not to be communicated but to such as have become proficient in the science connected with them, nor then but with proper caution and restriction; and often under the guard of heavy penalties. Charters of incorporation are granted by civil governments for their greater security, and patents for their encouragement. Nay, every government, every statesman, and every individual, has secrets which are concealed with prudent care, and confided only to the trusty and the true.

We [Freemasons] only claim a like indulgence,—that of conducting ourselves by our own rules, and of admitting to a participation of our secrets and privileges such as choose to apply for them on our own terms. So far from wishing to deprive any one of the light we enjoy, we sincerely wish all the race of men were qualified to receive it; and if so, our doors would never be shut against them, but our Lodge, our hearts and souls, would be open to their reception.

If the secrets of Masonry are replete with such advantage to mankind, it may be asked, Why are they not divulged for the general good? To this it may be answered—Were the privileges of Masonry to be indiscriminately dispensed, the purposes of the institution would not only be subverted, but our secrets, being familiar, like other important matters, would lose their value, and sink into disregard.

It is a weakness in human nature, that men are generally more charmed with novelty than with the intrinsic value of things. Innumerable testimonies might be adduced to confirm this truth. Do we not find that the most wonderful operations of the Divine Artificer, however beautiful, magnificent, and useful, are overlooked, because common and familiar? The sun rises and sets, the sea ebbs and flows, rivers glide along their channels, trees and plants vegetate, men and beasts act; yet these, being perpetually open to view, pass unnoticed. The most astonishing productions of Nature, on the same account, escape observation, and excite no emotion, either in admiration of the great Cause, or of gratitude for the blessing conferred. Even Virtue herself is not exempted from this unhappy bias in the human frame. Novelty influences all our actions and determinations. What is new, or difficult in the acquisition, however trifling or insignificant, readily captivates the imagination, and ensures a temporary admiration; while what is familiar, or easily attained, however noble or eminent, is sure to be disregarded by the giddy and the unthinking.

Did the *essence* of Masonry consist in the knowledge of particular secrets, or peculiar forms, it might, indeed, be alleged that our pursuits were trifling and superficial. But this is not the case; they are only the keys to our treasure, and, having their use, are preserved; while, from the recollection of the lessons which they inculcate, the well-informed Mason derives instruction: he draws them to a near inspection, views them through a proper medium, adverts to the circumstances which gave them rise, and dwells upon the tenets they convey. Finding them replete with useful information, he prizes them as sacred; and, being convinced of their propriety, estimates their value by their utility.

It has been well said by a reverend and learned brother, "In that awful day when the secrets of all hearts shall be disclosed, the gazing multitude who have curiously inquired our secret, shall be astonished to know that the greatest deep of Masonic secrecy was the unpublished act of doing good."

We may further observe that the Guilds or Incorporations of Craftsmen which in the thirteenth century rose into importance, and which in our own metropolis, although considerably altered, exist to this day, have every one laws as stringent for their government as those of our fraternity, and in some respects similar. We take the drapers' articles for instance. Strict rules are laid down for admission of members of the "Crafte:" on taking an apprentice, every brother has to present him to the wardens, and pay 13*s*. 4*d*. There is an ordinance forbidding "any broders of thes folyship to inform any strainger of the feitz of drapeire" (tem. 5 Edw. IV.). Keeping the secrets of the Craft was provided for by an ordinance entitled, "None to betray lytel things said in consell to other of the Crafte, ne no brother to inform any strainger." Relief of decayed brethren, or to those fallen in poverty, was provided for by 14*d*. a week from the box.

Religion was the foundation of the Guild: divine worship was the solid band of union of the association. The members were constantly reminded, that it was not to the contrivances of wit, or the strength of the labouring hand, that man owes his daily bread. Industry, they were taught, might be the appointed means, but God's providence was the only source of our subsistence; its increase the result of his blessing, not of our frugality; the alms, the testimony of our gratitude to Him from whom the bounty, unmerited and undeserved, is obtained. Imperfect as these institutions may have been, how much better calculated were they than those of our own time, to ameliorate the condition of the lower orders of the community! The modern operative belongs to a degraded, and therefore to a hostile order. His feelings, views, interests, are all in opposition to the manufacturer and capitalist, whom he considers as his tyrant and his enemy. But in the old time, the workman was the *brother*, the *companion* of his employer, perhaps poorer in purse, inferior in station, younger in age, but all united by the most kind and sociable bonds. They repeated the same creed, lighted their lamp before the same altar, feasted at the same board.

So with regard to the operative Freemasons of that age, MR. RUSKIN, in a public lecture on *Socialism in Architecture and its Effects*, tells us, "that several centuries back the architects who furnished the designs did not regard the men who executed them as mere machines, but all worked together with one mind, and that nothing great in architecture had been done, save by associated bodies, where all the faculties of mind and hand had been brought out to the utmost."

Many are deluded by the vague supposition that our mysteries are merely nominal; that the practices established amongst us are frivolous; and that our ceremonies may be adopted or waived at pleasure. On this false basis we find too many of the Brethren hurrying through all the degrees of the Order, without adverting to the propriety of one step they pursue, or possessing a single qualification to entitle them to advancement. Passing through the usual formalities, they consider themselves authorized to rank as masters of the art, solicit and accept offices, and even assume the government of the lodge, equally unacquainted with the rules of the institution that they pretend to support, and the nature of the trust which they are bound to perform. The consequence is obvious; anarchy and confusion ensue, and the substance is lost in the shadow.—Hence men who are eminent for ability, rank, and fortune, frequently view the honours of Masonry with indifference; and, when their patronage is solicited, either accept offices with reluctance, or reject them with disdain.

Masonry long laboured under these disadvantages, and every zealous friend to the Order earnestly wished for a correction of the abuse. Of late years, it must be acknowledged, our assemblies have been in general better regulated; of which the good effects are sufficiently displayed in the judicious selection of our members, and the more proper observance of our general regulations.

We do not hesitate to appeal to the world in justification of the purity of our moral system. Our constitutions are well known. We have submitted them freely to general investigation. We solemnly avow them as the principles by which we are governed, the foundation on which we build, and the rules by which we work. We challenge the most severe critic, the most precise moralist, the most perfect Christian, to point out any thing in these constitutions inconsistent with good manners, fair morals, or pure religion. We feel assured that every one who will take the pains to inquire into the subject must be convinced that the institution is friendly to the best interests of mankind—well calculated to ameliorate the disposition and improve the character—and to adorn its faithful adherents with every natural, moral, and social virtue.

By the use of the *universal language of Masons*, members of the fraternity of all nations communicate easily and freely with each other. On every part of the globe they can make known their wishes, and be sure of finding an attentive friend, a hospitable asylum, and liberal assistance. The Order, though composed of persons from various countries, separated by all the natural barriers which prevent men from combining into coherent masses, yet seems to be one body actuated by one soul. Thousands and thousands have but one heart, one hand,—the heart of benevolence, the hand of charity.

Sweet are the uses of Masonry in adversity! Then, when the offices of general philanthropy would not reach us, or our share in its benignities prove inadequate to our need—when *Friendship* grows cold, and its most zealous professor forsakes us—*Masonry* triumphs in the exercise of its lovely charities.

The brethren should ever bear in mind that the interests of Freemasonry are in their hands. They should therefore be careful not to blend with it their weaknesses nor to stain it with their vices. They should consider how much the world expects of them, and how unwilling it is to make any abatement. It is highly incumbent on them to "walk in wisdom towards them that are without;" doing nothing that should render their principles suspicious, or disgrace the institution in the eyes of the world. For assuredly, if the brethren, in their conduct, forget they are men, the world, with its usual severity, will remember they are Masons.

FRIENDLY ADMONITIONS.

As useful knowledge is the great object of our desire, let us diligently apply to the practice of the art, and steadily adhere to the principles which it inculcates. Let not the difficulties that we have to encounter check our progress, or damp our zeal; but let us recollect that the ways of wisdom are beautiful, and lead to pleasure. Knowledge is attained by degrees, and cannot every where be found. Wisdom seeks the secret shade, the lonely cell, designed for contemplation. There enthroned she sits, delivering her sacred oracles. There let us seek her, and pursue the real bliss. Though the passage be difficult, the farther we trace it the easier it will become.

Union and harmony constitute the essence of Freemasonry: while we enlist under that banner, the society must flourish, and private animosities give place to peace and good fellowship. Uniting in one design, let it be our aim to be happy ourselves, and contribute to the happiness of others. Let us mark our superiority and distinction among men, by the sincerity of our profession as Masons; let us cultivate the moral virtues, and improve in all that is good and amiable; let the Genius of Masonry preside over our conduct, and under her sway let us perform our part with becoming dignity; let us preserve an elevation of understanding, a politeness of manner, and an evenness of temper; let our recreations be innocent, and pursued with moderation; and never let irregular indulgences lead to the subversion of our system, by impairing our faculties, or exposing our character to derision. In conformity to our precepts, as patterns worthy of imitation, let the respectability of our character be supported by the regularity of our conduct and the uniformity of our deportment; then as citizens of the world, and friends to every clime, we shall be living examples of virtue and benevolence, equally zealous to merit, as to obtain, universal approbation.

CHAPTER V.

PRINCIPLES OF THE INSTITUTION OF FREEMASONRY.

"These men, skilled in divine and human knowledge, do not disclose to the vulgar the hidden significations contained under the natural appearances, but veil them under figures and emblems; yet they are ready to reveal them in a proper place and with due ceremonies to those who are deserving and worthy of being initiated. So far I am permitted to say with respect, preserving a reverential silence as to what further relates to these mystic rites."—HELIODORUS.

HAVING stated the nature and traced the rise and progress of Freemasonry, we would now call attention, as an authoritative exponent of the principles of the Institution in England, to the first two clauses of the ancient charges, as set forth in the Book of Constitutions:—

"A Mason is obliged, by his tenure, to obey the moral law; and if he rightly understand the art, he will never be a stupid atheist nor an irreligious libertine. He, of all men, should best understand that God seeth not as man seeth; for man looketh at the outward appearance, but God looketh to the heart. A Mason is, therefore, particularly bound never to act against the dictates of his conscience. Let a man's religion or mode of worship be what it may, he is not excluded from the Order, provided he believe in the glorious Architect of heaven and earth, and practise the sacred duties of morality. Masons unite with the virtuous of every persuasion in the firm and pleasing bond of fraternal love. They are taught to view the errors of mankind with compassion, and to strive, by the purity of their own conduct, to demonstrate the superior excellence of the faith they may profess. Thus Masonry is the centre of union between good men and true, and the happy means of conciliating friendship amongst those who must otherwise have remained at a perpetual distance.

"A Mason is a peaceable subject to the civil powers wherever he resides or works, and is never to be concerned in plots and conspiracies against the peace and welfare of the nation, nor to behave himself undutifully to inferior magistrates. He is cheerfully to conform to every lawful authority; to uphold, on every occasion, the interest of the community; and zealously promote the prosperity of his own country. Masonry has ever flourished in times of peace, and been always injured by war, bloodshed, and confusion; so that kings and princes, in every age, have been much disposed to encourage the Craftsmen on account of their peaceableness and loyalty, whereby they practically answer the cavils of their adversaries, and promote the honour of the Fraternity. Craftsmen are bound by peculiar ties to promote peace, cultivate harmony, and live in concord and brotherly love."

Masonry comprehends within its circle every branch of useful knowledge and learning, and stamps an indelible mark of pre-eminence on its *genuine* professors, which neither chance, power, nor fortune can bestow. When its rules are strictly observed, it is a sure foundation of tranquillity amid the various disappointments of life; a friend, that will not deceive, but will comfort and assist in prosperity and adversity; a blessing, that will remain with all times, circumstances, and places, and to which recourse may be had when other earthly comforts sink into disregard. Masonry gives real and intrinsic excellency to man, and renders him fit for the duties of society. It strengthens the mind against the storms of life, paves the way to peace, and promotes domestic happiness. It ameliorates the temper, and improves the understanding; it is company in solitude, and gives vivacity, variety, and energy to social conversation. In youth it governs the passions and employs usefully our most active faculties; and in age, when sickness, imbecility, and disease have benumbed the corporeal frame, and rendered the union of soul and body almost intolerable, it yields an ample fund of comfort and satisfaction. These are its general advantages; to enumerate them separately would be an endless labour. It may be sufficient to observe, that he who cultivates this science, and acts agreeably to the character of a Mason, has within himself the spring and support of every social virtue; a subject of contemplation that enlarges the mind and expands all its powers; a theme that is inexhaustible, ever new and always interesting.

The Rev. Charles Brockwell, a minister of the Church of England, in a sermon preached before a Grand Lodge more than a century back, said, "I have had the honour of being a member of this ancient and honourable society many years, have sustained many of its offices, and can and do own in this sacred place, and before the Grand Architect of the Universe, that I never could observe aught therein but what was justifiable and commendable, according to the strictest rules of society; this being founded on the precepts of the Gospel, the doing the will of God, and subduing the passions, and highly conducing to every sacred and social virtue. But not to insist on my own experience, the very antiquity of our institution furnishes a sufficient ground to confute all gainsayers. For no combination of wicked men for a wicked purpose ever lasted long; the want of virtue, on which mutual trust and confidence is founded, soon divides and breaks them to pieces. Nor would men of unquestionable wisdom, known integrity, strict honour, undoubted veracity, and good sense, though they might be trepanned into a foolish and ridiculous society, which could pretend to nothing valuable, ever continue in it, or contribute towards supporting and propagating it to posterity."

Again, the Rev. Brother Thaddeus Mason Harris says, "It interests us also in the duties and engagements of humanity; produces an affectionate concern for the welfare of all around us; and, raising us superior to every selfish view or party prejudice, fills the heart with an unlimited goodwill to man." He also writes, "In all countries and in all ages, 'the true and accepted' have been found to conduct themselves as peaceable citizens, and acknowledged to be the firm and decided supporters of good order, government, and religion. Its *laws* are reason and equity; its *principles*, benevolence and love; and its *religion*, purity and truth; its *intention* is peace on earth; and its *disposition* goodwill towards men."

The Rev. Dr. Milne, Grand Chaplain, in a sermon before the Grand Lodge of England, in 1788, says, "I think we are warranted in contending that a society thus constituted, and which may be rendered so admirable an engine of improvement, far from meriting any reproachful or contumelious treatment, deserves highly of the community; and that the ridicule and affected contempt which it has sometimes experienced can proceed only from ignorance or from arrogance; from those, in fine, whose opposition does it honour, whose censure is panegyric, and whose praise would be censure."

The Rev. Brother Dr. Oliver, who has laboured earnestly in the cause of the institution, says, "Freemasonry is neither an exclusive system of religion, nor does it tolerate the detestable principles of infidelity. It is a teacher of morality, and contributes its powerful aid, in that capacity, to the salvation of souls by recommending and enforcing the duties of the second table, and by demanding an acquiescence in the doctrines of the first. And this course of discipline is perfectly consonant with the teaching of Christianity. When the lawyer asked the subtle question, 'Which is the great commandment of the law?' Jesus said unto him, 'Thou shalt love the Lord thy God with all thy heart, and with all thy soul, and with all thy mind; and thy neighbour as thyself:' or, in other words, this is all that is required by the Jewish law for the salvation of man."

All the plans and ceremonies of Freemasonry are pacific. It breathes nothing but the spirit of love and charity to all mankind. It co-operates with true religion in regulating the tempers, in restraining the passions, and harmonizing the discordant interests of men. In one hand it holds the olivebranch of peace; in the other, the liberal offerings of universal charity. The distinguishing characteristic of our institution is charity in its most ample sense—that charity which has been justly described as the chief of all the social virtues.

This virtue includes a supreme degree of love to the great Creator and Governor of the universe, and an unlimited affection to the beings of his creation, of all characters and of every denomination. This last duty is forcibly inculcated by the example of the Deity himself, who liberally dispenses his beneficence to unnumbered worlds.

It is not particularly our province to enter into a disquisition of every branch of this amiable virtue; we shall, therefore, only briefly state the happy effects of a benevolent disposition toward mankind; and show that charity, exerted on proper objects, is the greatest pleasure man can possibly enjoy.

The bounds of the greatest nation, or the most extensive empire, cannot circumscribe the generosity of a liberal mind. Men, in whatever situation they are placed, are still, in a great measure, the same. They are exposed to similar dangers and misfortunes; they have not wisdom to foresee, or power to prevent, the evils incident to human nature; they hang, as it were, in a perpetual suspense between hope and fear, sickness and health, plenty and want. A mutual chain of dependence subsists throughout the animal creation. All of the human species are, therefore, proper objects for the exercise of charity.

Beings who partake of one common nature ought to be actuated by the same motives and interests. Hence, to soothe the unhappy by sympathizing with their misfortunes, and to restore peace and tranquillity to agitated spirits, constitute the general and great ends of the Masonic system. This humane, this generous disposition, fires the breast with manly feelings, and enlivens that spirit of compassion which is the glory of the human frame, and which not only rivals, but outshines every other pleasure that the mind is capable of enjoying.

All human passions, when directed by the superior principle of reason, tend to promote some useful purpose; but compassion toward proper objects is the most beneficial of all the affections, and excites more lasting degrees of happiness, as it extends to greater numbers, and alleviates the infirmities and evils which are incident to human existence.

Possessed of this amiable, this godlike disposition, Masons are shocked at misery, under every form and appearance. When they behold an object pining under the miseries of a distressed body or mind, the healing accents which flow from the tongue mitigate the pain of the unhappy sufferer, and make even adversity, in its dismal state, look gay. When pity is excited, the Mason will assuage grief, and cheerfully relieve distress. If a Brother be in want, every heart is moved; when he is hungry, we feed him; when he is naked, we clothe him; when he is in trouble, we fly to his relief. Thus we confirm the propriety of the title we bear; and convince the world at large that BROTHER, among Masons, is more than the name.

The principles above enunciated are, to a great extent, though not to the extent we desire, and which we shall ever labour to attain, developed by our benevolent institutions. It is not necessary for us to allude to these institutions further in this article than to say that they provide for the exigencies of every stage of life; through them we educate and clothe the young; we provide annuities, and an asylum in the decline of life, for the distressed brethren and their widows; whilst, for the relief of casual and sudden calamity, we have an income administered through the Board of Benevolence, of something like 4000*l.* a year.

The Rev. Brother Fawcett says, "Charity is a complete and consistent thing. It is not a *segment,* but a *circle.* Its affections stream from God, their *centre;* all mankind compose their circumference; they go forth not only in one, but in all directions, towards the production of others' good."

In carrying out the principles of charity to their full and legitimate extent, the Brethren are enjoined, as we shall hereafter show in our lectures, ever to bear in mind and act upon the dictates of brotherly love, relief, and truth; the first rendering us affectionate, the second generous, and the third just.

It must not be forgotten, that without bias to any particular creed, the connexion between Masonry and Religion is absolute, and cannot be destroyed. Masonry contributes to promote the social happiness of mankind in this world, by the practice of moral virtue. Religion gives us happiness in a future state. Hence Masonry must be considered the handmaid of Religion, because the practice of every social and moral virtue, though it cannot absolutely save, is an essential condition of salvation.

We may with truth say, if there be any country on the globe in which the proportions of the social edifice have not yet been harmoniously adjusted, so if there be any in which the conflicting elements of society have not yet subsided into calm and unruffled repose; of what inestimable value is such an institution as ours, receiving and inviting within its temple, all,—of every colour, and clime, and creed, and politics,—to hear there inculcated, and see practised, the doctrines of brotherly forbearance and Christian peace!

CHAPTER VI.

THE GOVERNMENT OF THE FRATERNITY.

"Freemasonry is a moral order, instituted by virtuous men, with the praiseworthy object of recalling to our remembrance the most sublime truths, in the midst of the most innocent pleasures, founded on liberality, brotherly love, and charity."—ARNOLD.

THE mode of government observed by the Fraternity will give the best idea of the nature and design of the Masonic institution.

Three classes are established among Masons, under different appellations. The privileges of each class are distinct; and particular means are adopted to preserve those privileges to the just and meritorious. Honour and probity are recommendations to the First Class; in which the practice of virtue is enforced, and the duties of morality are inculcated; while the mind is prepared for a regular progress in the principles of knowledge and philosophy.—Diligence, assiduity, and application, are qualifications for the Second Class; in which is given an accurate elucidation of science, both in theory and practice. Here human reason is cultivated, by a due exertion of the intellectual powers and faculties; nice and difficult theories are explained; new discoveries are produced, and those already known beautifully embellished.—The Third Class is restricted to a selected few, whom truth and fidelity have distinguished, whom years and experience have improved, and whom merit and abilities have entitled to preferment. With them the ancient landmarks of the Order are preserved; and from them we learn the necessary instructive lessons which dignify the art, and qualify the professors to illustrate its excellence and utility.

Such is the established plan of the Masonic system. By this judicious arrangement, true friendship is cultivated among different ranks of men, hospitality promoted, industry rewarded, and ingenuity encouraged.

The supreme power is vested in the Grand Master, as the organ of the Grand Lodge by which he is elected annually, the members of the Grand Lodge being the Masters, Wardens, and Past Masters of the several Lodges. The provinces, i. e., beyond ten miles from the metropolis, are each governed in like manner, the Provincial Grand Master being the Deputy of the Supreme Grand Master. The Supreme Grand Lodge is permanently established in the extensive premises known as Freemasons' Hall, in Great Queen Street, Lincoln's Inn Fields, where also the executive business of the Fraternity is transacted. The regular meetings of the Grand Lodge are held on the first Wednesday in the months of March, June, September, and December; the Grand Festival or Installation of the Grand Master is held on the Wednesday following St. George's Day or the 23rd of April. The Provincial Grand Lodges are, or ought to be, held annually, at such place as the Provincial Grand Master may please to appoint. The rule is to visit each Lodge in his province seriatim.

The laws for government are printed and published under the title of "Constitutions of the Ancient Fraternity of Free and Accepted Masons."

The style and title of the institution is "THE ANCIENT FRATERNITY OF FREE AND ACCEPTED MASONS." The word *Free* originally signified that the person so called was free of the company or guild of incorporated Masons; and those operative

Masons who were not free of the guild were excluded from working with those who were. We are told, by many authors, that this term was first used in the tenth century, when the travelling masons of Lombardy were incorporated by the Roman pontiff. *Accepted* we take to be equivalent to the term *initiated;* and it doubtless alludes to the *acceptance* into their society, by operative masons, of persons who were not *operatives.* An Accepted Mason is one who has been adopted into the Order, and has received the freedom of the society, in the same manner as the freedom of the city of London is now bestowed as a mark of honour on persons of distinguished rank, valour, or attainments. This is evident from the regulations made in 1663, under the Grand Mastership of the Earl of St. Albans, where the word is repeatedly used in this sense. Thus:—"No person hereafter, who shall be *accepted* a Freemason, shall be admitted into any Lodge or assembly, until he has brought a certificate of the time and place of his *acceptation* from the Lodge that accepted him, unto the Master of that limit or division where such Lodge is kept." And again:—"No person shall be *made* or accepted a Freemason, unless" &c.

A *Lodge* is generally understood to be the room in which a regularly constituted body of Freemasons assembles for the purposes connected with the Institution. The term is also used to designate the collection of Masons thus assembled, just as we use the word "church" to signify the building in which a congregation of worshippers meet, as well as the congregation itself. *Ragon* says that the word "Lodge" is derived from the Sanscrit *loga,* which signifies the *world.* Our lectures define a Lodge to be an assembly of Masons, *just, perfect,* and *regular,* who are met together to expatiate on the beauties and mysteries of the Order. It is *just,* because it contains the volume of the Sacred Law unfolded; *perfect,* from its numbers, every order of Masons being virtually present by its representatives, to ratify and confirm its proceedings; and *regular,* from its warrant of constitution, which implies that it meets and works under the sanction of the Grand Master of the country in which the Lodge is held.

A Lodge-room should always, if possible, be situated due east and west. Its form should be that of a parallelogram or oblong square. The approaches should be angular, for Oliver says,— "A straight entrance is un-Masonic." There should be two ante-rooms adjoining it, the one nearest being the preparation room, and the outer the Tyler's room.

Symbolically, a Mason's Lodge is a representation of the world. Its clouded canopy is an emblem of those mansions of unutterable bliss where the Grand Master of the universe for ever reigns, whose all-seeing eye beholds, with unceasing complacency, the efforts of His creatures to do His will. To that abode of the blessed the Mason is taught to aspire, while the path is indicated by the theological ladder, whose principal rounds are faith, hope, and charity. The sun—the eternal fountain of light, the unwearied ruler of the day—shines in the Lodge, a bright exponent of the great Creator's power; while the moon—the glorious orb of night—repeats the lesson of Divine munificence. Here, too, we are taught that the vast universe over which this omnipotence presides, was no work of chance, but that its foundations were laid in wisdom, supported by strength, and adorned with beauty. And as the presence of the Almighty illuminates with refulgent splendour the most distant recesses of the universe, so is the Lodge enlightened by the presence of His revealed will. And hence the Bible, as it is of all lights the most pure, is to the Mason most indispensable. And, finally, as this world, vast in its extent and complicated in its motions, is governed and regulated with unceasing concord and harmony,—so is the Lodge controlled and directed by the same spirit of peace, which, emanating from the exercise of brotherly love, relief, and truth, reaps its fruits in universal charity.

"The widow's tear, the orphan's cry,—
All wants our ready hands supply,
As far as power is given.
The naked clothe, the prisoner free,
These are thy works, sweet Charity!
Revealed to us from heaven."

The place of meeting is named in the Warrant of Constitution, and the Lodge can be held at no other place, unless its removal is sanctioned by the proper authorities. Some Lodges in the provinces have halls of their own, but the great majority are held at taverns. The provincial Grand Lodge meetings are generally held in the Town Halls.

The floor is said to be paved with *Mosaic* work, which consists of innumerable little stones of different colours, closely united together, so as to imitate a painting. The floor of Solomon's Temple was thus constructed, and the term *Mosaic* is supposed to have been derived from the fact that Moses so paved the floor of the Tabernacle. Mosaic or tessellated pavements were very common among the ancients; the Romans especially most ingeniously decorated their floors in this manner. Several have been discovered in various parts of England. In memory of the flooring of the Temple and Tabernacle the Mosaic pavement is always preserved as an ornament of the Lodge, in the tessellated border, which has in its centre a blazing star.

The Mosaic pavement of a Lodge is placed there to show the vicissitudes of human life; that however prosperity may favour us with smiles to-day, it is uncertain how long it will continue to bless us. Adversity may come when we least expect it, and penury and distress may follow joy and pleasure. The latter period of life may be subjected to want and misery, when we are most unfit to encounter it; and instead of resting in peace after a long and troublesome journey, we may be compelled again to encounter the burden and heat of the day.

All the decorations and symbols of Freemasonry are borrowed from the Tabernacle and Temple, and the phraseology from the art of architecture, which serve to characterize an institution which might justly claim more noble devices; at the same time they are used either as emblems or indications of the simplest and most important moral truths.

"Human life is chequered at the best,
And joy and grief alternately preside,
The good and evil demon of mankind."

This tessellated ornament or symbol at present exists only in the tracing board, but the important lesson it conveys ought not to be lost sight of; and we trust among the many attempts the brethren make to render their Lodges perfect, a tessellated carpet or floor-cloth will be in every Lodge ere long.

CHAPTER VII.

FORMATION OF A LODGE.

"There are some circumstances in the lot of mankind that show them to be destined to friendship and amity: those are their mutual need of each other; their mutual compassion; their sense of mutual benefits; and the pleasures arising in company."—SOCRATES.

EQUALITY is one of the landmarks of Freemasonry, and the peer and artisan acknowledge the sentiment by meeting on the square and parting on the level; but as we cannot alter the social distinctions of the country we inhabit, Masons necessarily form communities adapted to the social position they hold, and the means at their command. In the promiscuous concourse of many, it is sufficient that we have an opportunity of selecting our company. We turn away from those who do not engage us, and we fix our resort where the society is more to our mind. Hence it follows that men occasionally enter the institution, and find the members of the Lodge do not occupy the same position in the social scale as themselves, or whose habits and pursuits are not congenial with their own, or whose conversation does not reach the standard of their own perfection. These and various other causes will occur to withdraw brethren from their mother Lodge; and if there is not in their own locality a suitable Lodge, they are led to form one that shall offer a prospect agreeable to their feelings. Or it does happen that two or three in a town or neighbourhood meeting in promiscuous intercourse, finding themselves members of the Order, and there being no Lodge near, determine on founding one. Now it is very desirable that among the founders should be a brother of some experience in the craft, as we have seen Lodges formed in haste, without an expert and skilful Past Master united with them, struggle on for years and never arrive at any mark in the Order; and generally those Lodges have shown signs of progress most readily, in which the Master first entrusted with the warrant is a well-skilled Past Master.

Masonry is an art useful and extensive. In every art there is a mystery, which requires a progress of study and application before we can arrive at any degree of perfection. Without much instruction, and more exercise, no man can be skilful in any art; in like manner, without an assiduous application to the various subjects treated in the different lectures of Masonry, no person can be sufficiently acquainted with the true value of the institution.

From this remark it is not to be inferred, that those who labour under the disadvantage of a confined education, or whose sphere of life requires assiduous attention to business or useful employment, are to be discouraged in their endeavours to gain a knowledge of Masonry. To qualify an individual to enjoy the benefits of the society at large, or to partake of its privileges, it is not absolutely necessary that he should be acquainted with all the intricate parts of the science: these are only intended for persons who may have leisure and opportunity to indulge the pursuit.

Masonry, according to the general acceptation of the term, is an art founded on the principles of Geometry, and directed to the service of mankind. But Freemasonry, embracing a wider range, and having a nobler object in view, namely, the cultivation and improvement of the human mind, may with more propriety be called a science, although its lessons are for the most part veiled in allegory and illustrated by symbols, inasmuch as, veiling itself under the terms of the former, it inculcates principles of the purest morality.

To draw aside this veil, therefore, or more properly speaking, to penetrate through its mysteries, is the object of the Lectures, and by a faithful and appropriate attention to them, every Mason may hope ultimately to become acquainted with all its mysteries.

Some may be more able than others, some more eminent, some more useful; but all, in their different spheres, may prove advantageous to the community; and our necessities, as well as our consciences, bind us to love one another. To persons, however, whose early years have been dedicated to literary pursuits, or whose circumstances and situation in life render them independent, the offices of the Lodge ought principally to be restricted. The industrious tradesman proves himself a valuable member of society, and worthy of every honour that we can confer; but the nature of every man's profession will not admit of that leisure which is necessary to qualify him to become an expert Mason, so as to discharge the official duties of the Lodge with propriety. And it must also be admitted, that those who accept offices and exercise authority in the Lodge ought to be men of prudence and address, enjoying the advantages of a wellcultivated mind and retentive memory. All men are not blessed with the same powers and talents; all men, therefore, are not equally qualified to govern. He who wishes to teach, must submit to learn; and no one can be qualified to support the higher offices of the Lodge, who has not previously discharged the duties of those which are subordinate. Experience is the best preceptor. Every man may rise by gradation, but merit and industry are the first steps to preferment. Masonry is wisely instituted for different ranks and degrees of men; and every brother, according to his station and ability, may be employed in the Lodge, and class with his equal. Actuated by the best principles, no disquietude is found among the professors of the art. Each class is happy in its particular association; and when all the classes meet in general convention, one plan regulates the whole: neither arrogance nor presumption appear on the one hand, nor diffidence nor incivility on the other; but every brother vies to excel in promoting that endearing happiness which constitutes the essence of civil society.

The selection of men in the founding of a Lodge is a task of considerable nicety; hence it is essentially necessary the brother who undertakes it should be conversant with the habits and opinions of every one he purposes to connect himself with, as one ill-mannered, ill-tempered, or contemptuous person, will throw all prospective harmony into discord.

It should ever be borne in mind we ought to be as careful whom we introduce into a Lodge as to our own fireside, and one we would not admit to intimate intercourse with our own domestic circle, is unfit for a seat in our Lodge. One who is addicted to intemperance, with gambling propensities, a scoffer at religion, or debauchee of any kind, is unworthy of admittance within our portals.

The necessary measure to accomplish this object is thus defined in *The Book of Constitutions.*

OF CONSTITUTING A NEW LODGE.

Every application for a warrant to hold a new Lodge must be by petition to the Grand Master, signed by at least seven regularly registered Masons; and the Lodges to which they belong, or formerly belonged, must be specified. The petition must be recommended by the officers of a regular Lodge, and be transmitted to the Grand Secretary, unless there be a Provincial Grand Master in the district or province in which the Lodge is proposed to be holden, in which case it is to be sent to him or to his deputy, who is to forward it, with his recommendation or opinion thereon, to the Grand Master. If the prayer of the petition be granted, the Provincial Grand Master may issue a dispensation, authorizing the brethren to meet as a Lodge, until a warrant of constitution shall be signed by the Grand Master.

The following is the form of petition:—

"To the M. W. Grand Master of the United Fraternity of Ancient Free and Accepted Masons of England:

"We, the undersigned, being regular registered Masons of the Lodges mentioned against our respective names, having the prosperity of the craft at heart, are anxious to exert our best endeavours to promote and diffuse the genuine principles of the art; and, for the conveniency of our respective dwellings and other good reasons, we are desirous of forming a new Lodge, to be named . In consequence of this desire, we pray for a warrant of constitution, empowering us to meet as a regular Lodge, at on the of every month, and there to discharge the duties of Masonry, in a constitutional manner, according to the forms of the Order and the laws of the Grand Lodge: and we have nominated and do recommend Brother [A. B.] to be the first Master, Brother [C. D.] to be the first Senior Warden, and Brother [E. F.] to be the first Junior Warden of the said Lodge. The prayer of this petition being granted, we promise strict obedience to the commands of the Grand Master and the laws and regulations of the Grand Lodge."

The warrant or dispensation being granted, it is entrusted to some skilful brother, who is specially deputed by the Grand Master, or Provincial Grand Master, to open and consecrate in solemn form the new Lodge.

CHAPTER VIII.

CONSECRATION OF A LODGE.

THE deputy of the Grand Master being ready, a procession is arranged from the ante-room, and he is conducted into the apartment in which the Lodge is to be held; he takes his position in the east, having a representative D. G. M. on his right, and the Chaplain on his left; he directs two brethren, being Past Masters, to fill the Wardens' chairs, and forthwith opens the Lodge in the three degrees, and an ode is sung.

Brother Preston says, "The Master, and his officers, accompanied by some dignified clergyman, having taken their stations, and the Lodge, which is placed in the centre, being covered with white satin, the Consecration ceremony commences, all devoutly kneel, and the preparatory prayer is rehearsed."

Although the practice is not universal, an extemporary prayer is generally adopted at the opening of the ceremony. From the mass of odes, we give one written by Brother Dunckerley, a Mason of great and deserved celebrity, and as the air is patent to the British people, it is easy of adoption:—

TUNE—"*God save the Queen.*"

Hail! universal Lord!
By Heaven and Earth adored;
　　All hail! great God!

Before Thy name we bend,
To us Thy grace extend,
And to our prayer attend.
All hail! great God!

The Deputy Grand Master is then informed by the Secretary (*pro tem.*) that the brethren present desire to be formed into a new Lodge, and, having presented a petition for a warrant, or Charter of Constitution, which has been granted, pray it may be constituted in ancient and solemn form. The Deputy Grand Master orders the petition and the warrant (or the dispensation) to be read; which done, next, the minutes of the proceedings of the petitioners are to be read, and these are to be approved and confirmed, and signed by the Deputy Grand Master, who then inquires of the brethren approved of the officers nominated in the warrant to preside over them. This being signified, the Deputy Grand Master delivers an address on the nature and design of the Institution suitable to the time or locality.

The Chaplain then offers a prayer:—

Almighty Father, God Most High, the Grand Geometrician and Great Architect of the Universe, we implore Thy blessing with every confidence in Thy providence and protection upon this Lodge, convened for the sacred object of solemnly dedicating its House of Assembly to Thy honour and glory. We pray most fervently that all who meet within these walls may be ever endued with the lofty principles of brotherly love, relief, and truth; and, above all, of devotion to Thee, through whose bounty our cups overflow with corn, wine, and oil in plenteousness; from whom we have received the heart to feel, the hand to labour, the eye to behold; the ear to hear, the tongue to proclaim; and all the faculties which make us susceptible of every moral and natural good. May the blessed volume of Thy matchless wisdom be the *square* to regulate all our conduct, the *compasses* within whose hallowed circle we may ever walk with peace and safety, the infallible *plumb-line* of rectitude and truth. Enable us to fill each sphere of duty with integrity and honour; to win the love of our personal associates, by amiable attention to all the sweet and endearing charities of human life,—and as fathers, husbands, friends, and Masons to exalt the profession in which we glory. And while we invoke Thy heavenly grace in behalf of our Order, wherever established on the face of the globe, we especially beseech Thee to bless the Grand Master of our native land, and his representatives at home and abroad; endue them in this world with peace, honour, and length of days; let Thine arm protect them, and Thy wisdom counsel them in all that may tend to the furtherance of all noble principles: and when at Thy summons they shall lay down the gavel of Masonry here, admit them, we pray Thee, to the grand and perfect Lodge above, which is now veiled in clouds and darkness at the summit of the ladder, there to behold that bright Morning Star, whose auspicious rising brings peace and salvation to the faithful and obedient of the human race.

Omnes.—All Glory be to God on high,
Peace on Earth,
Good will towards men.—*So mote it be.*

Grand honours.

The tracing board lying in the centre, which in the Consecration Ceremony is denominated *The Lodge*[1], and covered with a fair linen cloth, is now unveiled. The consecrating vessels being prepared, an ode or anthem is sung. Then to slow and solemn music the corn, wine, and oil are diffused by three Past Masters, saying:—

1st. "Glory be to God on high."

[1] At the Union Grand Lodge, held in 1813, we are told there was a piece of furniture constructed under the direction of Brother John Soane, Treasurer Superintendent of Works, to represent the Ark of the Covenant, and this was denominated *The Lodge.*

2nd. "Peace on earth."

3rd. "Good will towards men."

Omnes. "So mote it be."

Sanctus. "Glory be to Thee, O Lord."

The Chaplain then takes the censer three times round the Lodge, and halting in the east gives prayer.

The Deputy Grand Master then delivers Solomon's Invocation, 1 Kings viii. 23, "Lord God of Israel," to end of ver. 43, and ver. 49 to end of ver. 53.

ANTHEM. (Psalm cxxxiii.)

Behold! how pleasant and how good,
For Brethren such as we,
Of the "Accepted" Brotherhood,
To dwell in unity.

'Tis like the oil on Aaron's head,
Which to his feet distils;
Like Hermon's dew, so richly shed
On Zion's sacred hills.

For there the Lord of light and love,
A blessing sent with power;
Oh ! may we all this blessing prove,
E'en life for evermore.

On friendship's altar rising here,
Our hands now plighted be,
To live in love, with hearts sincere,
In peace and unity.

The Deputy Grand Master then solemnly dedicates the Lodge to God, to Masonry, and to benevolence and universal charity, and constitutes it in form. The Hallelujah Chorus closes the ceremony.

It is customary at Consecrations that the distinguished Brother to whom the duty is entrusted should, in course of the ceremony, address the brethren present on the occasion. The address is generally adapted to the circumstances or locality. The address which follows is by the accomplished and eloquent Rev. Brother Thaddeus Mason Harris:—

BRETHREN,

The ceremonies we are about to perform are not unmeaning rites, nor the amusing pageants of an idle hour; but have a solemn and instructive import. Suffer me to point it out to you, and to prepare your minds for those important sentiments they are so well adapted to convey.

This Hall, designed and built by wisdom, supported by strength, and adorned in beauty, we are first to consecrate in the name of the great Jehovah; which teaches us in all our works begun and finished to acknowledge, adore, and magnify Him. It reminds us, also, in His fear to enter the door of the Lodge, to put our trust in Him while passing its trials, and to hope in Him for the reward of its labours.

Let, then, its altar be devoted to his service, and its lofty arch resound with his praise! May the eye which seeth in secret witness here the sincere and unaffected piety, which withdraws from the engagements of the world to silence and privacy, that it may be exercised with less interruption and less ostentation.

Our march round the Lodge reminds us of the travels of human life, in which Masonry is an enlightened, a safe, and a pleasant path. Its tessellated pavement of Mosaic work intimates to us the chequered diversity and uncertainty of human affairs. Our step is time; our progression, eternity.

Following our ancient constitutions, with mystic rites, we dedicate this Hall to the honour of Masonry.

Our best attachments are due to the Craft. In its prosperity we find our joy, and in paying it honour we honour ourselves. But its worth transcends our encomiums, and its glory will outsound our praise.

Brethren, it is our pride that we have our names on the records of Masonry. May it be our high ambition that they should shed a lustre on the immortal page!

The Hall is also to be dedicated to virtue.

This worthy appropriation will always be duly regarded while the moral duties which our sublime lectures inculcate with affecting and impressive pertinency, are cherished in our hearts and illustrated in our lives.

As Freemasonry aims to enliven the spirit of philanthropy and promote the cause of charity, so we dedicate this Hall to universal benevolence; in the assurance that every Brother will dedicate his affections and his abilities to the same generous purpose; that while he displays a warm and cordial affection to those who are of the fraternity, he will extend his benevolent regards and good wishes to the whole family of mankind.

Such, my Brethren, is the significant meaning of the solemn rites we are now to perform, because such are the peculiar duties of every Lodge. I need not enlarge upon them now, nor show how they diverge, as rays from a centre, to enlighten, to improve, and to cheer the whole circle of life. Their import and their application is familiar to you all. In their knowledge and their exercise may you fulfil the high purposes of the Masonic Institution!

How many pleasing considerations, my Brethren, attend the present interview! Whilst in almost every other part of the world political animosities, contentions, and wars interrupt the progress of humanity and the cause of benevolence, it is our distinguished privilege, in this happy region of liberty and peace, to engage in the plans and to perfect the designs of individual and social happiness. Whilst in other nations our Order is viewed by politicians with suspicion, and by the ignorant with apprehension, in this country, its members are too much respected and its principles too well known, to make it the object of jealousy or mistrust. Our private assemblies are unmolested, and our public celebrations attract a more general approbation of the fraternity. Indeed, its importance, its credit, and we trust its usefulness, are advancing to a height unknown in any former age. The present occasion gives fresh evidence of the increasing affection of its friends; and this noble apartment, fitted up in a style of elegance and convenience which far exceed any we have among us, does honour to Masonry, as well as the highest credit to the respectable Lodge for whose accommodation and at whose expense it is erected.

We offer our best congratulations to the worshipful Master, Wardens, Officers, and Members of the Lodge. We commend their zeal, and hope it will meet with the most ample recompense. May their Hall be the happy resort of piety, virtue, and benevolence! May it be protected from accident, and long remain a monument of their attachment to Masonry! May their Lodge continue to flourish, their union to strengthen, and their happiness to abound! And when they and we all shall be removed from the labours of the earthly Lodge, may we be admitted to the brotherhood of the perfect, in the building of God, the Hall not made with hands, eternal in the heavens!

At Consecrations, the aid of music, Vocal and Instrumental, is essential. Besides those Anthems introduced, any of the following may be used:—

ANTHEMS.

'LET there be light!'—the Almighty spoke,
Refulgent streams from chaos broke
  To illume the rising earth!
Well pleased the Great Jehovah stood—
The Power Supreme pronounced it good,
  And gave the planets birth!
    In choral numbers Masons join,
      To bless and praise this light divine.

Parent of light! accept our praise!
Who shedd'st on us thy brightest rays,
  The light that fills this mind.
By choice selected, lo! we stand,
By Friendship join'd, a social band!
  That love—that aid mankind!
    In choral numbers, &c.

The widow's tear—the orphan's cry—
All wants our ready hands supply,
  As far as power is given!
The naked clothe—the prisoner free!
These are thy works, sweet Charity!
  Reveal'd to us from heaven!
    In choral numbers, &c.

BLEST Masonry! thy arts divine
  With light and truth inform the mind,
The virtues in thy temples shine,
  To polish and adorn mankind:
Sprightly pleasures, social love,
  In thy triumphant domes unite;
'Tis these thy gallant sons improve,
  And gild the day, and cheer the night.

Dark bigots may with anger gaze,
  And fools pretend thy rites to blame,
But worth is still deserving praise,
  And Pallas' self will speak thy fame.
Apollo bids the tuneful choir
  Prepare their songs, and sweetly sing,
The music sound from every lyre,
  And all the hills with Pæans ring.

The pure unrivall'd joys of life,
  Love and Friendship 'mongst us reign;
We banish Discord far, and strife,
  From Masonry! thy blest domain.
As in fair nature's works, the whole
  Is moved with harmony and art,
So order sanctifies the soul,
  And truth and candour warm the heart.

This night another dome we raise,
  And consecrate to Hiram's laws;
Let all unite, your voices raise,
  Sing triumph to the glorious cause.
We scorn the blind's censorious pride,
  Masons united ever stand,
Nor guilt nor faction can divide
  The faithful and illustrious band.

[Tune—"*Rule Britannia.*"]

To Heaven's high Architect, all praise,
  All praise, all gratitude be given;
Who deign'd the human soul to raise
  By mystic secrets sprung from heaven.

CHORUS.

Sound aloud the great Jehovah's praise;
To him the dome, the temple raise.

HAIL to the Craft! at whose serene command
The gentle Arts in glad obedience stand:
Hail, sacred Masonry! of source divine,
Unerring sov'reign of th' unerring line:

Whose plumb of truth, with never-failing sway,
Makes the join'd parts of symmetry obey:
Whose magic stroke bids fell confusion cease,
And to the finish'd Orders gives a place:
Who calls vast structures from the womb of earth,
And gives imperial cities glorious birth.
To works of Art her merit not confined,
She regulates the morals, squares the mind;
Corrects with care the sallies of the soul,
And points the tide of passions where to roll:
On virtue's tablet marks her moral rule,
And forms her Lodge an universal school;
Where Nature's Mystic laws unfolded stand,
And Sense and Science, join'd, go hand in hand.
O may her social rules instructive spread,
Till Truth erect her long-neglected head!
Till through deceitful night she dart her ray,
And beam full glorious in the blaze of day!
Till men by virtuous maxims learn to move,
Till all the peopled world her laws approve,
And Adam's race are bound in Brothers' love.

Then follows the installation of the W. M.

CHAPTER IX

THE CEREMONY OF OPENING AND CLOSING THE LODGE.

IN all regular assemblies of men which are convened for wise and useful purposes the commencement and conclusion of business is accompanied with some form. In every country of the world the practice prevails, and is deemed essential. From the most remote periods of antiquity it is traced, and the refined improvements of modern times have not abolished it.

Ceremonies, simply considered, are little more than visionary delusions; but their effects are sometimes important. When they impress awe and reverence on the mind, and attract the attention to solemn rites by external forms, they are interesting objects. These purposes are effected when judicious ceremonies are regularly conducted and properly arranged. On this ground they have received the sanction of the wisest men in all ages, and consequently could not escape the notice of Masons. To begin well, is the most likely means to end well: and it is justly remarked, that when order and method are neglected at the beginning, they will be seldom found to take place at the end.

The ceremony of opening and closing the Lodge with solemnity and decorum is therefore universally adopted among Masons; and though the mode in some meetings may vary, and in every

Degree must vary, still an uniformity in the general practice prevails in the Lodge; and the variation (if any) is solely occasioned by a want of method, which a little application will easily remove.

To conduct this ceremony with propriety ought to be the peculiar study of all Masons, especially of those who have the honour to rule in our assemblies. To persons who are thus dignified, every eye is directed for regularity of conduct and behaviour; and by their example other brethren, less informed, may naturally expect to derive instruction.

From a share in this ceremony no Mason is exempted; it is a general concern, in which all must assist. This is the first request of the Master, and the prelude to business. No sooner has it been signified, than every officer repairs to his station, and the brethren rank according to their degrees. The intent of the meeting becomes the object of attention; and the mind is insensibly drawn from the indiscriminate subjects of conversation which are apt to intrude on our less serious moments.

Our first care is directed to the external avenues of the Lodge; and the officers, whose province it is to discharge that duty, execute the trust with fidelity. By certain mystic forms, of no recent date, it is intimated that we may safely proceed. To detect impostors among ourselves, an adherence to order in the character of Masons ensues, and the Lodge is opened or closed in solemn form.

At opening the Lodge, two purposes are effected: the Master is reminded of the dignity of his character, and the brethren of the homage and veneration due to him in their sundry stations. These, however, are not the only advantages resulting from a due observance of the ceremony; a reverential awe for the Deity is inculcated, and the eye is fixed on that object from whose radiant beams alone light can be derived. Hence, in this ceremony, we are taught to adore the Great Architect of the universe, and to supplicate that the labours then begun in order, may be continued in peace, and closed in harmony.

At closing the Lodge, a similar form takes place. Here the less important duties of the Order are not passed unobserved. The necessary degree of subordination which takes place in the government of the Lodge is peculiarly marked; while the proper tribute of gratitude is offered up to the beneficent Author of life, whose blessing is invoked, and extended to the whole Fraternity, thus:—

"Brethren, let us express our gratitude to the Great Architect of the universe, for favours already received, and may He continue to support our Order by cementing and adorning it with every moral and social virtue. *So mote it be.*"

Each brother then faithfully locks up in his own repository the treasure which he has acquired; and, pleased with his reward, retires to enjoy, and disseminate among the private circle of his friends, the fruits of his labour and industry in the Lodge.

These are faint outlines of a ceremony which universally prevails among Masons, and distinguishes all their meetings. It was the custom some years back to read the ancient charges at every meeting, and although the practice does not hold at the present time, they are too valuable to be lost sight of, as they form an invaluable code for our moral government, and are moreover not unfrequently referred to.

THE ANCIENT CHARGES.

ON THE MANAGEMENT OF THE CRAFT IN WORKING.

[To be rehearsed at opening the Lodge.]

Masons employ themselves diligently in their sundry vocations, live creditably, and conform with cheerfulness to the government of the country in which they reside.

The most expert Craftsman is chosen or appointed Master of the work, and is duly honoured in that character by those over whom he presides.

The Master, knowing himself qualified, undertakes the government of the Lodge, and truly dispenses his rewards according to merit.

A Craftsman who is appointed Warden of the work, under the Master, is true to Master and Fellows, carefully oversees the work, and the brethren obey him.

The Master, Wardens, and Brethren, are just and faithful, and carefully finish the work they begin, whether it be in the First or Second Degree; but never put that work to the First which has been appropriated to the Second Degree.

Neither envy nor censure is discovered among Masons. No brother is supplanted, or put out of his work, if he be capable to finish it; for he who is not perfectly skilled in the original design, can never, with equal advantage to the Master, finish the work which has been begun by another.

All employed in Masonry meekly receive their rewards, and use no disobliging name. "Brother" is the appellation they bestow on each other. They behave courteously within and without the Lodge, and never desert the Master till the work be finished.

LAWS FOR THE GOVERNMENT OF THE LODGE.

You are to salute one another in a courteous manner, agreeably to the forms established among Masons; you are freely to give such mutual instructions as shall be thought necessary or expedient, not being overseen or overheard, without encroaching upon each other, or derogating from that respect which is due to a gentleman were he not a Mason; for though, as Masons, we meet as brethren on a level, yet Masonry deprives no man of the honour due to his rank or character, but rather adds to his honour, especially if he have deserved well of the Fraternity, who always render honour to whom it is due, and avoid illmanners.

No private committees are to be allowed, or separate conversations encouraged: the Master or Wardens are not to be interrupted, or any brother who is speaking to the Master; but due decorum is to be observed, and a proper respect paid to the Master and presiding officers.

These laws are to be strictly enforced, that harmony may be preserved, and the business of the Lodge be carried on with order and regularity. *So mote it be.*

CHARGE ON THE BEHAVIOUR OF MASONS.

[To be rehearsed at closing the Lodge.]

When the Lodge is closed, you are to enjoy yourselves with innocent mirth, but carefully avoid excess. You are not to compel any brother to act contrary to his inclination, or give offence by word or deed, but enjoy a free and easy conversation. You are to avoid immoral or obscene discourse, and at all times support with propriety the dignity of your character.

You are to be cautious in your words and carriage, that the most penetrating stranger may not discover what is not proper to be intimated; and, if necessary, you are to waive the discourse, and manage it prudently, for the honour of the Fraternity.

At home, and in your several neighbourhoods, you are to behave as wise and moral men. You are never to communicate to your families, friends, or acquaintances, the private transactions of our different assemblies; but, on every occasion, consult your own honour, and the reputation of the Fraternity at large.

You are to study the preservation of health, by avoiding irregularity and intemperance; that your families may not be neglected and injured, or yourselves disabled from attending to your necessary employments in life.

If a stranger apply in the character of a Mason, you are cautiously to examine him, in such a method as prudence may direct, and agreeably to the forms established among Masons; that you may not be imposed upon by an ignorant false pretender, whom you are to reject with contempt; and beware of giving him any secret hints of knowledge. But if you discover him to be a true and genuine brother, you are to respect him; if he be in want, you are, without prejudice, to relieve him, or direct him how he may be relieved; you are to employ him, or recommend him to employment: however, you are never charged to do beyond your ability; only to prefer a poor *Mason,* who is a good man and true, before any other person in the same circumstances.

Finally, These rules you are always to observe and enforce, and also the duties which have been communicated in the lecture; cultivating brotherly love, the foundation and copestone, the cement and glory of this ancient Fraternity; avoiding, on every occasion, wrangling and quarrelling, slandering and backbiting; not permitting others to slander honest brethren, but defending their characters, and doing them good offices, as far as may be consistent with your honour and safety, but no farther. Hence all may see the benign influence of Masonry; as all true Masons have done from the beginning of the world, and will do to the end of time.

CHAPTER X.

THE ENTERED APPRENTICE, OR THE FIRST DEGREE.

"Know that they are neither public nor private, neither published nor unpublished; seeing they are only intelligible to those who have been my listeners."—AULUS GELLIUS.

"Ask, and it shall be given to you; seek, and you shall find; knock, and it shall be opened unto you."—MATT. vii. 7.

ANCIENT Craft Masonry consists of but three degrees, viz. Entered Apprentice, Fellow-Craft, and Master Mason. There are many rites connected with Freemasonry, and the degrees vary in number, but they all commence with these three. In all ancient mysteries there were progressive degrees, and the object of these steps of probation was to test the character of the aspirant, and at the same time by gradual revelations prepare him for the important knowledge he was to receive at the final moment of his adoption.

The laws regarding the admission of persons into the Fraternity are very stringent.

OF PROPOSING MEMBERS. MAKING, PASSING, AND RAISING.

Great discredit and injury having been brought upon our ancient and honourable Fraternity from admitting members and receiving candidates, without due notice being given, or inquiry made into their characters and qualifications, and from passing and raising Masons without due instruction in the respective

The Entered Apprentice.

degrees, it is declared that a violation or neglect of any of the following laws shall subject the Lodge offending to erasure, and no emergency can be allowed as a justification. [A dispensation cannot be granted except in cases specially provided for.]

1. No brother shall be admitted a member of a Lodge without a regular proposition in open Lodge, nor until his name, occupation, and place of abode, as well as the name and number of the Lodge of which he is or was last a member, or in which he was initiated, shall have been sent to all the members in the summons for the next regular Lodge meeting; at which meeting the brother's Grand Lodge certificate, and also the certificate of his former Lodge is to be produced, and the decision of the brethren ascertained by ballot. When a Lodge has ceased to meet, any former member thereof shall be eligible to be proposed and admitted a member of another Lodge, on producing a certificate from the Grand Secretary, stating the fact and specifying whether the brother has been registered and his quarterage duly paid.

2. No person shall be made a Mason without a regular proposition at one Lodge, and a ballot at the next regular Lodge; which shall not take place unless his name, addition, or profession, and place of abode shall have been sent to all the members in the summons.

In cases of emergency, the following alteration is allowed. Any two members of a Lodge may transmit in writing to the Master the name, &c. of any candidate whom they may wish to propose, and the circumstances which cause the emergency; and the Master, if it be proper, shall notify the same to every member of his Lodge; and may summon a Lodge to meet at a period of not less than seven days from the issuing of the summons, for the purpose of balloting for the candidate; and if the candidate be then approved, he may be initiated into the first degree. The Master shall, previous to the ballot being taken, cause the proposition, and emergency, to be recorded in the minute-book of the Lodge.

3. No man shall be made a Mason in any Lodge under the age of twenty-one years, unless by dispensation from the Grand Master, or Provincial Grand Master. Every candidate must be a free man, his own master, and, at the time of initiation, in reputable circumstances. Previous to his initiation, he must subscribe his name at full length to a declaration of the following import (any individual who cannot write is consequently ineligible to be admitted into the Order), viz.

To the Worshipful Master, Wardens, Officers, and Members of the Lodge of

No.

I being a free man, and of the full age of twenty-one years, do declare, that, unbiassed by the improper solicitation of friends, and uninfluenced by mercenary or other unworthy motive, I freely and voluntarily offer myself a candidate for the mysteries of Masonry; that I am prompted by a favourable opinion conceived of the institution, and a desire of knowledge; and that I will cheerfully conform to all the ancient usages and established customs of the Order. Witness my hand, this day of

Witness

4. No person can be made a Mason in, or admitted a member of a Lodge, if, on the ballot, three black balls appear against him; but the bye-laws of a Lodge may enact that one or two black balls shall exclude a candidate.

5. Every candidate shall, on his initiation, solemnly promise to submit to the constitutions, and to conform to all the usages and regulations of the Craft.

6. No Lodge shall on any pretence initiate into Masonry more than five persons on the same day, unless by a dispensation, which shall specify the total number to be initiated.

7. No Lodge shall confer more than one degree on any brother on the same day, nor shall a higher degree be conferred on any brother at a less interval than four weeks from his receiving a previous degree, nor until he has passed an examination in open Lodge in that degree.

8. No other Lodge shall initiate any non-commissioned officer or corporal belonging to a regiment or battalion to which a military Lodge is attached, nor shall any Lodge initiate any military person below the rank of a corporal, except as a serving brother, or by dispensation from the Grand Master, or Provincial Grand Master.

9. No person shall be made a Mason for less than three guineas exclusive of the registering fee, nor shall a Lodge on any pretence remit or defer the payment of any part of this sum. The member who proposes a candidate must be responsible to the Lodge for all the fees payable on account of the initiation.

This is not to extend to the making of serving brethren, who may be initiated by the Lodge which they are to serve, provided that no fee or reward be taken, and that a dispensation from the Grand Master or Provincial Grand Master be first obtained, which shall be specified in the return made to the Grand Secretary; but a brother so initiated cannot be a member of the Lodge in which he was initiated, though eligible to become a subscribing member of any other Lodge, and, upon being registered as a joining member of such other Lodge, and paying his contributions in like manner with other members, he is entitled to all the privileges and benefits of the Craft.

If, however, there be no other Lodge in the vicinity of his

dwelling of which he can become a member, he may be permitted to pay through the Lodge in which he was initiated the quarterly dues to the fund of benevolence; and after having served the Lodge and paid such dues for four years at least, may be considered eligible to be relieved in case of distress, and entitled to the other privileges of the Craft in the same manner as if he had been a regular subscribing member.

As it generally happens that first impressions are too powerful to be obliterated by time or circumstances, it is of vital importance that the most reverential attention be paid by every brother in the Lodge during the ceremony of initiation: no one therefore ought to preside who has not a clear enunciation and ready and reverential delivery. The degree is remarkable for the beauty of the morality which it inculcates, and for the practical lesson enforced on the mind of the neophyte in the exercise of Beneficence and Charity.

The Entered Apprentice is the first degree in Masonry, and although it supplies no historical knowledge, it is replete with information on the internal structure of the Order. It is remarkable for the beauty of the morality which it inculcates. In this degree the neophyte has impressed on his mind,— by symbolic ceremonies too important in their character ever to be forgotten,—a lesson of humility and contempt of worldly riches and earthly grandeur. The beauty of holiness and charity are depicted in emblematic modes, stronger and more lasting than mere language can express; and the convert is directed to lay a corner-stone of virtue and purity, upon which he is charged to erect a superstructure alike honourable to himself and to the Fraternity into which he is admitted.

On the threshold, the candidate for the mysteries and privileges of Freemasonry is required to declare that he presents himself of his own free will and accord, that it is under no influence exercised by others to enter the Order, and he promises that if admitted he will submit to the laws and constitutions of the Order.

The first sound the aspirant then hears is prayer. The Divine aid in his favour is thus invoked:—

"Vouchsafe thine aid, Almighty Father and supreme Ruler of the Universe, to this our present convention, and grant that this candidate for Masonry may dedicate and devote his life to thy service, and become a true and faithful Brother amongst us! Endue him with a competency of thy Divine wisdom; that by the secrets of this Art, he may the better be enabled to display the beauties of godliness, to the honour and glory of thy Holy Name! *So mote it be.*"

It is a duty incumbent on the Master of a Lodge, before the ceremony of initiation takes place, to inform the candidate of the purpose and design of the Institution; to explain the nature of his solemn engagements; and in a manner peculiar to Masons, to require his cheerful acquiescence to the tenets of the Order.

BENEFICENCE and CHARITY, which are the distinguishing characteristics of Masonry, were enjoined on the Israelites in the 25th chapter of *Leviticus*, wherein is the law for the institution of the *jubilee*, or year of liberty, which was to be a season of national rest, festivity, and joy, when care ceased and labour was suspended. "If thy brother be waxen poor and fallen into decay with thee, thou shalt relieve him; yea, though he be a stranger or sojourner, that he may live with thee."

The eminent Apostle of the Christian Church reiterates the sentiment of the Jewish legislator in the language that demonstrates this virtue to be the cementing bond of Freemasonry. "Though I speak with the tongue of men and of angels, and have not charity, I become as sounding brass or a tinkling cymbal. And though I have the gift of prophecy and understand all mysteries and knowledge, and have all faith, so that I could remove mountains, and have not charity, I am nothing." (1 Cor. xiii.)

Charity is the chief corner-stone of our Temple, and upon it is to be erected a superstructure of all the other virtues, which make the good man and the good Mason. This charity of which our Order boasts, is not alone that sentiment of commiseration which leads us to assist the poor with pecuniary donations. The true Mason will be slow to anger and easy to forgive. He will stay his falling brother by gentle admonition, and warn him with kindness of approaching danger. He will not open his ear to slanderers, and will close his lips against all reproach. His faults and his follies will be locked in his breast, and the prayer for mercy will ascend to Jehovah for his brother's sins. Nor will these sentiments of beneficence be confined to those who are bound to him by ties of kindred or worldly friendship alone, but extending them throughout the globe, he will love and cherish all who sit beneath the broad canopy of our Universal Lodge. For it is the boast of our institution, that a Mason, destitute and worthy, may find in every clime a brother, and in every land a home.

Charity in its benevolent signification forms the basis of the Masonic Institution, and Freemasonry has especial regard to the three stages of destitution—infancy, unavoidable misfortune, and extreme old age: for all these, when proved worthy, relief is at hand. The destitute orphans of deceased brethren are placed in schools, where they are clothed, taught, and fed; where they are brought up in the practice of religion and virtue, and afterwards placed in situations where their previous training will make them good and worthy members of society; and for our aged brethren who have passed their lives in the practice of Masonic principles, and in the decline of life misfortune overtakes them, they are entitled to the provisions of an Asylum and an Annuity Fund. For sudden misfortune or calamity, there is a large fund for immediate relief to the distressed brother or his widow and children, or for the assistance of a Foreign Mason whose case is properly vouched for.

To use the symbolic language, Masons meeting on the Square ought to part on the Level. The neophyte enters the institution to seek a master, and from him to gain instruction. The first principle inculcated is the perfect spirit of *Equality* among the brethren. The universality of Masonry is illustrated by the sun, the glorious luminary being, according to the Copernican system, the centre, the earth constantly revolving round on its axis; and Freemasonry being universally spread over its surface, it necessarily follows that the sun must always be at its meridian with respect to Freemasonry.

A thorough knowledge of the Holy Scriptures is requisite to make a perfect Mason; and hence, as having its origin in an association of builders, the construction of a Lodge is symbolically a rebuilding of the glorious Temple erected by the Grand Master, King Solomon, who is represented by the Master of the Lodge. The descriptive language is derived from the Sacred Volume.

A knowledge of Geometry is highly beneficial to the free and accepted Mason. To the operative Mason it is an essential study. Much of the teaching is by geometrical rule, as by right lines and angles Masons are taught to live upright lives and practise well-squared actions.

The first objects to which the eyes of the newly admitted brother are directed are the three great emblematic lights of Masonry,— the *Volume of the Sacred Law*, the *Square*, and the *Compasses*, which by their emblematic teaching instruct man in the great duties of life,—to his God, his neighbour, and himself. Subordinate to these great lights there are in Masonry three lesser lights, viz. the representatives of the Sun as ruling or enlightening the day; the Moon, as the ruler or illuminator of the night, and the Master of the Lodge as the instructor of the brethren: these lights from their position have also an astronomical reference, as showing the course of the sun, which, rising in the east, gains its due effulgence in the south, and sets in the west.

As on his first admission the young Mason has but generalities presented to his attention, the only reference to the building of the Temple is to the curiously constructed pillars placed at the grand entrance, as described in 2 Chron. iii. 15 — 17: "He made before the house two pillars of thirty and five cubits high, and the chapiter that was on the top of each of them was five cubits. And he made chains as in the oracle, and put them on the heads of the pillars; and made an hundred pomegranates, and put them on the chains. And he reared up the pillars before the temple, one on the right hand, and the other on the left; and called the name of that on the right hand Jachin, and the name of that on the left Boaz."

The badge of the Entered Apprentice Mason is by its whiteness a symbol of purity, and has ever been esteemed as more valuable for its antiquity than any other badge, and more worthy of regard than the sovereign Order of the Garter, the highest prized order of knighthood in the world. The lambskin, or white leather apron is the first gift bestowed by the Master on the newly initiated apprentice. It resembles the apron worn by the operative Masons to preserve their garments, but we, as speculative Masons, use it for a more noble purpose. By the whiteness of its colour, and the innocence of the animal from which it is obtained, we are admonished to preserve that blameless purity of heart and conduct, which will alone enable us hereafter to present ourselves before the Grand Master of the Universe, unstained with sin and unsullied with vice.

Eumolpus of Thrace was initiated in the mysteries of Ceres, at Eleusis (1350 B.C.), and made Hierophantes or High Priest, and the office remained in his family for 1200 years. It was he who instituted the lamb-skin as a symbol of peace and good will. Hence our ancient brethren insisted on our badge being only worn when love and harmony prevailed, and the practice has been held through all time to this day. Thus, it is truly asserted, it is more ancient than the Roman Eagle or Golden Fleece.

The first tools put into the hand of the young operative Mason are the 24-inch rule, the hammer, and the chisel. These are used to measure his work, to knock off all superfluities, and to smoothen the surface of the stone. The speculative Mason morally uses them thus: by the 24-inch rule he measures the natural day, and divides it in portions for the three great duties of life, which throughout the whole human scheme are ever presented to view—prayer to the Most High; labour and necessary refreshment, with repose; and service to his brother or neighbour in time of need. The stone-mason's hammer, or gavel, as it is termed, is a symbol of conscience or man's knowledge of his thoughts and premeditated actions, which should curb all vanity and worldly-mindedness which interfere with that purity of heart essential to a good Mason. The chisel is an emblem of the advantages of education, which enables man to cultivate his intellectual powers, and thus fit him for society.

"Man, like the generous vine, supported lives;
The strength he gains is from the embrace he gives."

The initiation of the Apprentice Mason being completed, he is then further instructed in Masonic requirements with the following charge:—

BROTHER,

As you have now passed through the ceremonies of your initiation, allow me to congratulate you on being admitted a member of our ancient and honourable society. Ancient, no doubt, it is, as having subsisted from time immemorial; and honourable it must be acknowledged to be, because by a natural tendency it conduces to make all those honourable who are strictly obedient to its precepts. Indeed, no institution can boast a more solid foundation than that on which Freemasonry rests—the practice of social and moral virtue: and to so high an eminence has its credit been advanced, that in every age monarchs themselves have become the promoters of the Art; have not thought it derogatory from their dignity to exchange the sceptre for the trowel; have patronized our mysteries, and even joined in our assemblies.

As a Mason, I would first recommend to your most serious contemplation the volume of the Sacred Law: charging you to consider it as the unerring standard of truth and justice, and to regulate your actions by the divine precepts it contains. Therein you will be taught the important duties you owe to God, to your neighbour, and to yourself. To God, by never mentioning his name, but with that awe and reverence which are due from the creature to his Creator; by imploring his aid on all your lawful undertakings, and by looking up to Him in every emergency for comfort and support. To your neighbour, by acting with him upon the square; by rendering him every kind office which justice or mercy may require; by relieving his distresses and soothing his afflictions; and by doing to him, as, in similar cases, you would wish he should do to you. And to yourself, by such a prudent and well-regulated course of discipline, as may best conduce to the preservation of your corporeal and mental faculties in their fullest energy; thereby enabling you to exert the talents wherewith God has blessed you, as well to his glory, as to the welfare of your fellowcreatures.

As a citizen of the world, I am next to enjoin you to be exemplary in the discharge of your civil duties, by never proposing, or at all countenancing, any act that may have a tendency to subvert the peace and good order of society; by paying due obedience to the laws of any state which may for a time become the place of your residence, or afford you its protection; and above all, by never losing sight of the allegiance due to the

Sovereign of your native land; ever remembering that nature has implanted in your breast a sacred and indissoluble attachment to that country from which you derived your birth and infant nurture.

As an individual, I am further to recommend the practice of every domestic as well as public virtue. Let Prudence direct you! Temperance chasten you! Fortitude support you! and Justice be the guide of all your actions. Be especially careful to maintain, in their fullest splendour, those truly Masonic ornaments, which have already been amply illustrated, Benevolence and Charity.

Still, however, as a Mason, there are other excellencies of character to which your attention may be peculiarly and forcibly directed. Among the foremost of these are, Secrecy, Fidelity, and Obedience.

Secrecy may be said to consist in an inviolable adherence to the obligation you have entered into, never improperly to reveal any of those Masonic secrets which have now been, or may at any future time be, entrusted to your keeping; and cautiously to shun all occasions which might inadvertently lead you so to do.

Your Fidelity must be exemplified by a strict observance of the constitutions of the Fraternity; by adhering to the ancient landmarks of the Order; by never attempting to extort, or otherwise unduly obtain, the secrets of a superior degree; and by refraining to recommend any one to a participation of our secrets, unless you have strong grounds to believe that by a similar fidelity, he will ultimately reflect honour on our choice.

So must your Obedience be proved by a close conformity to our laws and regulations; by prompt attention to all signs and summonses; by modest and correct demeanour whilst in the Lodge; by abstaining from every topic of religious or political discussion; by ready acquiescence in all votes and resolutions duly passed by the brethren; and by perfect submission to the

Master and his Wardens, whilst acting in the discharge of their respective offices.

And, as a last general recommendation, let me exhort you to dedicate yourself to such pursuits as may enable you to become at once respectable in your rank of life, useful to mankind, and an ornament to the Society of which you have this day been admitted a member; that you would more especially devote your leisure hours to the study of such of the liberal arts and sciences as may lie within the compass of your attainment; and that, without neglecting the ordinary duties of your station, you would consider yourself called upon to make a daily advancement in Masonic knowledge.

Whatever business may have been entered upon, or in whichever degree the Lodge may have been opened, the final close is in the first degree, in order to give the Apprentice Mason his share in the proceedings of the meeting; and the Master invariably solicits the sentiments of each member on any point of interest, either to the Craft generally or the particular Lodge, and concludes the meeting by one and all offering up their thanks to the Great Architect of the Universe for favours received, and a supplication to the same high Power that He will by his beneficence continue his support to the Order, by cementing its members in love and unity, adorning them with all the Divine virtues.

REMARKS ON THE FIRST LECTURE.

Having illustrated the ceremony of opening and closing the Lodge, and inserted the Prayers and Charges usually rehearsed in our regular assemblies on those occasions, we shall now enter on a disquisition of the different Sections of the Lectures which are appropriated to the three Degrees of the Order; giving a brief summary of the whole, and annexing to every Remark the particulars to which the Section alludes. By these means the industrious Mason will be better instructed in the regular arrangement of the Lectures, and be enabled with more ease to acquire a competent knowledge of the Art.

The First Lecture is divided into Sections, and each Section is subdivided into Clauses. In this Lecture, virtue is painted in the most beautiful colours, and the duties of morality are strictly enforced. Here we are taught such wise and useful lessons as prepare the mind for a regular advancement in the principles of knowledge and philosophy; and these are imprinted on the memory by lively and sensible images, well calculated to influence our conduct in the proper discharge of the duties of social life.

The First Section of this Lecture is suited to all capacities, and may, and ought to be known by every person who wishes to rank as a Mason. It consists of general heads, which, though they be short and simple, will be found to carry weight with them. They not only serve as marks of distinction, but communicate useful and interesting knowledge when they are duly investigated. They qualify us to try and examine the rights of others to our privileges, while they demonstrate our own claim; and as they induce us to inquire minutely into other particulars of greater importance, they serve as a proper introduction to subjects which are more amply explained in the following Sections.

The Second Section makes us acquainted with the peculiar forms and ceremonies which are adopted at the initiation of candidates into Masonry; and convinces us, beyond the power of contradiction, of the propriety of our rites; whilst it demonstrates to the most sceptical and hesitating mind their excellence and utility.

The Third Section, by the reciprocal communication of our marks of distinction, proves the regularity of our initiation, and inculcates those necessary and instructive duties which dignify our character in the double capacity of Men and Masons.

The Fourth Section rationally accounts for the origin of our hieroglyphical instruction, and points out the advantages which accompany a faithful observance of our duty. It illustrates, at the same time, certain particulars, our ignorance of which might lead us into error, and which, as Masons, we are indispensably bound to know. It illustrates, also, the symbolic pillars by which the Lodge is supported, and the moral virtues of faith, hope, and charity, allegorically described as the three principal staves of the Masonic ladder.

To make daily progress in the Art is a constant duty, and expressly required by our general laws. What end can be more noble than the pursuit of virtue? what motive more alluring than the practice of justice? or what instruction more beneficial than an accurate elucidation of symbols which tend to improve and embellish the mind? Every thing that strikes the eye more immediately engages the attention, and imprints on the memory serious and solemn truths. Masons have, therefore, universally adopted the plan of inculcating the tenets of their Order by typical figures and allegorical emblems, to prevent their mysteries from descending within the familiar reach of inattentive and unprepared novices, from whom they might not receive due veneration.

The usages and customs of Masons have ever corresponded with those of the ancient Egyptians, to which, indeed, they bear a near affinity. Those philosophers, unwilling to expose their mysteries to vulgar eyes, concealed their particular tenets and principles of polity and philosophy under hieroglyphical figures; and expressed their notions of government by signs and symbols, which they communicated to their Magi alone, who were bound *by oath*[1] never to reveal them. Pythagoras seems to have established his system on a similar plan; and many Orders of a more recent date have copied the example. Masonry, however, is not only the most ancient, but the most moral Institution that ever subsisted; as every character, figure, and emblem depicted in the Lodge has a moral meaning, and tends to inculcate the practice of virtue on those who behold it.

The Fifth Section explains the nature and principles of our Institution, and teaches us to discharge with propriety the duties of the different departments which we are appointed to sustain in the government of the Lodge. Here, too, our ornaments are displayed, and our jewels and furniture specified; while a proper attention is paid to our ancient and venerable patron.

To explain the subjects treated in this Section, and assist the industrious Mason to acquire them, we can only recommend a punctual attendance on the duties of the Lodge, and a diligent application to the lessons which are there inculcated.

The Sixth Section strengthens those which precede, and enforces, in the most engaging manner, a due regard to character and behaviour, in public as well as in private life, in the Lodge as well as in the general commerce of society.

This Section forcibly inculcates the most instructive lessons. *Brotherly Love, Relief*, and *Truth* are themes on which we here expatiate.—By the exercise of *Brotherly Love* we are taught to regard the whole human species as one family, the high and low, the rich and poor; who, as children of the same Parent, and inhabitants of the same planet, are to aid, support, and protect each other. On this principle Masonry unites men of every country, sect, and opinion; and conciliates true friendship

[1] Pythagoras used the triangle as a symbol to administer the oath of secrecy, deriving it, doubtless, from the Jews, who used this form, as a perfect symbol, each side answering to the fourlettered name YHVH, I AM, was, and ever shall be.

among those who might otherwise have remained at a perpetual distance.—*Relief* is the next tenet of the profession; and though to relieve the distressed is a duty incumbent on all men, it is more particularly so on Masons, who are linked together by an indissoluble chain of sincere affection. To soothe calamity, alleviate misfortune, compassionate misery, and restore peace to the troubled mind, is the grand aim of the true Mason. On this basis he establishes his friendships, and forms his connexions. —*Truth* is a divine attribute, and the foundation of every virtue. To be good and true is the first lesson we are taught in Masonry. On this theme we contemplate, and by its dictates endeavour to regulate our conduct. Influenced by this principle, hypocrisy and deceit are unknown in the Lodge, sincerity and plain-dealing distinguish us; while the heart and tongue join in promoting the general welfare, and rejoicing in each other's prosperity.

To this illustration succeeds an explanation of the four cardinal virtues, TEMPERANCE, FORTITUDE, PRUDENCE, and JUSTICE.

Temperance is that due restraint upon our affections and passions which renders the body tame and governable, and frees the mind from the allurements of vice. That virtue should be the constant practice of every Mason, as he is thereby taught to avoid excess, or contract any licentious or vicious habit, the indulgence of which might lead him to disclose some of those valuable secrets which he has promised to conceal and never reveal, and, consequently, subject him to the contempt of all good Masons.

Fortitude is that noble and steady purpose of the soul, equally distant from rashness and cowardice; it enables a man to undergo any labour, pain, danger, or difficulty, when thought necessary. By fortitude we are taught to resist temptation and encounter danger with firmness and resolution.

Prudence teaches us to regulate our lives and actions by the dictates of reason, and is that habit of mind by which men wisely judge on all things relative to their temporal and eternal happiness. It should therefore be the distinguishing characteristic of every Free and Accepted Mason. On this virtue all others depend; it is, therefore, the chief jewel that can adorn the human frame.

Justice is that station or boundary of right which teaches us to render to every man his just due, and that without distinction. This virtue is not only consistent with divine and moral law, but is likewise the standard and cement of civil society. Without the exercise of justice, universal confusion would ensue, lawless force would overcome the principles of equity, and social intercourse no longer exist. So, as the practice of justice in a great measure constitutes the real good man, it ought to be the invariable habit of every Mason never to deviate from it in the smallest way, but be just and upright in all things

The explanation of these virtues is accompanied with some general observations on the equality observed among Masons. In the Lodge no estrangement of behaviour is discovered. Influenced by the same principle, an uniformity of opinion, which is useful in exigencies, and pleasing in familiar life, universally prevails, strengthens the ties of friendship, and promotes love and esteem. Masons are brethren by a double tie, and among them, as brothers, no invidious distinctions exist; merit being always respected, and honour rendered to whom honour is due.—A king in the Lodge is reminded that, although a crown may adorn the head, or a sceptre the hand, the blood in the veins is derived from the common parent of mankind, and is no better than that of the meanest subject.—The statesman, the senator, and the artist are there taught that, equally with others, they are, by nature, exposed to infirmity and disease; and that an unforeseen misfortune, or a disordered frame, may impair their faculties, and level them with the most ignorant of their species. This checks pride, and incites courtesy of behaviour. —Men of inferior talents, or who are not placed by fortune in such exalted stations, are instructed to regard their superiors with peculiar esteem; when they discover them voluntarily divested of the trappings of external grandeur, and condescending, in the badge of innocence and bond of friendship, to trace wisdom and follow virtue, assisted by those who are of a rank beneath them. Virtue is true nobility, and Wisdom is the channel by which Virtue is directed and conveyed; Wisdom and Virtue only mark distinction among Masons.

The Seventh and last Section is an elucidation of the two denominations of Masons, Free and Accepted, and Operative; with an examination in detail of the points which peculiarly mark the former; and concluding with the following illustration of what is and ought to be the distinguishing characteristics of every Free and Accepted Mason, viz., *Virtue, Honour,* and *Mercy.*

VIRTUE.—In perusing the records of ancient Rome, we find that the Consul Marcellus intended to erect a temple to be dedicated both to Virtue and Honour, but was for a time prevented carrying the project into execution, and he afterwards founded two temples, so situate, the only avenue to the temple of Honour was through that of Virtue, thereby leaving an excellent moral to posterity. *Virtue* is the highest exercise and improvement of reason, the integrity, harmony, and just balance of affection, the health, strength, and beauty of the soul. The perfection of Virtue is to give Reason its full scope, to obey the dictates of conscience with alacrity, to exercise the defensive talents with fortitude, the public with justice, the private with temperance, and the whole of them with prudence; that is, in a due proportion to each other, with a calm and diffusive benevolence; to love and adore our Creator with sincerity, and to acquiesce in all the dispensations of Divine Providence with cheerful resignation. Every approach towards this standard is a step towards perfection and happiness; a deviation therefrom leads to vice and misery.

HONOUR is the most manly and dignified sentiment or impulse of the soul which Virtue can inspire; and the actions of all good men are regulated by Honour, inasmuch as it renders unnecessary the forms that are found requisite to bind those who are destitute of this refined principle. It is also the highest incentive to the performance of the most heroic and disinterested actions, as it implies the united sentiments of Faith, Truth, and Justice, carried by an enlightened mind far beyond the moral obligations which the laws of our country require, or can punish the violation of. Honour, although a different principle from Religion, is that which produces similar effects; for the lines of action, although differently drawn, terminate in the same point. Religion embraces Virtue as it is enjoined by the laws of God, Honour as it is graceful and ornamental to human nature: the religious man fears, the man of honour scorns, to do an ill act; the one considering vice as beneath him, the other as offensive to the Deity; the one as unbecoming, the other as that which is forbidden. Thus Honour may be justly considered the noblest branch that can spring from the glorious stock of virtue; for a man of honour will not content himself with a literal discharge of his duty as a man and a citizen, but he exalts and dignifies it to magnanimity: he gives where he might with propriety refuse, and he forgives where he might with strict justice resent. Thus Virtue and Honour united have hitherto been, and we trust will continue to be, the characteristics of a Mason.

MERCY has ever been held sacred by all good men. If possessed by a monarch, it adds a brilliancy to every gem that adorns his crown; it gives glory to his ministers, and an unceasing freshness to the wreath which decks the warrior's brow. It is the companion of true honour and the ameliorator of justice, on whose bench, when enthroned, she interposes a shield of defence on behalf of the victim impenetrable to the sword. As the vernal showers descend from heaven to enliven and invigorate the vegetable world, so Mercy, resting on the heart of man, when its vital fluids are condensed by revenge, by its exhilarating warmth restores perverse nature to its original source in purer streams. It is the chief attribute of that Deity, on whom the best as well as the wisest of us must rest his hopes and dependence. To show mercy and forgiveness is highly pleasing in the sight of our Creator; we are told that "blessed are the merciful, for they shall obtain mercy," not only in this transitory life, but at the final day of retribution, when summoned before God's awful tribunal, when the actions done in this life are unfolded to view; and although justice may demand the fiat, let us hope His mercy will avert the awful doom.

Such is the arrangement of the Sections in the First Lecture, which, including the forms adopted at opening and closing the Lodge, comprehends the whole of the First Degree.

On taking a retrospective view of this Lecture, it will be apparent that the cause of Freemasonry is connected with the best interests of mankind, and that by a strict attention to the tenets of the Order, and the principles of Truth and Virtue which are inculcated in the Lecture, Masons cannot fail to elevate themselves in the scale of intellectual beings, and become better members of society.

SONGS APPROPRIATE TO THE ENTERED APPRENTICE.

COME, let us prepare, we Brothers that are
  Assembled on merry occasion,
To drink, laugh, and sing; for our wine has a spring:
  Here's a health to an Accepted Mason.

The world is in pain our secrets to gain,
And still let them wonder and gaze on:
Till they're shown the Light, they'll ne'er know the right
Word or sign of an Accepted Mason.

'Tis this, and 'tis that, they cannot tell what,
Nor why the great men of the nation
Should aprons put on, and make themselves one
With a Free and an Accepted Mason.

Great kings, dukes, and lords, have laid by their swords,
Our myst'ry to put a good grace on;
And thought themselves famed to hear themselves named
With a Free and an Accepted Mason.

Antiquity's pride we have on our side,
To keep up our old reputation;
There's nought but what's good to be understood
By a Free and an Accepted Mason.

We're true and sincere, and just to the fair,
Who will trust us on any occasion;
No mortal can more the ladies adore
Than a Free and an Accepted Mason.

Then join hand in hand, by each Brother firm stand,
Let's be merry and put a bright face on;
What mortal can boast so noble a toast } *Chorus*
As a Free and an Accepted Mason? } *3 times.* } *Standing.*

HERE'S a health to each one, from the king on the throne,
To him that is meanest of station,
If he can contend to have lawfully gain'd
The name of an Accepted Mason.

The glories of kings are poor empty things,
  Though empires they have in possession,
If void of the fame of that noblest of names,
  A Free and an Accepted Mason.

It is ancienter far than other arts are,
  Surpassing all other profession:
There's none can pretend to discover a friend
  Like a Free and an Accepted Mason.

The world is amazed, their wonder is raised
  To see such concurring relation
Among us: they cry, The devil is nigh
  When one is accepted a Mason.

But let them say on, to us 'tis well known
  What's true or false in the relation;
Let's drink his health round that is secret and sound,
  And a Faithful and Accepted Mason.

JUST straight from his home see yon candidate come,
  Prepared for the time and occasion:
Of all that can harm we will him disarm,
  That he no ways may hurt a Freemason.

His eyes cannot search out the way of his march,
  Nor yet where his steps he must place on:
When him we receive, he cannot perceive
  How he came to be made a Freemason.

Then he'll danger defy, and on heaven rely
  For strength to support the occasion;
With the blessing of pray'r he banishes fear,
  And undaunted is made a Freemason.

When he makes his demand, by the Master's command,
  To know if he's fit for the station,
Around he is brought, ere he get what he sought
  From a Free and an Accepted Mason.

When girded with care, by the help of the square,
  The emblem of truth and of reason,
In form he is placed, while to him are rehearsed
  The mysteries of a Freemason.

Then full in his sight doth shine the grand light,
  To illumine the works which we trace on;
And now, as his due, he's cloth'd in full view
  With the badge of an Accepted Mason.

Now, hark! we enlarge on the duties and charge,
  Where his conduct and walk he must place on;
Then a bumper we'll fill, and show our good will
  To a Free and an Accepted Mason.

WHEN a Lodge of Freemasons are cloth'd in their aprons,
  In order to make a new Brother,
With firm hearts and clean hands they repair to their stands,
  And justly support one another.

Trusty Brother, take care, of eaves-droppers beware,
  'Tis a just and a solemn occasion;
Give the word and the blow, that workmen may know
  You are going to make a Freemason.

The Master stands due, and his officers too,
  While Craftsmen are plying their station;
The Deacons do stand right for the command
  Of a Free and an Accepted Mason.

Now traverse your ground, as in duty you're bound,
  And revere the authentic oration,
That leads to the way, and proves the first ray
  Of the light of an Accepted Mason.

Here are words, here are signs, here are problems and lines,
  And room too for deep speculation:
Here virtue and truth are taught to the youth
  When first he is bound to a Mason.

Hieroglyphics shine bright, and light reverts light
  On the rules and the tools of vocation;
We work and we sing, the Craft and the King,
  'Tis both duty and choice in a Mason.

What's said or is done is here truly laid down,
  In this form of our high installation;
Yet I challenge a man to know what I mean,
  Unless he's an Accepted Mason.

The ladies claim right to come into our light,
  Since the apron, they say, is their bearing;
Can they subject their will, can they keep their tongues still,
  And let talking be changed into hearing?

This difficult task is the least we can ask,
  To secure us on sundry occasions;
When with this they comply, our utmost we'll try
  To raise Lodges for lady Freemasons.

Till this can be done, must each Brother be mum,
  Though the fair one should wheedle and teaze on;
Be just, true, and kind; but still bear in mind
  At all times that you are a Freemason.

CHAPTER XI.

THE SECOND DEGREE, OR FELLOW-CRAFT.

"Thus he showed me: and behold the Lord stood upon a wall made by a plumb-line, with a plumb-line in his hand. And the Lord said unto me, Amos, what seest thou? And I said, A plumb-line. Then said the Lord, Behold, I will set a plumb-line in the midst of my people Israel: I will not pass by them any more."—AMOS vii. 7, 8.

MASONRY is a progressive science, and is divided into different classes, or degrees, for the more regular advancement in the knowledge of its mysteries. According to the progress we make, we limit or extend our inquiries; and, in proportion to our talents, we attain to a lesser or greater degree of perfection.

Masonry includes almost every branch of polite learning under the veil of its mysteries, which comprehend a regular system of virtue and science. Many of its illustrations may appear unimportant to the confined genius; but the man of more enlarged faculties will consider them in the highest degree useful and interesting. To please the accomplished scholar and ingenious artist, the institution is well suited; and in the investigation of its latent doctrines, the philosopher and mathematician may experience equal satisfaction and delight.

To exhaust the various subjects of which Masonry treats, would transcend the powers of the brightest genius: still, however, nearer approaches to perfection may be made; and the man of wisdom will not check the progress of his abilities, though the task he attempts may at first seem insurmountable. Perseverance and application will remove each difficulty as it occurs; every step he advances, new pleasures will open to his view, and instruction of the noblest kind attend his researches. In the diligent pursuit of knowledge great discoveries are made; and the intellectual faculties are wisely employed in promoting the glory of God and the good of mankind.

SUCH IS THE TENDENCY OF ALL THE ILLUSTRATIONS IN MASONRY. REVERENCE FOR THE DEITY AND GRATITUDE FOR THE BLESSINGS OF HEAVEN ARE INCULCATED IN EVERY DEGREE. This is the plan of our system and the result of our inquiries.

The Entered Apprentice duly qualified by time is thus in open Lodge required to undergo an examination as to his preparation for being initiated, when and where he underwent the ceremony, his knowledge of what he had been entrusted with, with proofs, and also what Freemasonry was.

The candidate having satisfactorily replied to these inquiries, or any other method of proof deemed necessary, he is then, under a solemn promise of secrecy, entrusted with a password to enable him to present himself at the portal of a Fellow-Craft's Lodge.

The First Degree being intended to enforce the duties of morality, and imprint on the memory the noblest principles which can adorn the human mind, the Second Degree extends the plan, and comprehends a more diffusive system of knowledge. Practice and theory are united, to qualify the industrious Mason to share the pleasures which an advancement in the art necessarily affords. Listening with attention to the opinions of experienced men on important subjects, the mind of the Craftsman is gradually familiarized to useful instruction, and he is soon enabled to investigate truths of the utmost concern in the general transactions of life.

From this system proceeds a rational amusement. While the

The Fellow Craft.

mental powers are fully employed, the judgment is properly exercised; a spirit of emulation prevails; and every brother vies who shall most excel in promoting the design of the Institution.

During the candidate's absence a Lodge of Fellow-Crafts is opened, and as this degree is particularly devoted to science, the blessing of the Creator is thus invoked:—

"We supplicate the Grand Geometrician of the Universe that the rays of Heaven may shed their benign influence over us, to enlighten us in the paths of nature and of science. *So mote it be.*"

On the Entered Apprentice being admitted into the Lodge, he is directed by the Master to kneel while the blessing of Heaven is thus invoked:—

"We supplicate, O Lord, a continuance of thy Divine aid in behalf of the brother who now kneels before Thee; and grant that the work to be done in thy name be continued to thy glory. *So mote it be.*"

The brother who has been admitted into the Second Degree is informed by the Master that as a Craftsman he is expected to make the liberal arts and sciences his future study, that he may be the better enabled to discharge his duties as a Mason, and estimate the wondrous works of the Almighty Creator.

The Master then admonishes him on the progression by which he had been advanced, and that it is equally his duty to bear in mind and practise the moral virtues inculcated in the First Degree, as well as those demonstrative sciences which are the objects of the Second Degree.

The working tools of a Craftsman are then presented to him. Their operative and speculative uses are thus described:

The *Square* is an important implement to operative Masons, for by it they are enabled to correct the errors of the eye, and to adjust with precision the edges, sides, and angles of their work, and thus assist in bringing rude matter into due form. The nicest joints are by its means adjusted, and stones are fitted with accuracy to fill their destined positions.

The *Level* is an instrument by which Masons' work is adjusted in the same line or plane, or to lay the work in true horizontal level.

The *Plumb* is an instrument made use of for the purpose of erecting perpendicular lines, or to try and adjust all uprights while fixing on their proper basis.

To the speculative Mason the *square* teaches morality,—the *level* equality, and the *plumb* justness and uprightness of life and actions: and thus by square conduct, level steps, and upright intentions, we hope to ascend to those immortal mansions whence all goodness emanates.

The Lodge in this degree is closed by the Master exhorting the brethren to remember wherever they are, whatever they do, the all-seeing eye of the Grand Geometrician is ever over all, and that while they continue to act as Fellow-Craft Masons, they must discharge their duties with fervency and zeal.

The Second Degree is, it is to be observed, particularly devoted to science. The lessons or instructions in the First Degree are entirely given to piety, morality, and brotherly love. In the Second Degree the Craftsman's attention is directed to the study of science, the beauties of which, and the wonders of nature and art, are by degrees unfolded to his view in the Lectures. Many Masons are of opinion this degree completed ancient Jewish Masonry, and that the Third, or Master Mason's Degree was an ordination of the New Covenant.

The Book of Constitutions declares, "No Lodge shall confer more than one degree on any brother on the same day, nor shall a higher degree be conferred on any brother at a less interval than four weeks from his receiving a previous degree, nor until he has passed an examination in open Lodge in that degree."

The Lecture of this degree is divided into five Sections, and the whole are devoted to human science, and to trace the goodness and majesty of the Creator by minutely analyzing his works.

The First Section of the Second Degree elucidates the mode of introduction into this class; and instructs the diligent Craftsman how to proceed in the proper arrangement of the ceremonies which are used on that occasion. It enables him to judge of the importance of those rites, and convinces him of the necessity of adhering to all the established usages of the Order. Here he is entrusted with particular tests, to prove his title to the privileges of this degree; and satisfactory reasons are given for their origin. The duties which cement, in the firmest union, well-informed brethren, are illustrated; and an opportunity is given to make such advances in the Art, as will always distinguish the talents of able Craftsmen.

Besides the ceremony of passing to the Second Degree, this Section contains many important particulars, with which no officer of the Lodge should be unacquainted.

Formerly, the following charge was delivered to the Craftsman on passing this degree:—

BROTHER,

Being advanced to the Second Degree of the Order, we congratulate you on your preferment. The internal, and not the external, qualifications of a man, are what Masonry regards. As you increase in knowledge, you will consequently improve in social intercourse.

It is unnecessary to recapitulate the duties which, as a Mason, you are now bound to discharge; or enlarge on the necessity of a strict adherence to them; as your own experience must have established their value. It may be sufficient to observe, that your past behaviour and regular deportment have merited the honour which we have conferred; and in your new character it is expected that you will not only conform to the principles of the Order, but steadily persevere in the practice of every virtue.

The study of the liberal arts, that valuable branch of education, which tends so effectually to polish and adorn the mind, is earnestly recommended to your consideration; especially the science of Geometry, which is established as the basis of our Art. Geometry, or Masonry, originally synonymous terms, is of a divine and moral nature, and enriched with the most useful knowledge. Whilst it proves the wonderful properties of nature, it demonstrates the more important truths of morality.

As the solemnity of our ceremonies requires a serious deportment, you are to be particularly attentive to your behaviour in our regular assemblies; you are to preserve our ancient usages and customs sacred and inviolable; and induce others, by your example, to hold them in due veneration.

The laws and regulations of the Order you are strenuously to support and maintain. You are not to palliate, or aggravate, the offences of your brethren; but, in the decision of every trespass against our rules, judge with candour, admonish with friendship, and reprehend with mercy.

As a Craftsman, in our private assemblies you may offer your sentiments and opinions on such subjects as are regularly introduced in the Lecture, under the superintendence of an experienced Master, who will guard the landmarks against encroachment. By this privilege you may improve your intellectual powers, qualify yourself to become an useful member of society, and, like a skilful brother, strive to excel in what is good and great.

All regular signs and summonses, given and received, you are duly to honour, and punctually obey, inasmuch as they consist with our professed principles. You are to encourage industry and reward merit; supply the wants and relieve the necessities of brethren and fellows, to the utmost of your power and ability; and on no account to wrong them, or see them wronged, but timely to apprise them of approaching danger, and view their interest as inseparable from your own.

Such is the nature of your engagements as a Craftsman; and these duties you are now bound, by the most sacred ties, to observe.

The Second Section of this degree presents an ample field for the man of genius to perambulate. It cursorily specifies the particular classes of the Order, and explains the requisite qualifications for preferment in each. In the explanation of our usages, many remarks are introduced, which are equally useful to the experienced artist and the sage moralist. The various operations of the mind are demonstrated, as far as they will admit of elucidation, and a fund of extensive science is explored throughout. Here we find employment for leisure hours; trace science from its original source; and, by drawing the attention to the sum of perfection, contemplate with admiration the wonderful works of the Creator. Geometry is displayed, with all its powers and properties; and in the disquisition of this science, the mind is filled with rapture and delight.

Geometry is the science which investigates the relations existing between parts of space, whether linear, superficial, or solid. The history of the rise of this science, by the Egyptians, having their landmarks yearly destroyed by the inundations of the Nile, being obliged to invent the art of land-surveying in order to preserve the memory of the bounds of property, is transmitted to us by tradition, but without any proof that they were more of Geometers than Astronomers. We have no historic evidence of the knowledge and practice of this science by any people earlier than the Greeks. Thales, born at Miletus in Ionia, of Phœnician parents, travelled in pursuit of knowledge, and when in Egypt taught the people how to measure the pyramids. He founded the earliest school for Geometry and Astronomy. Thales, who is enumerated among the Seven Wise Men, we may rank as the first natural philosopher. He is recorded to have made many physical discoveries. He determined the magnitude of the sun to be 720 times that of the moon, and fixed the length of the year at 365 days. He predicted the great eclipse which took place when the armies of Cyrus and Alyattes were engaged in battle. Diogenes records one of his sayings:—"The most ancient of things existing is God, for He is uncreated; the most beautiful thing is the Universe, for it is God's creation." He died about B.C. 548.

Pythagoras, some few years after, gave Geometry the form of a science; he was followed by other eminent men, among whom may be more particularly named Plato and Euclid. The mathematical works of the latter are in use to this day.

Geometry is the first and noblest of sciences, and the basis on which the structure of Freemasonry is erected.

The contemplation of this science in a moral and comprehensive view fills the mind with rapture. To the true Geometrician, the regions of matter with which he is surrounded afford ample scope for his admiration, while they open a sublime field for his inquiry and disquisition. Every blade of grass which covers the field, every flower that blows, and every insect which wings its way in the bounds of expanded space, proves the existence of a First Cause, and yields pleasure to the intelligent mind.

The symmetry, beauty, and order, displayed in the various parts of animate and inanimate creation are pleasing and delightful themes, and naturally lead to the source whence the whole is derived. When we bring within the focus of the eye the variegated carpet of the terrestrial creation, and survey the progress of the vegetative system, our admiration is justly excited. Every plant that grows, every flower that displays its beauties or breathes its sweets, affords instruction and delight. When we extend our views to the animal creation, and contemplate the varied clothing of every species, we are equally struck with astonishment; and when we trace the lines of Geometry drawn by the Divine pencil in the beautiful plumage of the feathered tribe, how exalted is our conception of the heavenly work! The admirable structure of plants and animals, and the infinite number of fibres and vessels which run through the whole, with the apt disposition of one part to another, is a perpetual subject of study to the true Geometrician; who, while he adverts to the changes which all undergo in their progress to maturity, is lost in rapture and veneration of the Great Cause that produced the whole, and which continues to govern the system.

When he descends into the bowels of the earth, and explores the kingdom of ores, minerals, and fossils, he finds the same instances of Divine wisdom and goodness displayed in their formation and structure; every gem and every pebble proclaims the handy-work of an Almighty Creator.

When he surveys the watery element, and directs his attention to the wonders of the deep, with all the inhabitants of the mighty ocean, he perceives emblems of the same Supreme Intelligence. The scales of the largest whale, and the pencilled shell of the most diminutive fish, equally yield a theme for his contemplation, on which he fondly dwells; while the symmetry of their formation, and the delicacy of the tints, evince to his discerning eye the wisdom of the Divine Artist.

When he exalts his view to the more noble and elevated parts of Nature, and surveys the celestial orbs, how much greater is his astonishment! If, on the principles of Geometry and true philosophy, he contemplates the sun, the moon, the stars, and the whole concave of heaven, his pride is humbled, and he is lost in awful admiration. The immense magnitude of those bodies, the regularity and rapidity of their motions, and the vast extent of space through which they move, are equally inconceivable; and, as far as they exceed human comprehension, baffle his most daring ambition, till, lost in the immensity of the theme, he sinks into his primitive insignificance.

By Geometry, then, we curiously trace Nature, through her various windings, to her most concealed recesses. By it we discover the power, the wisdom, and the goodness of the Great

Artificer of the Universe, and view with delight the proportions which connect this vast machine. By it we discover how the planets move in their different orbits, and demonstrate their various revolutions. By it we account for the return of seasons, and the variety of scenes which each season displays to the discerning eye. Numberless worlds are around us, all framed by the same Divine Artist, which roll through the vast expanse, and are all conducted by the same unerring law.

A survey of Nature, and the observation of her beautiful proportions, first determined man to imitate the Divine plan, and study symmetry and order. This gave rise to societies, and birth to every useful art. The architect began to design; and the plans which he laid down, improved by experience and time, produced works which have been the admiration of every age.

The Second Section concludes with this eloquent illustration of the six days' work of Creation:—

When we consider that the formation of this world was the work of that Divine Being who created the beautiful system of the Universe, and caused all nature to be under his supreme command, how ought we to magnify and adore his Holy Name for his goodness to the children of men! Before the Almighty was pleased to command this vast whole into existence, the elements and materials of the Creation lay blended together without form or distinction; darkness was on the face of the great deep, and the Spirit of God moved on the surface of the waters. The Almighty, as an example to man that things of moment should be done with due deliberation, was pleased to be six days in commanding it from chaos to perfection.

The first instance of his supreme power was made manifest by commanding light. Being pleased with this new operation, He distinguished it by a name, calling the light day, and the darkness He called night. In order to keep this new-framed matter within just limits, the second period was employed in laying the foundation of the Heavens, which He called firmament, designed to keep those waters which were within the clouds, and those beneath them, asunder. On the third period those waters were commanded into due limits; on the retreat of which dry land appeared, which He called earth, and the gathering together of the mighty congregated waters He called seas. The earth being, as yet, irregular, barren, and uncultivated, God spake the word, and it was immediately covered with a beautiful carpet of grass, designed as pasture for the brute creation. Trees, shrubs, and flowers of all sorts succeeded in full growth, maturity, and perfection. On the fourth period those two grand luminaries, the sun and moon, were created,—the sun to rule the day, and the moon to govern the night. And the sacred historian informs us they were ordained for signs, for seasons, for days and years. The Almighty was also pleased to bespangle the ethereal concave with a multitude of stars, that man, whom He intended to make, might contemplate thereon, and justly admire his majesty and glory.

On the fifth period He caused the waters to bring forth a variety of fish for our use; and in order to imprint on man a reverential awe of his Divine omnipotence, He created great whales, which, together with other inhabitants of the great deep, multiplied exceedingly after their kind. On the same period He caused the birds to fly in the air, that man might delight his eyes and ears, with some for their beautiful plumage, and others for their melodious notes.

On the sixth period He created the beasts of the field, and the reptiles that crawl on the earth. And here we may plainly perceive the wisdom, power, and goodness of the Grand Geometrician of the Universe made manifest throughout the whole of his proceedings. He produced what effects He pleased without the aid of natural causes, such as giving light to the world before He had created the sun, and making the earth fruitful without the influence of the heavenly bodies. He did not create the beasts of the field until He had provided them with sufficient herbage for their support, neither did He make man until He had provided him with a dwelling, and every thing requisite for life and pleasure. Then to dignify the works of his hands still more He made man, who came into the world with greater pomp than any creature that had preceded him. They came with only a single command. God spake the word, and it was done; but at the formation of man, we are told, there was a consultation, in which God said, Let us make man. He was immediately formed out of the dust of the earth; the breath of life was breathed into his nostrils, and man became a living soul. Now in this one creature was a combination of every thing that was excellent throughout the whole creation, such as the quality and substance of an animate being, the life of plants, the sense of beasts; but, above all, the understanding of angels,—formed after the immediate image of God, thereby intimating to him that integrity and uprightness should ever influence him to adore his Divine Creator, who had so liberally bestowed on him the faculty of speech, and further endued him with that noble instinct called reason.

The Almighty as his last and best gift to man created woman; under his forming hand a creature grew, man like, but different in sex,

> "All kind and soft, all tender and divine,
> To mend our faults and mould us into virtue."

On she came, led by her Heavenly Maker, though unseen yet guided by his voice, adorned with all that Heaven could bestow to make her amiable. Grace was in all her steps, Heaven in her eye, and in every gesture dignity and love. The Almighty having finished his six days' work, on the seventh He rested, blessed, hallowed, and sanctified it. He has therefore taught man to work six days industriously, but strictly commanded him to rest on the seventh, the better to contemplate on the beautiful works of the creation, to adore Him as their Creator, to go into his sanctuaries, and offer praises for life and every blessing he so amply enjoys at his all-bountiful hands.

The Third Section has reference to the building of King Solomon's Temple, particularly detailing the construction of the two remarkable pillars that stood at the entrance. This Section is short, but of great importance to the Craftsman. The information it contains is founded on reason and sacred record; in fact, it is almost entirely derived from the historical books of the Old Testament.

Hanway, in his Journal of Travels, published in 1753, mentions as being in the Cabinet of Curiosities at Dresden a model of the Temple of Solomon cut in cedar, according to the description in the Book of Kings. The Sanctum Sanctorum, the Ark, &c., are all represented.

The Fourth Section, after illustrating the formation of a Fellow-Craft's Lodge, describes the FIVE NOBLE ORDERS OF ARCHITECTURE, and the seven liberal arts and sciences.

The Five Orders in Architecture are the Tuscan, Doric, Ionic, Corinthian, and Composite; and in the history of mankind there are few things more remarkable than that Masonry and Civilization have ever gone hand in hand together, and in earlier times it may be affirmed the Orders in architecture marked their growth and progress.

By Order, in architecture, is meant a system of the members, proportions, and ornaments of columns and pilasters; or it is a regular arrangement of the projecting parts of a building, which, united with those of a column, form a beautiful, perfect, and complete whole. Order in architecture may be traced from the first formation of society. When the rigour of seasons obliged men to contrive shelter from the inclemency of the weather, we learn that they first planted trees on end, and then laid others across, to support a covering. The bands which connected those trees at top and bottom are said to have suggested the idea of the base and capital of pillars; and from this simple hint originally proceeded the more improved art of architecture.

The five Orders are thus classed: the Tuscan, Doric, Ionic, Corinthian, and Composite.

The *Tuscan* is the most simple and solid of the five orders. It was invented in Tuscany, whence it derives its name. Its column is seven diameters high; and its capital, base, and entablature have but few mouldings. The simplicity of the construction of this column renders it eligible where solidity is the chief object, and where ornament would be superfluous.

The *Doric* order, which is plain and natural, is the most ancient, and was invented by the Greeks. Its column is eight diameters high, and it has seldom any ornaments on base or capital, except mouldings, though the frieze is distinguished by triglyphs and metopes, and the triglyphs compose the ornaments of the frieze. The solid composition of this order gives it a preference in structures where strength and a noble but rough simplicity are chiefly required.

The *Ionic* bears a kind of mean proportion between the more solid and delicate orders. Its column is nine diameters high; its capital is adorned with volutes, and its cornice has denticles. There is both delicacy and ingenuity displayed in this pillar; the invention of which is attributed to the Ionians, as the famous Temple of Diana at Ephesus was of this order. It is said to have been formed after the model of an agreeable young woman, of an elegant shape, with her hair dressed, as a contrast to the Doric order, which was formed after that of a strong robust man.

The *Corinthian,* the richest of the five orders, is deemed a masterpiece of art, and was invented at Corinth by Callimachus. Its column is ten diameters high, and its capital is adorned with two rows of leaves and eight volutes, which sustain the abacus. The frieze is ornamented with curious devices, and the cornice with denticles and modillions. This order is used in stately and superb structures.

The *Composite* is compounded of the other orders, and was contrived by the Romans. Its capital has the two rows of leaves of the Corinthian, and the volutes of the Ionic. Its column has the quarter-round as the Tuscan and Doric orders, is ten diameters high, and its cornice has denticles or simple modillions. This pillar is generally found in buildings where strength, elegance, and beauty are united.

These observations are intended to induce the industrious Craftsman to pursue his researches into the rise and progress of Architecture, by consulting the works of the best writers on the subject.

As the seven liberal arts and sciences are illustrated in this Section, it may not be improper to give a short explanation of them:

Grammar teaches the proper arrangement of words, according to the idiom or dialect of any particular people; and that excellency of pronunciation, which enables us to speak or write a language with accuracy, agreeably to reason and correct usage.

Rhetoric teaches us to speak copiously and fluently on any subject, not merely with propriety, but with all the advantages of force and elegance; wisely contriving to captivate the hearers by strength of argument and beauty of expression, whether it be to entreat or exhort, to admonish or applaud.

Logic teaches us to guide our reason discretionally in the general knowledge of things, and direct our inquiries after truth. It consists of a regular train of argument, whence we infer, deduce, and conclude, according to certain premises laid down, admitted or granted; and in it are employed the faculty of conceiving, judging, reasoning, and disposing; which are naturally led on from one gradation to another, till the point in question is finally determined.

Arithmetic teaches the powers and properties of numbers; which is variously effected by letters, tables, figures, and instruments.

By this art, reasons and demonstrations are given for finding out any certain number, whose relation or affinity to others is already known.

Geometry treats of the powers and properties of magnitudes in general, where length, breadth, and thickness are considered. By this science the architect is enabled to construct his plans; the general, to arrange his soldiers; the engineer, to mark out ground for encampments; the geographer, to give us the dimensions of the world, delineate the extent of seas, and specify the divisions of empires, kingdoms, and provinces; and by it, also, the astronomer is enabled to make his observations, and fix the duration of times and seasons, years and cycles. In short, Geometry is the foundation of architecture, and the root of the mathematics, and the basis on which the superstructure of Freemasonry is erected.

"The spacious firmament on high,
With all the blue ethereal sky,
And spangled heavens, a shining frame,
Their great Original proclaim.

"Th' unwearied sun, from day to day,
Does his Creator's praise display,
And publishes to every land
The work of an Almighty Hand.

"Soon as the evening shades prevail,
The moon takes up the wondrous tale,
And nightly, to the listening earth,
Repeats the story of her birth;

"While all the stars that round her burn,
And all the planets in their turn,
Confirm the tidings as they roll,
And spread the truth from pole to pole.

"What though in solemn silence all
Move round the dark terrestrial ball;
What though nor voice nor minstrel sound
Among their radiant orbs be found;

"With saints and angels they rejoice,
And utter forth their glorious voice;
For ever singing as they shine,
'The hand that made us is Divine.' "

Music teaches the art of forming concords, so as to compose delightful harmony, by a proportional arrangement of acute, grave, and mixed sounds. This art by a series of experiments is reduced to a science, with respect to tones and the intervals of sound only. It inquires into the nature of concords and discords, and enables us to find out the proportion between them by numbers.

In praise of this science Shakspeare says,

"The man that hath no music in himself,
Nor is not moved with concord of sweet sounds,
Is fit for treasons, stratagems, and spoils;
The motions of his spirit are as dull as night,
And his affections dark as Erebus:
Let no such man be trusted."

Astronomy is that art by which we are taught to read the wonderful works of the Almighty Creator in those sacred pages, the celestial hemisphere. Assisted by Astronomy, we observe the motions, measure the distances, comprehend the magnitudes, and calculate the periods and eclipses of the heavenly bodies. By it we learn the use of the globes, the system of the world, and the primary law of nature. While we are employed in the study of this science, we perceive unparalleled instances of wisdom and goodness, and through the whole of creation trace the glorious Author by his works.

The Fifth Section has reference to the institution at the time of building the Temple of Solomon, and may be said especially to refer to the payment of the workmen there employed, the government and division of classes among our ancient brethren, and the period that remarkable building was constructing, and its final completion and dedication.

Thus ends the Lecture in the Second Degree, which, besides the historical information relative to the house of God erected by King Solomon, contains a complete theory of philosophy and physics, and a regular system of science, demonstrated on the clearest principles, and established on the firmest foundation.

SONGS APPROPRIATE TO THE FELLOW-CRAFT.

TUNE—"*Goddess of Ease.*"

GENIUS of Masonry, descend,
   And with thee bring thy spotless train;
Constant our sacred rites attend,
   While we adore thy peaceful reign;
Bring with thee Virtue, brightest maid,
   Bring Love, bring Truth, bring Friendship here;
While social Mirth shall lend her aid,
   To smooth the wrinkled brow of care.

Come, Charity, with goodness crown'd,
   Encircled in thy heavenly robe,
Diffuse thy blessings all around,
   To every corner of the globe.
See where she comes, with power to bless,
   With open hand and tender heart,
Which wounded feels at man's distress,
   And bleeds at every human smart.

Envy may every ill devise,
   And falsehood be thy deadliest foe,
Thou, Friendship, still shalt towering rise,
   And sink thine adversaries low:
Thy well-built pile shall long endure,
   Through rolling years preserve its prime,
Upon a rock it stands secure,
   And braves the rude assaults of time.

Ye happy few, who here extend,
   In perfect lines from east to west,
With fervent zeal the Lodge defend,
   And lock its secrets in each breast:
Since ye are met upon the square,
   Bid love and friendship jointly reign;
Be peace and harmony your care,
   Nor break the adamantine chain.

Behold the planets how they move,
   Yet keep due order as they run;
Then imitate the stars above,
   And shine resplendent as the sun:
That future Masons, when they meet,
   May all our glorious deeds rehearse,
And say, their fathers were so great,
   That they adorn'd the universe.

TUNE—"*Rule, Britannia.*"

HAIL, Masonry, thou craft divine!
   Glory of earth, from heav'n reveal'd;
Which doth with jewels precious shine,
   From all but Masons' eyes conceal'd:
      Thy praises due, who can rehearse,
      In nervous prose, or flowing verse?

All Craftsmen true distinguish'd are;
  Our code all other laws excels:
And what's in knowledge choice and rare,
  Within our breasts securely dwells.
    The silent breast, the faithful heart,
    Preserve the secrets of the art.

From scorching heat and piercing cold,
  From beasts, whose roar the forest rends;
From the assaults of warriors bold,
  The Mason's art mankind defends.
    Be to this art due honour paid,
    From which mankind receives such aid.

Ensigns of state that feed our pride,
  Distinctions troublesome and vain,
By Masons true are laid aside—
  Art's free-born sons such toys disdain;
    Ennobled by the name they bear,
    Distinguish'd by the badge they wear.

Sweet fellowship, from envy free,
  Friendly converse of brotherhood;
The Lodge's lasting cement be,
  Which has for ages firmly stood.
    A Lodge thus built, for ages past
    Has lasted, and shall ever last.

Then let us celebrate the praise
  Of all who have enrich'd the art;
Let gratitude our voices raise,
  And each true Brother bear a part.
    Let cheerful strains their fame resound,
    And living Masons' healths go round.

TUNE—"*In Infancy.*"

LET Masonry from pole to pole
  Her sacred laws expand,
Far as the mighty waters roll,
  To wash remotest land.
That Virtue has not left mankind,
  Her social maxims prove;
For stamp'd upon the Mason's mind
  Are unity and love.

Ascending to her native sky,
  Let Masonry increase;
A glorious pillar raised on high,
  Integrity its base.
Peace adds to olive boughs, entwined,
  An emblematic dove,
As stamp'd upon the Mason's mind
  Are unity and love.

LET drunkards boast the power of wine,
  And reel from side to side;
Let lovers kneel at beauty's shrine,
  The sport of female pride:
Be ours the more exalted part,
To celebrate the Mason's art,
  And spread its praises wide.

To dens and thickets, dark and rude,
  For shelter beasts repair;
With sticks and straws the feather'd brood
  Suspend their nests in air:
And man untaught, as wild as these,
Binds up sad huts with boughs of trees,
  And feeds on wretched fare.

But science dawning in his mind,
  The quarry he explores;
Industry and the Arts combined
  Improved all nature's stores:
Thus walls were built, and houses rear'd—
No storms nor tempests now are fear'd
  Within his well-framed doors.

When stately palaces arise,
  When columns grace the hall,
When towers and spires salute the skies,
  We owe to Masons all:
Nor buildings only do they give,
But teach men how within to live,
  And yield to Reason's call.

All party quarrels they detest;
  For Virtue and the Arts,
Lodged in each true Freemason's breast,
  Unite and rule their hearts:
By these, while Masons square their minds,
The state no better subjects finds,
  None act more upright parts.

When Bucks and Albions are forgot,
  Freemasons will remain;
Mushrooms, each day, spring up and rot,
  While oaks stretch o'er the plain:
Let others quarrel, rant, and roar;
Their noisy revels when no more,
  Still Masonry shall reign.

Our leathern aprons we compare
  With garters red and blue;
Princes and Kings our brothers are,
  While they our rules pursue:

Then drink success and health to all
The Craft around this earthly ball;
May Brethren still prove true!

IN all your dealings take good care,
Instructed by the friendly square,
To be true, upright, just, and fair,
And thou a Fellow-craft shalt be.

The level so must poise thy mind,
That satisfaction thou shalt find,
When to another Fortune's kind:
And that's the drift of Masonry.

The compass t'other two compounds,
And says, though anger'd on just grounds,
Keep all your passions within bounds,
And thou a Fellow-craft shalt be.

Thus symbols of our Order are
The compass, level, and the square;
Which teach us to be just and fair:
And that's the drift of Masonry.

CHAPTER XII.

THE FIVE ORDERS OF ARCHITECTURE.

"First unadorn'd,
And nobly plain, the manly Doric rose;
The Ionic then, with decent matron grace,
Her airy pillar heaved; luxuriant, last,
The rich Corinthian spread her wanton wreath."

ASSOCIATED as the symbolic degrees are with the building of the House of God at Jerusalem, and our allegorical instruction in the tools used by operative Masons, our Lectures, from the earliest time, have ever required some explanation of the different styles of Architecture.

Architecture is sometimes defined to be the art of building, and we find the Greek term ἀρχιτέκτων (architectōn) is employed by Herodotus as the word Architect is now. He says, Rhœcus, a Samian, was the architectōn of the great Temple of Samos (built B.C. 986). Leaving out of our inquiry the earlier constructions, such mounds of earth as that of Alyattes or of Silbury Hill, or those remarkable monuments like Stonehenge, we briefly notice the characteristics that distinguish the different styles of Architecture.

Egyptian architecture is so purely monumental or historical as to be of little use to the student. Presuming that the pyramids are of a date long prior to any other structures now existing, we find at the entrance to the great pyramid a proof that the method of constructing an arch was known to these

The Doric.

The Ionic.

The Five Orders

The Corinthian.

The Tuscan. The Composite.

of Architecture.

people, as four enormous masses of stone, placed thus, support

the stupendous pile of rude stones, which are laid in without order above. These masses, as far as can be judged by comparison, are not less than twenty-five feet by twelve. At Thebes there are arches formed of four courses of bricks.

Some writers have claimed for the Etruscans the invention of the arch; it is found in their sepulchral monuments, gates, &c. The date of these people is, however, only about six centuries before Christ, whereas the great pyramid was constructed above 300 years earlier, according to the account of Herodotus.

These wondrous structures, the pyramids, as well as the temples in Egypt, which are astounding both for their gigantic vastness, and the prodigious solidity of the materials and mode of construction employed, are, to the eye accustomed to Grecian and modern architecture, utterly devoid of beauty of proportion, and uncouthly sublime.

Of the immensity of all the structures of the ancient Egyptians, we only notice the vast hall of Karnak, which is 340 feet by 170 in extent; it has 134 columns disposed in nine parallel rows one way, and sixteen the other, the smaller pillars being nine feet in diameter, and the larger eleven feet. In comparison with such enormous dimensions, in every respect—for the whole structure extended several thousand feet—all other works of ancient and modern architecture shrink into insignificance.

There appears, as far as we can judge, one peculiarity which identifies Egyptian architecture with that of the Israelites: before the Temple were placed a pair of colossal pillars or obelisks.

Of Jewish Art or Architecture, beyond the descriptions of the Books of Kings and Chronicles, the sole memorials in existence are the sculptured transcripts on the Arch of Titus at Rome. But every description in the sacred records, from the calf of the wilderness to the twelve oxen of the molten sea, or the lions of the throne of Solomon,—these latter the work of our Master, Hiram,—evinces the taste of the former bondsmen of Pharaoh.

In Egypt, a country destitute of wood, even the most ancient erections are of stone, and were in imitation of the natural caves in which the rude inhabitant had sought a wretched shelter. In Asia, the land of the Israelites, wood was abundant, and accordingly we find from the descriptions in Holy Writ, that this material was much employed in the most sacred and important buildings; for though few details capable of giving any just architectural notions are preserved of Solomon's Temple, it is plain that cedar wood was the chief material, both for roof and columns—that is, for supported and supporting members. Hence the temples of Palestine were less durable than those of Egypt. Of this we have a striking proof in the House of Dagon, which was wholly overturned by Samson pulling down two pillars. Of course such a catastrophe could not have occurred with a structure of stone.

In the oldest ruin existing in Asia—Persepolis—the marble columns evidently bear marks of having been connected with cross-beams of wood, and doubtless supported a roof of the same material. Hence the easy conflagration of this abode of the Persian kings in a debauch of Alexander.

Without further speculation on the styles of Architecture of other ancient nations, as Babylonian or Hindoo, we shall enter on a rather brief description of the Science of Architecture, as first framed by the Greeks, and afterwards enlarged by the Romans.

We first describe Architecture according to the scientific arrangement accepted by artists of all countries, and the height of the columns according to the universal mode. This is followed by noticing the most remarkable samples of the Orders whose remains exist; and we close our narration by a popular account, chiefly derived from Brother Preston.

Orders in Architecture.—What is termed an Order consists of two principal divisions, the *Column* and the *Entablature,*— i. e. the upright support, and the horizontal mass supported by it; the former being divided into *Base, Shaft,* and *Capital* (except in the Doric Order, where the shaft rests immediately upon the flooring); the latter, also, into three parts, *Architrave, Frieze,* and *Cornice.* These together constitute an Order, which is further distinguished as belonging either to the *Doric,* or *Ionic,* or *Tuscan,* or *Corinthian,* or *Composite.*

Of the *Doric* there are two kinds. The *Greek,* the column of which is generally executed without a base; the flutings of the shaft are twenty in number, very shallow and without fillets; but some examples are fluted only at the upper and lower extremities. The capital consists of a solid-looking *abacus,* the uppermost member, without a moulding, but supported by a very elegant echinus moulding, which swells gradually out of the line of the shaft, having three annulets or rings at the bottom. The features of the entablature are very simple, being plain and without ornament; the triglyphs are invariably placed over the centre line of the column, except the columns at the angles, when the triglyphs form the extremity of the frieze. Other triglyphs are placed in the centre between those before mentioned.

The *Roman Doric Base* is sometimes only a simple fillet; the shaft springs from it by a small curve; as at others it consists of a square plinth, a torus moulding, and fillet, from which the shaft springs in like manner. The *Shaft* is terminated by a neck moulding, composed of a fillet and astragal (a small ring moulding), and from this springs the *Capital,* commencing with a neck sometimes enriched with pateras and buds. The *Architrave* consists of one or more plain faces separated from the frieze above, with guttæ under the triglyph. The *Frieze* is divided into compartments by a triglyph over each column, and one or more between, according to the width between them. The *Cornice* completes the Order, of which the principal features are a cavetto (or hollow) on a cyma recta, a corona and bed moulding on the frieze, all of which are enriched or plain. There are sundry minor details, which are not needed in our description.

The *Tuscan* Order, which is simple in its design, has a base formed of a plinth or squared piece of stone as a foundation, and a torus above it surmounted with a fillet. The architrave is a plain face, with a broad fillet. The frieze also is a plain face. The cornice consists of an ogee, a fillet, an ovolo, forming the bed-mould of the cornice, which consists also of the corona and fillet, surmounted by a cymatium.

The *Ionic* has an Attic base. The flutings of the shaft are twenty-four in number, with fillets. The capital is distinguished by being formed with two volutes (a kind of spiral scroll) on two faces, front and back, and the volutes are connected by horizontal, straight, and curved lines. The architrave is divided into two faciæ. The frieze is usually plain. The cornice is supported by an ogee and other enriched mouldings. The cornice itself consists of a corona, with a small ogee and fillet, on which is placed a cyma recta.

The general proportions of the *Corinthian* and *Composite* columns are the same, and they differ only in their mouldings and enrichments. The base of both is occasionally Attic; the flutings of the shaft are the same as the Ionic. The capital of the Corinthian is composed of two rows of acanthus leaves, eight in each row; and the upper row is placed between and over the divisions of the lower row; four spiral volutes in each face rise out of two bunches of the acanthus leaf, and two of these on each facia are connected at the angles, and support the abacus. The frieze is enriched with figures or ornaments. The cornice is distinguished by its modillions and dentils; the former are supported by an enriched echinus and astragal, and the latter by an ogee and astragal enriched. Richness of decoration distinguishes both these Orders. The *Composite,* as its name implies, is a compound; the chief difference between it and the Corinthian is, that the volutes have the characteristic of the Ionic Order.

The General Post Office, London, erected from the designs of Sir Robert Smirke, is a correct copy of the Attic Ionic Order.

Grecian Doric.—Of the remains of this style may be noticed the ponderous ruins at Selinus, in Sicily, which consist of no less than six Temples, one of which, 331 feet in length, composed of a double peristyle of columns sixty feet high, must have presented one of the sublimest objects ever reared by human art. At Agrigentum, also in Sicily, are the ruins of the Temple of Juno, most picturesque now, and of concord most perfect: there are also the ruins of the grand Temple of Olympian Jove, one of the most stupendous buildings of the ancient world, and whose buried materials swell into hills, or subside into valleys, so as to make the traveller ignorant whether he tread upon the prostrate labours of man, or the workings of nature. There is also at Gela, the Temple of Apollo. It is found that all these enormous piles arose in little more than a century, embracing the greater part of the fifth, and early part of the fourth century before our present era.

Of the Temple of Minerva or Parthenon, at Athens, erected about

450 B.C., we may form some judgment by the remains now in the British Museum, and a model, reduced, in its perfect state. It was built under the direction of Phidias, by Ictinus, to whom also is ascribed the most perfect vestige of antiquity in existence, the Temple of Apollo Epicurus in Arcadia, and which is reported to have been one of the most splendid buildings of the Peloponnesus. The magnificent columns which

"Crown Sunium's marble steep,"

ruins of the Temple of Minerva, belong to the same era.

The propylæum of Grecian Doric, on an imposing scale, erected by Brother Hardwick, at the Railway Terminus, Euston Square, is the grandest architectural specimen in England; its model was the entrance to the market-place at Athens.

Ionic Order.—There are but few remains of the Order now extant in Greece, or her colonies; but we may notice the Temple of Juno, in the Isle of Samos, raised about eight centuries before the present era, and which in the age of Herodotus was the grandest building in Greece. The earliest example of the true Ionic was the Temple of Bacchus, at Teos, erected about 440 B.C. At Athens are the remains of the Temples of Minerva Polias, and Erectheus, of unknown date; near Miletus, in Ionia, is the Temple of Apollo; at Priene, another city of Ionia, is a Temple of Minerva. In other parts of Asia Minor also are remains of this Order, the names and dates of which cannot be ascertained. St. Pancras Church, London, erected about 1819, is worthy of notice, as the finest copy of Erectheum Ionic.

Corinthian Order.—The earliest building of this Order is the magnificent Temple of Minerva, at Tegea, in the Peloponnesus, of which Scopas was the architect: it was erected about 400 B.C. The circular erection of Lysicrates, called the Choragic Monument, is one of the most exquisite and perfect gems of architectural taste, and the purest specimen of the Order which has reached our time. Its minuteness and unobtrusive beauty has preserved it almost entire amid the ruin of the mightiest piles of Athenian art: it was erected 342 B.C. Also may be noticed at Athens the magnificent ruins of the Temple of the Olympian Jupiter, the columns of which are of the best age of Greece; they are composed of the finest white marble, and of the most perfect workmanship, with an elevation of nearly 60 feet, and belong to an edifice 400 feet long.

Originally there were but three Orders, all of Grecian origin: the Doric, Ionic, and Corinthian. They exhibit three essentially distinct styles of composition, and they alone show invention, and particular character. To these the Romans added the Tuscan, which they made plainer than the Doric, and the Composite, which was more ornamental than the Corinthian. As now classed, the Five Orders are, the Tuscan, Doric, Ionic, Corinthian, and Composite.

The *Tuscan* is the most simple and solid, and is placed first in order, on account of its plainness. Its column is seven diameters high; the base, capital, and entablature have but few mouldings. The simplicity of the construction of this column renders it eligible where solidity is the chief object, and where ornament would be superfluous. It may be said to be no other than the Doric more deprived of ornament.

The *Doric,* although of the earliest date, is placed second. Its column, agreeably to modern proportions, is eight diameters high, and has no ornament except mouldings on either base or capital; though the frieze is distinguished by triglyphs and metopes, and the cornice by mutules. The solid composition of this Order gives it a preference in structures where strength and a noble but rough simplicity are chiefly required.

The *Ionic* bears a kind of mean proportion between the more solid and delicate Orders. Its column is nine diameters high;

its capital is adorned with volutes, a kind of spiral scroll, and, which is the characteristic ornament of the Order, its cornice has denticles. There is both delicacy and ingenuity displayed in this column, and when pure it is indeed most elegant. It is poetically suggested to have been formed after the model of a young female of elegant shape with her hair dressed, as a contrast to the Doric Order, which was formed after that of a strong robust man.

The *Corinthian,* the richest of the Five Orders, is generally considered to be a masterpiece of art, and its invention attributed to the poet Callimachus, in the following anecdote, which, if not true, is too pretty to be thrown aside. He observed on the grave of a young lady recently interred a basket of toys—left as a tribute by her nurse—covered with a tile placed over an acanthus, a herb with broad prickly leaves; as the plant grew the leaves encompassed the basket, till arriving at the tile they met with an obstruction, and bent downwards. Callimachus, struck with the object, set about imitating it, and it was adopted as a new Order in architecture; the vase of the capital represented the basket, the abacus the tile, and the volutes the bending leaves. It is Vitruvius who tells this pretty traditional story; but the plant was always a favourite with the poets. Theocritus, describing a cup of Ætolian manufacture, says, "The plant acanthus is expanded all round the cup," and represents a vase of bronze, covered with acanthus leaves wrought in gold. Virgil mentions the plant in several places; and in the Bucolics describes two beechen cups, on which was carved the scene of Orpheus enchanting the trees, with "the soft acanthus folded round the handles." The frieze of the Corinthian capital is covered with ornamental devices, and the cornice with dentils and modillions. There is something stately in this column.

The *Composite,* as its name imports, is compounded of the other Orders. Its capital has two rows of the acanthus leaves of the Corinthian, and the volutes of the Ionic Order. The column is ten diameters high, and its cornice has dentils and simple modillions. This style is adapted for buildings where strength, elegance, and beauty are sought for. Painting and sculpture strained every nerve to decorate the buildings fair science had raised, while the curious hand designed the furniture and tapestry; music, eloquence, and poetry lent their aid, beautifying and adorning them with temperance, fortitude, justice, virtue, honour, and mercy, beside many other Masonic emblems; the splendour however of all was eclipsed by the double triangle, on which were exhibited faith, hope, and charity, united with brotherly love, relief, and truth.

Relative Proportions of the Five Orders.

	Height of Shaft.	Base, including Plinth.	Capital.	Architrave.	Frieze.	Cornice.	Height of Cornice.
Tuscan	12.0	.30	.30	.31½	.31½	.42	.42
Doric	13.28	.30	.32	.30	.45	.45	.57
Ionic	16.9	.30	.21	.40½	.40½	.54	.54
Corinthian	16.20	.30	.70	.45	.45	.60	.58
Composite same as Corinthian.							

The distinction of "Order" belongs, strictly speaking, to the style of the column and external part of the building. Although in ecclesiastical structures the roof has also the support of arches, they are not always supported by columns of any marked character. A style of architecture which does not belong exclusively to either of the "Five Orders," has obtained so much notoriety in our own days, that for the claim we now set forth it must not be omitted in a work devoted to Freemasonry.

This style, which has the various appellations of 'Gothic,' 'Pointed,' or 'Christian,' is marked by the full development and consistent application of the pointed arch. During the twelfth century first appeared an innovation of the rounded or circular arch, by the introduction of the lancet or sharply pointed: and as several churches were erected almost simultaneously, no authority we have consulted awards to any one a priority of date. Hence it has been a matter of dispute among writers on the subject of architecture, as to whence this style was derived. Walpole claims it as English, as its first adoption was in the cathedrals of our own land; and it is difficult to displace this claim, but he offers no suggestion as to who the builders were. Lord Aberdeen maintains that the style is of Oriental growth, and that it was brought in by the Crusaders. Sir Christopher Wren thinks it was invented by the Society of Freemasons who travelled throughout Europe erecting churches.

Now had either of these commentators reviewed the entire subject impartially, he would necessarily have seen his opponent's views were equally correct as his own. And if we allow that the first examples were in England, that the designers derived the idea from something they had seen in the East during the holy wars, and that those architects were members of the religious and military orders, we think the conclusion we shall arrive at is, that Sir Christopher Wren's theory is the true one. The Freemasons invented the style in question. We have undoubted evidence that the Abbey Church of St. Ouen in Rouen, which may claim pre-eminence for lightness and elegance over every other structure, was designed by Alexander de Berneval "the Freemason." He began the building in the early part of the twelfth century, and died when the building had only advanced as far as the transept. Berneval intended, it appears, to flank the western front by two magnificent towers, ending by a combination of open arches and tracery, corresponding with the outline and fashion of the central tower. Peterborough is the only English cathedral possessing this feature, which adds greatly to the magnificence of the building.

The Crusaders, in visiting Constantinople, must have gazed with wonder at the magnificence displayed in the buildings, as, before it was despoiled by successive vandals—we do not refer to the barbarians so called, but the Venetians as well as the Turks,—many of the glorious structures of Asia Minor, of which now only ruined fragments remain, were in some state of completeness, if not perfect. Some vestiges of the fortresses erected by the Templars and Hospitallers are now in existence in the Holy Land, which have defied the hand of time, as they did the Turks. The Church of the Templars in London, as also some few others in our own land, remain to testify the architectural skill of the soldier monks.

There are also in Britain remains of a like disposition to erect stately structures in the Hospitallers; and at Marienburg and Thorn in Prussia, the Teutonic Knights have left permanent records of their capabilities as builders.

By whatever name it is designated, this system of architecture was perfected and diffused all over Europe within a comparatively brief space of time, by a small society of artists, who were closely connected with each other. But whoever might be the builders, this much is certain, that they were not mere heapers together of stones, but they all had thoughts which they meant to embody in their labours. Let a building be ever so beautiful, if it be destitute of meaning, it cannot belong to the fine arts. The proper display of purpose, the immediate expression of feeling, are indeed denied to this eldest and most sublime of all the arts. It must excite the feelings through the medium of thought; but perhaps the feelings which it does excite are on that account only so much the more powerful. All architecture is symbolical, but none so much as the Christian architecture of the middle ages. The first and greatest of its objects is to express the elevation of holy thoughts, the loftiness of meditation set free from earth, and proceeding unfettered to heaven. It is this which stamps itself on the spirit of the beholder, however little he may himself be capable of analyzing his feelings when he gazes on those far-stretching columns and airy domes. But this is notable; every part of the structure is as symbolical as the whole; and of this we can perceive many traces in the writings of the times. The altar is directed towards the rising of the sun, and the three great entrances are meant to express the conflux of visitors from all the regions of the earth. Three towers express the Christian mystery of the triune Godhead; the choir rises like a temple within a temple, with redoubled loftiness; the shape of the cross is in common with the Christian churches even of the earlier times. The round arch was adopted in the earlier Christian architecture, but laid aside on account of the superior gracefulness supposed to result from the crossing of arches. The rose is the most essential part of all the ornaments of this architecture; even the shape of the windows, doors, and towers may be traced to it, as well as the accompanying decorations of flowers and leaves. When we view the whole structure from the crypt to the choir, it is impossible to resist the idea of earthly death leading only to the fulness, the freedom, and the solemn glories of eternity.

A writer in the "Builder," in referring to the ORIENTAL SOURCE OF WESTERN ARCHITECTURE, says, "I remember once standing before the magnificent front of Peterborough Cathedral with an old Indian officer, when he said, 'Why this is just what we see throughout the East; huge pointed portals running up to the top of the building; spires, pinnacles—every thing like the minarets; the aspiring character of Mussulman architecture.' " And this style came into general use shortly after the great Crusade. We do not say that the dogma, *post hoc, ergo propter hoc,* is always correct; but surely it is in this instance.

While noticing the various styles of architecture, it may not be out of place to refer to what may be considered the oldest in existence—the pyramidal: and as belonging to that character,

Mr. FERGUSON, in his *Handbook of Architecture,* says, "Whatever value may be placed upon the Buddhist monuments as works of art, there can be no question of their historical value. Of the styles still practised it is the oldest, having been constantly in use for more than 2000 years; and it is the style of a religion, which even now when its greatest glory has passed away, still reckons among its votaries, if not the greatest, at least as great a number of followers as any religion that exists on the face of the globe."

Of Masonic symbols we may notice one on the front of the Tomb of Solon at Dagon Lu. Solon flourished 600 years B.C.

CHAPTER XIII.

MARK MASON.

"*Mark Masons,* all appear
Before the chief overseer;
View there *the stone,*
On which appears *the name*
That raises high the fame
Of all to whom the same
Is truly known."

THIS rank or degree was unquestionably among our ancient brethren attached to the Fellow-Craft, or lay between him and the Master Mason. For a long period it has been abandoned by the Grand Lodge of England, and we believe it is out of use in France, if even it ever was practised in that country. It has always been practised in Ireland, Scotland, and America. But they all differ in the ritual. The Mark Degree has, however, to a certain extent been restored to English Masonry, but not formally, as the Grand Lodge does not at present acknowledge it. This restoration has been brought about by warrant of constitution from Scotland, and the ceremonial is of that country's practice. This is called the *Mark Master,* and the chief distinction between the *Man* and the *Master*—or the Irish and Scottish practice—is, that the ceremonial of the former is made the legend in the latter. The legend narrates the discovery of the missing key-stone of the arch, which had been rejected by the assistant overseers, as not being a truly squared stone. The workman, when made known by his *mark,* was rewarded and honoured. The legend is exceedingly interesting, and it is very desirable the Mark should be restored to the Fellow-Craft.

The degree of the *Mark Man* is practised under the Irish Constitution only, and the Albany Lodge at Newport in the Isle of Wight holds its warrant from the Irish Lodge. The historical legend shows, that during the building of Solomon's Temple, among the workmen employed, one, on presenting the result of his labours to the overseer, had the stone rejected when tried by the square; it was consequently cast aside, and its artist treated with contumely. Some time after, when the arch, the work on which they were then employed, was near its completion, the key-stone or centre could not be found,—the master overseer having given out the work,—until after a diligent search the stone which the assistant overseer had rejected was discovered to be that wanting, and its contriver being known by his mark being cut upon it, was honoured and rewarded, and proclaimed entitled to the degree of a skilled craftsman. The ritual is strictly in harmony with this narrative, and all who have witnessed its performance acknowledge it to be not only interesting, but strictly in harmony with Craft Masonry.

The Mark Degree, as far as can be learned from a cubical stone over a century old, contained illustrations of the seven liberal sciences, viz., Grammar, Arithmetic, Logic, Rhetoric, Music, Astronomy, and Geometry, which are now referred to in the Second Degree. The stone in question bears also on its face symbols which seem to show Astrology was included in the system of instruction. The angelic influences on the actions of men formed a portion of belief with many nations and religions; it is prominent in the Mohammedan faith, and, by the Cabala, at one period with the Jews.

In the degree of the Knight of the Sun, 28° of the Ancient and Accepted Rite, these same celestial names appear as junior officers, and they have a mallet in one hand and a sword in the other. We have been told that this degree was formerly in practice in England. The evidence furnished by the stone in question, and the use of one of the working implements of the Mark Mason, bears it out; for this, the first implement put into the hands of the young Mason, appears no where beyond the symbolic degrees.

Our transatlantic brethren hold the mark in high estimation, and so also it is looked upon in Scotland; but the former seek to connect it by illustration with the *Tessera Hospitalis* of the ancient Romans, but without logical argument, as with the ancients the practice was the breaking a die in two parts, a totally different matter to each selecting a peculiar and distinguishing mark of his own, and as we well know, originated when the capability of writing their names was confined to the few, we may say to the learned clerks. There is abundant evidence of the use of the Mason's mark in ecclesiastical structures all over the world, and especially those erected during the middle ages and after the Crusades. More than thirty different marks were found on the various buildings in Malta, some of which are in the alphabet character; among the ruined structures in Syria a traveller copied as many; and further, of a building called the Old Khan, he says, "This is a large and imposing quadrangular building, constructed of *square* blocks of limestone, each marked with a Mason's monogram."

The use of the mark was general in Great Britain, and those who entered the higher degrees always accompanied their signature of attendance with their Mason's mark. On the Bible which Robert Burns gave to his Highland Mary at their last parting, is his Mason's mark.

Thus it must be conceded that the Mark was the operative part of Craft Masonry, for in early times the architects were generally ecclesiastics, and especially high dignitaries, as our celebrated countryman William of Wykeham, and they were the Master Masons. The skilled artisan or workman was not slighted or neglected, and the record of his labours was preserved in his mark on the stone. In those days the architect and the workman worked with one heart and one mind, not as in these latter times in distinct classes; and by this unity and brotherhood it was that the glorious structures to God and his service, that cover our own and other lands, were constructed.

Mr. Ainsworth, in his notice of the city of Al Hadha, in Mesopotamia, whose walls are covered with Masonic Marks, in reference to its plan of construction says, "A square within a circle, and in its exact centre, certainly points out that a system was observed in its construction."

Mr. Godwin, in a paper read before the Antiquarian Society, referring to this subject, says "that these marks are to be found in great abundance on all the ancient buildings of England and France, and that in his opinion, these marks, if collected and compared, might assist in connecting the various bands of operatives, who, under the protection of the Church mystically united, spread themselves over Europe during the middle ages, and are known as Freemasons." He observes also, that in conversation in September, 1844, with a Mason at work on the Cathedral of Canterbury, he found that many masons, who were all Freemasons, had their mystic marks handed down from generation to generation; this man had his mark from his father, and he received it from his grandfather.

It has been noticed that by the evidence of the Cubical Stone, Astrology formed part of, or was connected with, the Mark Degree. The practice of this science, which is now confined to the impostors who pretend to reveal the future, found universal belief among all the nations of antiquity except the Greeks, and prevailed through the whole world during the middle ages. This science is based upon the supposition that the heavenly bodies are the instruments by which the Creator regulates the course of events in this world, giving them different powers according to their different positions.

ASTRONOMY and ASTROLOGY seem to have been used by the Greeks in the same sense, and Cicero uses the word *Astrologia* to express astronomical knowledge. Astrology may properly be taken to mean the science of the stars, and Astronomy their order and arrangement. These sciences were studied in unison by the learned mathematicians of bygone times, as the books of the Rosicrucians show. There was doubtless in Astronomical and Masonic symbols much in common, and the two sciences were practised by the same men. In the ritual of the present day, Astronomy is alluded to as the "mirrored study, wherein you are enabled to contemplate the intellectual faculties, and trace them from their development through the paths of heavenly science, even to the throne of God Himself."

The Jewel of the Mark Degree is a Key-stone, with initials of a sentence running around the centre, in which the brother's mark ought to be engraved.

CHAPTER XIV.

THE THIRD DEGREE, OR THE MASTER MASON.

"Every one shall answer these three questions: How hast thou entered? How hast thou wrought? How hast thou lived? and if he can assoile these, and hath laud therein, he may be raised, and honoured, and rewarded."—ANCIENT MS.

THE Fellow-Craft who is duly qualified by time, on presenting himself as a candidate for the Third Degree, has to submit himself to an examination of his qualifications as a Craftsman, which examination proving satisfactory, he is duly admitted as a Master Mason.

In this degree, which is the perfection of symbolic or ancient Craft Masonry, the purest truths are unveiled amid the most awful ceremonies. Hutchinson says, "The Master Mason represents a man under the Christian doctrine, saved from the grave of iniquity, and raised to the faith of salvation." The Third Degree, when taken into connexion with the other two, proves that Freemasonry embraces a fund of information, that not only tends to modify the manners and disposition of mankind in this world, but possesses a direct influence on their preparation for the world beyond the grave.

In treating with propriety on any subject, it is necessary to observe a regular course. In the former degrees we have recapitulated the contents of the several sections rather fully, as the making them known violates no rule of the Order; but the sections in this degree embody the most important points of the institution, and hence must be concealed from the outer world.

The Lecture in this degree has now but three sections, and they are exclusively devoted to illustrating the ritual. A most impressive lesson on the duties Masons owe to each other, is in this degree illustrated in a manner calculated to imprint it indelibly on the mind of every one to whom it is administered. The candidate is instructed that his admission in a state of helpless indigence was emblematic of the birth of man, who at his entrance into this mortal existence is equally helpless, and indebted to others for the preservation of his life. And it further symbolizes the principles of active benevolence for relief and consolation in the hour of affliction. Above all, he was taught to bend with humility and resignation before the Great Architect of the Universe; to purify his heart from the operation of passion and prejudice, and to prepare it for the reception of truth from the precepts of wisdom, to His glory and the good of his fellow-creatures. He is further told, that by the Second Degree of Masonry he was enabled to contemplate the high distinction at which he might arrive by the application of his intellectual faculties to the study of heavenly science; and that the secrets of nature and the principles of moral truth were unveiled, for the purpose of impressing upon him a just estimate of those wondrous faculties with which he was endowed; that he may feel the duty which is thereby imposed upon him, of cultivating them with unremitting care and attention, that he may become an useful and happy member of society. When his mind has thus been modelled to virtue and science, the Third Degree presents him with another great and useful lesson—the knowledge of himself. It prepares him by contemplation for the closing hours of existence; and when, by means of that contemplation, it has conducted him through the chequered scenes of prosperity and adversity, incident to this mortal life, it finally instructs him how to die.

Thus it will be seen that death and the resurrection to life eternal, are the objects symbolized in the Master Mason's Degree, and the aspirant for its honours is invited to reflect on these awfully important subjects; the allegory has direct reference to them. Such teaching cannot fail to suggest to the attentive Mason, that the degree must have been framed under the New Covenant; for besides the forcible illustration it contains of the duty to our neighbour, as promulgated by Him who spake as never man spake, the resurrection of the body to life eternal, which is its crowning object, was unknown to the Jews.

In all the ancient mysteries there was a period of darkness in which the aspirant was placed, his release from which was called the act of regeneration, and he was said to be born again or raised from the dead. Hence, Hutchinson says, Masons, remembering that they are brought out of darkness into light, are admonished to let the light which is in them so shine before all men, that their good works may be seen, and the Great Fountain of that light be glorified.

Mosheim says that in chemical language the + was an emblem of light, because it contains within its figure the forms of the three letters of which the Latin LVX (Light) was composed.

The most prominent symbol in this degree is the five-pointed star, or pentalpha, which is a geometrical figure representing an endless triangle. It was by Pythagoras used as an emblem of health; it is also called the pentangle of Solomon, and is said to have constituted the seal or signet of our Royal Grand Master. With Freemasons at the present day it represents the Five Points of Fellowship.

The Divine construction put upon this emblem is intended, not only to teach the Master Mason the principle by which he is raised from darkness; so it is also the emblem of moral duties professed by the Mason, which in all ages have been most religiously performed.

The Master Mason imposes a duty on himself, full of moral virtue and Christian charity, by enforcing that brotherly love which every man should extend to his neighbour.

The pentangle of Solomon was used as the banner of Antiochus Soter, and in ancient times all over Asia was employed as a charm against witchcraft, and this belief extended to Europe, as we learn from Goethe that this figure was scratched on the threshold of a newly built house by the builder. He makes Faust tell Mephistophiles to enter his dwelling; the latter replies, "Why you must know I am hindered egress by a quaint device upon the threshold—that five-toed damned spell." It was in early times among the Jews in use as a symbol betokening safety; and to this day the English shepherd cuts it on the grass in the green sward, little thinking its ancient signification; the entire figure representing the Greek characters υγεια, *health*. Bishop Kennett says, "When the pentangle of Solomon is delineated on the body of a man, it is supposed to point out the five places wherein our Saviour was wounded."

The FIVE POINTS of FELLOWSHIP are these,—

First. That when the calamities of our brother call for our aid, we should not withdraw the hand that might sustain from sinking; but that we should render him those services, which, not encumbering or injuring our families or fortunes, charity and religion may dictate for the saving of our fellow-creature;

Second. For which purpose, indolence should not persuade the foot to halt, or wrath turn our steps out of the way; but forgetting injuries and selfish feelings, and remembering that man was born for the aid of his generation, and not for his own enjoyments only, but to do that which is good, we should be swift to have mercy, to save, to strengthen, and execute benevolence.

Third. As the good things of this life are partially dispensed,

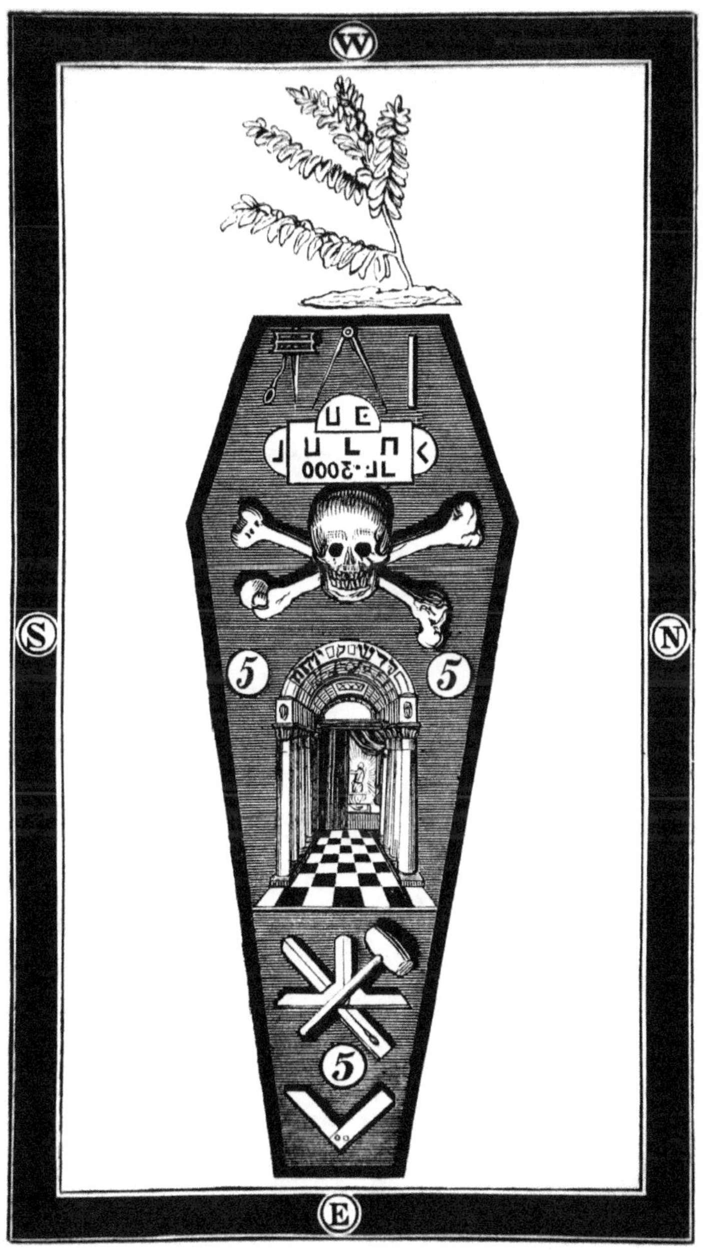

The Master Mason.

and some are opulent whilst others are in distress, such principles also enjoin a Mason, be he ever so poor, to testify his good will towards his brother. Riches alone do not allow the means of doing good; virtue and benevolence are not confined to the walks of opulence: the rich man, from the many talents entrusted to his charge, is required to make extensive works under the principles of virtue; and yet poverty is no excuse for an omission of that exercise; for as the cry of innocence ascendeth up to heaven, as the voice of babes and sucklings reacheth the throne of God, and as the breathings of a contrite heart are heard in the celestial regions, so a Mason's prayers devoted to the welfare of his brother, are required of him.

The *Fourth* principle is never to injure the confidence of your brother, by revealing his secrets; for perhaps that were to rob him of the guard which protects his property or life. The tongue of a Mason should be void of offence and without guile; speaking truth with discretion, and keeping itself within the rule of judgment, maintaining a heart void of uncharitableness, locking up secrets and communing in charity and love.

Fifth. A Mason should regard a brother's character as sacred as his own; he should not wrongfully revile him himself, nor suffer another to do so, if in his power to prevent it, but should repel all attacks on his good fame. He is bound to respect the chastity of all the near and dear relatives and connexions of his brother Masons. This last and great social duty is so well respected by the Fraternity, that instances of its violation are very rare. By these sacred admonitions Freemasons are linked together in an indissoluble bond of fraternal affection and brotherly love, and preserved they cannot fail to distinguish the Fraternity from those who are strangers to the institution, and thus demonstrate to the world that the term "Brother" is something more than an empty name.

Intimately associated as the Master Mason's Degree is with the Holy Royal Arch, it necessarily follows that some of the symbols belong to both; the more noticeable are the CIRCLE and the CUBE.

The POINT WITHIN a CIRCLE—although now explained as representing—the *point* the individual brother, and the *circle* the boundary of his duty,—had astronomical and other meanings, as it is found in the rites of very ancient times. With the Egyptians it represented the phallus as the symbol of fecundity, and it is conjectured that the temples of the Druids, which were circular, had a single stone erected in the centre. Among the Scandinavians, the hall of Odin contained twelve seats disposed in the form of a circle for the principal gods, with an elevated seat for Odin in the centre. In course of time the symbol became with astronomers a representation of the sun, and it is to this day the chemical symbol of gold.

The CUBE is defined to be a regular solid body, consisting of six square and equal faces or sides, and the angles all right angles. In what is termed (incorrectly) a double cube, four of the faces are oblong squares.

The CUBE which now appears as the *perfect ashlar,* has ever been a Masonic symbol, and belongs especially to Craft Masonry, and every Mason, as he advances beyond the Third Degree, will observe that this important geometrical figure becomes of considerable use. In the Royal Arch, in the Knight Templar, and Rose Croix degrees, the cube is referred to. It was a most important symbol in the teaching of Pythagoras.

Cœsar in his Commentaries informs us, that the Druids worshipped *Mercury.* Besides the well-known symbol of the winged rod, with the serpents twined around it, there was another mode of representing *Hermes* among the Druids. It was by a cubical figure of marble. These cubical statues were placed in the vestibules of their temples, and were intended as expressive emblems of the God of eloquence and truth, since they were polished squares on every side equal, which way soever they were turned.

Pausanias tells us that the inhabitants of Phares in Achaia, around the statue of their principal divinity Mercury, erected in the forum of that city thirty cubes of polished marble in honour of that deity, whose symbol was a cube.

Borlase, in his account of Cornwall, says, "A cubic stone was the Druid's symbol for Mercury, who, as the messenger of the Gods, was esteemed the index, or symbol, of truth, always like itself, as it is with a cube."

The ancient pagan altars were of a cubical form; and it was customary among the ancients to engrave the names of the architects who built their temples upon cubical pedestals, as was the case in the Temple of Vulcan at Memphis, built by Menes, whose name was placed on the cubical pedestal of the altar: also in the Temple of Jupiter Olympius at Athens, the name of the architect was engraved in a similar manner; and at the rebuilding of the Temple of Diana at Ephesus, the labourers, when digging for the second foundation, found the names of the two principal architects who built the first temple, engraved on a cubical pedestal, deposited in a square vault, exactly under the most sacred place of the first temple.

Another emblem is the ACACIA.

The custom of planting an Acacia, or sprig of that shrub, on a grave amongst the Hebrews, arose from this circumstance. Agreeably to their laws no dead bodies were allowed to be interred within the walls of their cities. The cohens or priests were forbidden to cross a grave, and the Jews always avoided doing so from a belief that evil would happen, and they therefore placed the ACACIA to mark the spot where a body was interred. The species called *mimosa nilotica* grows profusely about Jerusalem. This custom explains our adoption of the plant. One of the characteristics of the genus is the sensibility of its leaves to the touch of human hands. The Greek word ἀκακία signifies innocence, and *Hutchinson* (Spirit of Masonry) supposes the Third Degree to be Christian, exemplifying the rise of the Christian dispensation after the destruction of the Mosaic. Alluding to this Greek meaning of Acacia he says, "The word signifying innocence or being free from sin, implies that the sins and corruptions of the Old Law, and devotees of the Jewish altar, had hid religion from those who sought her, and she was only to be found where innocence survived, and under the banner of the Divine Lamb." There is sufficient authority in the ancient Jewish custom for the adoption of the Acacia, without Brother Hutchinson's theory. It is to be observed that in all the ancient mysteries some plant was adopted for a symbol, as the mistletoe by the Druids, the palm by the Egyptians, and the myrtle by the Greeks.

Brother Hutchinson in his summary of the Third Degree says, "As Moses was commanded to pull his shoes from off his feet on Mount Horeb, because the ground whereon he trod was sanctified by the presence of the Divinity, so the Mason who would prepare himself for this third stage of Masonry, should advance in the naked paths of truth, be divested of every degree of arrogance, and come as a true ACACIAN, with steps of innocence, humility, and virtue, to challenge the ensigns of an Order, whose institutions arise on the most solemn and sacred principles of religion."

CHAPTER XV.

THE CEREMONY OF INSTALLATION OF MASTER OF A LODGE.

"All preferment among Masons is grounded upon real worth and personal merit only; that so the Lord may be well served, the brethren not put to shame, nor the royal craft despised; therefore no Master or Warden is chosen by seniority, but for his merit."—ANCIENT CHARGES.

IT is a prominent advantage of the popular form of government, that the grounds of distinction and advancement being chiefly personal qualities, men are classed according to their individual abilities and merit. This is strikingly illustrated in the system of Freemasonry, which to a certain extent inculcates the doctrine of equality; but although each brother has equal pretensions to power, yet to every Lodge there must of necessity be a head. This ruler is the Master, to whom is entrusted for one year the entire responsibility of government. On the completion of his year of office he falls into the ranks of the Past Masters, who may be considered a select council, assisting the Master in the general control of the affairs and accounts of the Lodge, and at all times exercising a vigilant care over its wellbeing. Thus, although the democratic principle is to a certain extent allowed, yet the most perfect equality of rights can never prevent the ascendancy of superior minds, displayed (according to the Masonic theory) in those members who have passed the ordeal of the chair.

The Book of Constitutions declares:—

"The officers of a Lodge are the Master and his two Wardens, with their assistants the two Deacons, Inner Guard, and Tyler. There must also be a Treasurer and Secretary. A Chaplain, Master of the Ceremonies, and Stewards may be appointed.

"Every Lodge shall annually elect its Master and Treasurer by ballot, such Master having regularly served as Warden of a warranted Lodge for one year; and, at the next meeting after his election, when the minutes are confirmed, he shall be duly installed in the chair according to ancient usage, after which he shall appoint his Wardens and other officers, except the Treasurer; the Tyler is to be chosen by the members of the Lodge."

All Lodges have a fixed day for the installation, when more than ordinary exertions are made to do honour to the occasion; all the members generally endeavour to be present, and visitors from other Lodges are invited. There must be at least three Past Masters present at an installation; and the brother who undertakes the performance of the ceremony (not necessarily a member of the Lodge) ought to be well skilled in the craft, and possess a thorough acquaintance with all the ceremonies. The Lodge being opened in due form, the Master elect is presented by a Past Master of the Lodge (as duly elected) for installation, his merit and services being his recommendation for the high office of a ruler in the craft. The installing Master informs the Master elect that the choice of the brethren has been approved and confirmed, and imparts to him the necessary qualifications of a Master:—That he should be of good report, true and trusty, and be held in high estimation by the brethren. That he should be exemplary in conduct, easy in address, courteous in manner, but steady and firm in principle. That he must have been regularly initiated, passed, and raised in the several degrees of Freemasonry, and have served the office of Warden in a warranted Lodge for twelve months. That he should be well skilled in the science, and able and willing to undertake the work. He should be well versed in the ancient charges and landmarks of the Order. He must have been duly elected by ballot of the brethren in open Lodge assembled, and presented before a board of installed Masters, by whom the choice of the brethren must be approved.

Brother Oliver says,—"I am decidedly of opinion that much general knowledge is necessary, to expand the mind, and familiarize it with Masonic discussions and illustrations, before a brother can be pronounced competent to undertake the arduous duty of governing a Lodge. A master of the work ought to have nothing to learn. He should be fully qualified, not only to instruct the younger brethren, but to resolve the doubts of those who are more advanced in Masonic knowledge,—to reconcile apparent contradictions,—to settle chronologies,—and to elucidate obscure facts or mythic legends, as well as to answer the objections, and to render pointless the ridicule of our uninitiated adversaries."

The power of a Master in his Lodge is absolute; he is the supreme arbiter on all questions of order, so far as the meeting is concerned, nor can any appeal be made from his decision to that of the Lodge. He is amenable for his conduct to the Grand Lodge alone.

The Master elect having, in the presence of the Lodge, consented to undertake the office with all its responsibilities, the installing Master directs the Secretary to read the ancient charges and regulations from the Book of Constitutions, to each clause of which the future Master gives his assent:—

"1. You agree to be a good man and true, and strictly to obey the moral law.

"2. You are to be a peaceable subject, and cheerfully to conform to the laws of the country in which you reside.

"3. You promise not to be concerned in plots or conspiracies against government, but patiently to submit to the decisions of the supreme legislature.

"4. You agree to pay a proper respect to the civil magistrate, to work diligently, live creditably, and act honourably by all men.

"5. You agree to hold in veneration the original rulers and patrons of the Order of Freemasonry, and their regular successors, supreme and subordinate, according to their stations; and to submit to the awards and resolutions of your brethren in general Lodge convened in every case consistent with the Constitutions of the Order.

"6. You agree to avoid private piques and quarrels, and to guard against intemperance and excess.

"7. You agree to be cautious in your carriage and behaviour, courteous to your brethren, and faithful to your Lodge.

"8. You promise to respect genuine and true brethren, and to discountenance impostors and all dissenters from the original plan of Freemasonry.

"9. You agree to promote the general good of society, to cultivate the social virtues, and to propagate the knowledge of the mystic art as far as your influence and ability can extend.

"10. You promise to pay homage to the Grand Master for the time being, and to his officers when duly installed, and strictly to conform to every edict of the Grand Lodge.

"11. You admit that it is not in the power of any man or body of men to make innovation in the body of Masonry.

"12. You promise a regular attendance on the communications and committees of the Grand Lodge, upon receiving proper notice thereof; and to pay attention to all the duties of Freemasonry upon proper and convenient occasions.

"13. You admit that no new Lodge can be formed without permission of the Grand Master or his Deputy, and that no countenance ought to be given to any irregular Lodge, or to any person initiated therein; and that no public processions of

Masons clothed with the badges of the Order can take place without the special licence of the Grand Master or his Deputy.

"14. You admit that no person can regularly be made a Freemason or admitted a member of any Lodge without previous notice and due inquiry into his character; and that no brother can be advanced to a higher degree except in strict conformity with the laws of the Grand Lodge.

"15. You promise that no visitor shall be received into your Lodge without due examination, and producing proper vouchers of his having been initiated in a regular Lodge."

At the conclusion the Installing Officer addresses the Master elect as follows:—"Do you submit to and promise to support these charges and regulations as Masters have done in all ages?" Upon his answering in the affirmative the ceremony of installation proceeds.

He is then required, by solemn obligation, to accept the office and to govern his Lodge according to the laws of the Grand Lodge of England, neither himself to introduce, nor to allow in others, any deviation from the ancient usages and landmarks of the Order, but, on the contrary, to preserve the same in their integrity; and in all respects faithfully to discharge his duties as a ruler. This obligation is undertaken for one year, or until a new Master shall have been duly elected and installed in his stead.

The Lodge is then opened in the superior degree, and all, except installed Masters, having retired, a board of installed Masters is declared, and the ceremony of installation proceeds, and on this solemn occasion the Divine aid is thus invoked:—

"Almighty, Eternal, and Most High God, vouchsafe thine aid to this our solemn rite, and grant that the worthy and distinguished brother who is now about to be numbered amongst the rulers of the craft, may be endowed with wisdom to comprehend, judgment to define, and firmness to enforce obedience to thy law. Sanctify him with thy grace, strengthen him with thy power, and enrich his mind with genuine knowledge, that he may be enabled to enlighten the brethren, and consecrate our meetings to the honour and glory of thy most holy Name. So mote it be."

The Master is next invested with the badge of a Past Master —the highest honour in the power of the Lodge to bestow,— and also with the jewel of the Master of the Lodge. This jewel represents the *square,* because as the square is employed by operative Masons to fit and adjust the stones of a building, that all the parts may properly agree, so the Master of the Lodge is admonished, by the symbolic meaning of the square upon his breast, to preserve that moral deportment among the members of his Lodge which should ever characterize good Masons, and to exert his authority to prevent any ill-feeling or angry discussion arising to impair the harmony of their meetings.

Next is presented to him the gavel, which is also called the *hiram,* because as Solomon controlled and directed the workmen in the Temple by the assistance of Hiram the builder, so does the Master preserve order in the Lodge by the aid of the gavel. The true form of the gavel is that of a stone-mason's hammer. It is to be made with a cutting edge, that it may be used to break off the corners of rough stones,—an operation which could never be effected by the common hammer or mallet. It derives its name from its shape, that of the old gable or gavel end of a house. The distinction between this implement and the settingmaul is understood by every Master Mason.

The Master is then entrusted with the Warrant of the Lodge, which is committed to his keeping during his period of office— which cannot extend beyond two years in succession, nor can the same brother be Master of more than one Lodge at the same time.

He has then his attention directed to the various implements of the profession, emblematical of our conduct in life, and upon this occasion they are carefully enumerated.

The volume of the Sacred Law—that great light in Masonry —will guide you to all truth; it will direct your path to the temple of happiness, and point out to you the whole duty of man.

The *square* teaches us to regulate our actions by rule and line, and to harmonize our conduct by the principles of morality and virtue.

The *compass* teaches us to limit our desires in every station, that rising to eminence by merit, we may live respected, and die regretted.

Finally to the Worshipful Master are presented the Book of Constitutions as his guide at all times in cases of difficulty, and the By-laws of the Lodge, which he is required to cause to be read once in the year, so that none may plead ignorance of their contents.

The Worshipful Master then invests his immediate Past Master, who acts as his assistant in his absence as well as in his presence; it being the established custom when the Master is unable to be present that his immediate predecessor should preside.

After being saluted, as an installed Master, with grand honours, and also in token of respect as a master of arts and sciences, the board of installed Masters is closed.

The brethren below the chair are then admitted—Master Masons first, the others in succession; the installing Master proclaiming the Worshipful Brother in the east, west, and south, as duly installed.

The new Master enters immediately on the duties of his office by appointing his officers, who are separately conducted to the pedestal—generally by the installing brother. The Worshipful Master then invests each newly-appointed brother with the collar and jewel of his office in the following form:—

"Brother C. D., I appoint you Senior Warden of the Lodge, and invest you with the ensign of your office—the level—which will remind you, while presiding over the labours of the Lodge, that it is your duty to see that every brother meets upon the level, and that the principle of equality is preserved during the work, without which, harmony, the chief support of our institution, cannot be preserved. Your regular attendance on our stated meetings is essentially necessary, as in my absence you may be called to rule the Lodge, and in my presence to assist me in its government. I firmly rely on your knowledge of the Art and attachment to the Lodge, for the faithful discharge of the duties of the office.

"Brother E. F., I appoint you Junior Warden of the Lodge, and invest you with the collar and jewel of office; that jewel, the plumb-rule being an emblem of uprightness and integrity, will teach you the peculiar correctness of conduct that is expected from you, particularly in the introduction of visitors. To you is committed the superintendence of the brethren during the hours of refreshment; it is, therefore, indispensably necessary that you should not only be temperate and discreet in the indulgence of your own inclinations, but carefully note that none others be suffered to convert the purposes of refreshment into intemperance and excess. Your regular attendance is particularly requested; and I have no doubt that you will faithfully execute every duty."

The Treasurer, who has been elected by the Lodge, is next invested with the jewel of his office, the Worshipful Master thus addressing him:—

"Brother G. H., I have the pleasure of investing you with the jewel of the office to which you have been elected by the brethren; and I am sure you will do honour to their selection."

The Secretary is then presented and invested, the Worshipful Master thus addressing him:—

"I appoint you, Brother J. K., Secretary of the Lodge. It is your province to record the minutes and issue the summonses for our meetings. Your good inclinations to Masonry and the

Lodge will, no doubt, induce you to discharge the duties of the office with fidelity, and by so doing you will merit the esteem and applause of the brethren."

The Deacons are then named and invested; the Master addressing them as follows:—

"Brothers L. M. and N. O., I appoint you Deacons of the Lodge. It is your province to attend on the Master, and assist the Wardens in the active duties of the Lodge; such as the reception of candidates in the different degrees, and in the immediate practice of our rites."

The next officer appointed is the Inner Guard, whom the Master addresses thus:—

"Brother P., I appoint you Inner Guard of the Lodge. Your duty is to admit Masons on proof, to receive candidates in due form, and to obey the commands of the Junior Warden."

The Tyler is invested, and with his instrument of office, the Master gives him a short charge on his duties.

The investiture of officers being completed, the installing Master addresses the Master, Wardens, and brethren, somewhat to the following effect:—

"W. M., the brethren having unanimously elevated you to the chair, you cannot be insensible of the obligations which devolve on you as their head, nor of your responsibility for the faithful discharge of the important duties annexed to the appointment. The honour, reputation, and usefulness of your Lodge, will materially depend on the skill and assiduity with which you manage its concerns; whilst the happiness of its members will be generally promoted in proportion to the zeal and ability with which you propagate the genuine principles of our institution. For a pattern of imitation, consider the great luminary of nature, which, rising in the east, regularly diffuses light and lustre to all within its circle. In like manner it is your province to spread and communicate light and instruction to the brethren of your Lodge. Forcibly impress on them the dignity and high importance of Masonry, and seriously admonish them never to disgrace it. Charge them to practise out of the Lodge those duties they are taught within it, and by amiable, discreet, and virtuous conduct, convince mankind of the goodness of the institution; so that when a person is said to be a member of it, the world may know that he is one to whom the burthened heart may pour forth its sorrows, to whom distress may prefer its suit, whose head is guided by justice, and whose heart is expanded by benevolence. In short, by a diligent observance of the by-laws of your Lodge, the Constitutions of Masonry, and, above all, the volume of Sacred Law which is given as a rule and guide of your faith, you will acquit yourself with honour and reputation, and lay up a crown of rejoicing which will continue when time shall be no more.

"Brother Wardens, you are too well acquainted with the principles of our institution to warrant any distrust that you will be found wanting in the discharge of your respective duties. Suffice it to say, that what you have seen praiseworthy in others, you should carefully imitate; what in others may appear defective, you should yourselves amend. You should be examples of good order and regularity; for it is only by a due regard to the laws in your own conduct, that you can expect obedience to them from others. You are assiduously to assist the Master in the discharge of his trust; diffusing light, and imparting knowledge to all whom he shall place under your care. In the absence of the Master you may succeed to higher duties; your acquirements, therefore, must be such, as that the brethren never suffer for want of proper instruction. From the spirit which you have hitherto evinced, I entertain no doubt that your future conduct will be such as to merit the applause of the brethren, and the testimony of a good conscience.

"Brethren, such is the nature of our institution, that some must of necessity rule and teach, so others must of course learn to submit and obey: humility in both is an essential duty.

The officers who are appointed to govern your Lodge, are sufficiently conversant with the rules of propriety, and the laws of the institution, to avoid exceeding the powers with which they are entrusted; and you are of too generous a nature to envy their preferment. I trust, therefore, you will have but one aim —to please each other, meeting in the grand design of being happy and conferring happiness. Finally, my brethren, as this association has been formed and perfected in such unanimity and concord, in which we greatly rejoice, so may it long continue, and remain a monument of wisdom, strength, and beauty, which ages cannot wither, nor adversity decay. May you long enjoy every satisfaction and delight which disinterested friendship can afford: may kindness and brotherly affection distinguish your conduct as men and Masons; within these peaceful walls may your children's children celebrate with joy and gratitude, the annual recurrence of this auspicious solemnity; and may the tenets of our Order be transmitted through your Lodge from generation to generation."

CHAPTER XVI.

THE SUPREME ORDER OF THE HOLY ROYAL ARCH.

"The philosophers (Pythagoreans) concealed their sentiments of the Nature of things under the veil of divine allegories; lest, being accused of impiety by the priests (which often happened), they might be exposed, in their turn, to the hatred, if not to the fury, of the vulgar."—TOLAND.

THE Book of Constitutions at its outset says, "By the solemn act of union between the two Grand Lodges of Freemasons of England, in December, 1813, it was declared and pronounced that pure and ancient Masonry consists of three degrees and no more, viz., those of the Entered Apprentice, the Fellow-Craft, and the Master Mason, *including* the Supreme Order of the Holy Royal Arch."

By this declaration the Royal Arch would appear, as we are told, to be only the completion of the Master Mason's Degree; and yet there is a different governing body in the Grand Chapter, another establishment beyond his Lodge into which the candidate must be admitted, different regalia, and another certificate.

What the Royal Arch was at the period of this declaration it is not easy to decide, as we have seen five different rituals of various dates within the last century, and neither bears much resemblance to the present degree.

The present ceremony was arranged by the Rev. Brother Adam Brown at the instance of his late R. H. the Duke of Sussex, and the object the Grand Master had in view was effected, as every

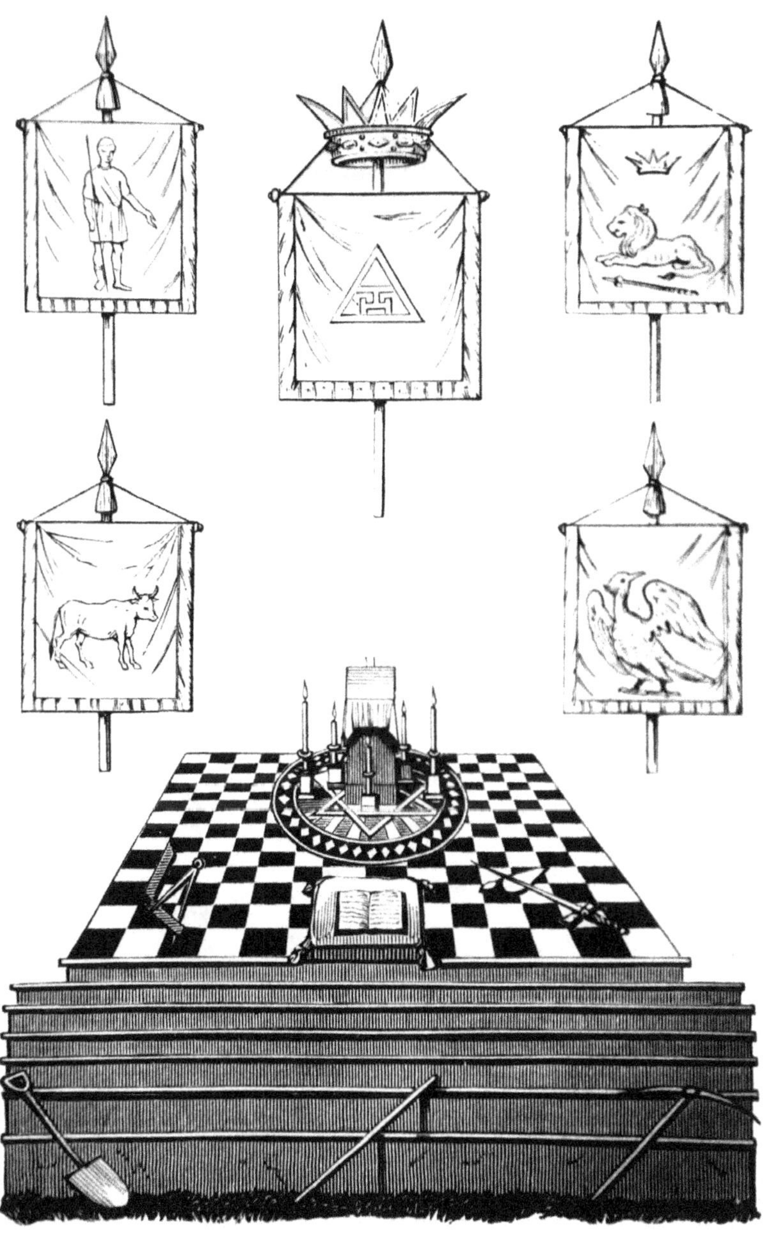

The Holy Royal Arch.

R. A. Mason will perceive when he has attained the rank of Past First Principal of a Chapter.

In the preceding degrees we learn how Solomon built that magnificent Temple which was justly esteemed as the most wonderful structure ever known, and for its regal splendour and unparalleled lustre far transcended all ideas that we can form of it at the present period. After the death of Solomon, his kingdom, as threatened by the Most High, was divided; ten of the tribes of Israel revolted from his son Rehoboam; the tribes of Judah and Benjamin, however, continued faithful to the house of David, and were ruled by the descendants of Solomon.

Whilst the Jews continued to serve God with that purity of worship and sincere devotion which characterized their early progenitors, the Almighty was pleased to grant them many signal instances of his divine favour and protection, by preserving their holy city from the horrors of war, but when they forsook the God of their fathers and followed the false gods of their heathen neighbours,—when, as God, by the prophet Isaiah, complains, "they forsook the fountains of living waters, and hewed out for themselves broken cisterns that could hold no water," they were justly punished for their perverse and rebellious spirit, for their wicked apostasy and blind idolatry. It almost exceeds the power of belief, but it is but the proof of the depravity of human nature, that his favoured people, for whom, when in Egypt, God wrought by the hand of Moses a series of the most astonishing miracles; to whom He displayed from Mount Sinai "the Divine Majesty of his glory, and the excellence of his magnificence;" and who heard the Almighty speaking with an audible voice out of the midst of the fire, and who had also the glorious Shechinah, the visible symbol of his presence, constantly with them,—that they should have debased themselves by idolatry and polluted their worship by the adoration of false gods. Having tried the patience and long-suffering of the Most High for many ages, during which they had divers warnings of his displeasure, He at length declared by his prophet He would execute summary punishment for their wickedness.

In the fourth year of the reign of Jehoiakim, king of Judah, the word of the Lord came to Jeremiah the prophet, empowering him to declare the vengeance of the Lord of Hosts, "Because ye have not heard my words, Behold, I will send Nebuchadrezzar the king of Babylon against this land, and against the inhabitants thereof. I will take from them the voice of mirth, and the voice of gladness, the voice of the bridegroom, and the voice of the bride, the sound of the mill-stones, and the light of the candle. And this whole land shall be a desolation and an astonishment, and their nation shall serve the king of Babylon for seventy years. And it shall come to pass, when seventy years are accomplished, that I will punish the king of Babylon, and the land of the Chaldeans, for their iniquity, saith the Lord, and will make it perpetual desolations." (Jeremiah xxv.) This threatened judgment was verified in the eleventh year of the reign of Zedekiah, when the armies of Nebuchadnezzar, king of Babylon, captured the city, and having plundered the holy Temple of its sacred vessels, razed it to the ground, and carried away the whole population, except a few of the menial tribes who were left to till the land.

After the death of Jeremiah, God raised up Daniel to be his prophet, and the instructor of his disobedient but now repentant people. Daniel in his youth was taken amongst his countrymen into captivity, and in course of time, by being enabled to interpret the handwriting exhibited to Belshazzar the king, on the wall of his banqueting-room, was exalted to favour, and became one of the king's chief officers. After this Babylon fell into the hands of the Persians, and Cyrus, who succeeded to the government of the whole country, was by Daniel made acquainted with the prophecy of Isaiah,—wherein he, Cyrus, is described by name more than 200 years before his birth, and the circumstances of the taking of Babylon, and the restoration of the Jews, are foretold with wondrous minuteness and accuracy. "Thus saith the Lord to his anointed, to Cyrus, whose right hand I have holden, to subdue nations before him; and I will loose the loins of kings, to open before him the two-leaved gates; and the gates shall not be shut . . . I have raised him up in righteousness, and I will direct all his ways; he shall build my city and let go my captives, not for price nor reward, saith the Lord of Hosts;" and further, "He saith of Cyrus, He is my shepherd, and shall perform all my pleasure: even saying to Jerusalem, Thou shalt be built; and to the Temple, Thy foundation shall be laid."

Daniel, who directed the attention of Cyrus to this grand prediction, could not fail to enforce and explain those declarations concerning God which it contains. Cyrus, who, it is evident, was a remarkable character, and who, it has been assumed by Dr. Hales, worshipped the one true God as known to the patriarchs, readily adopted the office designed for him, and issued his proclamation:—"Jehovah, the God of heaven, has given me all the kingdoms of the earth, and He has charged me to build Him a house at Jerusalem." He accordingly gave permission to the Jews to return to their own land. Besides giving the captives their liberty, he furnished them with money to prosecute the great and glorious undertaking, and also restored all the vessels of gold and silver belonging to the house of God, which had been taken by Nebuchadnezzar.

Josephus tells us, "that the number of those who came out of captivity to Jerusalem was forty-two thousand four hundred and sixty-two."

The progress of the restoration of the Temple was, however, hindered by the Samaritans, who, not being allowed to participate in the work, represented to Cambyses (who succeeded his father Cyrus), that the Jews were a seditious and rebellious people. But when Darius Hystaspes[1] ascended the throne, Zerubbabel reminded him of the vow he had made to rebuild Jerusalem and its Temple: the result was that the king issued a decree to effect this purpose without delay, and he ordered all his subjects to give every assistance to the work.

The accuracy with which this prophecy was fulfilled is shown by the respective dates according to the best received chronology:—the Jews were subjected by Nebuchadnezzar, B.C. 605, and the first year of the reign of Cyrus over all the East was B.C. 536, and between these dates we find a difference of sixty-nine years, and therefore allowing for any inaccuracy of current and complete years, the result is sufficiently satisfactory.

The conduct of the proceedings was entrusted to Zerubbabel, who, as a prince of the tribe of Judah, and a descendant of David, had the kingly office in his person, and joined with him was Joshua the High Priest; the prophet Haggai aiding by his eloquent appeals to the people. It was then the Sanhedrim of the Jews was first instituted, doubtless in imitation of the great council of elders who were appointed by God to assist Moses in the discharge of his judicial functions. Over this Sanhedrim presided Zerubbabel, prince and governor of Judea, Haggai the prophet, and Joshua the High Priest.

The three degrees of Craft Masonry refer to the building of the first Temple erected by Solomon. The Royal Arch Degree refers especially to the second Temple, and the circumstances connected therewith.

Thus the Chapter is a representation of the great Sanhedrim convened for the purpose of building the second Temple; and as they tried the merits of those who sought to be admitted to a participation in that great and glorious undertaking, so it is the

[1] Hystaspes, the father of Darius, a noble Persian of the family of Achæmenides, was the first who introduced the learning and mysteries of India into Persia.

province of members to examine the qualifications of those who seek admission to this sublime degree.

The legend of the degree is framed in consistency with the narrative we derive from the Old Testament. The exaltation into this degree is concluded by explanations of the three Principals.

The Historical (by Joshua).—There are three epochs in Royal Arch Masonry which especially merit attention, viz., the history of the three ancient Lodges or Chapters which we commemorate: the First, or Holy Lodge; the Second, or Sacred Lodge; and the Third, or Grand and Royal Lodge. The First, or Holy Lodge, was opened A.L. 2515, by Moses, Aholiab, and Bezaleel, on consecrated ground, at the foot of Mount Horeb in the wilderness of Sinai, where the host of Israel pitched their tents and assembled to offer up their prayers and thanksgivings for their signal deliverance from the hands of the Egyptians. In this place the Almighty had before revealed Himself to his faithful servant Moses, when He commissioned him his high ambassador of wrath against Pharaoh and his people, and of freedom and salvation to the house of Jacob; here were delivered the forms of those mysterious prototypes, the Tabernacle, and the Ark of the Covenant; and also the Sacred Law, engraved by the hands of the Most High, with those sublime and comprehensive precepts of religious and moral duty; and here also were dictated those peculiar forms of civil and religious polity which, by separating his favourite people from all other nations, consecrated Israel a chosen vessel for his service. For these reasons we denominate this the First, or Holy Lodge.

Solomon, the king of Israel, Hiram, the king of Tyre, and Hiram Abif, presided over the Second or Sacred Lodge, which was held, A.L. 2992, in the bosom of the Holy Mount Moriah, in the very centre of the place where the sanctuary of the solemn Sanhedrim was afterwards erected. On this spot Abraham proved his intuitive faith by leading his only and beloved son Isaac a destined victim to the altar of his God, when it pleased the Almighty to provide a more fitting sacrifice. Here, also, on the threshing-floor of Araunah the Jebusite, David offered up that mediatorial prayer by which the plague was stayed; and here had revealed to him in a vision the plan of that magnificent Temple which was afterwards erected by his illustrious son, and where God had declared He would establish his most holy Name for ever. We therefore designate this the Second, or Sacred Lodge.

The Third, or Grand and Royal Lodge, was holden at Jerusalem, A.L. 3469, after the return of the Israelites from the Babylonish captivity, by Zerubbabel, the prince of the people, Haggai the prophet, and Joshua the son of Josedech the High Priest. Now in the person of Zerubbabel was the royal line of David and princely house of Judah restored, and thus it remained until the destruction of Jerusalem by the Romans under Titus, in the seventieth year of the present era; thereby verifying the prediction of Jacob, that "the sceptre should not depart from Judah, nor a lawgiver from between his feet, until Shiloh come." (Gen. xlix. 10.) To commemorate this restoration, this is called the Third, or Grand and Royal Lodge.

In all well formed and regularly constituted Chapters, are represented the grand originals, viz., Zerubbabel, Haggai, and Joshua, whose names they also bear. The two Scribes represent Ezra and Nehemiah, the selectors and expounders of the Sacred Law, and the attendants on the grand Sanhedrim, by whose names they are also designated. Yourselves represent the three sojourners who, for their zeal and fidelity in discovering and preserving the secrets of the Sacred Arch, were awarded seats in the august assembly. The people are represented by the rest of the companions.

The *symbols* are described by the Second Principal; of these we cannot here enter further than to remark, among them are the ensigns of the twelve tribes, figuratively denoting the peculiar blessings bequeathed to each by the patriarch Jacob, as recorded in the forty-ninth chapter of Genesis; also the standards of the four leading divisions of the army of Israel, the devices being those of a man, a lion, an ox, and an eagle. From the traditions of the Hebrews we learn that the standard of Reuben bore a man, Judah a lion, Ephraim an ox, and Dan an eagle. These four composed a cherubim; therefore God chose to sit upon cherubims bearing the forms of these animals, to signify He was the Leader and King of the cohorts of the Israelites.

Bochart (Hierozoicon, on the animals mentioned in the Bible) says that they represented the nature and ministry of Angels—by the lion's form is signified their strength, generosity, and majesty; by that of the ox, their constancy and assiduity in executing the commands of God; by their human shape, their humanity and kindness; and by that of the eagle, their agility and speed. Spencer and other authorities say that the cherubim had the face of a man, the wings of an eagle, the back and mane of a lion, and the legs and feet of an ox. This very closely approaches the gigantic forms we have received from the excavations at Nineveh, sent by Layard, and now in the British Museum. They guarded the portals of the temple and palace.

At Mourg-Aub in Persia, which is supposed to be the ancient sacred city Pasargada, where resided the Magi of old, and which contains the tomb of Cyrus, is the sculptured figure of a man with four large wings. This we must consider a representation of the celestial figure which Cyrus had derived from the Hebrew captives.

Moses Stuart, in his criticism on the Apocalypse (ch. iv. 7), suggests that the Throne of God in Heaven rested on the bodies of the four living things; in a word, that the living creatures, while they had each a particular face mentioned, had not the erect bodies of human beings, but that of brutes, or horizontal ones; and that it was upon these bodies that the throne rested, while the heads of the creatures projected beyond the throne.

In the works of *Philo-Judœus* there is an express dissertation upon the CHERUBIM, in which that writer repeatedly asserts that those two powers in God, which the Paraphrasts denominate the two hands of God, are symbolized by the *cherubic* figures of the ark, in allusion to which it is said, "God dwelleth between the cherubim." Let us, in the first place, attentively consider what is related concerning the *cherubim* in the prophetic vision of *Ezekiel,* and then advert to what *Philo* and *Josephus,* who must be supposed fully to know, and accurately to report, the sentiments of their nation, have observed upon this subject. It may be truly said of the description in *Ezekiel,* of which, however, since it extends through nearly the whole of the first chapter of that prophet, we can only state the outlines, that in grandeur of idea and energy of expression, it as far surpasses the loftiest strains of Homer, and the most celebrated Gentile authors, as, in the opinion of the great critic *Longinus,* the account which Moses gives of the Creation does all their relations of the Cosmogony. At the commencement of this sublime book, the prophet represents himself as sojourning amidst the sorrowful captives of Judah on the banks of the Chebar, when to his astonished view the heavens were opened, and he saw visions of God. This stupendous appearance of the glory of Jehovah, which immediately took place, is represented by him as preceded by a whirlwind from the north, attended with a great cloud, and a fire unfolding itself (that is, spiral), while a brightness issued from the centre of it, vivid and transparent as the colour of amber. The four sacred animals that supported the everlasting throne which resembled the sapphire, and on which sat the likeness of a man, whose appearance from his loins upwards, and from his loins downwards, was like that of an ardent flame encircled with variegated splendours, such as are visible in the bow that is in the cloud in the day of rain, exhibited to Ezekiel a fourfold aspect. They had each the face of a man, they had likewise the face of a lion and the face of an ox,—they four also had the face of an eagle. They had each four wings which were joined one to another, and the noise of those wings when they moved was loud as the noise of great waters, awful as the voice of the Almighty; and the likeness of the firmament upon the heads of the living creatures was as the colour of the terrible crystal stretched forth over their heads above. This magnificent chariot of the Deity is likewise said to have wheels of the colour of a beryl, that is, azure, or the colour of the sky, wheel within wheel, or (as Jonathan's paraphrase translates the word Ophannim) sphere within sphere,—and those wheels had rings or strakes full of eyes, so high, that they were dreadful, that is, their circumference was so vast as to raise terror in the prophet who beheld them. Such is the lofty description of the chariot that conveyed the personified Shechinah—the God-man who in the likeness of the rainbow sat upon the sapphire throne, and who, half human, half divine, in that appearance exhibited to the favoured prophet the mystery of the future incarnation of the Λόγος. Thus are the three Persons in the Holy Trinity shadowed out under the similitude of the three noblest animals in nature—the bull, the lord of the plain—the lion, the king of the forest—and the eagle, the sovereign of birds. But though each of the sacred cherubic figures had the aspect of those august animals, they had likewise the face of a man, to denote that the human nature was blended with the divine in that particular Person of the Divine Triad, who is emphatically called the Lion of the tribe of Judah. In another chapter of this prophet it is said, that their whole body, and their backs, and their hands, and their wings, as well as the wheels, were full of eyes round about. This must be considered as a striking and expressive emblem of the guardian vigilance of Providence, all-seeing and omniscient; while the multitude of wings with which they are adorned exhibits to us as direct symbols of that powerful, that all-pervading

Spirit, which, while it darts through nature with a glance, is every where present to protect and defend us. So attached to this heavenly symbol were the Jews, that when Solomon erected that stupendous Temple, which continued for so many ages the delight and boast of the Hebrew nation, we are told that he carved all the walls of the house round about with sculptured figures of cherubim.

In the splendid vision also which Ezekiel was permitted to have of the new Temple to be formed upon the model of the old, it is said that the walls were adorned with carved work of cherubim and palm-trees.

These symbolical representations of the cherubim, which appear in so many places in the Old and New Testament, have been the subject of endless doubt, and no satisfactory solution of the mystery has been arrived at. With the early Christians the four figures, in their separate and natural state, are symbols of the four Evangelists.

The first face, that of a man, signifies Matthew, who begins to write, as of a man, the book of the generation of Jesus Christ, the Son of David, the son of Abraham; the second, Mark, in which is heard the voice of the lion roaring in the desert, "Prepare ye the way of the Lord;" the third, that of the calf, prefigures Luke the Evangelist commencing his history from the priest Zechariah; and the fourth, the Evangelist St. John, who, having taken the wings of an eagle, and hastening to loftier things, speaks of the Word of God.

Their introduction into Masonry is a strong proof of the intimate connexion of our Order with the Holy Scriptures, and they have for a very long period formed the four quarters on the dexter side of the armorial bearings of the Fraternity, the sinister side being occupied by the bearings of the City of London Company of (Operative) Masons.

The description which Josephus gives of the nature of the cherubim, from the traditions of his time, represents them as *winged living animals,* of a form and aspect different from every thing that had been seen by man, as an assemblage of the great, the terrible, and the wonderful. It is however manifest that they bore some resemblance of the man, the lion, the bull, and the eagle, as far as the poets could pourtray, or the artists execute these subjects.

The cherubim of the ark were also known to the Arabians by tradition as winged creatures, something like the human form.

We may observe that there is an ancient Hebrew apothegm to this effect:—There are four superb creatures in the world,—the lion among the wild beasts, the ox among the tame, the eagle among the birds, and the man who surpasses them all.

At opening a Chapter none but Principals can be present; it is preceded by the Holy Communion Prayer, addressing the Most High in his triform attributes:—

"O Omnipotent, O Omnipresent, O Omniscient and Almighty Lord, unto whom all hearts are open, all desires known, and from whom no secrets are hid; cleanse the thoughts of our hearts by the inspiration of thy Holy Spirit, that we may perfectly love Thee, and worthily magnify thy Holy Name and Word. *So mote it be.*"

The Chapter is opened in solemn form, and the other companions are admitted. The formulas of reading and confirming minutes, entertaining propositions, &c., are in precisely the same manner as in a Lodge.

The officers of a Chapter are the First Principal, who represents Zerubbabel the prince of the people; the Second Principal, who represents Haggai the prophet; and the Third Principal, who represents Joshua the son of Josedech, the High Priest; two Scribes, one representing Ezra, and who performs the duties of Secretary, and the other named Nehemiah; there are also a Principal Sojourner and his two assistants; the serving companion without, is denominated the Janitor.

The ostensible object of the degree is to recover the lost word,—the Master Mason being only in possession of a substituted word,—and this is discovered in a secret vault which for a period of nearly five centuries was unknown, it being beneath the first Temple, and brought to light by the sojourners who were sent to prepare the foundation for the second Temple.

Thus it may be said that in this degree are brought to light the essentials of Masonry, which for a period of five centuries were buried in darkness.

A companion must have attained the rank of Master of a Lodge to be eligible for the Third Principal's chair, and he must also have served the office of Scribe or Sojourner. The other chairs can only be attained after intervals of twelve months. These restrictions, however, are not enforced in the formation of a new Chapter.

Although the legislative wisdom that framed the Book of Constitutions declares there are but 'three degrees and no more,' we must insist, that this is another degree, and that each of the Principals takes a new degree as he advances.

The badge of the Royal Arch consists of a sash and apron, the former being radiated with purple and crimson, the apron being bordered with the same, the triple Tau being delineated on both. The jewel worn on the left breast, suspended by a white ribbon (Principals wear red), is a double triangle within a circle of gold, with symbols and inscriptions engraved on it. It is only when he has passed the first chair, a companion obtains another jewel, which is a circle having on it a triangle, the back centre being a glory of rays, and on the whole a celestial crown, all of gold. The officers of a Chapter wear crimson collars, to which are suspended jewels, emblematic of their respective offices. The three Principals bear sceptres, emblematic of the regal, prophetical, and sacerdotal offices. The kingly robe is red, the prophetic purple, and the priestly blue. The other officers wear white robes, emblems of that purity of heart and mind that should ever distinguish those who are admitted into this supreme order.

The aim and end of this degree appears to be the bringing in one view before the Master Mason the traditional history of the

TRUE WORD, and the transmission of Masonry from the first formation of a Lodge by Moses to the era of the rebuilding of the Temple by order of Cyrus. The historical portion of the Lecture makes mention of three tabernacles designed for the dwelling-place of the Most High, the first of which was by his own command delivered to Moses; the second, that of Solomon—the whole plan and model of which was laid by the same Divine Architect, viz. God Himself (it was built of the same form as the first, but of course much larger, as providing for a greatly increased population); the third, the foundations of which were laid by Zerubbabel, according to Josephus, was similar to that of Solomon, but larger. We cannot conceive that it was this Temple of which the prophet Haggai says, "The glory of this latter house shall be greater than the former, saith the Lord of Hosts." It wanted the five principal things which invested Solomon's Temple with glory, viz. the Ark and Mercy-seat, the Divine Presence, or visible glory of the Shechinah, the Holy Fire on the altar, the Urim and Thummim, and the Spirit of Prophecy. But we may rather conceive it referred to the third or Herod's Temple, which in having the presence of the Lord, must have had greater glory than those buildings which preceded it. It was considerably larger than the Temple of Zerubbabel. It was built of white marble, and all the Jewish writers praise it for its beauty. Josephus says, "Its appearance had every thing that could strike the mind and astonish the sight; for it was covered on every side with solid plates of gold, so that when the sun rose upon it, it reflected such a strong and dazzling effulgence from it, that the eye was no more able to withstand its radiance than the splendour of the sun."

TACITUS calls it *immensœ opulentiœ templum,* a temple of immense opulence. On one of those days when our Blessed Lord taught the people in the sacred edifice, and preached the Gospel unto them, "some spake of the temple, how it was adorned with goodly stones and gifts; He said, As for these things which ye behold, the days will come, in the which there shall not be left one stone upon another that shall not be thrown down." (Luke xxi. 5, 6.) Within forty years this important prediction, which foretold the destruction of the Holy Place, was accomplished, and this splendid building, at once the envy and admiration of the world, passed away. It was entirely demolished by the Romans under Titus, A.D. 70, in the same month and the same day of the month that Solomon's Temple was destroyed by the Babylonians. The entire city was razed to its foundations, and its inhabitants slaughtered or carried away into captivity.

The companions are arranged in the form of an arch, and the newly-exalted companion is figuratively admitted through an arch of Masonry, and to a certain extent this has been the practice in all the rituals.

When every officer is in his place, and perfect in the business, and the Chapter properly arranged, the ceremony is not only impressive, but also instructive; and the reason it is not so universally held in esteem, consists in brethren having seen exaltations inefficiently and imperfectly rendered.

A perfect knowledge of the degree can only be attained by a companion passing regularly through the three chairs, and making himself a thorough master of the entire ritual, which necessarily requiring time and diligence, is not attained by all. We have heard objections raised to the alteration of the ritual, but such brethren were not acquainted with the fact of there having previously been no established rule, and hence the desirability of having regularity. Another fact they are ignorant of is, that the Royal Arch does contain every thing useful and proper, the various practices embodied, and also all the so-called higher degrees. Hence a perfect acquaintance with this degree will pass a Mason into any degrees on the Continent.

But independently of this, every *principle* of the old practice is included in the modern and now established custom. We have reason to believe that formerly the degree contained matter which, at the present day, would be decidedly objectionable.

In like manner, our ancestors were accustomed to witness in the miracle-plays sacred subjects treated with a familiarity that now could not be tolerated.

The present ritual of the Royal Arch in England differs from that of any other country. Scotland, Ireland, and the United States of America, although not quite alike, approach more to the system formerly in use among us. All the old rituals were very long. One we remember to have inspected would have required six hours to give perfectly; but it was the custom of the period, and it was when the author was exalted by the officials to read the ritual. The old ceremonial began with the first delivery of THE WORD to Moses at the Burning Bush, its loss and recovery in the Old Covenant, and its perfection in the New Covenant. Thus in the old lectures the three great lights represented the sublime word in three different points of view, but more particularly that superior light which shone forth in the Gospel revelation, when the mysteries of the Trinity were publicly displayed at the baptism of Christ.

The reason why we enter the Chapter upon the Holy Bible, and the interlacing equilateral triangle, refers to the roll of the law, which was found at the time of building the second Temple. This roll represented the Old Testament, and the equilateral triangle the New Testament, or, in other words, the Trinity in Unity. In the original formula of the Order we find it thus given:—

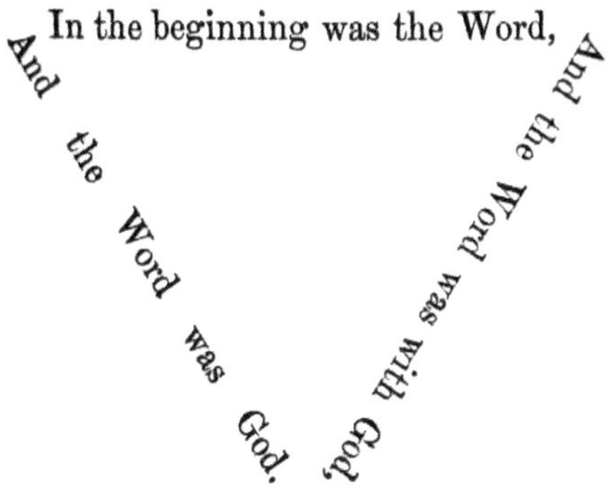

Hence this degree was in the strongest sense Trinitarian Christianity. All the old writers are loud in praise of the Royal Arch. Laurence Dermot calls it "the root, heart, and marrow of Freemasonry.

Webb says, "This degree is indescribably more august, sublime, and important, than all which precede it, and is the summit and perfection of ancient Masonry. It impresses on our minds a belief of the being and existence of the supreme Deity, without beginning of days or end of years, and reminds us of the reverence due to his Holy Name."

Brother Oliver, in his lectures, says, "If we pass on to the Royal Arch, we receive a wonderful accession of knowledge, and find every thing made perfect; for this is the *ne plus ultra* of Masonry, and can never be excelled by any humam institution."

The Royal Arch Degree, as far as can be learned from different authorities, lay dormant for a very long period, and, unless it formed a part of, and was the perfection of, the Master's Degree, does not appear in *Preston's volume;* but it must be observed, that that worthy brother terms the Lodge in the Third Degree A CHAPTER.

It has been suggested, that from the practice and legend the name was *Ark,* and the Ark of the Covenant is the sacred thing discovered. From Buxtorf we learn, that the Jews have a tradition that King Josiah, being foretold by Huldah the prophetess, that the Temple would be destroyed soon after his death, caused the Ark to be put in a vault underground, which Solomon, foreseeing the destruction, had caused to be built for the purpose of preserving the Ark. Josiah directs "the Levites to put the Holy Ark in the house that Solomon did build" (2 Chron. xxxv. 2); which they interpret to mean the *sacred vault,* where it remains to this day, and from thence shall be manifested and brought out again in the days of the Messiah.

At the union of the two Grand Lodges, it is to be remembered, that in the centre of the hall was the ark of the Masonic covenant, prepared under the direction of Brother John Soane, R.A., grand superintendent of the works for the edifice of the union, and in all time to come to be placed before the throne. "The two Grand Masters placed the act of union in the interior of the said ark."

Brother Fellowes, in his elaborate inquiry, insists on Freemasonry being derived from the mysteries of ancient times, all of which had astronomical reference; and he shows this degree owes its title to the imaginary arch made in the heavens by the course of the sun (*Osiris*) from the vernal to the autumnal equinox; the signs through which he passes in forming this semicircle, including those of the equinox, being seven, the number of grades or steps required to be taken by the Mason to entitle him to the honours of this degree.

The old emblem of the R.A. shows the arch with those seven signs upcn it; ♋ (*Cancer*) being the centre or key-stone, surmounting the pillars of wisdom and strength. This was abolished when the degree was reformed, and no arch now appears on the jewel. No reference to this astronomical symbol was made in the ritual. But although this theory of the origin of the degree is denied by modern Masons, the Grand Chapter of England preserves and exhibits some evidence of an acknowledgment of its astronomical origin in the carpet presented to the Grand Chapter by H. R. H. the Duke of Sussex, whom all allow to have been a most profoundly learned Mason. Further, the author was made acquainted with a very extraordinary application of the Tau figure, in measuring the celestial globe, the cardinal point being the Dog-star.

Among the more prominent symbols of this degree are to be noticed the circle and triangle.

Cudworth, in treating of the Egyptian Theology, says the following sublime definition of the Deity is to be found in the writings of Hermes Trismegistus: "*God is a circle,* whose centre is every where, but whose circumference is no where to be found." This geometrical figure was considered as the most perfect of all those made use of in that science, and as comprehending in itself all other imaginable figures whatever. Hence it arose, that nearly all the Egyptian hieroglyphics illustrative of the Divine nature were adorned with circular emblems; and that almost all the temples of Egypt were sculptured with this symbol, at once emblematic of the perfection of the Deity, as well as possibly allusive to the rapid circular motion by which all nature revolves.

In the *Equilateral Triangle,* also a geometrical figure, of which the three sides are equal in quantity, we have another symbol handed down to us from the Egyptians, which was by them used to describe the Numen triplex, or the Deity in his threefold character. In one of the ancient books of the Hebrews it is asserted that the three branches of the letter ש (*schin*) are a proper emblem of the three persons that compose the Divine essence. They sometimes call these three *Sephiroth,* spirits; at other times the three Δυναμεις or *powers,* and at other times the *three lights. Rabbi Hagahon* affirmed there were three lights in God,—the *ancient light,* the *pure light,* and the *purified light;* he says further there is one spirit of the living God, the voice, the spirit, and the word, which are *one.* Rabbi Akiba, who wrote sixteen centuries ago, says in almost similar terms, as quoted in the *Jetzirah,* "There is one spirit of the living God, the voice, the spirit, and the word; and this is the Holy Spirit."

The Ribbon, or Sash, as well as the Ribbon around the Badge of this degree, is composed of two of the colours of which the veil of the Temple was interwoven,—purple and scarlet,— and of the veils, which formerly were a marked feature in Royal Arch Masonry, and still are in Scotland and America, *Josephus,* in describing the Tabernacle, says that the veils of the Holy Place, composed of four different materials, were emblematic of the four elements; for the fine linen which was made of flax, the produce of the land, typified the earth; the purple tinge shadowed out the sea, because stained of that colour by the blood of a shell-fish; the deep blue was symbolical of the cerulean sky, or the air; and the scarlet is a natural emblem of fire.

Among the symbols descended to us from times of remote antiquity, and which prevailed throughout the East, and more particularly in Egypt, was the TAU or letter **T**. This emblem occurs very frequently on the Egyptian obelisks, and is represented by the learned as a most sublime hieroglyphic, a mysterious and powerful amulet endowed with astonishing virtue, as well as exhibiting one of the most complete mathematical figures, possessing at once both length and breadth. Most commentators agree that the *Tau* was the mark alluded to in *Ezekiel*. "And the Lord said unto the man which had the writer's inkhorn, Go through the midst of the city, through the midst of Jerusalem, and set a *Mark* upon the foreheads of the men that sigh and cry for all the abominations that be done in the midst thereof." The Vulgate gives this version,—"mark them on the forehead with the letter *Tau,*"—which affords room to suppose it was a symbol of more sacred import in the early patriarchal ages than is generally supposed. The **T** was among the ancients a hieroglyphic of eternal life. *Dr. Clarke* says it was the monogram of Thoth, the symbolical name of *hidden wisdom* among the Egyptians. In Hindostan, under the name of *"tiluk,"* it was marked upon the body of the candidate at his initiation, to show he was set apart for the sacred mysteries.

In this degree, adopting the prophet Ezekiel's mention of the symbol, we take it as a mark distinguishing those who were to be saved on account of their sorrow for their sins, from those who, as idolaters, were to be slain. It therefore may be assumed that the triple Tau is used in the Royal Arch Degree, as designating and separating those who know and worship the true name of God, from those who are ignorant of that august mystery.

Some have said it was the monogram of Hiram of Tyre, others that it is the initials TH, *Templum Hierosolymœ,* and it has been suggested to be a representation of three T squares, and that it alludes to the three Grand Masters, being their monogram.

The government of a Royal Arch Chapter is entrusted to the three Principals, who united form one triune head. The ceremony of the installation of the Principals is most impressive, and embodies much historical information. The illustration of important events in the career of the Israelites, by which the Royal Arch Mason is led by progressive steps to a more perfect knowledge of the wisdom, truth, and justice of the Most High, is such as cannot fail to impress every one admitted to the highest rank in the degree with awe and reverence for the great Jehovah. His majesty, might, and power, as well as his power to punish, are amply displayed in the Volume of the Sacred Law, and portions of the Scriptures are introduced at each step in the Supreme Degree, illustrative of the grade to which the companion is admitted.

In the ceremonial attached to the Third Chair, reference is made to the punishment of a rebellious people, when, under Korah, Dathan, and Abiram, they resisted the authority of God's chosen servants, and, led by "two hundred and fifty princes of the assembly, famous in the congregation, men of renown, gathered themselves against Moses and Aaron." "And the Lord spake unto Moses, saying, Get you up from among this congregation, that I may consume them as in a moment. And they fell upon their faces. And Moses said unto Aaron, Take a censer, and put fire therein from off the altar, and put on incense, and go quickly unto the congregation, and make an atonement for them: for there is wrath gone out from the Lord; the plague is begun. And Aaron took as Moses commanded, and ran into the midst of the congregation; and, behold, the plague was begun among the people: and he put on incense, and made an atonement for the people. And he stood between the dead and the living; and the plague was stayed. Now they that died in the plague were fourteen thousand and seven hundred, beside them that died about the matter of Korah. And Aaron returned unto Moses unto the door of the tabernacle of the congregation: and the plague was stayed."

It is to be observed, that upon ordinary occasions incense could only be offered on the golden altar in the Holy Place; but on this extraordinary occasion an extraordinary remedy was provided; and Aaron went out into the camp with the incense, and placing himself in the part where the destruction raged, and that which it might not have yet reached, the plague ceased on his offering the incense and making an atonement. God might have stayed the plague without the intervention of Aaron; but in this time of discontent, it pleased Him to afford another convincing testimony, that the High Priest was acting in his sacred office by his appointment and by his direction.

In illustration of the priestly office is read, "And the Lord spake unto Moses, saying, Take Aaron and his sons with him, and the garments, and the anointing oil, and a bullock for the sin offering, and two rams, and a basket of unleavened bread; and gather thou all the congregation together unto the door of the tabernacle of the congregation. And Moses did as the Lord commanded him; and the assembly was gathered together unto the door of the tabernacle of the congregation. And Moses said unto the congregation, This is the thing which the Lord commanded to be done. And Moses brought Aaron and his sons, and washed them with water. And he put upon him the coat, and girded him with the girdle, and clothed him with the robe, and put the ephod upon him, and he girded him with the curious girdle of the ephod, and bound it unto him therewith. And he put the breastplate upon him: also he put in the breastplate the Urim and the Thummim. And he put the mitre upon his head; also upon the mitre, even upon his forefront, did he put the golden plate, the holy crown; as the Lord commanded Moses. And Moses took the anointing oil, and anointed the tabernacle and all that was therein, and sanctified them. And he sprinkled thereof upon the altar seven times, and anointed the altar and all his vessels, both the laver and his foot, to sanctify them. And he poured of the anointing oil upon Aaron's head, and anointed him, to sanctify him."

PRAYER.

All-merciful Father, who hast assisted us this day to number this our companion among the rulers of the Order, grant that his life and actions may be guided by thy holy will and power. Inspire him and us with humility and a ready obedience to Thee and thy laws; and let that mercy shown to thy earlier people not be withheld from us, so that after the closing hours of existence we may be numbered among those elected unto the temple of eternal bliss and glory.

In the introduction to the Prophetical Office, the Second Principal, the following passages of Scripture are read:—

"And the child Samuel ministered unto the Lord before Eli. And the word of the Lord was precious in those days; there was no open vision. And it came to pass at that time, when Eli was laid down in his place, and his eyes began to wax dim, that he could not see; and ere the lamp of God went out in the temple of the Lord, where the ark of God was, and Samuel was laid down to sleep; that the Lord called Samuel: and he answered, Here am I. And he ran unto Eli, and said, Here am I; for thou calledst me. And he said, I called not; lie down again. And he went and lay down. And the Lord called yet again, Samuel. And Samuel arose and went to Eli, and said, Here am I; for thou didst call me. And he answered, I called not, my son; lie down again. Now Samuel did not yet know the Lord, neither was the word of the Lord yet revealed unto him. And the Lord called Samuel again the third time. And he arose and went to Eli, and said, Here am I; for thou didst call me. And Eli perceived that the Lord had called the child. Therefore Eli said unto Samuel, Go, lie down: it shall be, if he call thee, that thou shalt say, Speak, Lord; for thy servant heareth. So Samuel went and lay down in his place. And the Lord came and stood, and called as at other times, Samuel, Samuel. Then Samuel answered, Speak; for thy servant heareth. And the Lord said to Samuel, Behold, I will do a thing in Israel, at which both the ears of every one that heareth it shall tingle. In that day I will perform against Eli all things which I have spoken concerning his house: when I begin, I will also make an end. For I have told him that I will judge his house for ever for the iniquity which he knoweth; because his sons made themselves vile, and he restrained them not. And therefore I have sworn unto the house of Eli, that the iniquity of Eli's house shall not be purged with sacrifice nor offerings for ever. And Samuel lay until the morning, and opened the doors of the house of the Lord. And Samuel feared to show Eli the vision. Then Eli called Samuel, and said, Samuel, my son. And he answered, Here am I. And he said, What is the thing that the Lord hath said unto thee? I pray thee hide it not from me: God do so to thee, and more also, if thou hide any thing from me of all the things that he said unto thee. And Samuel told him every whit, and hid nothing from him. And he said, It is the Lord: let him do what seemeth him good. And Samuel grew, and the Lord was with him, and did let none of his words fall to the ground. And all Israel from Dan even to Beersheba knew that Samuel was established to be a prophet of the Lord. And the Lord appeared again in Shiloh: for the Lord revealed himself to Samuel in Shiloh by the word of the Lord."

"And when Abram was ninety years old and nine, the Lord appeared to Abram and said unto him, I am the Almighty God; walk before me, and be thou perfect."

"Wherefore I say unto the children of Israel, I am the Lord, and I will bring you out from under the burdens of the Egyptians, and I will rid you out of their bondage, and I will redeem you with a stretched out arm and great judgments."

"And Moses stretched out his hand over the sea: and the Lord caused the sea to go back by a strong east wind all that night, and made the sea dry land, and the waters were divided. And the children of Israel went into the midst of the sea upon the dry ground: and the waters were a wall unto them on their right hand and on their left. And the Egyptians pursued, and went in after them to the midst of the sea, even all Pharaoh's horses, his chariots, and his horsemen. And it came to pass, that in the morning watch the Lord looked unto the host of the Egyptians through the pillar of fire and of the cloud, and troubled the host of the Egyptians, and took off their chariot wheels, that they drave them heavily: so that the Egyptians said, Let us flee from the face of Israel; for the Lord fighteth for them against the Egyptians. And the Lord said unto Moses, Stretch out thine hand over the sea, that the waters may come again upon the Egyptians, upon their chariots and upon their horsemen. And Moses stretched forth his hand over the sea, and the sea returned to his strength when the morning appeared; and the Egyptians fled against it: and the Lord overthrew the Egyptians in the midst of the sea."

The effect of this extraordinary exhibition of the Divine power upon the Hebrews, proves the miraculous character of the transaction. When they saw the great work which the Lord had done to seal their redemption from Egypt, they believed in Him; and in after times, its stupendous and undoubted character occasioned their successive historians, prophets, poets, and didactic writers, more frequently to refer to this miracle than any other of the extraordinary manifestations of Divine power which the Sacred Volume records.

PRAYER.

Almighty Father, who in the hour of perplexity assistedst the people of Israel, and subduedst their enemies, bestow on us the continuance of thy kindness and protection; let the knowledge of thy goodness and power inspire us with gratitude for thy manifold blessings which we have already received, and grant that during our sojourn in this world of sin, we may overcome the powers of darkness, and live according to thy will and commandments, to the honour and glory of thy most holy Name.

On reaching the exalted position of Zerubbabel, the Companion elected to kingly power has his attention directed to the Lord's election of the youth David to fill the throne Saul was no longer worthy to occupy, as described in the Holy Scriptures:—

"And the Lord said unto Samuel, How long wilt thou mourn for Saul, seeing I have rejected him from reigning over Israel? fill thine horn with oil, and go, I will send thee to Jesse the Beth-lehemite: for I have provided me a king among his sons. And Samuel said, How can I go? if Saul hear it, he will kill me. And the Lord said, Take an heifer with thee, and say, I am come to sacrifice to the Lord. And call Jesse to the sacrifice, and I will show thee what thou shalt do: and thou shalt anoint unto me him whom I name unto thee. And Samuel did that which the Lord spake, and came to Beth-lehem. And the elders of the town trembled at his coming, and said, Comest thou peaceably? And he said, Peaceably: I am come to sacrifice unto the Lord: sanctify yourselves, and come with me to the sacrifice. And he sanctified Jesse and his sons, and called them to the sacrifice. And it came to pass, when they were come, that he looked on Eliab, and said, Surely the Lord's anointed is before him. But the Lord said unto Samuel, Look not on his countenance, or on the height of his stature; because I have refused him: for the Lord seeth not as man seeth; for man looketh on the outward appearance, but the Lord looketh on the heart. Then Jesse called Abinadab, and made him pass before Samuel. And he said, Neither hath the Lord chosen this. Then Jesse made Shammah to pass by. And he said, Neither hath the Lord chosen this. Again, Jesse made seven of his sons to pass before Samuel. And Samuel said unto Jesse, The Lord hath not chosen these. And Samuel said unto Jesse, Are here all thy children? And he said, There remaineth yet the youngest, and, behold, he keepeth the sheep. And Samuel said unto Jesse, Send and fetch him: for we will not sit down till he come hither. And he sent, and brought him in. Now he was ruddy, and withal of a beautiful countenance, and goodly to look to. And the Lord said, Arise, anoint him: for this is he. Then Samuel took the horn of oil, and anointed him in the midst of his brethren: and the Spirit of the Lord came upon David from that day forward. So Samuel rose up, and went to Ramah."

And in further illustration of the knowledge of the will of the Most High,—

"And God said unto Moses, I AM THAT I AM: and he said, Thus shalt thou say unto the children of Israel, I AM hath sent me unto you."

"Moreover he said, I am the God of thy father, the God of Abraham, the God of Isaac, and the God of Jacob. And Moses hid his face; for he was afraid to look upon God."

"And I appeared unto Abraham, unto Isaac, and unto Jacob, by the name of God Almighty, but by my name JEHOVAH was I not known to them."

The ritual of this Supreme Degree, when fully carried out, is not excelled by any other in the whole Masonic system. It inspires its members with the most exalted ideas of God, and leads to the exercise of the most pure and sublime piety and reverence for the incomprehensible JEHOVAH, the Eternal Ruler of the Universe, the Elemental Spring and Primordial Source of all its principles, the very Fountain of all its virtues.

ROYAL ARCH ODES.

WHEN orient Wisdom beam'd serene,
 And pillar'd Strength arose;
When Beauty tinged the glowing scene,
 And Faith her mansion chose;
Exulting bands the fabric view'd,
 Mysterious powers adored,
And high the triple union stood,
 That gave the mystic Word.

Pale Envy wither'd at the sight,
 And, frowning o'er the pile,
Call'd Murder up from realms of night,
 To blast the glorious toil.
With ruffian outrage join'd in woe,
 They form the league abhorr'd;
And wounded Science felt the blow
 That crush'd the mystic Word.

Concealment, from sequester'd cave,
 On sable pinions flew,
And o'er the sacrilegious grave
 Her veil impervious threw.
Th' associate band in solemn state
 The awful loss deplored;
And Wisdom mourn'd the ruthless fate
 That whelm'd the mystic Word.

At length through Time's expanded sphere
 Fair Science speeds her way;
And, warm'd by Truth's refulgence clear,
 Reflects the kindred ray.

A second fabric's towering height
  Proclaims the sign restored;
From whose foundation—brought to light,
  Is drawn the mystic Word.

To depths obscure the favour'd Trine
  A dreary course engage,
Till through the arch the ray divine
  Illumes the sacred page!
From the wide wonders of this blaze
  Our ancient signs restored;
The Royal Arch alone displays
  The long-lost mystic Word.

AIR—"*Rule, Britannia.*"

ALMIGHTY Sire! our heavenly King,
  Before whose sacred name we bend,
Accept the praises which we sing,
  And to our humble prayer attend!
    All hail, great Architect divine!
    This universal frame is thine.

Thou, who didst Persia's king command
  A proclamation to extend,
That Israel's sons might quit his land,
  Their holy temple to attend.
    All hail, &c.

That sacred place, where three in one
  Comprised thy comprehensive name;
And where the bright meridian sun
  Was soon thy glory to proclaim.
    All hail, &c.

Thy watchful eye, a length of time,
  The wondrous circle did attend;
The glory and the power be thine,
  Which shall from age to age descend.
      All hail, &c.

On thy omnipotence we rest,
  Secure of thy protection here;
And hope hereafter to be blest,
  When we have left this world of care.
      All hail, &c.

Grant us, great God! thy powerful aid
  To guide us through this vale of tears;
For where thy goodness is display'd,
  Peace soothes the mind, and Pleasure cheers.
      All hail, &c.

Inspire us with thy grace divine,
  Thy sacred law our guide shall be:
To every good our hearts incline,
  From every evil keep us free.
      All hail, &c.

CHAPTER XVII.

MARK MASTER.

"Blessed is the man whose God is good; who, initiated in divine ceremonies, hallows his life by rule."—*Euripides.*

IN England the Mark Degree is altogether a distinct institution, the only qualification being, that the candidate should be a duly certified Master Mason. It is to be regretted that the brethren who revived the degree did not take both the *Mark Man* as well as *Mark Master;* for the first we conceive to be a necessary prelude to the latter, as is to a certain extent shown by the legend of the Mark Man being given in the shape of a lecture.

In Scotland considerable importance is attached to the Mark Master in connexion with the Royal Arch.

Our transatlantic brethren also view the degree with considerable favour. The *Mark Master* is designated the first degree of *American Capitular Masonry.* The ritual would appear, from the erudite Brother Mackay, to be much more elaborate than our own.

The *Mark Master* was not required in England, its place being supplied by the *Installed Master,* which, when the Mark was in practice, did not exist. The Mark Master never can be restored to English Masonry by its Grand Lodge. Its Master is styled 'Right Worshipful,' which is that of the Deputy Grand Master of England or Grand Master of a Province.

This is decidedly objectionable. There are two differently constituted Lodges of Mark Masters, and one party has created itself a Grand Lodge.

The degree of *Mark Master,* which narrates the legend here described in a lecture from the Master at the end of the ceremony, differs in the ritual, and when it was framed was, we presume, the step a Mason gained to attain the rank similar to the Installed Master. It belongs to the Scottish Constitution, and ought not to have been introduced into English Masonry, where it can never be of any use.

From a discourse by the Rev. Bro. T. M. Harris (U.S.), from Rev. ii. 17, it would appear that the Mark Master Mason has given him the distinguishing symbol of the degree, a white stone, and he alludes to ancient custom with reference to its use; he quotes the anthem which is adopted in the ceremonial of admission.

THE ANTHEM.

[AIR—"*God save the Queen.*"]

MARK Masters, all appear
Before the Chief Overseer.
In concert move;
Let him your work inspect;
For the Chief Architect,
If there be no defect,
He will approve.

You who have pass'd the square,
For your rewards prepare.
Join heart and hand;
Each with his mark in view,
March with the just and true;
Wages to you are due,
At your command.

Hiram, the widow's son,
Sent unto Solomon
Our great key-stone;
On it appears the name
Which raises the high fame
Of all to whom the same
Is truly known.

Now to the westward move,
Where, full of strength and love,
Hiram doth stand;
But if impostors are
Mix'd with the worthy there,
Caution them to beware
Of the right hand.

CEREMONIES.

Now to the praise of those
Who triumph'd o'er the foes
Of Masons' art;
To the praiseworthy three,
Who founded this degree;
May all their virtues be
Deep in our hearts!

He says, "The stone which bears 'the mystic word' is legible only to those who have been taught the interpretation; by others it is rejected as insignificant, or considered as 'a stone of stumbling, and a rock of offence.'"

Now there has been a custom in the East of long date, and we are assured that it still abides with the Arabs, that on a traveller leaving a tent where he had been received with hospitality, he has presented to him a small square white stone, the possession of which will ensure him good treatment from the tribe he next visits. There are marks on it known only to the chiefs of the tribes in communication. The key-stone of the arch is a totally different affair, and the mark placed on it is known to each and all the Lodge.

Those brethren who have entered the Templar know the stone presented to them is in reference to the ancient custom.

A learned brother, Dr. Hopkins, is very eloquent on the ceremony of this degree. He says, "As Mark Masons it is especially our duty to make our conduct such as shall stand the test of the Grand Overseer's *square,* and fit us for the place for which we are destined in the building. Thus far as regards ourselves; with respect also to others, let us learn by this degree not to judge by appearances; let us remember our own ignorance, and be more ready to approve than to condemn. As the stone which the builders rejected became the head of the corner, so the man we despise to-day may control our destiny tomorrow."

The degree of Mark Master is historically considered of the utmost importance, since we are informed that, by its influence, each operative Mason at the building of the Temple was known and distinguished, and the disorder and confusion, which might otherwise have attended so immense an undertaking, was completely prevented. Not less useful is it in its symbolic signification. As illustrative of the Fellow-Craft, this degree is particularly directed to the inculcation of order, regularity, and discipline. It teaches us that we should discharge all the duties of our several stations with precision and punctuality; that the work of our hands and the thoughts of our hearts should be good and true—not unfinished and imperfect—not sinful and defective—but such as the Great Overseer and Judge of heaven and earth will see fit to approve as a worthy oblation from his creatures. If the Fellow-Craft's Degree is devoted to the inculcation of learning, that of the Mark Master is intended to instruct us how that learning can most usefully and judiciously be employed for our own honour and the profit of others. And it holds forth to the desponding the encouraging thought, that although our motives may sometimes be misinterpreted by our erring fellow-mortals—our attainments be underrated, and our reputations be traduced by the envious and malicious, there is One, at least, who sees not with the eyes of man, but may yet make that stone which the builders rejected, the head of the corner. The intimate connexion, then, between the second and fourth degrees of Masonry is this, that while one inculcates the necessary exercise of all the duties of life, the other teaches the importance of performing them with systematic regularity. The true Mark Master is a type of that man, mentioned in the sacred parable, who received from his master this approving language: "Well done, thou good and faithful servant; thou hast been faithful over a few things, I will make thee ruler over many things: enter thou into the joy of thy Lord."

CHARGE TO BE READ AT OPENING THE LODGE.

"Wherefore, brethren, lay aside all malice, and guile, and hypocrisies, and envies, and all evil speakings: if so be ye have tasted that the Lord is gracious. To whom coming, as unto a living stone, disallowed indeed of men, but chosen of God, and precious; ye also, as living stones, be ye built up a spiritual house, an holy priesthood, to offer up sacrifices acceptable to God.

"Wherefore, also, it is contained in the Scriptures, Behold, I lay in Zion for a foundation a tried stone, a precious cornerstone, a sure foundation; he that believeth shall not make haste. Judgment will I also lay to the *line,* and righteousness to the *plummet.* Unto you, therefore, which believe, it is an honour; and even to them which be disobedient, the stone which the builders disallowed, the same is made the head of the corner.

"Brethren, this is the will of God, that with well-doing ye

put to silence the ignorance of foolish men. As free, and not as using your liberty for a cloak of maliciousness, but as the servants of God. Honour all men; love the brotherhood; fear God; honour the King."

The *first section* explains the manner of convocating and opening a Mark Master's Lodge. It teaches the stations and duties of the respective officers, and recapitulates the mystic ceremony of introducing a candidate.

In this section are exemplified the regularity and good order which were observed by the craftsmen on Mount Libanus, and in the plains and quarries of Zeredatha, and ends with a beautiful display of the manner in which one of the principal events originated, which characterizes this degree.

In the *second section,* the Mark Master is particularly instructed in the origin and history of this degree, and the indispensable obligations he is under to stretch forth his assistant hand to the relief of an indigent and worthy brother, to a certain and specified extent.

The progress made in architecture, particularly in the reign of Solomon, is remarked; the number of artists employed in building the Temple of Jerusalem, and the privileges they enjoyed are specified; the mode of rewarding merit and of punishing the guilty is pointed out; and the marks of distinction, which were conferred on our ancient brethren, as the rewards of excellence, are named.

TEXTS OF SCRIPTURE INTRODUCED AND MASONICALLY EXPLAINED.

To him that overcometh will I give to eat of the hidden manna, and I will give him a *white stone,* and in the stone a *new name* written, which no man knoweth save he that receiveth it. (Rev. ii. 17.)

And we will cut wood out of Lebanon, as much as thou shalt

need; and we will bring it to thee in floats by sea to Joppa, and thou shalt carry it up to Jerusalem. (2 Chron. ii. 16.)

The stone which the builders refused, is become the head stone of the corner. (Ps. cxviii. 22.)

Did ye never read in the Scriptures, The stone which the builders rejected, the same is become the head of the corner? (Matt. xxi. 42.)

And have ye not read this scripture, The stone which the builders rejected, is become the head of the corner? (Mark xii. 10.)

What is this then that is written, The stone which the builders rejected, the same is become the head of the corner? (Luke xx. 17.)

This is the stone which was set at nought of you builders, which is become the head of the corner. (Acts iv. 11.)

He that hath an ear to hear, let him hear. (Rev. iii. 13.)

Then he brought me back the way of the gate of the outward sanctuary, which looketh toward the east, and it was shut. Then said the Lord unto me, This gate shall be shut, it shall not be opened, and no man shall enter in by it; because the Lord, the God of Israel, hath entered in by it; therefore it shall be shut. It is for the prince; the prince, he shall sit in it to eat bread before the Lord; he shall enter by the way of the porch of that gate, and shall go out by the way of the same.

And the Lord said unto me, Son of man, *mark well,* and behold with thine eyes, and hear with thine ears, all that I say unto thee concerning all the ordinances of the house of the Lord, and all the laws thereof: and *mark well* the entering in of the house, with every going forth of the sanctuary. (Ezek. xliv. 1—5.)

PARABLE.

For the kingdom of heaven is like unto a man that is an householder, which went out early in the morning to hire labourers into his vineyard. And when he had agreed with the labourers for a penny a day, he sent them into his vineyard. And he went out about the third hour, and saw others standing idle in the market-place, and said unto them, Go ye also into the vineyard; and whatsoever is right, I will give you. And they went their way. And again he went out about the sixth and ninth hour, and did likewise. And about the eleventh hour, he went out and found others standing idle, and said unto them, Why stand ye here all the day idle? They say unto him, Because no man hath hired us. He saith unto them, Go ye also into the vineyard; and whatsoever is right, that shall ye receive. So, when even was come, the Lord of the vineyard saith unto his steward, Call the labourers, and give them their hire, beginning from the last unto the first. And when they came that were hired about the eleventh hour, they received every man a penny. But when the first came, they supposed that they should have received more; and they likewise received every man a penny. And when they had received it, they murmured against the goodman of the house, saying, These last have wrought but one hour, and thou hast made them equal unto us, which have borne the burden and heat of the day. But he answered one of them, and said, Friend, I do thee no wrong; didst not thou agree with me for a penny? Take that thine is, and go thy way; I will give unto this last even as unto thee. Is it not lawful for me to do what I will with mine own? Is thine eye evil because I am good? So the last shall be first, and the first last: for many are called, but few chosen. (Matt. xx. 1—16.)

CHARGE.

Brother, I congratulate you on having been thought worthy of being promoted to this honorary degree of Masonry. Permit me to impress it on your mind, that your assiduity should ever be commensurate with your duties, which become more and more extensive as you advance in Masonry.

The situation to which you are now promoted will draw upon you not only the scrutinizing eyes of the world at large, but those also of your brethren, on whom this degree of Masonry has not been conferred; all will be justified in expecting your conduct and behaviour to be such as may with safety be imitated.

In the honourable character of Mark Master Mason it is more particularly your duty to endeavour to let your conduct in the Lodge, and among your brethren, be such as may stand the test of the Grand Overseer's square, that you may not, like the unfinished and imperfect work of the negligent and unfaithful of former times, be rejected and thrown aside, as unfit for that spiritual building, that house not made with hands, eternal in the heavens.

While such is your conduct, should misfortunes assail you, should friends forsake you, should envy traduce your good name, and malice persecute you; yet may you have confidence that, among Mark Master Masons, you will find friends who will administer relief to your distresses, and comfort in your afflictions; ever bearing in mind, as a consolation under all the frowns of fortune, and as an encouragement to hope for better prospects, that *the stone which the builders rejected* (possessing merits to them unknown) *became the chief stone of the corner.*

The working tools are the *mallet* and *chisel.* The *mallet* teaches us to correct the irregularities of temper, and, like enlightened reason, to curb the aspirations of unbridled ambition, to depress the malignity of envy, and to moderate the ebullition of anger. It relieves the mind from all the excrescences of vice, and fits it as a well-wrought stone for that exalted station in the great temple of nature, to which, as an emanation of the Deity, it is entitled.

The *chisel* is emblematic of the effects of education on the human mind. For as the artist, by the aid of this instrument, gives form and regularity to the shapeless mass of stone, so education, by cultivating the ideas, and by polishing the rude thoughts, transforms the ignorant savage into the civilized being.

Hymns for a Mark Masons' Lodge. Words by Bro. John Mott Thearle, P.M., No. 82, P.J.G.D. Herts. Set to Music by Bro. E. Hart.

OPENING HYMN.

GRACE this Lodge, Great Overseer,
  With all thy pure and earnest truth,
That it may flourish through all time
  Even with unabated youth.

Bless the advancing ones this night,
  That through their lives they'll onward go,
Marking progress by the light
  Acknowledged and derived from you.

Their Mark in hand, thy Mark at heart,
  O may they ever constant prove,
And in all time and circumstance,
  Unite in brotherhood and love!

CLOSING HYMN.

HAVE we mark'd well, Great Overseer?
  A work to last beyond all time;
Each his allotted task fulfill'd,
  The glory and the praise be thine.

In this degree we find the truth,
  On earth below, in heaven above,
The Corner-stone of every work
  Should be unselfish, lasting love.

Still will we work, and working pray,
  Trusting that in a better land
Our mystic Key-stone may be raised,
  And fitted by thy Master Hand.

CLOSING.

The ceremony of closing a Lodge in this degree, when properly conducted, is peculiarly interesting. It assists in strengthening the social affections; it teaches us the duty we owe to our brethren in particular, and the whole family of mankind in general, by ascribing praise to the meritorious, and dispensing rewards to the diligent and industrious.

CHAPTER XVIII.

THE ANCIENT AND ACCEPTED RITE.

"All under various names adore and love
One Power immense, which ever rules above."

DRYDEN.

"Let envy howl, while heaven's whole chorus sings,
And bark at honour not conferred by kings."

POPE.

THIS rite is by some authorities designated as the *Scotch Rite,* as having derived its first establishment from Scottish Masons. The earliest record we have of the practice of any of the degrees contained in the rite is that the Lodge "St. George de la Observance, No. 49, chartered by the Grand Lodge of England in 1736," stationed in Covent Garden, worked the "sublime degrees" in a body attached to their Lodge. The members were mostly of French or Italian extraction, and the authority to work these degrees, it is said, was derived from Scotland. But there is positive living testimony that some of the degrees in the rite, as the eighteenth, twenty-eighth, and thirtieth, were practised in the Midland Counties in the latter half of the last century, by brethren who were descendants of the Ancient York Masons; and at Nottingham, in particular, they were worked under the authority of Lord Rancliffe, who was Grand Master of the Templars.

Brother *Preston* says, "January 4, 1787, was opened in London the Grand Chapter of Harodim. Though of ancient date and practised in different parts of Europe, there is no record prior to this of its establishment in England. The mysteries of this Order are peculiar to the Institution itself, while the lectures include every branch of the Masonic system, and represent the Art of Masonry in a finished and complete form." The presiding officer was called the Chief Harod.

As far as can now be ascertained, the Chapter of Harodim appears to have been a combination of the system of the Ancient York Masons with other degrees imported from France, as got up by Ramsay and others.

Harodim is a Hebrew word, signifying princes or rulers; there were three hundred chief overseers whom Solomon appointed to set the people at work (2 Chron. ii. 18). After Preston's time we hear nothing of the Harodim Chapter.

Some of the degrees now embodied in the Ancient and Accepted Rite continued to be practised up to a very recent period, and little over thirty years since were conferred on brethren now living, at the Crown Tavern on Clerkenwell Green, Brother Goldsworthy being one of the acting directors of the proceedings. We have been told that this association was a Council of the Nine Excellent Masters, and thus might be analogous to the Supreme Council; but we are unable to learn what degrees were conferred, for, excepting as to the Ark Mariner or Noachite, and the Rose-Croix, the survivors have no knowledge. They gave no certificate.

The Old Kent Lodge, now No. 15, had a warrant from the late Duke of Kent, empowering it to confer seven degrees, among which was the Knight of the Sun; a price for each degree was named in the warrant. The warrant was one of confirmation for one of ancient date that had been lost. It is said that this warrant is now in the possession of a brother who was a member at the time, and we believe now living.

The Lodge of Fidelity, now No. 3, was the last Lodge that worked the old degrees; it met at the place named.

When the Duke of Sussex came into power, he exerted all his influence to suppress the practices we have referred to, and the degrees referred to were confined to a few brethren, survivors of the Ancient York Masons, of whom the present M. P. Sovereign of the Order, Dr. Leeson, was one.

At the death of the Duke of Sussex, it was thought desirable to assemble the scattered fragments of the ancient degrees, and by general consent of the remaining members of the Ancient Order, to form a general governing body of the Ancient and Accepted Rite. The present degrees of the Knight Templar and the Holy Arch not being found to exist amongst the ancient degrees of the Order as elsewhere described, it seemed impossible to combine them in the rite; and thus it was thought better to establish an independent conclave for the degree of Knight Templar by a general accordance of the various existing Encampments, a great majority of which acceded thereto, and those with one exception have since joined. It was then that an interview took place between the leaders, and it having been satisfactorily proved that none of the existing Encampments ever had any authority by warrant from any legally constituted authority to give the degrees of Rose-Croix and Kadosh, they being degrees of the Ancient and Accepted Rite, it was agreed to discontinue any assumption of authority over those degrees on the part of the Grand Conclave, whilst the Supreme Council, on their part, discontinued any authority or interference with the Templar Degree.

Among the leaders of this movement the present Sovereign Grand Commander of the Supreme Council was the most active, and in concert with a few others, commenced the necessary steps for the formation of a Council of the Ancient and Accepted Rite; whilst these were progressing, Brother Crucefix obtained a legal authority from the Supreme Council at New York, (now at

Boston,) giving him the first rank. Brother Leeson, as a descendant of the Ancient York Masons, was at the time in correspondence with another body for a like authority, but on the arrival of the New York power, overtures were made to him to forego his ancient privileges, and to assist in the establishment of a Supreme Council in this country under the authority of the American body.

The first members of the Council were,

1. Dr. Thomas Crucefix.
2. Dr. Henry Beaumont Leeson.
3. Henry Udall.
4. Richard Lee Wilson.
5. Rev. Dr. George Oliver.
6. David W. Nash.
7. Thomas Prior.
8. William Tucker.
9. Sir John Robinson, Bart.

Brothers Udall and Nash have been removed from the Council; Brothers Oliver and Robinson have resigned; Brothers Crucefix, Wilson, Prior, and Tucker are deceased: the present M. P. Sovereign alone survives of the original Council. The warrant of the New York Council was issued 26th October, 1845, and the Council was organized in March 1846. Brother Leeson went over to Paris to visit the governing bodies of the Order, by whom he was received with open arms: a warrant of recognition was at once granted to the English Council, and Brother Leeson was appointed the representative of the Grand Orient in this country. The Supreme Council of Ireland granted a like acknowledgment.

It cannot but be acknowledged that by the establishment of the Supreme Council the English Masons who had taken the degrees included in the rite are now in a more satisfactory position, inasmuch as they are in accordance with the Supreme Councils of Ireland, Scotland, France, Germany, and the Brazils.

The degrees in this rite are not innovations on pure symbolic Masonry, but are rather illustrations, and as such are full of much instructive speculation, combining many traditions of great interest to Masons, shedding great light on the object of the institution.

They were also cultivated on the continent of Europe in a similar way to that adopted in Great Britain, until their embodiment by Frederick the Great, King of Prussia.

It appears that, in 1740, soon after his ascension to the throne, Frederick chartered a Lodge at Berlin, by the name of "The Three Globes," and organized it as a Grand Lodge. The degrees of Craft Masonry were governed by this Grand Lodge, and the higher degrees of the rite of Harodim or Perfection, with its twenty-five degrees, were under the government of an "Inner East," whose members were elected by the Grand Lodge. This rite of Perfection or Harodim comprised eleven degrees, viz., Knight of the Sword (or East), Prince of Jerusalem, Knight of the East and West, Sovereign Prince Rose-Croix, and seven of the superior degrees belonging to the Consistories of Sublime Princes of the Royal Secret, including that last named.

Some few years after the degrees were increased in number to thirty-two, by making three grades of the thirty-second, and adding Noachite, or Prussian Knight, Knight of St. Andrew, and some preparatory degrees to the series.

These degrees—or rite—although extensively practised on the continent of America, had no governing head, until Frederick the Great condescended to become, and was acknowledged and proclaimed, chief, with the rank, as declared by the Constitutions of the Order, ratified at Berlin on the 25th of October, 1762, of "Sovereign Grand Inspector General and Grand Commander." These Constitutions were "proclaimed for the government of Sublime and Perfect Masons, chapters, councils, colleges, and consistories of the royal and military Art of

Freemasonry over the surface of the two hemispheres." From this body emanated authority to confer these degrees in France and America, and it is by one of these warrants, issued for New York, the Supreme Council now act.

On the 1st of May, 1786, the Grand Constitution of the Thirty-third Degree, called the Supreme Council of Sovereign Grand Inspectors General, was finally ratified by his Majesty the King of Prussia, who, as Grand Commander of the Order of Princes of the Royal Secret, possessed the sovereign Masonic power over the Craft. By the new constitution this high power was conferred on a Supreme Council composed of nine brethren in each nation, who possessed all the Masonic prerogatives in their own district that his Majesty individually possessed, and are sovereigns in Masonry.

The Supreme Council in the South United States declared, "Although many of the Sublime Degrees are a constitution of the Blue Degrees, yet there is no interference between the two bodies. The Sublime Masons never initiate into the Blue Degrees without a legal warrant for that purpose from a Symbolic Grand Lodge; but they communicate the secrets of the Chair to such applicants as have not already received them previous to their admittance into the Sublime Lodge; yet they are at the same time informed that it does not give them rank as Past Masters in the Grand Lodge."

The designation, as used by the "Supreme Council of the Thirty-third Degree for England and Wales and the Dependencies of the British Crown," differs as regards six of those of Prussia, but in practice we believe them to be the same, or but slightly altered. The degrees are stated as thirty-three in number, the first three being the symbolic, viz., the Entered Apprentice, Fellow-Craft, and Master Mason. The Mason who is possessed of the certificate of these last named is, according to the present usage, admissible to all degrees included below the Eighteenth Degree, which is the Sovereign Prince Rose-Croix of

Heredom. This must undoubtedly appear to the brother who has been exalted to the Royal Arch, and who has gone through the long course required to reach the chair of a Craft Lodge, to be a wholesale mode of conferring rank. We conceive that, according to strict rule, none but a regularly installed Master of a Craft Lodge is eligible to these degrees; in fact, the certificate of the Council begins by "certifying and acknowledging the brother to be an expert Master and Past Master of the Symbolic Lodges." In other countries we understand the Supreme Council claim the right to confer the rank of Past Master; but in England no attempt is made to interfere with the functions of the Grand Lodge, or to infringe its constitutions.

The formation of a Supreme Council of Sovereign Grand Inspectors General of the Thirty-third Degree is in this manner: the Inspector to whom the degree is first given regularly, is thereby authorized and empowered to confer it on another brother who is duly qualified by character and degrees to receive from him his obligation; these two give it in like manner to a third, when the three admit the rest by voting *viva voce*, beginning with the youngest Inspector; one nay excludes an applicant for ever, if the reasons given for such negative are deemed sufficient. After the first three the rules of reception must be regularly adhered to.

The first two admitted to the 33° should be the presiding officers of the Council; in case of death, resignation, or absence from the country not to return, of the first officer the M. P. Sovereign Grand Commander, the second officer or Lieutenant Grand Commander, takes his place, and appoints an Inspector General to succeed to his own office; in case of the like occurrences to the second officer, the M. P. Grand Commander appoints another Inspector General to succeed him who thus retires. The M. P. Sovereign Grand Commander in like manner appoints the Treasurer General, the Grand Master of Ceremonies, the Secretary General, the Captain of the Life Guards, and fills up all the vacancies as they may occur.

Every Inspector General previous to his election must pay into the Treasury the sum of ten guineas; the like sum has to be paid for the 32°, 31°, and 30°.

There must at all times, for any business in either of these degrees, be present three of the Supreme Council, of which one must be either of the two first officers.

The authority of the Ancient York Masons was transmitted, *viva voce*, from individual to individual, the oldest surviving Mason being considered for the time being as the chief Harod of the Order, whose duty it was to seek out some worthy brother to whom he could entrust the keys of the cypher and other documents necessary for the preservation of the Order, and it was the duty of that individual to conceal from the world generally the knowledge that he had been so entrusted, but it was known or generally understood by the members of the Order.

THE REGULATIONS OF THE SUPREME GRAND COUNCIL FOR ENGLAND AND WALES AND DEPENDENCIES OF THE BRITISH CROWN ARE AS FOLLOW:—

Brethren desirous of cultivating the Ineffable Degrees of the Ancient and Accepted Rite, from the 4th to the 18th inclusive, in any city, town, or place, where the same have not yet been established, under the authority of the Supreme Grand Council 33° for England and Wales and the Dependencies of the British Crown, must apply for a warrant to establish the same, by petition to the said Supreme Grand Council, addressed to the Illustrious Grand Secretary General for the time being; such petition to be signed by at least six Princes Rose-Croix, or members of the higher degrees holding allegiance to the Supreme Grand Council 33°, three of whom must be residents in the immediate vicinity of the place for which the warrant is required; such city, town, or place not being within the distance of ten miles from any other Chapter already legally established. A warrant for a Sovereign Chapter Rose-Croix will include authority to hold a Grand Lodge of Perfection and a Council of Princes of Jerusalem. The Grand Lodge of Perfection will govern the degrees from the 4th to the 14th inclusive; the Council of Princes of Jerusalem, the 15th and 16th Degrees; and the 17th and the 18th Degrees will be placed under the immediate administration of the Rose-Croix Chapter. A warrant cannot be removed from the city, town, or place, for which it was originally granted, without the permission of the Supreme Grand Council first had and obtained; and the charge for such removal shall be two guineas.

Form of Petition for a Warrant.—We, the undersigned Members of the Ancient and Accepted Rite, under the Supreme Grand Council 33° for England and Wales and the Dependencies of the British Crown, anxious to promote the welfare and extend the good of the Order, do hereby petition the Sovereign Grand Inspectors General 33° in council assembled, to grant a warrant to open and hold a Lodge of Perfection, a Council of Princes of Jerusalem, and a Sovereign Chapter Rose-Croix of H.R.D.M., to be named the

Chapter, at , in the {City or Town} of , in the County of And we do further recommend our Brother to be nominated the first Most Wise Sovereign of the same [our Brother to be the Most Equitable Sovereign Prince Master of the Council of Princes of Jerusalem; and our Brother to be the Thrice Potent Master of the Lodge of Perfection].

(Signed)

Dated

The fee for such warrant to be five guineas. Under necessary restrictions authorized Rituals may be obtained on payment of the expenses of preparing the same, which may be ascertained by application to the Illustrious Grand Treasurer General for the time being.

Whenever a warrant is granted by the Supreme Grand Council 33° to hold any Lodge of Perfection, Council of Princes of Jerusalem, or Sovereign Chapter Rose-Croix, application must be made to a Sovereign Grand Inspector General 33° to consecrate the same in ancient and solemn form.

Copies of such by-laws as may be agreed on by any Lodge of Perfection, Council of Princes of Jerusalem, or Sovereign Chapter Rose-Croix, shall be sent to the Illustrious Grand Secretary General for the time being, one to be retained by him, and the other to be deposited in the archives of the Order; and notice shall also be given to the Illustrious Grand Secretary General for the time being, whenever any alteration of such by-laws occurs.

N.B. By the Ancient Constitutions of the Order, no by-laws have any force or power unless sanctioned and approved by the Supreme Grand Council.

No Member of the 17th Degree shall be advanced to the rank of a Sovereign Prince Rose-Croix, H.R.D.M., for a less sum than three guineas.

Costume of the 18th Degree.—The brethren must be clothed in black, over which they should wear a dalmatic of white cloth, or stuff, bordered in black, with a Latin cross in red on the front and back.

Apron.—Of white satin bordered with red, and lined with black silk. On the satin is painted or embroidered the Jewel of the Order (the Pelican); on the lining a red cross.

Collar.—A waved or watered red ribbon, four inches wide, with narrow gold edging, lined with black; on the black side three red crosses, one on each side, and one at the point above a black rosette from which the jewel is to be suspended.

Jewel.—Compasses surmounted with an antique crown, points extended to 60°; a cross within the compasses; on one side of the jewel a pelican feeding its young; on the other, a white eagle with wings extended, as rising in the air: on both sides, on the joint of the compasses, a red rose.

In the first point the jewel should be covered with black crape.

No Lodge of Perfection, Council of Princes of Jerusalem, or Sovereign Chapter Rose-Croix, within the jurisdiction of the Supreme Council, can correspond, form any alliance, or hold any intercourse with any other Lodge of Perfection, Council of Princes of Jerusalem, or Sovereign Chapter Rose-Croix, nor *with any Masonic Body whatever, under any denomination whatever,* whether foreign or domestic, which professes to cultivate any of the degrees of the Ancient and Accepted Rite, or any other Rite, or any Sublime or Symbolic Degrees whatever, unless such Lodge, Council, or Chapter, or other Masonic Body, has been recognized as lawful and regular by the Supreme Grand Council.

In all cases of expulsion a vote of two-thirds of the members present shall be required, and such vote shall be submitted to the Supreme Grand Council 33° for confirmation.

Any brother having received the three first degrees of Craft Masonry in a duly-warranted Lodge, on the production of his Master Master's certificate, and on satisfactory assurance of his upright Masonic and moral character, is eligible for advancement to the degrees of the Ancient and Accepted Rite. But the Most Wise Sovereigns of Rose-Croix Chapters are earnestly cautioned to be very particular as to the social and Masonic character of those they admit to the privileges of this exalted degree.

No Lodge of Perfection, Council of Princes of Jerusalem, Sovereign Chapter Rose-Croix, or other meeting held under the authority of the Supreme Grand Council, can recognize the works of, or hold Masonic communication with, or receive as visitors, any brethren who have not taken the oath of allegiance to the Supreme Grand Council 33° (excepting brethren holding under foreign Supreme Councils duly recognized), unless such brethren shall take and sign such O.B., and be duly affiliated and regularized by special dispensations from the Supreme Grand Council, such dispensations bearing the signature of the Most Puissant Sovereign Grand Commander for the time being. Applications for such dispensations must be made at least fourteen days previous to the day of meeting, and must be forwarded by the Most Wise Sovereign of the Rose-Croix Chapter, accompanied by the fee of one guinea, to the Illustrious Grand Treasurer General for the time being; and a copy of the oath of allegiance, duly signed and certified by such Most Wise Sovereign, must accompany the application.

Every Lodge of Perfection, Council of Princes of Jerusalem, or Sovereign Chapter Rose-Croix shall, once in each year, in the month of November, fill up the printed form which will be sent, and return the same to the Illustrious Grand Secretary General for the time being, with the names, offices, and descriptions of subscribing and honorary members; and be particular to notify any death, resignation, or removal, which may have occurred since the last return. These returns are to be accompanied by the fee of one shilling for each subscribing member for verifying the register. The names and addresses of those who are advanced, admitted as joining members from other Chapters, or affiliated, must be sent without delay to the Illustrious Grand Treasurer General for the time being, with the fee of ten shillings each for registering and certificate. Unless this rule has been complied with, no brother can be received at any subsequent meeting of the Ancient and Accepted Rite. If no returns are made for the space of three years, the warrant of such Chapter shall be *ipso facto* forfeited, unless, on application duly made to the Supreme Grand Council 33°, such forfeiture be rescinded.

All Lodges of Perfection, Councils of Princes of Jerusalem,

and Sovereign Chapters Rose-Croix, shall take precedence according to the dates of their respective warrants.

By the Ancient Constitutions of the Order, no Chapter of Grand Elected Knights K.H. can be held except under the immediate authority of the Supreme Grand Council, three of whose members must be present. Such Chapters are held on the second Tuesdays in April and October, at their Grand East, London, when Candidates may be received. Recommendations for such must be sent from the Most Wise Sovereigns of the Rose-Croix Chapters of which such candidates are members, stating their names, residences, professions, &c. &c., to the Illustrious Grand Secretary General for the time being, on or before the second Tuesday in the months of March and September, in order that they may be submitted by him to the Supreme Grand Council 33°; and, if favourably received, notice will be sent to such candidates, with letters of admission to be by them presented on the day appointed for the meeting.

The brethren of the 30th Degree must be clothed in black, with white gloves; they should wear a white mantle bordered with black.

Sash.—To be a broad black ribbon, bordered with white, worn from the left shoulder to the right hip; upon it, opposite the breast, a red Teutonic Cross, with the letters K.H. in the centre, placed on two swords crossed as a Cross of St. Andrew.

Sword-belt.—Of black leather or velvet.

Jewel.—A black double-headed Spread Eagle, holding a Sword in its Claws; to be worn suspended round the neck from a flame-coloured ribbon.

All party spirit and cabal in any Council or Lodge is expressly forbidden, under pain of expulsion.

Soliciting votes at an election is strictly forbidden; and the brother doing it is liable to expulsion.

If a Prince give another Prince a challenge, he shall be excluded for ever.

Princes are strictly to observe the rule enforcing justice and good order, and their conduct in life should be irreproachable.

If any member of a Council or Lodge in this jurisdiction be guilty of any immoral or unmasonic conduct, or in any particular disobeys the Statutes and Regulations, Constitutions and Laws, of our Illustrious Order, he shall be reprimanded, suspended, or expelled, according to the aggravation of the offence.

All Sublime Masons who have received any degrees in a regular Lodge of Perfection, or Council of Princes of Jerusalem, in this jurisdiction, although for the time being they may not be members of any such Lodge or Council, shall be amenable for their conduct as Sublime Freemasons to the Council or Lodge nearest their places of residence.

If any member of a Council or Lodge within this jurisdiction shall be present at, or aid and assist in giving or receiving any of the Sublime or Symbolic Degrees in a clandestine or irregular manner, contrary to the true intent and meaning of the Statutes and Regulations of the said Supreme Grand Council, or of the Constitutions and Laws of True, Ancient, Free, or Accepted Masonry, he shall be expelled; and any Sublime Freemason, in and under this jurisdiction, who shall come to the knowledge of such illegal proceedings, shall immediately give information of the same to the Lodge or Council to which he belongs, under the penalty of suspension; that the honour, dignity, and legality of our Illustrious Order may be maintained, and the degrees of our Ancient and Accepted Rite be preserved in their purity and integrity.

A Prince of Jerusalem who visits an inferior Council or Lodge, should present himself clothed with the dress and ornaments of a Prince; and when his approach is announced, the Presiding Officer must send a Prince of Jerusalem to examine him; and if the officer report in his favour, he shall be received under the Arch of Steel, and be escorted by four brethren, and seated on the right hand of the Presiding Officer, An entry of his name and rank must be made on the minutes, that he may thereafter receive due honour without examination.

Princes have the right of being covered in all subordinate Lodges, Chapters, or Councils, and of addressing the Chair without first asking permission.

The Officers of all Councils of Princes of Jerusalem shall, in conformity with ancient usage, be styled and take rank as follows:—

1. Most Equitable Sovereign Prince Master. 2. High Priest. 3. Most Enlightened Senior Warden. 4. Most Enlightened Junior Warden. 5. Valorous Keeper of the Seals and Archives. 6. Valorous Treasurer. 7. Valorous Master of the Ceremonies. 8. Valorous Master of the Entrances. 9. Valorous Tyler.

At least five members are necessary to form a quorum for the transaction of business.

The Annual Meeting shall take place on a day to be fixed by the Council, and stated Meetings at such other times as shall be determined on.

The Officers shall be elected at the previous Meeting, and installed at the Annual Meeting.

No one shall be a member of any Council of Princes in this jurisdiction, who is not a member of a Lodge of Perfection under the superintendence of such Council.

It shall be the duty of every Council of Princes in this jurisdiction to inspect and watch over, with due care and fidelity, any and every Lodge of Perfection placed under its superintendence, and see that this work is done in conformity with the regulations and landmarks of the Order.

Every Council of Princes in this jurisdiction shall, for and in the name of the Supreme Grand Council of the 33rd and last Degree of the Ancient and Accepted Rite for England and Wales and the Dependencies of the British Crown, administer to all brethren admitted to any of the degrees conferred in their Council of Princes, and in the Lodges of Perfection under their superintendence, an obligation of fealty and allegiance to the said Supreme Grand Council, and submission to its decrees; and shall annually, immediately after their election of Officers, transmit to the said Supreme Grand Council every such obligation so taken, or a duplicate thereof, to be deposited in its archives.

Every letter of application from a Grand Elect, Perfect, and Sublime Mason, for the degrees of Knight of the East or Prince of Jerusalem, shall be accompanied with a certificate from the Treasurer of the Lodge of Perfection of which the applicant is a member, that all arrears of the applicant are paid up in the said Lodge; and shall enclose the required fee for elevation to those degrees. In the event of the rejection of any candidate, the amount of his enclosure shall be returned to him.

Notices of all suspensions and expulsions shall be given to the said Supreme Grand Council, as well as to all Councils and Lodges of inferior degree within the district.

No appeal, in any case of suspension or expulsion, can be made to the Supreme Grand Council from any Lodge of Perfection, until the matter in question shall have been submitted to the examination and decision of the Council of Princes of Jerusalem superintending such Lodge.

The Officers of Lodges of Perfection shall, in conformity with the most ancient usage, be styled and take rank as follows:—

1. Thrice Potent Master. 2. Hiram King of Tyre (his Deputy). 3. Senior Warden. 4. Junior Warden. 5. Keeper of the Seals. 6. Treasurer. 7. Secretary. 8. Orator. 9. Master of Ceremonies. 10. Captain of the Guards.

The Thrice Potent, on each election night, shall appoint one or two Tylers, also an Almoner.

The Annual Meeting shall take place on a day to be fixed by the Lodge, and stated Meetings at such other times as shall be determined on.

The Officers shall be elected at the previous Meeting, and installed at the Annual Meeting.

At all receptions the Orator shall make discourses in illustration of the Order, shall instruct the new brethren, and explain to them the mysteries, and exhort them to continue their zeal, fervour, and constancy. If he has observed any indiscretion or dispute, he shall inform the Lodge of it, and take measures accordingly.

If a brother is a prey to misfortune, it is the duty of every brother to endeavour to alleviate his distress.

The Almoner shall have the custody of the fund arising from the voluntary contributions of each night. He shall, before the closing of the Lodge, solicit the charitable contributions of the members. The sums so received shall be distributed by the Thrice Potent and Almoner, and shall be entered on the minutes at the next Meeting of the Lodge.

If any brother is taken sick, and it shall come to the knowledge of any member, he shall give early advice of it to the Almoner, and to the Lodge, that necessary succour may be administered. Should a brother die, all the brethren, if requested, are obliged to attend and assist at his funeral in the usual manner. It is most proper that the Lodge be then opened in the Perfect Master's Degree.

Secrecy, in reference to our Mysteries, as well as the transactions of the Lodge, regarding the character of a brother or applicant, being an indispensable obligation, the Thrice Potent shall always before closing the Lodge remind the brethren of their duty in this respect, and enforce it in the usual manner and form.

It shall be the duty of every Lodge of Perfection to place itself under the superintendence of the Council of Princes of Jerusalem sitting at its East.

It shall also be the duty of every Lodge, annually to make the reports and returns to such Council of Princes.

It is not the rule at present to practise any of the degrees below the 18th Degree; hence our explanations, being derived from a variety of sources partly written and partly oral, may not be considered precisely agreeable to some authorities, but in the main they will not be found to differ very widely. We must necessarily derive our authority from French sources.

Brother the Rev. Dr. Oliver, speaking upon this subject, says: —"The Ineffable Degrees are little known or esteemed in this country; for the evidences on which they rest are of doubtful authority; nor are these evidences essential to the well-being of Freemasonry, because the system is perfect without them, and they contain no typical references of any value either to improve the morals or amend the heart." We cannot in this matter entirely agree with our reverend brother, since we find that at this time the two degrees most practised, viz., the Rose-Croix and the Kadosh, are both well known and highly estimated; and as to the evidences of the degrees we are about to describe, although the greater part are certainly derived from sources not entirely trustworthy, some few have as certain an origin as other traditions the authenticity of which is not disputed; and in answer to Brother Oliver's last objection, we quote a small portion of one of the lectures:—

"What is the disposition of an Elect, Perfect, and Sublime Mason?—To keep his heart divested of jealousy, revenge, and every other evil passion; to be always ready to communicate benefits, and to have a tongue of good report.

"What kind of behaviour is recommended to you?—The most profound respect and submission to authority.

"Why are all Masons considered to be on equality?—Because they are equally subject to that Divine Being who is represented in our Lodges by the Sacred and Ineffable Name, and by the Equilateral Triangle."

The address which belongs to the Ineffable Degrees, derived from Brother Dalcho, is, as Brother Oliver himself allows, worthy of being adopted in the Symbolic Degrees. The Craft Masons use it in a Royal Arch Chapter, and, slightly altered, it is adopted by the Mark Masters.

"Brethren, you are now about to quit this sacred retreat of friendship and virtue, to mix again with the world. Amidst its concerns and employments forget not the duties you have heard so frequently inculcated and forcibly recommended in the Lodge. Be, therefore, diligent, prudent, temperate, and discreet. Remember also, that around this altar you solemnly and repeatedly promised to befriend and relieve, with unhesitating cordiality, so far as shall lie in your power, every brother who shall need your assistance; that you have promised to remind him, in the most tender manner, of his failings, and aid his reformation. Vindicate his character when wrongfully accused: suggest in his behalf, the most candid, favourable, and palliating circumstances, when his conduct is justly reprehended; that the world may observe how Masons love one another. These generous principles are to extend farther— every human being has a claim upon your kind offices; so that we enjoin it upon you to do good unto all, while we recommend it more especially to the household of the faithful. By diligence in the duties of your respective callings, by liberal benevolence and diffusive charity, by constancy and fidelity in your friendships, by uniformly just, amiable, and virtuous deportment— discover the beneficial and happy effects of this ancient and honourable institution. Let it not be supposed that you have here laboured in vain, and spent your strength for nought; for your work is with the Lord, and your recompense with your God. Finally, brethren, farewell: be ye all of one mind; live in peace; and may the God of love and peace delight to dwell with and to bless you."

But inasmuch as Masonry is professed in those nations which have not yet been converted to the Christian faith, and as it enkindles benevolence, and excites virtue, so accordant with the genius of the Gospel, it may eventually have no inconsiderable tendency towards introducing and propagating among them that most glorious system of revealed truth; at least, by humanizing the disposition, softening the manners, and removing the prejudices, may prepare the way for that most desirable event: in like manner to St. John the Baptist, who (our traditions assure us he was the first Christian Mason), was commissioned to prepare the way of the Lord, to smooth the road and remove the obstructions to the introduction of his truth.

The Sublime Degrees included in these rites, to which all the highly educated and intellectual of our Fraternity aspire, imply the recognition, and cannot be attained but through the acknowledgment, of Christianity.

From our description of the several degrees, our readers will discover that in some the canon of Scripture is the authority, in others, the apocryphal books; hence, if no other advantage is derived from a knowledge of the rite, at least it opens a vast field of inquiry to the diligent Mason. The brother who is admitted to the Ancient and Accepted Rite derives, in foreign Lodges, great benefit from its acquisition. Without the Rose-Croix, a Mason is held in but little esteem on the Continent. We must remark, that there are two systems adopted in France, the one identical with that practised in England, the other more usually designated "the French Rite" and "the Grand Orient." In the latter are seven degrees, three symbolic and four higher: viz., the three first, Craft; the fourth, the "Elect;" the fifth, the "Scotch Master;" the sixth, the "Knight of the East;" and the seventh, the Rose-Croix. This rite is also practised in Brazil. It was founded in 1786, by the Grand Orient of France.

With this introduction we shall now proceed to give some account of each degree, commencing with the Fourth Degree of the Rite, which is the first conferred by the Council, and is called—

SECRET MASTER.

In it is explained the mystic signification of those things which are contained in the *sanctum sanctorum* of the Tabernacle and the Temple; viz., the altar of incense, the golden candlestick, and the table of shewbread; and, also within the second veil, the ark of the testimony, and its lid and cover, called "the mercy-seat." For the forms of these holy things we have, besides the lucid description in the twenty-fifth chapter of Exodus, the authority of a bas-relief on the Arch of Titus at Rome, which was doubtless copied from the originals taken to that city by the triumphant army of the conqueror, after the destruction of Jerusalem: and although the ornaments which adorned the Temple of Solomon became a prey to the Chaldeans —if they were not, as is highly probable, all restored by Cyrus on the return of the Jews to their native land, it is certain that those used in the service of the second Temple were of a like pattern. The Master in this degree, as in the symbolic, represents Solomon, who now comes to the Temple to elect seven experts, or skilful practised Masons, to replace the loss of an illustrious character. The Master is styled Most Powerful; there is one Warden, who represents Adoniram, the overseer of the workmen on Mount Lebanon, and who was the first Secret Master. The Lodge is clothed in black, and illuminated by eighty-one lights. The badge is white, with a black edging, having a blue flap, on which an all-seeing eye is placed. The jewel of the degree is an ivory key, suspended from a white ribbon edged with black; on the key is engraved the letter Z, referring to Zadoc, who was the high priest in the reigns of David and Solomon.

PERFECT MASTER.

The Fifth Degree is that of PERFECT MASTER, and may be said to be a continuation of the preceding, being a tribute of respect to the worthy departed brother. In this the Right Worshipful Master represents Adoniram; he has also but one Warden, who is called "Inspector." The Deacon, or "Conductor" as he is called, represents Zabdiel, who was the father of Jashobeam, the first captain of the guards (1 Chron. xxvii. 2). The Hebrew of the Second Book of Samuel which speaks of Jashobeam, runs literally thus: "He who sat in the throne of wisdom, the head of the three, Adino of Ezni, who lifted up his spear against three hundred, whom he slew at one time." The badge is white, in the centre of which is embroidered within three circles a square stone or cube, on which the letter "J" is placed; the flap of the apron is green, symbolically to remind the Perfect Master that, being dead in vice, he must hope to revive in virtue. The jewel is a compass, extended sixty degrees, to teach him to act within measure, and ever pay due regard to justice and equity. The Perfect Master's Degree is founded on this traditional event. At the death of Hiram, the widow's son, Solomon, being desirous of paying a tribute of respect to his friend, requested Adoniram, the Grand Inspector, to make arrangements for his interment. The latter erected a superb tomb and obelisk of black and white marble, which he finished in nine days. The entrance to the tomb was between two pillars, supporting a square stone surrounded by three circles, on which was engraved the letter "J." The heart of the deceased was enclosed in a golden urn, to the side of which a triangular stone was fixed, inscribed with the letters "J.M.B." within a wreath of cassia. The urn was placed on the top of the obelisk. Three days after the interment, Solomon visited the tomb, and with solemn ceremonies, in the presence of the brethren, offered up a prayer, and with hands and eyes elevated to heaven, exclaimed, "It is accomplished!"

INTIMATE SECRETARY.

The Sixth Degree is the INTIMATE SECRETARY; in this there are only three officers, who represent Solomon, King of Israel,

Hiram of Tyre, and a captain of the guards. The ceremonial and legend are intended to preserve the remembrance of an instance of unlawful curiosity, the due punishment of the offender being averted only in consideration of his previous fidelity. Our brethren will readily perceive that these three degrees are a kind of commentary upon the historical traditions of the M.M. Degree, all having some reference to the event symbolized in that degree. The collar is crimson, and apron white with red border; on the flap is a triangle. The jewel is a triple triangle interlaced. In the degree of Intimate Secretary, the two persons who represent Solomon and Hiram of Tyre are clothed in blue mantles lined with ermine, with crowns on their heads, sceptres in their hands, and seated at a table on which are two naked swords, a roll of parchment, and a human skull. The rest of the brethren are considered only as Perfect Masters, and are termed Guards. They wear white aprons, lined and embroidered with crimson, and strings of the same, with crimson collars, to which is suspended a solid triangle. The degree relates to circumstances that occurred between Hiram and Joabert, when the fidelity of the latter was rewarded by Solomon with advancement to this rank.

The candidate is invested in open Lodge, and thus addressed by his superior: "My brother, I receive you as an Intimate Secretary, on your promise to be faithful to the Order into which you have just been admitted, and I trust that your fidelity will be proof against every temptation. I present you with a sword as a weapon of defence against the attacks of those who may try to extort from you the secrets which I am now about to communicate."

There is a tracing-board which is thus explained:—"The window in the clouds represents the vault of the Temple, and the letter 'J' which you see inscribed therein, indicates the Tetragrammaton, or sacred name of God. The door represents the principal entrance from the palace; the tears symbolize the repentance of Joabert in Solomon's chamber of audience, and are also emblematical of the lamentations of the king in the apartment hung with black, where he used to retire to lament the unhappy fate of Hiram; and here it was he received the King of Tyre."

PROVOST AND JUDGE.

This is the designation of the Seventh Degree. Traditional history relates its foundation by King Solomon for the purpose of strengthening his means of preserving order among the vast number of craftsmen engaged in the construction of the Temple. The presiding officer of the Lodge represents Tito, who was the first of the three hundred overseers called *Harodim,* a Hebrew word which signifies "princes" or "provosts" (see 1 Kings v. 16). In this degree there are six lights, which are so placed as to form a double triangle. The badge is white lined with red, and has a pocket; the collar is red; to it is suspended the jewel, a golden key, on the wards of which is engraved the letter "A." This degree appears out of place, as it has reference solely to the very first preparations for building the Temple; whereas those preceding it are connected with its construction and completion. Connected as these four degrees are with the historical traditions of the Third Degree, with the exception of the anachronism to which we are about to refer, they are unobjectionable and somewhat instructive. Are these traditions to be found in Preston's four sections of the Third Degree? Whence is derived the cognomen *Tito?*—it is clearly Latin or Italian. *Provost* comes from the Latin *prœpositus,* which denotes the chief of any society or community; the French word *prévôt* comes nearest to the form of the word, and the English expression "provost marshal," an officer attached to the army whose duty it is to seize and punish offenders against military discipline, has been adopted from the French *prévôt des maréchaux,* an officer who has similar functions. It has been suggested as probable that this degree was instituted among the Masonic crusaders, as it has more especial connexion with military government. The word "provost" is in England rarely used, we believe the only instances are those of the heads of certain colleges, &c.; in Scotland, it designates the chief magistrate in corporate cities, as the Lord Provost of Edinburgh, Glasgow, &c.

INTENDANT OF BUILDINGS.

The Eighth Degree is called INTENDANT of BUILDINGS, or "Master in Israel." The chief officers are a Thrice Puissant who represents King Solomon, the Senior Warden called Inspector, representing Tito the chief of the Harodim, and the Junior Warden who represents Adoniram. This arrangement of the Wardens would seem anomalous, as "Adoniram was set over the levy" of thirty thousand men sent by Solomon to Lebanon, while the Harodim were the three hundred overseers. The historical legend of this degree also affirms that the object of its institution was to supply the loss of Hiram, the widow's son. The badge is white, bordered with green and red. On the centre is a star of nine points, and on the flap a triangle with the initial of the degree. The Lodge is illuminated by twenty-seven lights, in three groups. The most noticeable character of this degree is the metaphorical use of the five points of fellowship in conjunction with the five orders of architecture. An Intendant of Buildings, we are told, must have made "the five steps of exactness, penetrated the inmost part of the Temple, and beheld the Great Light containing the three mysterious characters." The Intendant of Buildings, according to the modern acceptation of terms, is, doubtless, a most important office; but that post was filled most ably by Adoniram, and as there was but one building, the Harodim were under his control. Thus viewed, without better foundation than we are at present possessed of, the degree seems unsatisfactory.

ELECT OF NINE.

The Ninth Degree is ELECT of NINE. At this point we observe, for the first time, that the body is termed a "chapter." The chief officer is called Most Wise, he represents King Solomon; the second officer is the King of Tyre Most Puissant. The badge is of white satin, with a broad black border; on it are embroidered the emblems of the degree; the sash is black, bearing on it nine red roses; the jewel is a small poignard. The Lodge represents the secret chamber of King Solomon; it is illuminated by nine lights of yellow wax. The Lodge is called the Council of Nine Masters. The object of this degree is to exhibit the mode in which certain overseers, who, in order prematurely and improperly to obtain the knowledge of a superior degree, engaged in an execrable deed of villainy, received their punishment. It exemplifies the truth of the maxim that the punishment of crime, though sometimes slow, is ever sure; and it admonishes us, by the historical circumstances on which it is founded, of the binding nature of our Masonic obligation. The symbolic colours in the regalia are white, red, and black; the white being emblematic of the purity of the knights, the red of the atrocious crime committed, and the black of grief for its results. In the French Rite this is the Fourth Degree; it requires three chambers, and in some respects has similitude to the Seventeenth Degree of the Ancient and Accepted Rite, being also preparatory to the Rose-Croix. It is evident that the degree is an important one.

ELECT OF FIFTEEN,

or "Illustrious Elect of Fifteen," the Tenth Degree, also holds its meetings under the designation of "chapters," and in this the historical tradition, comprising the continuation and conclusion of the punishment inflicted on the traitors who, just before the completion of the Temple, had committed a crime of the most atrocious character, is more completely developed.

The three principal officers are a Most Illustrious Master, an Inspector, and the Introductor. The symbolic colour of the badge and collar is black strewed with tears.

SUBLIME ELECT.

The Eleventh Degree is that of SUBLIME ELECT, sometimes called "Twelve Illustrious Knights." This would appear to designate a new era in Masonry; as after vengeance had been taken upon the traitors mentioned in the preceding degrees, Solomon, to reward those who had remained faithful to their trust as well as to make room for the exaltation of others to the degree of Elect of Fifteen, appointed twelve of these latter, chosen by their companions, to constitute a new degree, on which he bestowed the name of Sublime Elect, and endowed them with a certain command over the workmen, who were, in imitation of the tribes of Israel, divided into twelve companies. The Sublime Elect rendered to Solomon daily an account of the work that was done in the Temple by their respective companies, and received the payment for them. The assembly is called a "Grand Chapter;" the presiding officer represents King Solomon, whose name he bears as Thrice Puissant; his two chief officers are a Grand Inspector and a Grand Master of Ceremonies. The apron is white, with a black border and lining, and on the flap is a red cross; there is also a black sash suspended from the right shoulder to the left hip, and on it hearts in flames. The costume resembles very closely that of the Knights Templar, differing only in the emblem. The room or place of meeting, which is called a Grand Chapter, is hung with black. We believe this degree is included with two others in the fourth of the French Rite. The title of Knights naturally suggests the idea that this degree could not have been formed before the Christian era, and is favourable to the suggestion that it was instituted by the military orders in Palestine. This degree in some form appears in different rites, and as three words belonging to it were adopted by the framers of the present H.R.A., there is every reason to suppose it was an important step in the high grades.

GRAND MASTER ARCHITECT

is the denomination of the Twelfth Degree. In this the principles of operative Masonry become prominent; it is a purely scientific degree, in which the rules of architecture and the connexion of the liberal arts with Masonry are dwelt upon. Although the lectures on the Fellow-Craft Degree illustrate architecture from the same point of view, the subject is susceptible of great extension, and under the "Grand Master Architect" numerous details illustrative of the Temple dedicated to the Most High by the wisest man, might be worked out. In the absence of distinct information upon many points, there is some exercise for the imagination in furnishing a complete description of the Temple of Solomon, which we must conclude was an astonishing and magnificent work for the time in which it was built; and it seems to have been distinguished from all other temples of remote antiquity by its sumptuousness of detail. The officers of this degree are the Master, who is denominated Most Powerful, and two Wardens. The Chapter is decorated with red and white hangings; the ornaments are the columns of the five orders of architecture, and a case of mathematical instruments. The jewel is a gold medal, on one side of which, in high relief, the five orders are represented, on the other a cube with triangle and other appropriate devices; this is suspended by a blue ribbon.

We think that every Mason who carefully studies the subject, will agree with us that this degree ought not to be laid aside. If it is not in its present state so full of interest as might be desired, the works of Josephus, Strabo, Calmet, and others afford abundance of illustrative materials of which the compilers of the Fellow-Craft lecture have made no use. The degree might also become a useful school of instruction in practical architecture, and by diffusing a correct taste among the Fraternity, and through them among the world at large, prevent the execution of unsightly structures and confusion of styles. But we must remark that the degree, so far as we can learn, never has been practised.

MASTER OF THE NINTH ARCH.

The Thirteenth Degree is denominated the MASTER OF THE NINTH ARCH, and sometimes, the "Ancient Royal Arch of Solomon." The historical traditions of this degree are represented as affording copious information on certain points in which the sacred volume is not entirely free from obscurity, and these have reference to the mode in which Enoch, notwithstanding the destruction caused by the deluge and the lapse of ages, was enabled to preserve important secrets that eventually were to be communicated to the first possessors of this degree. The *Book of Enoch* is one of the Hebrew scriptures designated apocryphal, that is, hidden books, from the fact that after the destruction of the Temple at Jerusalem by the Romans, the Jews, having established their sacred archives at Tiberias, hid there in a cell such books as it was considered expedient to withdraw from public inspection. The Scriptures now known as canonical, were deposited in a new chest, or ark of the covenant; but those holy books which were not included in this receptacle, and which at the close of the first century were suppressed by the Jews, and thus concealed, were called "the Apocrypha." The motive for this proceeding is said to be, that the predictions of the Messiah's advent and reign on earth contained in the *Book of Enoch,* are so direct and incontrovertible, that it was on this account concealed. The *Book of Enoch* appears to have been read by both Jews and Christians in the apostolic age; and this is seen in that passage of St. Jude's writings in which he says, "And Enoch also, the seventh from Adam, prophesied of these, saying, Behold, the Lord cometh with ten thousand of his saints, to execute judgment upon all, and to convince all that are ungodly among them of all their ungodly deeds which they have ungodly committed, and of all their hard speeches which ungodly sinners have spoken against Him." The *Book of Enoch* existed until the eighth century, when it unaccountably disappeared, save some fragments, until, in 1774, *Bruce* brought from Abyssinia three complete and beautiful copies of what was asserted to be the long-lost book. One of these he presented to the Bodleian library, and from this, in 1826, *Dr. Lawrence,* Professor of Hebrew, afterwards Archbishop of Cashel, produced a complete translation. The subject-matter of the book consists chiefly of relations of Enoch's prophetical and celestial visions, in the most remarkable of which the angel Uriel shows to the prophet various mysterious scenes in heaven, including a survey and explanation of the solar and lunar revolutions, according to the ancient astrological theory. *Eusebius* tells us that the Babylonians acknowledged Enoch as the inventor of astrology, and that he is the Atlas of the Greeks, who communicated to that people the knowledge of astronomy and the celestial globe. *Tertullian* endeavours to show that the *Book of Enoch* was preserved by Noah during the deluge. There have been many treatises by the learned on this book, but it must be allowed that although occasionally religious and moral precepts are enjoined, all sense of propriety is shocked by such preposterous combinations as continually appear in what is presented to us as the *Book of Enoch;* so that in comparison, even the metamorphoses of the pagan mythology appear to be rational. This explanation we consider necessary, as although the Thirteenth Degree is represented as most interesting and impressive, yet if its ritual be based upon the authority of the work described, we, as English Masons, cannot admit it to be of any great value.

The officers of this degree (which in France is called *Royale*

Arche) are a Thrice Puissant Grand Master who represents King Solomon; Hiram, King of Tyre, is also represented, attired as a traveller; there is a Grand Treasurer, representing Gibulum; a Grand Secretary, representing Joabert; and a Grand Inspector, who represents Stolkin;—who these worthies were we are unable to learn. The badge is white, with purple border. The jewel, a triangle, has in centre a representation of two people letting down a third through a square opening into an arch. English Royal Arch Masons must understand that this is the only Royal Arch Degree of the Continent.

GRAND SCOTCH KNIGHT, OR LODGE OF PERFECTION,

is the denomination now given in England to the Fourteenth Degree, but it appears to have been first called in the Scotch Rite, "Grand Elect, Perfect, and Sublime Mason;" in the United States it is designated "Perfection;" in France it is called "Grand Scotch Mason of Perfection of the Sacred Vault of James VI." The degree is considered to be the ultimate rite of ancient Masonry, as it is the last of the Ineffable Degrees that refer to the first Temple; its officers are a Thrice Potent Master, who represents King Solomon, Hiram, King of Tyre (his deputy), two Wardens, Keeper of the Seals, a Treasurer, Secretary, Master of Ceremonies, and Captain of the Guards. The apron is white, with red flames, bordered with blue, and bearing the jewel on the flap. The jewel is a pair of compasses extended on an arc of ninety degrees, surmounted by a crown, with a sun in the centre.

Brother Mackay gives the following history of this degree:—"By the completion of the Temple, the Masons who had been employed in constructing it acquired immortal honour. Their Order became more uniformly established and regulated than it had previously been. Their caution and reserve in admitting new members produced respect, and merit alone was required of the candidate. With these principles instilled into their minds, many of the Grand Elect left the Temple after its dedication, and dispersing themselves among the neighbouring nations, instructed all who applied and were found worthy in the Sublime Degrees of ancient Craft Masonry. The Temple was completed in the year of the world 3000. Thus far the wise King of Israel had proved worthy of his great office, and gained universal admiration; but in process of time, when he had advanced in years, his understanding became impaired; he grew deaf to the voice of the Lord, and was strangely irregular in his conduct. The Lord, who had appeared to Solomon in a dream after the dedication of the Temple, assured him He had accepted the building to be his house of sacrifice. He promised to bless him and his posterity if they were constant in his worship; if they did not remain faithful He would certainly punish them, and destroy the sacred edifice. The reign of Solomon was most prosperous; peace and plenty blessed the land; he extended the commerce of the country, and fitted out a fleet with which, aided by mariners from Tyre, he traded to Ophir for valuable commodities and the precious metals. His extended power and influence at length corrupted his virtue; he plunged into all manner of licentiousness, and the latter actions of his life inflicted a deep disgrace on his character; he took wives and concubines from among the idolatrous nations around him, who perverted his heart so that he worshipped Ashtoreth of the Sidonians, Moloch of the Ammonites, and Chemosh of the Moabites, to whom he built temples on the Mount of Olives; and the people, following his example, soon neglected the worship of the true God for that of idols. The Grand Elect and Perfect Masons saw this, and were sorely grieved, afraid that his apostasy would end in some dreadful consequences, and bring upon them those enemies whom Solomon had before defied. The day of the vengeance of the Most High did come; Jeroboam headed a rebellion against the king, and thirty years after the completion of the Temple Solomon died, and Rehoboam, his son by one of his Ammonite wives, succeeded; ten of the tribes revolted, and Shishak, King of Egypt, came with an army, carried off the treasures of the Lord's house and all the king's gold and silver, laying waste the whole country. After the lapse of four centuries from the death of Solomon, Nebuchadnezzar, the King of Babylon, sent his general Nebuzaradan with an army which desolated Judea with fire and sword; they took and sacked Jerusalem, razed the wall of the city, and destroyed the Temple. The conquerors carried the people captives to Babylon, leaving only a remnant of the lower class to till the land. The holy things of the Temple, its gold and silver vessels, were borne away."

All the degrees which we have thus described are conferred by name in a body called the LODGE OF PERFECTION, when the Rose-Croix is given, and included in the certificate of that degree. It is scarcely necessary for us to mention that the Royal Arch Degree, as such, forms no part of the Ancient and Accepted Rite, but its principles are doubtless to be found in the Thirteenth and Fourteenth Degrees; and although the present ritual differs very much from that in use previous to 1813, the Royal Arch, as far as we can discover, has for a very long period formed part of Masonic ceremonial in Great Britain.

We understand that it is intended by the Supreme Council to work this degree, as one governing Craft Masonry.

In the Degree of Perfection which is practised in the United States, among the decorations of the Lodge-room is a transparency, placed behind the chair of the Master, representing a burning bush enveloping a triangle, and the letters יהוה in the centre of the fire. In the west is a pillar of beauty. The pedestal is formed from the fragments of Enoch's pillar, which, being found in the ruins, were put together for that purpose. On a table is placed bread and wine and gold rings for the newly admitted brother. The position of the companions when seated forms a triangle; and the twenty-four lights are placed three and five in the west, seven in the north, and nine in the south.

The so-called historical leeture of this degree contains the following passages:—"At the death of Solomon, his kingdom was rent asunder, and ten of the tribes severed from the dominion of his son. But the evil did not rest here; for the fascinations and pleasures of the latitudinarian system which had so long prevailed under the influence of Solomon's pernicious example had become so agreeable to his subjects, that the whole ten tribes soon became confirmed idolaters; nor did Judah and Benjamin escape the infection. * * * When the time arrived that the Christian princes determined to free the Holy Land from the infidels, virtuous Masons voluntarily offered their services, on the condition that they should have a chief of their own election, which was granted. The valour and fortitude of those elected knights was such, that they were admired by all the princes of Jerusalem, who, believing that these mysteries inspired them with courage and virtue, were desirous of being initiated. The Masons complied with their request; and thus the royal Art became popular and honourable, was diffused throughout these various dominions, and has continued to spread through a succession of ages to the present time. * * * Whenever a Lodge of Perfection was held, nine Knights of the Ninth Arch tiled the nine arches which led to the sacred vaults, and so on in regular progression, the youngest taking his station at the first arch, which was near the apartment of Solomon. None were suffered to pass without giving the passwords of the different arches. There were living at that time several ancient Masters, who, excited by jealousy at the honours conferred upon the twenty-five brethren, deputed some of their number to wait upon Solomon, and request that they might participate in those honours. The king answered that the twenty-five Masters were justly entitled to the honours conferred on them, because they were zealous and faithful, and gave them also hopes that one day they would be rewarded according to their merits. This answer was not satisfactory, and one of the deputies warmly observed: 'What occasion have we for a higher degree? We know that the word has been changed, but we can still travel as Masters, and receive a Master Mason's wages.'

Solomon mildly replied, that those whom he had advanced to the Degree of Perfection had wrought in the difficult and dangerous work of the ancient ruins, had penetrated the bowels of the earth, and brought thence treasures to enrich and adorn the Temple of God; and desired the petitioners to go in peace, and aspire to perfection by good works. The deputies returned and reported their reception to the Masters. These Masters, displeased at the refusal, unanimously determined to go to the ancient ruins and search in the bowels of the earth, that they might have good pretext for making a re-application to Solomon for the required honours. The very next morning they removed the cubical stone, and descended into the cavern with a ladder of ropes by the light of torches; but no sooner had they all arrived at the bottom than the whole nine arches fell in upon them. The king, hearing of this accident, sent Joabert, Giblim, and Stolkin to make inquiries into the circumstance. At break of day they went to the place, but saw no remains of the arches, nor could they learn that any one of those who had descended had escaped to tell the tale. They carefully examined the spot, but found nothing except a few pieces of marble inscribed with hieroglyphics, by which Solomon discovered that these fragments formed a part of one of the pillars of Enoch."

The two oldest Lodges of Perfection in America were, one at Albany, constituted 20th December, 1767, by the Thrice Puissant Brother Henry Andrew Francken, D. G. Inspector General, from Kingston in Jamaica, and the other at Holmes' Hole, Martha's Vineyard, Massachusetts.

In our brief account of these degrees, of course we leave the brethren to form their own conclusions as to the value of any part of them; but since we know the source of this Fourteenth Degree, and as its contriver's name is rather conspicuous in the Masonic history of the last century, the introduction here of a notice of a remarkable individual will not appear out of place. The Chevalier Ramsay was born at Ayr, in Scotland, in 1686, and in early life went to France, where he became the intimate friend and associate of the celebrated Fénélon. He is said to have been a man of most extensive erudition, and to have cultivated most of the known sciences. Being of a restless and ambitions disposition, he engaged actively in political intrigues, and particularly devoted himself to the cause of the exiled princes of the house of Stuart, and conceived the idea of making use of the Masonic association to subserve the interests of their party. With this end in view, he endeavoured to obviate the objections of the French *noblesse* to the mechanical origin of the institution, at which their pride revolted, by asserting that it arose in the Holy Land during the Crusades as an order of chivalry. His theory was that the first Freemasons were a society of knights, whose business it was to rebuild the churches which had been destroyed by the Saracens; that the infidels, with the view of preventing the execution of this pious design, sent emissaries among them, who, disguised as Christians, became confounded with the builders and paralyzed their efforts; that the knights, having discovered the existence of these spies, became in future more careful, and instituted signs and words for the purpose of detection; and that, as many of their workmen were newly converted Christians, they adopted symbolic ceremonies with a view of instructing their proselytes more readily in the new religion. Finally, upon the Saracens gaining the upper hand, the Knights-Masons were compelled to abandon their original occupation; but being invited by the King of England to remove into his dominions, they had accepted the offer, and in this secure retreat devoted themselves to the cultivation and encouragement of architecture, sculpture, painting, and music.

In 1728 Ramsay attempted to lay the foundation of this new, and according to his idea improved, system of Masonry, and proposed to the Grand Lodge of England to substitute in place of the three ancient degrees others of his own invention, but which he asserted had been practised for time immemorial in the Lodge of St. Andrew at Edinburgh. His views being rejected in London, he carried them to Paris, where his degrees were adopted, not indeed as a substitute for, but as an addition to, ancient Craft Masonry. These degrees became popular, and in a short time gave birth to numerous others on the continent of Europe, the splendour of the decorations, and the gorgeous manner in which the ceremonials were conducted, captivating the senses. Ere long they fell into oblivion.

KNIGHT OF THE SWORD AND THE EAST,

which is the Fifteenth Degree, and especially refers to those valiant Masons who, with trowels in hand and swords by their sides, were ever ready and prepared to construct and defend the Holy City and Sanctuary, would appear to be one of very considerable interest, as it is founded on the circumstance of the assistance rendered by Darius to the Jews, who, liberated from their captivity, had been prevented by their enemies, after the death of Cyrus, from achieving their purpose of rebuilding the Temple. In this degree the meetings are designated "councils," and an important change takes place in the symbolic colours adopted; the hangings of the council chamber are water-green, in allusion to a circumstance hereafter referred to. The chamber is illuminated by seventy-two lights, in memory of the seventy-two years' captivity. The sash is a green watered ribbon, worn across the body from the right shoulder to the left hip, the figure of a bridge being in the front, having on it the letters Y and H; there are also sometimes other emblems painted on the ribbon. The apron is white, lined with red and bordered with green, and has on it emblems of war and its consequences. From Scripture and tradition is derived the following legend of this degree. The Knights of the East derive their origin from the captivity, when the whole land was "a desolation and an astonishment," and the nation did "serve the King of Babylon seventy years."

And when the seventy years were accomplished, the Israelites were restored to liberty by Cyrus, in fulfilment of the prophecy of Jeremiah. This prophecy was very remarkable, for it not only fixed the date for the return of the Hebrew people to their own land, but also for the overthrow of the Babylonian monarchy. "It shall come to pass, when the seventy years are accomplished, that I will punish the King of Babylon, and that nation, saith the Lord, for their iniquity, and the land of the Chaldeans, and will make it a perpetual desolation." And the last words of the prophet declare—"Thus shall Babylon sink, and shall not rise from the evil that I will bring upon her."

But to return to the historical events said to be connected with this degree. Cyrus permitted the Jews to return to Jerusalem for the purpose of rebuilding the Temple, and he caused all the holy vessels and ornaments which had been carried away by Nebuzaradan to "be restored, and brought again unto the Temple which is at Jerusalem, every one to his place, and place them in the house of God." (Ezra vi. 5.) The king committed the charge of the holy vessels, as well as of the returning captives, to Sheshbazzar, the prince of Judah; this is the Babylonian name of Zerubbabel, who was of the royal line of David, and a direct ancestor of our Lord Jesus Christ. When the Israelitish captives were assembled they numbered 42,360, exclusive of slaves and servants amounting to 7337.

This traditional history relates that Zerubbabel, for the protection of his people, armed 7000 Masons, and placed them in the van to repel such as should oppose their march to Judea. Their march was unimpeded as far as the banks of the Euphrates, where they found an armed force opposed to their passage. A conflict ensued, and the enemy was cut to pieces or drowned at the passage of the bridge. The emblematic colour of the degree is in allusion to this circumstance. The journey occupied four months, and in seven days from their arrival the work of restoring the Temple was commenced. The workmen were divided into classes, over each of which a chief, with two assistants, was placed. Every degree of each class was paid according to its rank, and each class had its distinctive modes of recognition. The works had scarcely commenced before the workmen were disturbed by the neighbouring Samaritans, who were determined to oppose the reconstruction of the edifice. Zerubbabel therefore ordered, as a measure of precaution, that the Masons should work with a sword in one hand and a trowel in the other, that they might be able at any moment to defend themselves from the attacks of their enemies. The second Temple occupied forty-six years in its construction, and was consecrated in a like manner to that of the Temple of Solomon. Those Masons who constructed it were created by Cyrus Knights of the East, and hence the title of this degree.

This appears in both the French Rites; in the Grand Orient it is the Sixth Degree; in both it is termed Knight of the East. The assembly is called a Council. Every thing bears a Hebrew character; there are the candlestick with seven branches, the brazen sea, and the table of shewbread, &c. There are seventy lights, in memory of the seventy years' captivity. The Chief of the Council is designated Sovereign, and represents Cyrus, King of Persia. The second officer is Nehemiah the Chancellor, Esdras is the Grand Orator, Mithridates the Grand Treasurer, and there is also a Grand General. Zerubbabel and two others appear to receive the authority from the King of Persia to rebuild the Holy City and Sanctuary. The sash, which is worn from right to left, is water-green, and on it are embroidered the symbols of the degree; to it is attached a small poignard. The apron is white satin with green border. The green colour has reference to the river Euphrates.

GRAND PRINCE OF JERUSALEM,

which is the Sixteenth Degree, is founded on certain incidents which took place during the rebuilding of the second Temple, at which time the Jews were much annoyed by the attacks of the neighbouring nations, as mentioned in the legend of the Fifteenth Degree.

The assembly is called the Grand Council, and the apartment should be separated into two parts. In the first is represented Darius the king, seated on a blue dais; this part represents the city of Babylon, and it should be hung with red. The other part represents the city of Jerusalem, where Zerubbabel presides.

In this degree the fact of the Valiant Masons who, at the building of the second Temple, were armed with sword and shield to protect the workmen, is especially referred to.

The saloons are illuminated by twenty-five candles in groups of five.

We find the following passage in Ezra iv.—"The people of the land weakened the hands of the people of Judah, and troubled them in building." It goes on to say that these enemies obtained a letter from King Artaxerxes, saying, "Give ye now commandment to cause these men to cease, and that this city be not builded until another commandment shall be given from me." And "so it ceased until the second year of the reign of King Darius," when the Israelites sent an embassy to that potentate to implore his protection and permission to resume the work, and succeeded in gaining the object of their petition.

The emblematic colour of the degree is yellow, the apron, which is red, being bordered and lined with that colour; the flap is yellow, having on it a balance on which are the letters D and Z. The jewel is a gold medal with a like emblem, and on the reverse a two-edged sword and five stars.

It is in contemplation to work this degree in England.

The first Grand Council of Princes of Jerusalem of which we find any record was formed at Charleston, in the United States, in 1788, and took the control of all subordinate degrees up to the fifteenth. The Council confers on a candidate for the 18th Degree all the degrees by name from the 4th to the 16th, previous to his being eligible for the 17th. The Statutes enact that the Council of Princes of Jerusalem have a right to visit all Lodges up to the 15th Degree.

KNIGHT OF THE EAST AND WEST,

which is the Seventeenth Degree, is entirely chivalric, and, as far as can be at present discovered, makes no pretence in its history to ancient Freemasonry. Its inventors asserted that it was organized by the Knights engaged in the Crusades; that in 1118—the same year that the Order of the Temple was instituted—eleven Knights took the vows of secrecy, friendship, and discretion, between the hands of Birinus, the patriarch of Jerusalem. The presiding officer is called Most Equitable Sovereign Prince Master, the other officers being High Priest, two Wardens, Keeper of the Seals and Archives, Treasurer, Master of the Ceremonies, Master of the Entrances, and Tyler. The badge is yellow bordered with red, having for its emblem a twoedged sword. The jewel is a heptagon of silver, having at each angle a golden star; in the centre is a lamb on a book with seven seals; the reverse has a two-edged sword between the scales of a balance; it is suspended from a blue ribbon.

As somewhat more deference is paid by the Supreme Council to this degree than any which precede it, and as it is distinctly conferred by an authoritative body, and forms a portion of the ceremonial of the Eighteenth Degree, it is necessary that we should give some explanation of it. The practice in conferring the degree of Rose-Croix, is to give, first, the degrees by name from the fourth to the fourteenth inclusive, in a Grand Lodge of Perfection; then to declare a Grand Lodge of Princes of Jerusalem opened, and confer the Fifteenth and Sixteenth Degrees, also by name; having closed that, a Grand Lodge of the Knights of the East and West is opened, and that degree is given by name, accompanied by secrets and password; thus we perceive that some importance is attached to the degree by the Supreme

Council. From the following description it will be seen that were this degree practised in accordance with the ritual, the grand council chamber of the Order would have a most gorgeous appearance. It must be hung with red, spangled with golden stars: in the east, under a canopy, is placed a throne elevated on seven steps, supported by the figures of four lions and four eagles, between which is placed an angel with six wings. On one side of the throne is displayed a transparency of the meridian sun, on the other, of the lustrous orb of night. In the east also are two vases, one containing water and the other perfume. On the south and north sides are canopies for the Ancients; while in the west are two seats with canopies, raised five steps, for the Venerable Wardens, who in conjunction with the Most Puissant act as the Grand Council. Twenty-four Knights are necessary to form a full council. On a pedestal in the east is placed a large Bible, from which are suspended seven seals. The covering of the floor displays a heptagon within a circle, over the angles of which appear certain initials; in the centre is the figure of a man clothed in a white robe, with a golden girdle around his waist; his right hand, which is extended, is surmounted by seven stars; he wears a long white beard; his head is surrounded with glory, and from his mouth issues a twoedged sword. Seven candlesticks stand around him, bearing the mysterious initials. The seven stars by which his hand is surmounted, are explained to signify the seven qualities which ought to distinguish a Freemason, viz., friendship, union, submission, discretion, fidelity, prudence, and temperance. But there is a higher meaning attached to the symbol of the seven stars, derived from passages in the Old Testament; they represent the seven eyes mentioned by Zechariah, which typify the care of Divine Providence, ever watchful to promote the welfare of his creatures; and the seven lamps of the Apocalypse, which symbolize the Holy Spirit of God, whence are also derived the seven spiritual gifts of a Christian man.

The candidate being in possession of the password of the Seventeenth Degree, then presents himself for admission to the Rose-Croix Chapter.

SOVEREIGN PRINCE OF ROSE-CROIX HEREDOM,

the Eighteenth Degree, is the most ancient and most generally practised of the historical degrees of Masonry. It is found in all the principal rites, and where (like the Royal Arch) it does not exist by name, its place is supplied by others whose symbols do not differ materially from it. To those who have not gone beyond the symbolic degrees, the name is perhaps more familiarly known than any other of the higher degrees. Of its origin, nothing satisfactory is known; one writer supposes it to have been instituted by the Knights Templar in Palestine, in the twelfth century, and asserts that Prince Edward, afterwards King Edward I., was there admitted into the Order; he also says that the Order was derived from an Egyptian priest converted to Christianity. *Ragon,* in his treatise entitled "Orthodoxie Maçonnique," has most elaborately investigated the subject, and attributes its origin to a pious monk, named John Valentine Andreä, who flourished in the early part of the seventeenth century. Andreä wrote, among other works, two treatises, one entitled "Judicorum de Fraternitate R. C.;" the other, "Noces Chimiques de Rozen Crutz." *Ragon* says that Andreä, grieved at seeing the principles of Christianity forgotten in idle and vain disputes, and that science was made subservient to the pride of man instead of contributing to his happiness, passed his days in devising what he supposed to be the most appropriate means of restoring each to its legitimate moral and benevolent tendency. *Clavel* absurdly affirms that the degree was founded by the Jesuits, for the purpose of counteracting the insidious attacks of freethinkers upon the Romish faith, but offers no evidence in support of his assertion: when in fact they were the great enemies of Masonry, and so far from supporting

porting it, wrote treatises against the Order. Many of the Rosicrucians were amongst the reformers of the age, and hence the hostility of the Romish Church. The almost universal recognition of this degree in all countries would favour the theory of its being of long standing.

The ceremonies of the degree are of the most imposing and impressive character, and it is most eminently a Christian degree. Its ritual is remarkable for elegance of diction, while the symbolic teaching is not only pleasing, but consistent with the Christian faith, figuratively expressing the passage of man through the valley of the shadow of death, accompanied and sustained by the Masonic virtues—faith, hope, and charity—and his final reception into the abode of light, life, and immortality.

The officers of a Rose-Croix Chapter are, the Most Wise Sovereign, a High Prelate, the First General, the Second General, who may be assimilated to Wardens; a Grand Marshal, who presents the candidates for admission; Raphael, their conductor during the ceremony; and the Captain of the Guard, who has charge of the entrance. The candidate, previous to his admission, if he has not already done so, must sign a declaration of fealty and allegiance to the Supreme Council; and on his admission, prior to the ceremonial, he promises this more fully in the presence of the Chapter. To give this degree in the full perfection of its ceremonies, several chambers are required, and the aid of powerful and solemn music; the rooms must also be large and lofty. There are two badges worn in this degree, or rather one, which is reversible; the first may be called the badge of mourning, and is of black silk, having in its centre the passion cross; the other side is of white satin, on which the cross with roses is worked in embroidery richly ornamented; it has a rose-coloured border; the collar is of rose-coloured satin, richly embroidered. The jewel includes the most important symbols of the degree; it is a golden compass, extended on an arc to twenty-two and a half degrees, or the sixteenth part of a circle; the head of the compass is surmounted by a crown with seven emerald points; it encloses a cross of Calvary, formed of rubies or garnets, having on its centre a full-blown rose. whose stem twines round the lower limb of the cross. At the foot of the cross is a pelican wounding her breast to feed her young, which are in a nest beneath. On the reverse, instead of a pelican there is a figure of an eagle. On the arc of the circle is engraven in cypher the password of the degree. The symbols of which the jewel is composed will satisfy our readers of the Christian character of the degree.

When the Rose-Croix Degree is conferred, the recipient is created and constituted "a Knight of the Pelican and Eagle, and Prince of the Order of Rose-Croix." The Degree of Knight of the Eagle and Pelican appears to be the name by which the Rose-Croix is elsewhere known, its ritual and legend being somewhat similar; but by the Council of the Ancient and Accepted Rite in England and Wales, both pass as one degree. The eagle on the jewel, it is ingeniously suggested, is a symbol of Christ, in his divine character, bearing the children of his adoption on his wings, teaching them with unequalled love and tenderness to spread their new-fledged wings, and soar from the dull corruptions of earth to a higher and holier sphere.

In Deuteronomy xxxii. 11, there is a beautiful comparison of the care and paternal affection of the Deity for his people with the natural tenderness of the eagle for her young—

"As the eagle stirreth up her nest,
Fluttereth over her young,
Expandeth her plumes, taketh them,
Beareth them upon her wings;
So Jehovah alone did lead him,
And there was no strange god with him."

The pelican is appropriately adopted as an emblem of the Saviour who shed his blood for the salvation of the human race, from the custom attributed by the poets to this bird of tearing open its breast to feed its offspring with its own blood. *Ragon* says that in the hieroglyphic monuments of the ancients the eagle was the symbol of a wise, and the pelican of a benevolent man; he therefore considers the eagle and pelican of this degree to be intended to symbolize perfect wisdom and perfect charity. The 102nd Psalm, which was written towards the end of the captivity, alludes to the lonely situation of the pelican in the wilderness, as illustrative of the poignancy of the writer's grief at witnessing the desolation of his country and the prostration of her sacred altars. In this view the pelican is a fitting symbol for the degree.

The cross was from the earliest ages, with the Egyptians, a symbol of eternal life; but since the crucifixion it has been peculiarly adopted as an emblem of Him who suffered on it; in this latter signification only it is adopted as an emblem in this degree—and hence its form. The rose, in Scripture, is applied as a figurative appellation of Christ; in the Canticles He is called "the Rose of Sharon." The cross alludes to his death; the rose on the cross is, therefore, an emblem of the death of the Saviour for the sins of mankind.

The rose, in ancient mythology, was consecrated to Harpocrates, the god of silence, and in the mysteries the hierophant wore a crown of roses, as emblems of silence and secrecy. Following this idea, *Ragon* suggests that as the cross was, in Egypt, an emblem of immortality, and the rose of secrecy, the rose followed by the cross was the simplest mode of writing "the secret of immortality."

Another theory of the origin of Freemasonry assigns to the union of the rose and the cross this explanation—that as the rose was the emblem of the female principle, and the cross or triple phallus of the male, the two together, like the Indian lingam, symbolized universal generation. Without entering upon the question of the age of our institution, we may notice the undoubted fact that both the rose and the cross were used as symbols from the most remote antiquity.

Whatever may have been the origin of the Rose-Croix Degree, it now bears universally an entirely Christian character; it is, indeed, a bold attempt to christianize Freemasonry, and to apply the rites, symbols, and traditions of ancient Masonry to the last and greatest dispensation; to add to the Temples of Solomon and Zerubbabel a third—that to which Christ alluded when He said, "Destroy this temple, and in three days I will raise it up." Many commentators on our institution insist that *all* degrees of Freemasonry allude directly to the religion of Christianity. If this be granted, it may certainly be asserted that the light on the subject becomes clearer in each succeeding degree, and displays its full effulgence in the exquisite mysteries of the Rose-Croix. Jehovah says, "I am come down to deliver my people;" He is said to come down in the person of Jesus Christ; in this degree the divine glory is symbolically asserted to have been manifested at the period when the word was recovered, the cubical stone being changed into the mystical rose, attended with the appearance of a blazing star, dispelling darkness, restoring the true light, and making the new law visible in our works. The brother who is admitted to the Rose-Croix will observe that the great discovery made in the early degrees of Masonry ceases to be of any value in this degree; for the Wisdom, Strength, and Beauty which supported the Temple of Solomon are replaced by the Christian pillars of Faith, Hope, and Charity; the three great lights of the Royal Arch of course remain, but the three lesser give place to thirty others, which, added to the three greater lights, allude to the years of the Messiah's sojourn upon earth. In short, from beginning to end, every thing bears the impress of Christianity. At its meetings the brethren break bread and eat salt with one another, and on the goblet of fraternal affection invoke the blessing of Him who is the Rose of Sharon, to aid on earth their progress to that state of perfection which will enable them, when bursting from the tomb, to join their Great Emmanuel in the skies, and be there united in a happy eternity.

Music lends its assistance to give this degree a character of sublimity, and at the closing of a chapter, after "Gloria in excelsis Deo," this anthem is sung:—

"Grateful notes and numbers bring,
While the name of God we sing,
Holy, holy, holy Lord,
Be thy glorious name adored.
Men on earth and saints above
Sing the great Redeemer's love:
Lord, thy mercies never fail,
Hail, hail, celestial Goodness, hail!

"While on earth ordain'd to stay,
Guide our footsteps in thy way:
Mortals, raise your voices high,
Till they reach the echoing sky.
Men on earth and saints above
Sing the great Redeemer's love:
Lord, thy mercies never fail,
Hail, hail, celestial Goodness, hail!"

In concluding our remarks on this impressive ceremony we feel bound to say, that if Christian Freemasonry, as with the ancient brotherhoods, is to be admitted, then certainly the Rose-Croix is a most beautiful rite. Conducted as we have witnessed it in the Metropolitan and other Chapters, it cannot fail to impress every brother with its sublimity and beauty.

To this degree has been attached the significant designation of *ne plus ultra.* In the original form of the Order of Knights

Templar in this country it was the next step taken above the simple Templar Degree, and was followed by that of the Kadosh. All encampments being qualified to give those degrees, the emblems of all are engraved on the certificates issued prior to 1851, and the seal confirms the grant. The "Ne plus ultra" is at the top of the Masonic ladder; the "K. D. S. H." uniting the whole structure. But at the present day, so desirous is the Supreme Council to disavow the Knights Templar, that the candidate for the Rose-Croix is, at the time of receiving the degree, allowed to wear the jewels of any Masonic rank he may have attained except that of the Knight Templar. The Rose-Croix Degree possesses similar characteristics to the Templar; the object in both degrees is the same; the Templar, perhaps, confining itself more to fact, while the Rose-Croix displays more of the allegory; hence in the latter was afforded a better opportunity of interweaving the symbols of Craft Masonry with an emblem of the Christian faith. The older Masons are united in the opinion that these degrees ought never to have been separated. The high consideration in which the Rose-Croix is held is shown in the circumstance that its ritual has met with universal acceptance; the Symbolic Degrees are in all countries identical, so also is the Rose-Croix—and this cannot be said of any other degree.

We can no where find a satisfactory explanation of the word *Heredom*. *Ragon*, in the second edition of his "Orthodoxie Maçonnique," says it was invented by the Stuart party, and is a corruption of the mediæval Latin word *hœredium*, which signified "a piece of ground fallen by inheritance." *Mackay* observes that, in an old MS. of the Scotch Rites, he has discovered the following explanation—that *Heroden* is the name of a mountain situate in the north-west of Scotland, where the first or Metropolitan Lodge of Europe was held, and supposes that the present orthography may be the French mode of spelling it. Dr. Oliver calls the H.R.D.M. and R.S.Y.C.S. two degrees; he states that the Royal Order of Heredom was founded on the dissolution of the Order of the Knights Templar, A.D. 1314, and that the Rose-Croix was, by the Grand Chapter of the former degree, added in 1736. In Scotland, the Rose-Croix Degree is given under the rite of the "Royal Order of Heredom and Rosy Cross," as well as under the sanction of the Supreme Council of the Thirty-third Degree. To be eligible for this Order, the brother must be acknowledged as a Royal Arch Mason by the Grand Chapter of Scotland.

In connexion with this degree it may be observed that the initials of the Latin inscription placed on the cross, I. N. R. I., representing *Jesus Nazarenus Rex Judœorum*, were by the Rosicrucians used as the initials of one of their hermetic secrets: *Igne Natura Renovatur Integra*—by fire nature is perfectly renewed. They also adopted them to express the names of their three elementary principles, salt, sulphur, and mercury, by making them the initials of the sentence *Igne Nitrum Roris Invenitur*. A learned Mason finds in the equivalent Hebrew letters ינרי the initials of the Hebrew names of the ancient elements, *Iaminim*, water; *Nour*, fire; *Ruach*, air; and *Iebschah*, earth.

In the first part of the ceremony, on the floor is a painting representing seven circles in white on a black ground, and in the centre a pelican, the circles representing the seven periods of the world's existence, through which the aspirant for honours has to pass. This symbol is doubtless of long date, for we learn from a traveller in the island of Ceylon, that in the ancient city of Amurajapura, there is in the sacred enclosure of a Dagobah or Temple, a circular slab of dark bluish granite, and on it are sculptured seven concentric rings; within each of these are different sacred emblems, and in the seventh, or inner, are a cow, a lion, a horse, and an elephant, also a peculiar long narrow leaf. The centre is occupied by ∴ which forms the letter I of the Lath alphabet.

The antiquity of this degree is shown in Rosetti's work on the secret societies which preceded the Reformation, especially in the extract which follows:—

"St. Paul, in the second chapter of his Epistle to the Galatians, calls the three Apostles—who attended their Divine Master in his most divine moments, and who witnessed his transfiguration on Mount Tabor, and his devotion in the garden,—*pillars;* and following that passage of the Apostle, the Paulicians[1] made them three pillars, emblematic of the three theological virtues: St. Peter was *faith,* St. James, *hope*, and St. John, *charity*. In a rite which is supposed to have descended from the Albigenses, three pillars appear, with the names of those virtues on them. The candidate is obliged to travel for thirty-three years (thus they call the thirty-three turns he takes, in allusion to the age of our Lord), to learn the beauties of the *new law*. His leader takes round the three columns, repeating successively the name of each virtue, and afterwards asks him what he has learnt in his pilgrimage; to which he answers that he has learnt the three virtues of faith, hope, and charity, and that by them he intends to govern himself. The Master assures him that they are the principles and *pillars* of the new *mystery*. In these same rites of the pilgrimage undertaken by the candidate who is thirty-three years of age, which extends through thirty-three years, the tragedy of Good Friday and the events of the following days are rehearsed, and Christ dies and rises again under his eyes. This new mystery, or new law, is the essence of Dante's *Vita Nuova*. In the Paradise we find this rite described exactly. Before the last vision, St. Peter examines him on faith, St. James on hope, and St. John on charity; relating to the three pilgrimages,—of the palmers, or Templars, to St. John of Jerusalem; of the pilgrims, or Albigenses, to St. James in Gallicia; and of the Romei, or Ghibbelines, to St.

[1] The Paulicians, who are generally considered to be a branch of the Manichæans, first appeared in Armenia in the seventh century.

Peter's in Rome: and at the examination presides Beatrice, who, by a far-fetched comparison, is likened to Christ, when transfigured before the eyes of his three Apostles."

"Wishing to let us know that these things are all mystical, he says in the Convito, 'There is one thing which should be very attentively observed by readers, for their own and their pupils' benefit: we read that when Christ went up into the mount to be transfigured, He took only three apostles with Him out of the twelve; and by that we are to understand that, in *very* secret things, we should have but few companions.'"—*Rosetti.*

The Rose-Croix Degree is alluded to in the works of Henry Cornelius Agrippa, a man of great learning and talent, of a noble family at Cologne, born 1486. His works were printed at Leyden in 1550. He practised as a physician and astrologer, and by the ignorance of the age was considered to be addicted to magical arts. He visited England in 1510.

Amongst the earliest known to have belonged to the Rose-Croix Brotherhood, was John Gower, the friend of Chaucer, whose sumptuous monument in St. Mary Overies' Church, or, as it is now called, St. Saviour's, Southwark, shows the recognition of the degree in the purple and gold band with fillets of roses which encircles his head: in Gower's works also the degree may be traced. The initiated in the Rose-Croix Degree will, by careful study, find allusions to it in the poems of Chaucer.

St. Saviour's Church is perhaps one of the least known in the great metropolis; it is well deserving of a visit. England does not contain a more elegant Gothic structure, and there are many memorials of interest to Masons: an effigy of a cross-legged Knight Templar; the stone effigy of an emaciated man wrapped in a shroud, which is drawn up in a very curious manner, at the back of the head, into a projecting knot: in the window of the south transept is, in beautiful stone tracery, the double triangle; and now placed upon the organ are the shields of Templars.

THE ROSE-CROIX CHAPTERS IN ENGLAND.

Metropolitan Chapter, held at Freemasons' Hall, London.

Coryton Chapter, at Axminster, Devon.

All Souls' Chapter, at Weymouth.

Mount Calvary Chapter, at the "Ship and Turtle," Leadenhall-street, London.

Vernon Chapter, Dee's Hotel, Birmingham.

St. Peter and St. Paul, at Bath.

Palestine Chapter, held alternately at Bolton, Liverpool, and Manchester.

Royal Kent Chapter, Newcastle-upon-Tyne.

Vectis Chapter, Masonic Hall, Ryde, Isle of Wight.

Royal Naval Chapter, Portsmouth.

Invicta Chapter, Masonic Hall, Woolwich.

GRAND PONTIFF

is the denomination of the Nineteenth Degree, and an appellation more decidedly papal could scarcely be found. Except in this and some other Masonic degrees, the modern title of pontiff would appear to be applied exclusively to the head of the Romish Church. Yet it can be undoubtedly traced to the early days of ancient Rome, when Numa Pompilius (B.C. 710—672) founded the college of priests, and instituted the office of *Pontifex Maximus*. The pontiffs stood in the place of an ecclesiastical court at Rome, having superintendence and power over all persons in matters connected with religion and ceremonial laws; and amongst their numerous duties was the government of the vestal virgins, and the superintendence of their moral conduct: the brethren who reach this Masonic degree, however, are not, as we are advised, possessed of any of these extraordinary powers, but are occupied in an examination of the Apocalyptic mysteries of the New Jerusalem, as set forth in Revelation xxi. and xxii. There are two chief officers: a Thrice Puissant in the east, who is seated on a throne under a canopy of blue, wearing a white satin robe, and the Warden in the west, who bears a staff of gold. All the members are clothed in white, and wear blue fillets embroidered with twelve golden stars. The decorations or hangings of the Lodge represent the vault of heaven—celestial blue, with stars of gold. The sash is crimson with golden stars; to it is suspended the jewel, a square, on one side of which is Alpha, and on the other Omega.

GRAND MASTER AD VITAM, OR GRAND MASTER OF ALL THE SYMBOLIC LODGES,

is the imposing name bestowed on the Twentieth Degree. Here the brother is again led to temple-building. The historical lecture refers to the period of the destruction of the third Temple by Titus, A.D. 70. The Christian Freemasons then in the Holy Land, filled with sorrow, departed from their home with the determination of erecting a fourth Temple—a spiritual edifice; and dividing themselves into different Lodges, dispersed over the various countries in Europe. A considerable number went to Scotland, and made choice of the town of Kilwinning, where they established a Lodge and built an abbey, in which the records of the Order were deposited; we are not informed where these worthy brethren were travelling during the period between A.D. 70 and 1140, when this magnificent abbey was founded, in which we have tolerably good proof that a Masonic Lodge was founded by the builders engaged in constructing the edifice. The presiding officer is styled Venerable Grand Master, and represents Cyrus Artaxerxes. Who is the personage meant we are at a loss to imagine; the younger Cyrus was the younger brother of Artaxerxes, second king of Persia of that name, and died in his 24th year, B.C. 358. Taylor says, on the suggestion of Prideaux, that the period of Artaxerxes Longimanus, who died B.C. 358, corresponds with the Ahasuerus of Scripture, mentioned in the book of Esther, whose wife was the daughter of Cyrus I. This is one of those numerous instances of anachronism in dates and persons that occur in the traditional history of the symbolic and historical degrees, and annoy the inquirer in his researches; they have arisen through the superficial acquaintance the framers had with ancient history, and could easily be set right. The names of Cyrus and Artaxerxes did not belong to the same individual. The Lodge, when perfect, is composed of nine Grand Masters; they all wear collars of yellow and blue. The jewel is a triangle, on which is engraved initials of the words.

NOACHITE, OR PRUSSIAN KNIGHT,

or, *the Very Ancient Order of Noachites,* is the Twenty-first Degree. We now find the traditional history carried back to an earlier date than in any other degree in Masonry, either symbolical or historical, for it commemorates the destruction of the Tower of Babel. It is stated that the meetings in this degree are holden only on the night of the full moon, and that no other light is permitted than what is derived from that luminary. The meeting is called a Chapter, and it is presided over by a Knight Commander Lieutenant, who represents Frederick II., King of Prussia. The other officers of the degree are five knights—the first being called Knight of Introduction; the second, of Eloquence; the third, of Finances; the fourth, of Chancery; and the fifth, of Defence. The badge is white satin with a yellow border. The Knights wear a black sash from right to left, and on the front is the jewel, an equilateral triangle crossed by an arrow.

The Noachites profess to be descendants of Peleg, who, they say, was the chief architect of the "tower whose top was to reach to heaven." This is a gratuitous assumption, for all that Moses tells us is, "that his father named him Peleg (*division*) for (or, because) in his days the earth was divided." This Order of the Noachites was first established in Prussia in 1755. There must have been formerly in English Masonry some matters connecting the name of the survivor of the deluge with its traditional history, (probably "the Ark and Mark," and "Ark and Dove" Degrees, were then used,) for we find in *Ahiman Rezon*, published in 1764, by Laurence Dermot, the first of the old charges, which is as follows:—

"*Concerning God and Religion.*—A Mason is obliged by his tenure to observe the moral law as a true *Noachida* (son of Noah, the first name of Freemasons); and if he rightly understand the Craft, he never will be a stupid atheist, nor an irreligious libertine, nor act against conscience. In ancient times, the Christian Masons were charged to comply with the Christian usages of each country where they travelled or worked; being found in all nations, even of divers religions. They are generally charged to adhere to that religion in which all men agree (leaving each brother to his own particular opinion), that is, to be good men and true, men of honour and honesty, by whatever names, religions, or persuasions they may be distinguished; for they all agree in the three great articles of *Noah,* enough to preserve the cement of the Lodge. Thus Masonry is the centre of their union, and the happy means of conciliating persons that otherwise must have remained at a perpetual distance."

It is to be observed that in the genealogical table of Jesus Christ, as given by St. Luke, Phaleg is called Phalec; there may be some further reference to him, on that account, in the historical traditions of the degree. Our ancient brethren evidently called themselves Noachidæ, or sons of Noah, and his precepts were preserved among them, the three first of which are: 1. Renounce all idols. 2. Worship the only true God. 3. Commit no murder. On this head Brother Oliver says, "The spurious Masons of antiquity, in all their mysteries, commemorated the descent of Noah into the ark, and his subsequent exodus. The entrance into initiation was symbolic of his entrance into the vessel of his salvation; his detention in the ark was represented by the darkness and the *pastos* (coffers, or couch) in which the aspirant was placed; and the exit of Noah, after the forty days of deluge, was seen in the manifestation of the candidate, when, being fully tried and proved, he was admitted to full light, amid the surrounding initiates, who received him in the *sacellum* or holy place."

It is not improbable that the ancient Masons, real or spurious, derived the connexion of "our father Noah" from the Egyptian mysteries; as, according to Bishop Cumberland, Mizraim, the son of Cham, grandson of Noah, was the first king of Egypt, and the name Osiris was his appropriated title, signifying "prince."

PRINCE OF LEBANON, OR KNIGHT OF THE ROYAL AXE.

The Twenty-second Degree, Thory asserts, was instituted by Pierre Riel, Marquis of Bournonville, who, when in command of the island of Bourbon in 1778, was there elected Grand Master of all the French Lodges in India. The legend of this degree states that it was instituted to record the memorable services rendered to Masonry by the mighty cedars of Lebanon, as the Sidonian architects cut down the cedars for the construction of Noah's ark[1]. Our ancient brethren, indeed, do not tell us how the Israelites had the wood conveyed to them from the land of promise to the mountains in the wilderness. They further say, that the descendants of the Sidonians were employed in the same offices, and in the same place, in obtaining materials for the construction of the ark of the covenant; and also, in later years, for building Solomon's Temple; and lastly, that Zerubbabel employed labourers of the same people in cutting cedars of Lebanon for the use of the second Temple. The tradition adds that the Sidonians formed colleges on Mount

[1] The best authorities consider that the descriptive term *gopher wood* agrees with the cypress; *shittim wood,* from Jerome's description, is doubtless the black acacia, which is very common about Mount Sinai, and on the mountains that border the Red Sea.

Libanus, and always adored the G.A.O.T.U. Sidon was one of the most ancient cities of the world, and even in the time of Homer, the Sidonians were celebrated for their trade and commerce, their wealth and prosperity. But their worship was not that of the true and living God, for medals are in existence bearing the inscription "to the Sidonian goddess," and this agrees with the appellation in 1 Kings xi., "Ashtoreth, goddess of the Sidonians." The allusion to the "colleges" on Mount Libanus may have some reference to the secret sect of the Druses, who still exist in that country, and whose mysterious ceremonies, travellers affirm, have considerable affinity to Freemasonry.

There are two apartments; the first representing a workshop at Lebanon, with axes, saws, mallets, wedges, and such like implements; the Master is Most Wise, his Wardens, Wise Princes. This apartment is lighted by eleven lamps, and this assembly is a "college." Each brother is armed with an axe. The second apartment represents the council of the Round Table; the presiding officer is Grand Patriarch, the others Patriarchs: the room is hung with red; a round table, in the centre, has on it the square, compass, and other mathematical instruments: each Patriarch is armed with a sword.

The collar belonging to this degree is celestial blue, lined and bordered with stars: the badge, which is white, has on it represented a table, upon which are laid several architectural plans. The jewel is an axe, crowned in gold.

CHIEF OF THE TABERNACLE,

the Twenty-third Degree commemorates the institution of the order of priesthood in Aaron and his sons Eleazar and Ithamar; and the ceremonial was in some degree founded on the instruction delivered to Moses in Exodus xxix. and xl. In many rites the degree of High Priest is to be found; in the old ritual of the Holy Royal Arch, the High Priest was the chief officer, and we still retain in that portion of English Masonry, as well as in the Master Mason's Degree, reference to him who only had the privilege of entering the sanctuary once in the year, on the day of solemn expiation, to make atonement for the sins of the whole people; so that doubtless this was a genuine Masonic degree, and not unworthy of practice at the present day. The installation of the Third Principal of a Royal Arch Chapter has undoubtedly been derived from this or some similar ceremonial. In the United States the order of High Priest, conferred on the immediate Past First Principal, somewhat resembles that of Past Master of a Lodge; the ceremony, when duly performed, is exceedingly impressive—when celebrated in ample form, the presence of at least nine High Priests is required. In America, as was formerly the case in England, High Priest is the title given to the First Principal.

In this degree there are three chief officers, viz.: a Sovereign Grand Sacrificer and two High Priests, and the members are called Levites. They wear a white badge, lined with scarlet, and bordered with a tricoloured ribbon—red, purple, and blue: in the centre is embroidered a representation of the "candlestick of pure gold, with three branches on the one side, and three branches on the other side," and on the flap a violet-coloured myrtle. The jewel, which is a thurible, or censer, is suspended from a broad sash of four colours—yellow, purple, blue, and scarlet, and worn from the left shoulder to the right hip.

The Lodge is hung with white, ornamented with columns of red and black, ranged in pairs at equal distances; the Holy Place is separated by a railing and curtain. There is a red altar, on it the Book of Wisdom and a poignard: the throne is elevated on seven steps. There is the altar of burnt offering and the incense; also two chandeliers of five lights each. There is the obscure chamber, which is hung with black; it has one lamp, an altar, and a stool on which are three skulls, also a skeleton with this inscription: "If you are fearful, go from hence; it is not permitted for men who cannot brave danger without abandoning virtue."

The Grand Sacrificer wears a long red robe over a yellow tunic, which is without sleeves; on his head is a mitre of cloth of gold. He wears a black scarf with silver fringe. The Levites wear white robes with red scarfs.

In the prophecy of Zechariah there is an account of the splendid and significant emblem used in this degree, presented in a vision which will abundantly reward an attentive examination: the principal object that met the eyes of the prophet was "a candlestick all of gold, with a bowl on the top of it and seven lamps." The image is evidently taken from the candlestick in the tabernacle. This candlestick is the scriptural symbol of the universal Church.

PRINCE OF THE TABERNACLE,

the name which is given to the Twenty-fourth Degree, is intended to illustrate the directions for constructing the tabernacle which Moses built for God by his express command, partly to be a palace of his presence as the King of Israel, and partly to be the locality of that most solemn worship which the people were to pay to Him. This was a moveable chapel, if we may so call it, so contrived as to be taken to pieces and put together at pleasure, for the convenience of carrying it from place to place, during the wanderings of the Israelites in the wilderness for forty years. This moveable fabric, which may properly be called the sacred tent, was nevertheless built with extraordinary magnificence and at a prodigious expense, that it might be in some measure suitable to the dignity of the King whose palace it was, and to the value of those spiritual and eternal blessings of which it was designed as a type or emblem. The value of the gold and silver alone, used for the work, amounted, according to Bishop Cumberland's estimate, in English money, to 182,528*l*. The immense sum required for its completion was raised by presents and voluntary contributions, and by a poll-tax of half a shekel for every male Israelite above twenty years old, which tax amounted to the sum of 35,359*l*. 7*s*. 6*d*. sterling. The Lodge is called a "hierarchy," and its officers are a Most Powerful Chief Prince, representing Moses, and three Wardens whose style is Powerful, and who respectively represent Aaron, Bezaleel, and Aholiab. There are two apartments necessary for this degree: the first, or vestibule, is decorated with the various attributes of Masonry; the second, which is of circular form, is hung with tapestry, representing a colonnade. The sun is represented on the Mosaic pavement, and in the centre is the chandelier with seven branches.

The members wear short cloaks of blue taffata, edged with gold embroidery, and a robe of cloth of gold. They have a coronet environed by stars and surmounted by a luminous triangle. The badge is white, lined with scarlet, and bordered with green; in the centre is embroidered a representation of the tabernacle; the flap is sky-blue.

The Twenty-third and Twenty-fourth Degrees, it will be seen, have been based upon the official duties of the priests. In the former we find the ark, altar, and golden candlestick; the Wardens are styled High Priests, while the presiding officer has the title of Grand Sovereign Sacrificer. The assembly is termed a "hierarchy." In the latter degree there are three Wardens, placed in the south, west, and north. The officers represent Moses, the lawgiver; Aaron, the High Priest; Bezaleel and Aholiab, the cunning artists under whose direction the tabernacle was constructed. The candidate represents Eleazar, who succeeded Aaron in the priesthood. The brother who is admitted to the degree of High Priesthood is thus addressed:—"The station you are called upon to fulfil is important, not only as it respects the correct practice of our rites and ceremonies, and the internal economy of the Chapter over which you are called upon to preside; but the public reputation of the institution will generally be found to rise or fall, according to the skill, fidelity, and discretion, with which its concerns are managed, and in proportion as the conduct and character of its principal officers are estimable or censurable."

In the First Degree of Scotch Knighthood, the adept is informed that he has been elevated to the degree of High Priest, which entitles him to receive the following information: that in future he has to adore the Deity under the name of *Jehovah,* which is much more expressive than the word *Adonai;* that in this degree he receives the Masonic science as descended from Solomon and revived by the Templars. In the Second Degree the royal Art is traced to the creation, from which period it has been transmitted through Noah, Abraham, Moses, Solomon, and other worthies, down to Hugo de Payens, the founder of the Knights Templar, and Jaques de Molay, their last Grand Master. In the next degree the *great word* is revealed to him, discovered by the Knights Templar when building a church at Jerusalem. It is related, that in digging under the spot whereon had been placed the holy of holies, in the bosom of Mount Moriah, they discovered three stones, on one of which was this word engraven. The Templars, on leaving the Holy Land, carried with them these relics, and on their arrival in Scotland, deposited them, on St. Andrew's day, as the foundation-stones of their first Lodge, whence they assumed the name of Knights of St. Andrew. The tradition adds that their successors, being entrusted with this secret, are perfect Masters of Freemasonry at the present day, and High Priests of Jehovah.

Our Royal Arch brethren will readily trace in this legend a resemblance to certain parts of the ceremonial belonging to that Supreme Degree; and in reference to the place in which the discovery was made, it is to be observed that Josephus speaks of some vaulted chambers that existed on the holy spot in his time. The old traveller Maundrell also says that in a garden situate at the foot of Mount Moriah he was shown several large vaults running at least fifty yards underground: they were built in two aisles arched at the top with a huge firm stone, and sustained by two pillars, each consisting of a single stone two yards in diameter.

KNIGHT OF THE BRAZEN SERPENT,

the Twenty-fifth Degree, is of long standing, and founded upon the events described in the book of Numbers xxi. 6—9:—"And the Lord sent fiery serpents among the people, and they bit the people; and much people of Israel died. Therefore the people came to Moses, and said, We have sinned, for we have spoken against the Lord, and against thee; pray unto the Lord, that he take away the serpents from us. And Moses prayed for the people. And the Lord said unto Moses, Make thee a fiery serpent, and set it upon a pole: and it shall come to pass, that every one that is bitten, when he looketh upon it, shall live. And Moses made a serpent of brass, and put it upon a pole, and it came to pass, that if a serpent had bitten any man, when he beheld the serpent of brass, he lived."

The ritual says that Moses, in obedience to the divine command, placed the brazen serpent upon the *tau,* and every one who looked upon it was directed to pronounce the word *hatathi,* "I have sinned;" and having done this he was immediately healed. Commentators regard the word, rendered "pole" in our translation, to mean *standard,* and the earliest form of the standard, of which we have a representation, the Persian, is the figure of the tau. The hangings of the Lodge are red and blue. A transparency, representing the burning bush, with the incommunicable Name in the centre, is placed over the throne. There is only one light; in the centre of the apartment there is a mount accessible by five steps; upon the summit is placed the

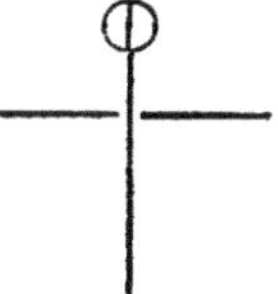

symbol of the degree. The Lodge is named the "Court of Sinai." The presiding officer is styled Most Powerful Grand Master, and represents Moses; the Wardens are called Ministers, and represent Aaron and Joshua; the Orator is styled Pontiff, the Secretary Grand Graver, and the Candidate "a Traveller." The jewel, which is suspended by a red ribbon, is a serpent entwined around a tau cross standing on a triangle, with the inscription יהוה.

The legend states that this degree was founded in the time of the Crusades, by John Ralph, who established it in the Holy Land as a military and monastic order, and gave it the name it bears, in allusion to the healing and saving virtues of the brazen serpent among the Israelites in the wilderness,—it being part of the obligation of the knights to receive and gratuitously nurse sick travellers, protect them against the attacks of the infidels, and escort them safely through Palestine.

The brazen serpent which Moses set up was preserved as a memorial of this miracle till the time of Hezekiah—more than 700 years—who, in extirpating idolatry, "removed the high places, and brake the images, and cut down the groves, and brake in pieces the brazen serpent that Moses had made; for until those days the children of Israel did burn incense to it." This was a bold measure; for some kings, however bent on the extirpation of idolatry, would have hesitated at the destruction of that which was certainly in itself an interesting memorial of a remarkable manifestation of the power of God.

It is not improbable that the influence of the example of the Egyptians, combined with the remembrance of the benefits derived from this particular brazen serpent, induced the Israelites to adopt the practice of serpent-worship. In the wilderness their fathers had been directed to look on it and live—they did so and lived. And this direction and its consequence, misunderstood and perverted, may have formed the foundation of the idolatry into which they fell. In what manner they worshipped the serpent does not appear, but it is most probable that, with a recollection of its origin, they regarded it as symbolizing the Divine healing power, and as such burned incense before it when attacked with disease, much in the same manner as the classical ancients resorted on similar occasions to the serpent-symbol of the healing god.

The worship of the serpent is supposed by *Bryant* to have commenced in Chaldæa, and to have been the first variation from the purer Zabaism. That it was intimately connected with Zabaism cannot be doubted, for the most prevailing emblem of the solar god was the serpent; and wherever the Zabæan idolatry was the religion, the serpent was the sacred symbol. But the universality of serpent-worship, and the strong traces which it has left in astronomical mythology, seem to attest an origin coeval with Zabaism itself. The earliest authentic record of serpentworship is to be found in the astronomy of Chaldæa and China: but the extensive diffusion of this remarkable superstition through the remaining regions of the globe, where Chinese wisdom never penetrated, and Chaldæan philosophy was but feebly reflected, authorizes the inference that neither China nor Chaldæa was the mother, but that both were the children of this idolatry.

Few ancient nations of any celebrity will be found which have not, at some time or other, admitted the serpent into their religion either as a symbol of divinity, or a charm, or an oracle, or a god.

The universality of serpent-worship is alluded to by *Lucan,* in these memorable lines:—

> "Vos quoque, qui *cunctis* innoxia NUMINA *terris*
> Serpetis, aurato nitidi fulgore, DRACONES."

Diodorus informs us that in the Temple of Bel or Belus, in Babylon, "was an image of the goddess Rhea, sitting on a golden throne; at her knees stood two lions, and near her very large serpents of silver, thirty talents each in weight. There was also an image of Juno, holding in her right hand the head of a serpent."

Herodotus says, "In the vicinity of Thebes there are sacred serpents, not at all troublesome to men; they are very small, but have two horns on the top of their head. When they die they are buried in the Temple of Jupiter, to whom they are said to belong."

In his notice of the Egyptian mythology, *Bryant* says, "The symbolical worship of the serpent was in the first ages very extensive, and was introduced into all the mysteries wherever celebrated. It is remarkable that wherever the Ammonians founded any places of worship, there was generally some story of a serpent."

Serpent-worship, under some form or other, was one of the most widely diffused modes of idolatry of the ancient world; it was the deified symbol of something good and beneficent. Among the Greeks and Romans it symbolized the good genius, and their worship of the healing power (the god Æsculapius), under the same figure, was but an extension of the same general idea. In various points of view Æsculapius corresponds to the Egyptian deities Serapis and Horus. In the monuments upon which these divinities are figured, they bear serpents as the emblems of health, and carry the chalice or salutary cup of nature surrounded by serpents.

There was a remarkable superstition in regard to a serpent of enormous bulk, which girded the world, current in the mythology of almost every nation where ophiolatria prevailed. This idea perhaps originated in the early consecration of the serpent to the sun, and the subsequent conversion of a serpent biting his tail, into an emblem of the sun's path. This hierogram was again considered as *typical of eternity,* partly from the serpent being a symbol of *Deity;* partly from the perfect figure of *a circle* thus formed, *without beginning or end;* and partly from an opinion of the *eternity of matter.*

Remains of this superstition were observed by *Bishop Pococke,* when he visited the banks of the Nile. "The next day we came to Raigny, where the religious sheikh of the famous serpent, Heredy, was at the side of the river to meet us. He went with us to the grotto of the serpent. He said it had been there ever since the time of Mahomet. He comes out of the grotto only during the four summer months, and it is said they sacrifice to it."

In the ancient Persian mysteries the statue of Mithra stood erect on a globe, out of which issued a serpent, the emblem of life, which, twining in numerous folds around the body of the deity, marked the convolutions of his orb, and the cycles of revolving time. When the honours of initiation were conferred on the candidate, a golden serpent was placed in his bosom, as an emblem of his being regenerated and made a disciple of Mithra; for this animal renewing its vigour in the spring of every year, by casting its skin, was not only considered as an apt symbol of renovated and reviviscent virtue, but of the sun himself, whose genial heat is annually renewed when he revisits the vernal signs.

THE PRINCE OF MERCY,

or "Scotch Trinitarian," is the name given to the Twenty-sixth Degree, which of course clearly designates its character and intention. It is a highly philosophical degree, and its ritual very impressive. The assembly is styled the Thrice Heavenly Lodge; the Chief Prince, whose title is Most Excellent, represents Moses; the Senior Warden represents Aaron; the Junior, Eleazar; and the candidate, Joshua. The jewel is a gold equilateral triangle, within which is a heart, also of gold, inscribed with the Hebrew letter ה, one of the symbols of the tetragrammaton; it is suspended from a tricoloured ribbon of green, white, and red. The apron is red, bordered with white fringe, and has a blue flap; on the flap is embroidered the jewel.

This is a Christian degree, and its ritual speaks of the triple alliance which the Eternal has made with man, and alludes in the first place to the covenant entered into with Abraham by circumcision; secondly, to that with his people in the wilderness through Moses; and thirdly, to that which He made with mankind by the mediation of his Son Jesus Christ.

With regard to the word "covenant," we may notice that Mr. *Taylor,* in his edition of Calmet's Dictionary, says, the word *testamentum* is often used in Latin to express the Hebrew בריה, *berith,* which signifies "covenant;" whence the titles *Old and New Testament* are used improperly to denote the *Old and New Covenant.* Without discussing the doctrine advanced in the ritual of this degree, we may remark that the first covenant between God and man was made with Adam at his creation, when he was prohibited to eat a certain fruit. A second covenant God made with man, after his fall, promising not only forgiveness on his repentance, but also a Messiah, who should redeem the human race from the death of sin and from the second death. A third covenant was with Noah, when the Lord directed him to build the ark, and which was renewed. These covenants were general; but that made with Abraham was limited; the seal or confirmation was the circumcision of all the males in Abraham's family. The effects of this covenant appear throughout the Old Testament; the coming of the Messiah is the consummation and end of it. The covenant of God with Adam forms what we call a state of nature; that with Abraham, explained further under Moses, constitutes the law; that ratified through the mediation of Jesus Christ is the kingdom of grace. In common discourse, we usually say the Old and New Testaments; the covenant between God and the posterity of Abraham, and that which He has made with believers by Jesus Christ; because these two covenants contain eminently all the rest.

The most solemn and perfect of the covenants of God with men, is that made through the mediation of our Redeemer, which must subsist to the end of time. The Son of God is the guarantee of it, it is confirmed with his blood; the end and object of it is eternal life, and its constitution and laws are infinitely more exalted than those of the former covenant.

GRAND COMMANDER OF THE TEMPLE

is the Twenty-seventh Degree. The assemblage is called a "Court," and altogether the degree has a character dissimilar to every other that precedes it; every thing about it is of the chivalric and military class. The presiding officer is styled Most Puissant, the Wardens are Sovereign Grand Commanders, and even the Knights are designated Commanders. The chamber is hung with red, having black columns surmounted by torches; on an altar is placed the Book of the Evangelists, with a sceptre and naked sword; on a pedestal is placed a lustre bearing twenty-seven lights. The members ought to be placed in a circle, and if there is no reception, at a round table. The badge is red satin, lined and edged with black; with a Teutonic cross encircled by a wreath of laurel, and a key beneath, all embroidered in black, upon the flap. The scarf is white, bordered with red, hanging from the right shoulder to the left hip, and bears on it a Teutonic cross in red. The jewel is a golden triangle, on which is engraved the Ineffable Name in Hebrew; it is suspended from a white collar bound with red, and embroidered with four Teutonic crosses. The accounts we have from the French writers all concur in connecting this degree with the Knights Templar, and it certainly has much of the character of that Order. It is generally considered to have been intended to supply the Templar Degree under this rite, but as we shall enter fully into the subject under its proper head, as a distinct rite, it is not necessary to say more in this place.

KNIGHT OF THE SUN

is the designation of the Twenty-eighth Degree. It is highly philosophical; it also bears other names, being sometimes called Prince of the Sun, Prince Adept, and Key of Masonry, or Chaos Disentangled. *Ragon,* who in his "Cours Philosophique" speaks disparagingly of the high degrees, says this is not a modern invention, but is of the highest antiquity, and was, in fact, the last degree of perfect initiation, teaching, as it did, the doctrines of natural religion, which formed an essential part of the ancient mysteries. The ceremonies and lecture, which are of great length, furnish a history of all the preceding degrees, and explain in the fullest manner the various Masonic emblems. The great object of this degree is the inculcation of truth, and as this virtue is one of the three great tenets of Masonry, we need scarcely say it deserves commendation. To be true and trusty is one of the first lessons in which the aspirant is instructed—it is the prime essential of the Master. All mortal affairs are transitory, but truth alone is immutable and eternal; it is the attribute of Him in whom there is no variableness nor shadow of changing. This might with propriety be called the Degree of Perfection; for truth, like a substance or reality, is opposed to typical representations, which are but as shadows; the law was given by Moses, but the grace and truth—the reality of the promised blessings—came by Jesus Christ. Every man should speak truth to his neighbour; that is—honestly, sincerely, with integrity. Truth on the part of God is united with mercy and goodness, because fidelity to promises being one great test of truth, and goodness and mercy being implied in the divine promises, when God realized any special good, He did but show Himself faithful and true, fulfilling the desires, or acting for the advantage of those who confided in Him and in his word. The love of truth is one of the noblest characteristics of the Christian, or truly pious man of any creed; and as genuine piety, wherever it prevails, will banish falsehood, so we find a real love of truth, and the conformity of a man's conduct with the regulations of truth, to be always the most desirable—the most favourable—the most decisive proofs of genuine religion; which, being itself a system of truth, delights in nothing more than in truth, whether of heart, discourse, or conduct.

The principal officers of this degree are styled Thrice Perfect Father Adam and Brother Truth; there are seven subordinate officers, who are named after the seven chief angels—Zaphiel, Camael, Anael, Michael, Gabriel, Raphael, Zaphriel.

Four apartments are requisite for the due ceremonial of this degree. The first represents a grotto; in the centre is a column, to which is attached a chain; on one side is a table, having on it a Bible and a small lamp. Over the entrance to the next apartment is inscribed, "Ye who have not power to subdue your passions, flee this sanctuary." This chamber is hung with black, and lighted by three candles in the east, west, and south. The fourth chamber is hung with red, and is illuminated by eleven candles. The last chamber is azure blue, and has but one light, which is very powerful, being a large illuminated glass globe, representing the sun—the symbol of the Great All, from whom flow all philosophical principles. The collar is white, having on it a chain suspending the jewel, a triangle of gold, with an eye in the centre. The Master wears a red robe and yellow tunic; he has a sceptre with golden globe on the top.

The historical legend describes the seven cherubim, whose names are written in the circle of the first heaven, to represent the corporeal pleasures of this life which the Eternal presented to man at the Creation, when He taught him to enjoy and to obey; these are—seeing, hearing, smelling, tasting, feeling, tranquillity, and thought.

In the Holy Scriptures we frequently read of missions and appearances of angels, sent to declare the will of God, to correct, teach, reprove, or comfort. Reference to these angelic missions is made in this degree, and we will describe those to which the allusion applies. In the apocryphal book of Tobit, Raphael tells Tobias that he is one of the seven angels who attend in the presence of God. The holy St. John saw seven angels standing before the Lord (Rev. viii. 2); and in that sublime and mysterious book, the Apocalypse, we find the number seven ever prominent. "The seven stars are the angels of the seven churches; and the seven candlesticks are the seven churches."

The number seven, among all nations, has been considered as a sacred number, and in every system of antiquity we find a frequent reference to it. In one of the lectures of the high degrees, it is stated that the different Masonic grades originally were seven in number, from the example of the G.A.O.T.U. who created all things in six days and rested on the seventh. Enoch, it is said, employed six days in constructing the arches, and on the seventh, having deposited the secret treasure in the lowest arch, was translated to the abode of the blessed. Solomon, who had been employed somewhat more than six years in building the Temple, celebrated its dedication in the seventh with every solemnity that was due to the Divine Being in whose honour it had been erected. The Pythagoreans called this a venerable number, because it referred to the creation, and because it made up the two perfect figures—the triangle and the square. The radical meaning of שבע is "sufficiency," or "fulness," and the number seven was thus denominated, because it was on the seventh day that God completed his work of creation; and hence, says *Parkhurst,* seven was, both among believers and heathens, the number of sufficiency or completion. In Freemasonry, seven is an essential and important number, and throughout the whole system the septenary influence extends itself in a thousand different ways.

This degree, as already mentioned, was worked by the Kent Lodge. We think it very probable that it was some knowledge of this degree which induced Rosetti to connect the theology of Swedenborg with Freemasonry. The degree is noticed by him in illustration of the Purgatory of Dante. It was formerly in extensive practice; and one of those preserved by the Ancient Masons in England, as already mentioned.

KNIGHT OF ST. ANDREW,

the Twenty-ninth Degree, is the preparation for the "Kadosh." This degree has also been called "Patriarch of the Crusades," in allusion to its supposed origin during those wars, and it had also the name of "Grand Master of Light." There are a Master and two Wardens. The Lodge, as in the degree of Secret Master, is illuminated by eighty-one lights arranged by nine times nine, but the hangings of the room are red. The assembly is called Grand Lodge, the Grand Master is called Patriarch, the other officers Worshipful Masters. The Master and officers are attired in scarlet robes with scarfs of purple, from which is suspended the jewel, a triple triangle, having in its centre the compasses, beneath it a square reversed; in the angle is a poignard. The Knights wear purple collars, to which the jewel, a Cross of St. Andrew, is attached; they also wear a white sash with gold fringe. The Grand Master and his two officers are on thrones covered with red drapery with gold fringe; above that of the Master is a transparency of a luminous triangle, bearing within emblems of the degree.

This is the first of the degrees which Ramsay proposed to substitute in place of the ancient Symbolic Degrees, and as a full explanation of his theory has been already given, under the degree of the Grand Scotch Knight, it is unnecessary to do more here than remark the inconsistency of this system. We have here, placed within four degrees of the pinnacle of his fabric, a degree intended to supersede the very first step in Freemasonry.

A *hierogram,* in this degree, is thus explained. The triangle or delta is the mysterious figure of the Eternal. The three letters which you see signify as follows:—G at the top of the

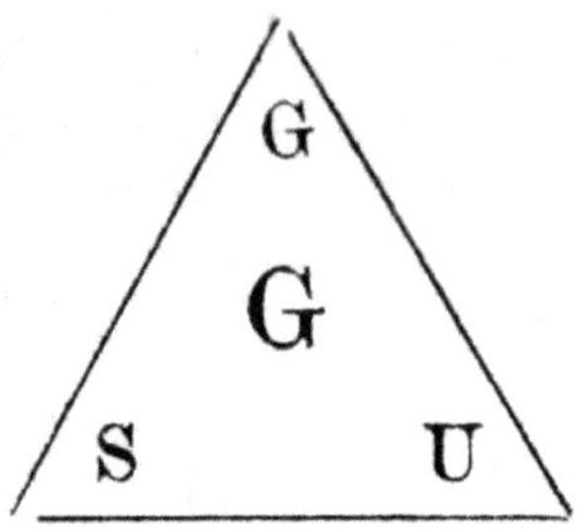

triangle refers to the *Grand Cause* of the Masons, S on the left hand the *submission* to the same order, and U at the right hand to the *union* that ought to reign among the brethren; which all together make but one body, or equal figure in all its parts. This is the triangle called equilateral. The G placed in the centre of the triangle signifies the Great Architect of the universe, who is God; and in this ineffable name is found all the divine attributes. This letter is placed in the centre of the triangle that we may understand the imperative requirement for every true Mason to bear it profoundly impressed upon his heart. The hierogram, though thus explained in the ritual, means in reality, *God, the Grand Superintendent of the Universe.* When we compare this clumsy contrivance with the beautiful simplicity of the ancient Symbolic Degrees—in which the Mason is gradually advanced step by step in knowledge, being taught the whole duty of man to God, his neighbour, and himself, before he is plunged into the mysteries of triangles and other geometrical symbols—and examine the system which Ramsay proposed to set up in its place, we can but conclude that those degrees in the rite he put forward which really possess merit, were not devised by himself, but gathered from other systems.

GRAND ELECTED KNIGHT KADOSH,

called also KNIGHT OF THE BLACK AND WHITE EAGLE, the Thirtieth Degree, is acknowledged to be very important, being found in many rites. Previously to the adoption of the Ancient and Accepted Rite, the Kadosh Degree formed, we believe, a part of the ceremonial of the Knights Templar. *Ragon* mentions the Kadosh as having been established at Jerusalem in 1118, in which case it must, of course, have belonged to the Templars.

The word from which this degree takes it name, has been a

considerable difficulty with all commentators—its first appearance in the volume of the Sacred Law is where we read that "God blessed the seventh day and sanctified it." (Gen. ii. 3.) He separated and distinguished it from the days of the week, setting it apart for the purposes of a sabbath, agreeably to the primary meaning of the word which is here made use of, קדש, *kodesh,* signifying "separated" or "consecrated." In the law, as delivered by Moses, we find the following precept concerning the feasts and sacred assemblages:—"Six days' work shall be done; but the seventh day is a Sabbath of rest, a holy convocation;" מקרא־קדש, *mikra-kodesh.* (Lev. xxiii. 3.) Mr. Taylor says, the word *kadesh,* as he writes it[1], signifies "holy" or "holiness," and is equivalent to the Greek ἱερὸς, "sacred." The name is also applied to certain places, where, probably, there had been a Divine appearance, as Meribah in Kadesh (Numbers xxvii. 14), and Meribah-Kadesh (Deut. xxxii. 51); and in Ezekiel xlvii. 19, it is used in the plural, Meriboth-Kadesh. In its application to this degree, we must consider it to be derived from the appointments of the priestly office. Exodus xxviii. 36—38: "And thou shalt make a plate of pure gold, and grave upon it, like the engravings of a signet, HOLINESS TO THE LORD. And thou shalt put it on a blue lace, that it may be upon the mitre; upon the forefront of the mitre it shall be. And it shall be upon Aaron's forehead, that Aaron may bear the iniquity of the holy things, which the children of Israel shall hallow in all their holy gifts; and it shall always be upon his forehead, that they may be accepted before the Lord." This plate had engraven on it, ליהוה קדש, *kodesh-laihovah,* which is rendered in our translation, and agreeably to the ancient versions, "Holiness to the Lord." The size and form are not defined by Moses, but the Jewish doctors say it was two fingers broad, and made in a circular form, adapted to the shape of the head, and so long that it reached from ear to ear, and was

[1] The word is differently rendered by translators.

fastened by a blue lace or ribbon, which was tied behind the head.

The mitre was a turban of fine linen, furnished in front with a plate of pure gold, bearing the inscription we have mentioned. In chap. xxxix. this ornament is called נזר, *nezer,* from a root signifying "to separate;" hence it denotes a crown, as a mark of separation or distinction.

It was formerly the custom in Royal Arch Chapters for the Third Principal to wear a mitre of this description, and also a similar head-plate, as well as the breast-plate ordained to be worn by the High Priest. These two ornaments—the head-piece and breast-plate, as worn by that officer in the Mount Sion Chapter (the oldest in London),—are now in the possession of a Past Principal; their use, as well as that of some other regalia, has been discontinued.

We are induced to believe that in the Kadosh was formerly comprised the degree—if it may be so called—of High Priest; and that it is not unlikely to have been adopted by the military and religious orders in Palestine, and conferred on the principal clerical members of those orders. We can suggest no better theory for the connexion of priestly and knightly rank in the degrees of chivalry.

We are told by *Pluche*, that in the East, a person preferred to honours bore a sceptre, and sometimes a plate of gold on the forehead, called a *kadosh,* to apprise the people that the bearer of these marks of distinction possessed the privilege of entering into hostile camps without fear of losing his personal liberty.

We have already observed that the Kadosh Degree—prior to the establishment of the Supreme Council of the Ancient and Accepted Rite in this country—was always conferred in encampments of Knights Templar; the preamble of the certificates issued up to the year 1851, runs thus:—"Royal and Exalted Religious and Military Order of H.R.D.M., Grand Elected Masonic Knights Templar, K.D.O.S.H. of St. John of Jerusalem,

Palestine," &c. By this title, the Order would also appear to assume a derivation from the Hospitallers. The ritual, however, connects the degree with the Knights Templar, and furnishes the history of the destruction of the Knights by the atrocious Philip of France and his minion Clement V. The Knights' costume should be black, worn as an emblem of mourning for the death of the illustrious Jaques de Molay, the martyred Grand Master. These remarks are not strictly applicable to the present practice in this country, as no reference is made to the death of Jaques de Molay.

The presiding officer of this degree is styled Most Illustrious Grand Commander; there are two Lieutenant Grand Commanders, a Grand Chancellor, a Grand Marshal, a Grand Treasurer, a Grand Secretary, and Grand Master of Ceremonies. In France, there is also recognized an officer called Minister of State. The officers are Grand and Perfect, the rest Grand Knights.

When the ritual is duly celebrated in ample form, three chambers are required, besides an ante-room for the reception of the candidate. According to the mode prescribed, and, we believe, adopted in France, the first room is hung with white drapery, and displays neither dais nor altar: at the bottom of the apartment is seen a statue of Wisdom, dimly visible by the pale light of a spirit-lamp placed over a chafing-dish. In England the chamber is hung with black; the Grand Sacrificateur here receives the candidate and his conductor. The second chamber, which is called the "Areopagus," is hung with black; at the farther end of the room is a table, covered with blue cloth, behind which are placed the two Lieutenants and an officer called the Orator; these three form the "Council of the Areopagus." The first Lieutenant, seated in the centre, presides, holding a golden sceptre; the other Lieutenant, on his right, bears the golden scales of justice, while the Orator, who is on the left, displays a sword; on either side of the room are ranged the seats of the Knights; three yellow candles light this chamber. The third hall, which is called the "Senate," is hung with red; in the east is the dais, on which is placed the throne, bearing on its canopy the double-headed eagle, crowned, and holding a poignard in his claws; a drapery of red and black, interspersed with red crosses, descends from the wings of the eagle, and forms a pavilion. On each side of the throne are placed the standards of the cross: one, white, with a green cross, bears the motto, "God wills it;" the other, black, with a shield charged on one side with a red cross, and on the other a doubleheaded eagle, has the motto, "Conquer or die." The hall of the Senate is illuminated by eighty-one lights, which are dispersed in a peculiar way: here is placed the mysterious ladder, which is symbolic of virtue and science; one of the supports is dedicated to the love of God, and the other to the love of our neighbour; the steps represent justice, candour, truth, wisdom, patience, and prudence; the platform is the *ne plus ultra;* the descending steps are grammar, rhetoric, logic, arithmetic, geometry, music, and astronomy. This symbol of the Order appears also on the old Knight Templar certificates.

The Knights wear a broad black sash, suspended from the left shoulder, ornamented and edged with silver fringe; on it is embroidered the Teutonic cross in crimson, and crossed swords. The jewel is a naked poignard of silver with a Teutonic cross of red enamel, in the centre of which are the figures 30. Some adopt the Eagle of the superior degrees, the distinguishment being that the extremities are tipped with gold.

We may here observe, that in the practice of our French brethren this is the last of the degrees which has its teaching engraved on the cubical stone, which is divided into eighty-one points—the square of nine, and the pyramid bearing the initials $_{P}{}^{N}{}_{U}$ i. e. *ne plus ultra,* which is variously applied to this and the Eighteenth Degree.

The degree in England at the present time can only be

conferred in the presence of at least three of the Supreme Council.

It is to be observed that the description of the ceremonial is derived from a French MS. of the middle of the last century, some portions differing in England. The degree is somewhat shorn of its dignity and importance in England, perhaps for want of proper apartments to conduct the ceremonial. It is now purely philosophical.

We cannot but think the degree is of high antiquity, though not perhaps in its present form, for, as now practised, there appears a want of unity of design. Thus we find the emblematic ladder prominent in the Symbolic Degrees as well as in the Rose-Croix; while the admixture of the military and religious ceremonies is more conspicuous in this than in any other degree. In its present form it bears evident traces of Teutonic origin; and most probably it was devised by the German knights. One standard used in this rite bears a green cross, which designated that nation in the Holy Land; the motto is the same as was borne by the pilgrims in the first crusade. The red cross belonged to the Templars, and was assumed by the two other orders on the extermination of the Templars. To this ceremonial additions were made in the eighteenth century, when the Ancient and Accepted Rite was established.

Although much importance is attached to the degree, it will not bear comparison with the Rose-Croix. There are several inconsistencies which strike us upon examining this degree—we may, for instance, inquire why the second chamber is named after the celebrated seat of justice at Athens. That court took cognizance of all crime and immorality, and idleness as the cause of vice: it heard causes in the darkness of night, that its members might not be prepossessed in favour of either plaintiff or defendant by their appearance: it allowed only a plain statement of facts, and hence its decisions were most just and impartial. We can see no possible connexion between the degree and the Greek tribunal. Again, the third chamber bears a Roman name, and one not applicable to a body which acknowledges a superior council. Other anachronisms might be noticed, but these are sufficient to illustrate the weak points of the degree.

It will be seen from the preceding remarks that the philosophical part of the degree is alone retained, and all reference to Jaques de Molay discarded; but the results of research into this and the Templar Degree prove that, if not identical, they were intimately connected. The allegory of the three days is more in harmony with the Rose-Croix; hence some desire that the Templar Degree should be brought into the Ancient and Accepted Rite, which it appears might be accomplished if the 30° were restored to its original fulness.

All degrees beyond the Rose-Croix are designated *Philosophical,* as they are particularly directed to the philosophical explanation of the Masonic system, which in all the inferior degrees receives a moral signification.

THE SOVEREIGN TRIBUNAL OF THE THIRTY-FIRST DEGREE, OR GRAND INQUISITOR COMMANDER.

It is not an historical degree, but is simply administrative in its character; the duties of the members being to examine and regulate the proceedings of the subordinate Lodges and Chapters. The meeting is designated a "Sovereign Tribunal," and is composed of nine officers, viz., a Most Perfect President, a Chancellor, a Treasurer, and six Inquisitors—one being elected to perform the functions of Inspecting Inquisitor. The decoration of the Lodge is white, with eight golden columns; on the dais above the presiding officer's throne are the letters J.E.; there is also an altar covered with white drapery. In the east, on a low seat, is placed a case containing the archives of the Order covered with blue drapery, having on its front a large red cross; on the right of the altar is the table of the Chancellor, on the left, that of the Treasurer. The floor of the Sovereign Tribunal is covered by a painting, the centre of which represents a cross, encompassing all the attributes of Masonry. As regalia, the members wear a white collar, on which is embroidered a triangle with rays, having in its centre the number 31, to which is suspended a Teutonic cross. In France the regulations direct a white apron, with *aurore* (yellow) flap, embroidered with the attributes of the degree. In England there is no badge used.

SUBLIME PRINCE OF THE ROYAL SECRET

is the Thirty-second Degree, and until the year 1786 (when Frederick the Great instituted the Thirty-third) this was the summit of the rite. The Lodge is styled a "Grand Consistory," and should be held in a building of two stories. We first enter the chamber of the Guards, and next, a room for preparing thc candidates. The third, in which the Lodge is held, is hung with black; on the draperies are represented skeletons, tears, and emblems of mortality, embroidered in silver. In the east is a throne, elevated on seven steps, which is the seat of the President; the throne, also, is draped with black satin, bearing similar emblems to the hangings; on a table covered with black satin are the actual emblems of mortality; the covering has the letters J.M., in memory of Jaques de Molay. It is somewhat remarkable that, with the numerous references to the chivalric orders in this and the other degrees, the rite ignores, as such, the Templar Degree.

The seats of the two principal officers are covered with crimson satin, bordered with black, and strown with tears of silver; in the front are embroidered certain letters. The officers are—a Thrice Illustrious Commander, two Illustrious Lieutenants Grand Commanders, a Minister of State, a Grand Chancellor, a Grand Treasurer, and a Grand Secretary. The

Chief wears a robe of royal purple, and he, as well as the Lieutenants, wear swords. The collar of this degree is black, lined with purple, with a black cross embroidered with silver, and suspended is a silver double-headed eagle over a Teutonic cross of gold.

The badge is of white satin, with a double border of black; on the flap is a trophy, with the double-headed eagle; in the centre of the badge is represented a camp of the Crusaders. The form of the camp is thus explained:—it is composed of an enneagon, within which is inscribed a heptagon, within that a pentagon, and in the centre an equilateral triangle, within which is a circle. Between the heptagon and pentagon are placed five standards, in the designs of which we find five letters, which form a particular word. On the first standard is emblazoned the ark of the covenant, with a palm-tree on each side; the ark has the motto *Laus Deo.* On the second is a lion of gold, holding in his mouth a golden key, with a collar of the same metal; the ground is blue, and on it is the device, *Ad majorem Dei gloriam.* The third standard displays a heart in flames, with two wings; it is surmounted by a crown of laurels; the field is silver. The next bears a double-headed eagle crowned, holding a sword in his right claw, and a bleeding heart in his left; the field is a water green. The last bears a black ox, on a field of gold. On the sides of the enneagon are nine tents; the colours are distinguished by numbers. On the tents are certain letters, which form the secret word. The tents are designed to represent the different degrees of Masonry, as follows:—1. Esdras typifies the Three First Degrees; with blue streamer. 2. Joshua, Perfect Master; green flag. 3. Aholiab represents the Sixth and Eighth Degrees; has a red and green flag. 4. Joiada, the Seventh Degree; has a red and black flag. 5. Peleg, the Ninth and Twelfth Degrees; has a black flag. 6. Joakim, a black and red flag, represents the Tenth and Eleventh Degrees. 7. Nehemiah, for the Fourteenth Degree, a red flag. 8. Zerubbabel, a flag of bright green, represents the Knight of the East, the Sword, or the Fifteenth Degree. 9. Malachi represents the Rose-Croix, as well as the Sixteenth and Seventeenth Degrees; it has a white flag with red stripes. The practice in England is to dispense with the badge, the emblems described being embroidered on the collar.

THE THIRTY-THIRD DEGREE, OR SOVEREIGN GRAND INSPECTOR GENERAL.

Its members constitute the "Supreme Council," which is the chief tribunal in this rite. The degree was, as already mentioned, instituted in 1786; and not more than one Supreme Council can exist in any one nation, which must be composed of nine members, not less than three of whom constitute a quorum, for the transaction of business.

The members of the Supreme Council of England and Wales, and the offices they fill, are at the present time as follow:—

Dr. Henry Beaumont Leeson, Most Puissant Sovereign Grand Commander.
Charles John Vigne, Lieutenant Grand Commander.
Henry Atkins Bowyer, Grand Treasurer.
Sir John George De la Pole, Bart., Grand Chancellor.
Henry Charles Vernon, Grand Secretary.
Robert James Shuttleworth, Captain General.

There are three vacancies at present.

Honorary (Retired) Members.
Col. George Augustus Vernon.
Dr. George Oliver.
Sir John Robinson, Bart.
John Axtell Deacon Cox.
George Beauchamp Cole.

William Hyde Pullen, 32°, Grand Secretary General.

The Lodge is hung with purple drapery, which sustains representations of emblems of mortality. In the east is the dais, having in its rear a transparency bearing the Sacred Name in Hebrew characters. In the centre of the chamber is a square pedestal, covered with crimson, supporting a Bible, upon which a sword is laid across. In the north is another pedestal, displaying a skeleton which holds a poignard in the right hand, and the drapery of the Order in the left. In the west is a throne, elevated on three steps, before which is a triangular altar, covered with crimson. Over the entrance door is inscribed in letters of gold the motto of the Order, *Deus meumque jus*. The chamber is illuminated by eleven lights, five in the east, two in the south, three in the west, and one in the north.

The Most Puissant Sovereign wears a royal robe of crimson satin, and on his head is a regal crown.

The badge of the degree is a white sash, four inches broad, edged with gold fringe, and suspended from the right shoulder to the left hip. At the bottom is a red and white rosette; and on the part that covers the breast is a triangle of gold, surrounded by rays, within which are the figures 33: on each side of this emblem is a drawn dagger. The jewel is the double-headed eagle, of silver, with a golden beak, and crowned with an imperial crown in gold, holding in his claws a naked sword.

We have already noticed the ingenious proceedings of the Chevalier Ramsay, and the theory which he set up respecting the rite of which we are treating; but it appears that as early as 1715, on raising the standard of revolt in Scotland, the adherents of the House of Stuart made many efforts to enlist Freemasonry as an auxiliary to their cause. The better to carry out this purpose, it was affirmed that the great legend of the Order alluded to the violent death of Charles I., and that

Cromwell, Bradshaw, and Ireton were alluded to as the traitors the Masons were to condemn. New degrees were invented in furtherance of the project, named Irish Master, Perfect Irish Master, &c., and all had a political bias. They doubtless were favourably received by those of the Fraternity who were attached to the Jacobite cause; and if they did not give Ramsay the idea, must have furnished him with materials and encouragement to set his great scheme on foot. These Irish degrees, like all worthless and spurious imitations of Masonry, soon died out; but the Ancient Rite which we are now considering, although its value is deteriorated, as we have shown, by some objectionable points, yet, with the exceptions we have alluded to, these degrees are not to be considered innovations on pure symbolic Masonry, but rather as illustrations of it. Connected with them are many interesting traditions and instructive speculations which could hardly fail to be useful in shedding light upon the character and objects of the institution. We have said that the greater part of these degrees are not practised; and we do not consider it advisable that they should all be brought into use, for the most retentive memory is sufficiently taxed to accomplish all the present working; indeed, of any brother who is perfect in these degrees it may well be said that

"the wonder grew,
That one small head should carry all he knew."

Still something might be made of this mass of historic lore; the traditions and mysteries of this rite would furnish admirable subjects for lectures, when a Lodge has no work before it; of course omitting all reference to doctrinal points which might offend the peculiar religious views of any brother present. Our French brethren saw the uselessness of retaining a number of degrees in name, when not more than a quarter of them could be practised, and wisely reduced the rite into a reasonable compass.

CHAPTER XIX.

THE ROYAL, EXALTED, RELIGIOUS, AND MILITARY ORDER OF MASONIC KNIGHTS TEMPLAR.

"This the scope was of our former thought,
Of Sion's fort to scale the noble wall,
The Christian folk from bondage to have brought,
Wherein, alas! they long have lived in thrall.
In Palestine, an empire to have wrought,
Where godliness might reign perpetual;
And none be left, that pilgrims might denay
To see Christ's tomb, and promised vows to pay."

THERE is much difference of opinion as to the origin of this degree of the Masonic Institution, and without attempting to show that the form of conferring the degree is identical with that of the gallant and devoted soldier-monks of the Crusades, it cannot be controverted that their Institution possessed some features of similarity to Freemasonry. The connexion between the Knights Templar and the Masonic Institution has been repeatedly asserted by the friends and enemies of both. Brother Lawrie says, "We know the Knights Templars not only possessed the mysteries, but performed the ceremonies, and inculcated the duties of Freemasons;" and he attributes the dissolution of the Order to the discovery of their being Freemasons, and assembling in secret to practise the rites of the Order. He endeavours to show that they were initiated into the Order by the Druses, a Syrian fraternity which existed at that date, and indeed now continues.

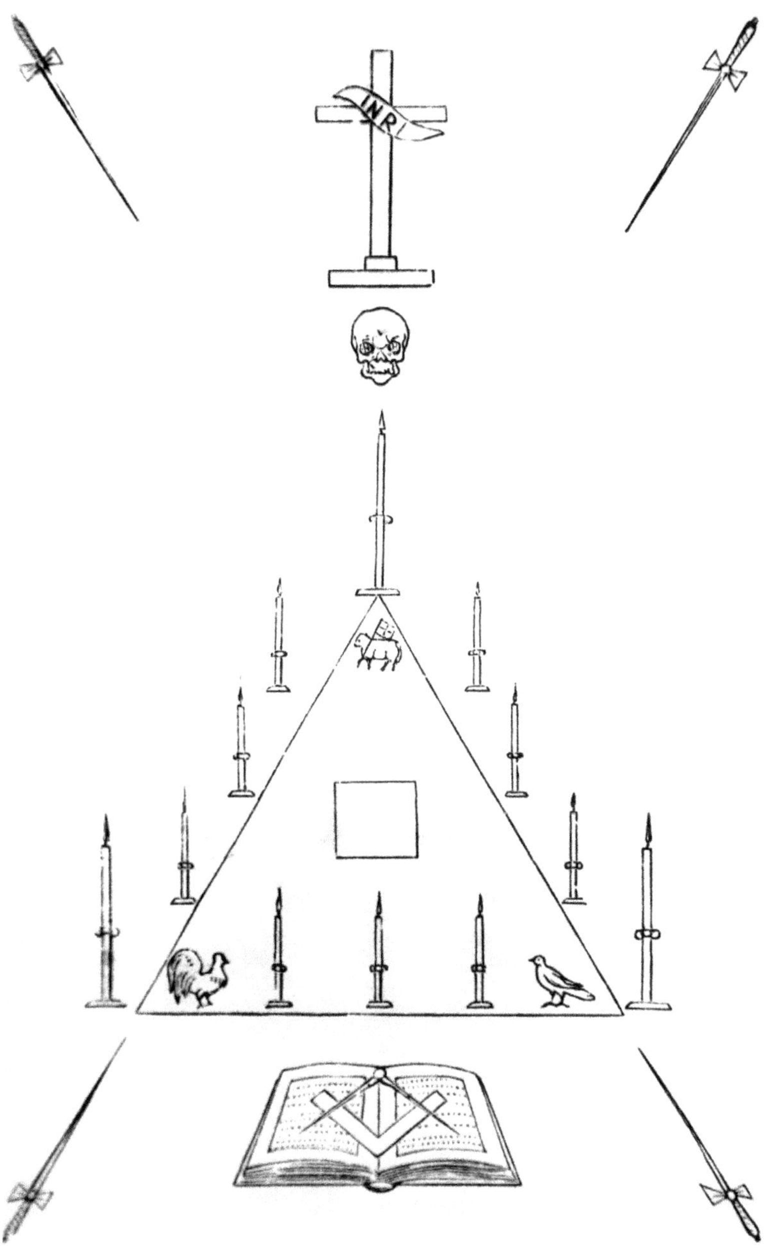

The Knight Templar.

In a French MS. ritual of about 1780, in the degree of Black and White Eagle (30°), the transmission of Freemasonry by the Templars is most positively asserted. The history of the Templars and their persecution is minutely described in the closing address, and the Grand Commander adds, "This is my illustrious brother, how and by whom Masonry is derived and has been transmitted to us. You are now a Knight Templar, and on a level with them."

This is not the practice of the degree in England at the present time, but it was, doubtless, when it was acknowledged to be connected with the Templar Degree.

The Order of the Temple, in the twelfth century, was divided into three classes: Knights, Priests, and Serving Brethren. Every candidate for admission into the first class must have received the honour of knighthood in due form, and according to the laws of chivalry, and consequently the Knights Templar were all men of noble birth. The second class, or the Priests, were not originally a part of the Order, but by the bull of Pope Alexander, known as the bull *omne datum optimum,* it was ordained that they might be admitted, to enable the knights more commodiously to hear divine service, and to receive the sacraments. Serving Brothers, like the Priests, were not a part of the primitive institution. They owed their existence to the increasing prosperity and luxury of the Order.

Over this society, thus constituted, was placed a presiding officer, with the title of Grand Master. His power, though great, was limited. He was in war the commander-in-chief of all the forces of the Temple. In his hands was placed the whole patronage of the Order, and as the vicegerent of the Pope, he was the spiritual head and bishop of all the clergy belonging to the society. He was, however, much controlled and guided by the Chapter, without whose consent he was never permitted to draw out or expend the money of the Order.

The Grand Master resided originally at Jerusalem; afterwards, when that city was lost, at Acre, and finally at Cyprus. His duty always required him to be in the Holy Land; he consequently never resided in Europe. He was elected for life from among the knights in the following manner. On the death of the Grand Master, a Grand Prior was chosen to administer the affairs of the Order until a successor could be elected. When the day which had been appointed for the election arrived, the Chapter usually assembled at the chief seat of the Order; three or more of the most esteemed knights were then proposed, the Grand Prior collected the votes, and he who had received the greatest number was nominated to be the electing Prior. An Assistant was then associated with him in the person of another knight. These two remained all night in the chapel, engaged in prayer. In the morning, they chose two others, and these four, two more, and so on until the number of twelve (that of the Apostles) had been selected. The twelve then selected a chaplain. The thirteen then proceeded to vote for a Grand Master, who was elected by a majority of the votes. When the election was completed, it was announced to the assembled brethren, and when all had promised obedience, the Prior, if the person was present, said to him, "In the name of God the Father, the Son, and the Holy Ghost, we have chosen, and do choose thee, Brother N., to be our Master." Then, turning to the brethren, he said, "Beloved sirs and brethren, give thanks unto God, behold here our Master."

The remaining officers were a Marshal, who was charged with the execution of the military arrangements on the field of battle. The Prior of Jerusalem, called the Grand Preceptor of the Temple, was the Treasurer of the Order, and had charge of all the receipts and expenditures. The Draper had the care of the clothing department, and distributed the garments to all the brethren. The Standard-bearer bore the glorious Beauseant to the field. The Turcopilar was the commander of a body of light horse called Turcopoles, who were employed as skirmishers and light cavalry. And lastly, to the Guardian of the Chapel was entrusted the care of the portable chapel, which was always carried by the Templars into the field.

Each Province of the Order had a Grand Prior, who was in it the representative of the Grand Master: and each House was governed by a Prior or Preceptor, who commanded its knights in time of war, and presided over its chapter in peace.

The mode of reception into the Order is described to have been exceedingly solemn. A novitiate was enjoined by the canons, though practically it was in general dispensed with. The candidate was received in a Chapter assembled in the chapel of the Order, all strangers being rigorously excluded. The Preceptor opened the business with an address to those present, demanding if they knew of any just cause or impediment why the candidate should not be admitted. If no objection was made, the candidate was conducted into an adjacent chamber, where two or three of the knights, placing before his view the rigour and austerities of the Order, demanded if he still persisted in entering it. If he persisted, he was asked if he was married or betrothed, had made a vow in any other Order, if he owed more than he could pay, if he was of sound body, without any secret infirmity, and free? If his answers proved satisfactory, they left him and returned to the Chapter, and the Preceptor again asked, if any one had any thing to say against his being received. If all were silent, he asked if they were willing to receive him. On their assenting, the candidate was led in by the knights who had questioned him, and who now instructed him in the mode of asking admission. He advanced, and kneeling before the Preceptor with folded hands, said, "Sir, I am come before God, and before you and the brethren; and I pray and beseech you, for the sake of God, and our sweet Lady, to receive me into your society and the good works of the Order, as one who, all his life long, will be the servant and slave of the Order." The Preceptor then inquired of him if he had well considered all the trials and difficulties which awaited him in the Order, adjured him on the Holy Evangelists to speak the truth, and then put to him the questions which had already been asked of him in the preparation-room, further inquiring if he was a knight, and the son of a knight and gentlewoman, and if he was a priest. He then asked him the following questions: "Do you promise to God and Mary, and our dear Lady, obedience, as long as you live, to the Master of the Temple, and the Prior who shall be set over you? do you promise chastity of the body? do you further promise a strict compliance with the laudable customs and usages of the Order now in force, and such as the Master and Knights may hereafter add? will you fight for and defend, with all your might, the Holy Land of Jerusalem, and never quit the Order but with the consent of the Master and Chapter? and lastly, do you agree that you never will see a Christian unjustly deprived of his inheritance, nor be aiding in such a deed?" The answers to all these questions being in the affirmative, the Preceptor then said, "In the name of God, and of Mary, our dear Lady, and in the name of St. Peter of Rome, and of our Father the Pope, and in the name of all the brethren of the Temple, we receive you to all the good works of the Order, which have been performed from the beginning, and will be performed to the end, you, your father, your mother, and all those of your family whom you let participate therein. So you, in like manner, receive us to all the good works which you have performed and will perform. We assure you of bread and water, the poor clothing of the Order, and labour and toil enow." The Preceptor then took the white mantle, with its ruddy cross, placed it about his neck, and bound it fast. The Chaplain repeated the 133rd Psalm: "*Behold, how good and how pleasant it is for brethren to dwell together in unity?*" and the prayer of the Holy Spirit, "*Deus qui corda fidelium;*" each brother said a *Pater,* and the Preceptor and Chaplain kissed the candidate. He then placed himself at the feet of the Preceptor, who exhorted him to peace and charity, to chastity, obedience, humility, and piety, and so the ceremony was ended.

The secret mysteries of the Templars, most of the historians say, were celebrated on Good Friday; and what those mysteries were, we discover from those who still carry them on as their heirs, the Order as kept up in France and other countries on the Continent—not the Masonic Institution. They are accustomed in these secret rites to act over the events which took place on the Thursday, Friday, and Saturday of the Holy Week, and then solemnize with great pomp the resurrection of Christ, the deliverer of mankind out of the servitude imposed by sin.

Bartolo, in his treatise concerning the cause brought before our Lord Jesus Christ, between the Virgin Mary on the one side and the Devil on the other, chose the same three days for the hearing of the cause; and on Easter-day, the day of the resurrection, he describes that Judge proclaiming mankind freed from Satan's power.

Dante also, from the opening of his sublime poem to the end of his first pilgrimage, spent the same three days in visiting the servants of Satan (in purgatory). On the third day he rose from the dead, and on Easter-day he saw the Star of Love shining before him.

Rosetti observes, "In the *Ne plus Ultra*—a Rose-Croix Degree—there is reference to the three days, the Thursday, Friday, and Saturday of the Holy Week, during which time they represent the Last Supper with the Apostles, and the death on the Cross at Calvary."

It is to be observed that, during the persecution of the illustrious Knights of the Temple, which was set on foot by the infamous Clement, assisted by the no less infamous Philip le Bel of France, a most prominent charge against the Order was, that they maintained a secret doctrine which was subversive of Christianity. The accusation of irreligion the Templars most strenuously denied, but not so the fact of their possessing certain secrets, which was true beyond all doubt—and secrets they have remained (as far as the outer world is concerned) from that day to this—not the slightest information has ever been obtained concerning them from any source. Thus much, however, we do know, that the Templars and all the other orders of knighthood possessed certain mysteries and peculiar forms, which were confined to themselves; and the rites observed in receiving and affiliating members approached, in a remarkable degree, to the practice of Freemasonry. They had, for instance, gradations in rank, which may be taken to answer to the degrees in our Craft; some religious ceremonial was used in communicating each additional secret of the Order: and to each was attached a solemn obligation.

One writer, indeed (*M. Rosetti*), distinctly asserts that the Templars were a branch of the Masonic Institution, whose great object in that age was the overthrow of the papal tyranny, and the monstrous fabric it had erected of idolatry, superstition, and impiety; and hence he traces the determination of the Pope to crush, at all hazards, the Order of the Temple, with all its daring innovations. Though there is a great probability, if not a certainty, that Masonry was a leading feature in the Templar institution, we are inclined to believe that the mysteries of the Craft were the only secrets of their practice. *Rosetti,* in his work On the Anti-papal Spirit of the Secret Societies of Italy in the Middle Ages, especially alludes to the brethren of the Rose-Croix, who, he says, were framed for the purpose of pulling down the triple crown. It was against the temporal power of the papacy they were opposed, not against the Church or the Pope as Bishop of Rome, but against that power inaugurated by Hildebrand, which dethroned kings, excommunicated the nations, and parted husband and wife. Bishop Hurd gives like testimony of those learned ecclesiastics who were members of the Rose-Croix, but who, to conceal their objects, called themselves Brotherhood of the Holy Ghost. The whole conduct of the

Knights refutes the charge of any attempt to subvert either Christianity or the Church; in fact, until the attack made upon the Templars by King Philip, the Orders of chivalry had always been considered by the Church of Rome as her strongest bulwarks; the esteem in which they were held by her is amply shown in the privileges which were granted to them in every state in Europe, exempting them from all authority except that of the Pope himself, and which in course of time increased the power and pride of the Knights to an extent which could not fail to bring upon them the combined jealousy and envy of all the reigning princes of the age, and was one of the principal causes of their downfall.

The wonderful architectural and engineering works which, both in Asia and Europe, were constructed under the direction of the Templars and Hospitallers—more particularly the former—are, it seems to us, very striking evidence of the Masonic origin of the Knights. *Gervase of Canterbury*, who wrote in the twelfth century, speaks of both French and English artificers, skilful to work in stone and in wood, who travelled in guilds or societies, for the purpose of proffering their services wherever the architect's and builder's art required to be exercised. These were the only men who possessed the requisite knowledge, and from their ranks kings and princes frequently impressed by violence workmen whom they required to construct their palaces or fortresses. They were the operative Freemasons, to whose surpassing skill, and knowledge of the laws of beauty and just proportion, we are indebted for the magnificent cathedrals which adorn this country and the Continent. They met in Lodges close tiled from the vulgar gaze, and pursued the practice of their mystic rites under the sanction of the throne and the Church. During the first Crusade we have no record of any building constructed by the warrior pilgrims; but at a later date, after the institution of the Orders of the Temple and St. John, castles, churches, palaces, and hospitals speedily arose on all sides. Their fortresses were of wondrous strength, and showed great skill in engineering. Thorn in Poland is indebted for its foundation to Herman Balk, Grand Master of the Teutonic Order, who, on his arrival in 1231, strongly fortified the ancient castle of Turno at Old Thorn, and in 1235 removed to the site of the present town. The Gothic cathedral was built by the German Knights. The chief seat of the Order was soon after removed to Marienburg: the ancient castle with the lofty towers and parapets, which are the remains of the old fortifications, show the strength of head-quarters of the Order. The remains of the palace of the Grand Master are extremely grand, and the late King of Prussia caused it to be repaired and partially restored to its ancient splendour. This town was built by the Knights in 1276.

Now, let it be observed, that the ranks of the Knights of all the Orders were recruited from the military but uneducated classes, both noble and plebeian, but who as such were little likely to have any knowledge of the science of architecture, or the art of fortifying with skill the most valuable strategic posts which presented themselves in their progress of conquest; yet to the present day the remains of their structural labours testify to the perfection they attained, both as architects and engineers. To what source, then, are we to attribute their skill? Let us see whether the peculiar condition of the Masonic body at that time will not afford an elucidation of the problem.

The travelling bodies of Freemasons, which we have mentioned, consisted of brethren well skilled in every branch of knowledge; among their ranks were many learned ecclesiastics, whose names survive to the present day in the magnificent edifices which they assisted to erect. The Knights of the Temple, themselves a body of military monks, partaking both of the character of soldiers and priests, preserved in their Order a rank exclusively clerical, the individuals belonging to which took no part in warfare, who were skilled in letters, and devoted themselves to the civil and religious affairs of the Order,—they were the historians of the period, and we know that all the learning of the time was in their keeping, in common with the other ecclesiastics of the time. From the best information we are possessed of regarding the Order, we believe there can be little doubt that these learned clerks introduced the whole fabric of Craft Masonry into the body of the Templars, and that not only was the speculative branch of the science by them incorporated with the laws and organization of the Knights, but to their operative skill were the Templars indebted for their triumphs in architecture and fortification. And it is worthy of remark, that in the records of the Order we find no mention of individual architects or builders; we may therefore not unfairly draw the inference, that the whole body were made participators in the knowledge and mysteries of the Craft.

A far different origin and organization than that of Freemasonry has been attributed to the Order of Templars; and to this we will shortly allude, more perhaps to the amusement than the edification of our readers. The argument which we are now about to examine, is curious as showing how far the power of prejudice can warp the mind and opinions of a learned and industrious student. *Von Hammer,* who has acquired a welldeserved and extended celebrity as an antiquary and historian, has actually attempted to identify the Templars and Freemasons with the celebrated eastern sect of Assassins. Speaking of the extent and influence of the latter body, he says:—

"The Templars incontrovertibly stand in the next rank to them; their secret maxims, particularly in so far as relates to the *renunciation of positive religion,* and the extension of their power by the acquisition of castles and strong places, seem to have been the same as those of the Order of Assassins. The accordance, likewise, of the *white dress* and *red fillet* of the Assassins, with the *white mantle* and *red cross* of the Templars, is certainly remarkably striking." * * * "The Assassins were a branch of the Ismaelites, the proper *illuminati* of the East. The institution of their Lodge, with the various grades of initiation, agree completely with what we have heard and read in our own days concerning secret revolutionary societies; and they coincide not less in the form of their constitution, than in the common object of declaring all kings and priests superfluous! The ostensible object of this institution was in itself sufficiently laudable, and the exoteric doctrine had merely for its object the extension of knowledge and the mutual support of the members. The greater number of the members were certainly deceived into good faith by the fair exterior of a beneficent, philanthropical knowledge, spreading far and wide; they were a kind of Freemasons. As in the west, *revolutionary societies arose from the bosom of the Freemasons,* so in the east, did the Assassins spring from the Ismaelites."

We shall not so far insult the common sense and intelligence of our readers as to enter upon any refutation of the absurdities contained in this extract. The writer's comparison of the costume of the Assassins and Templars is simply puerile—while the slanderous assertion of the irreligious and revolutionary principles which he attributes to Freemasonry would be laughable, were we not moved rather to pity his ignorance and malice. However, as Masons we can well afford to treat with contempt attacks of this kind, well knowing that the principles of our Order have for so many centuries blazed forth with undimmed lustre, even in the eyes of the profane, that an ignorance of its undoubted virtues can hardly be otherwise than assumed, and as such may be left to a well-merited contempt.

We have, however, entered upon this subject in consequence of another author (*Adler*), of a very different kind, having suggested that Freemasonry was introduced into Europe from the East by the Templars, who had received it from the Ismaelites. We think, on the contrary, that there is abundant evidence that it was carried to the East by the learned men who joined the second Crusade. It is not however by any means improbable, that the Templars, in the course of their long sojourn in Asia, during the frequent truces between the infidels and the Christians, became acquainted (as far as men of differing faith could honestly do) with the Ismaelites, which body doubtless, in its constitution and government, had some points of resemblance to their own. Of this tribe (the Ismaelites) little is distinctly known, and we are inclined to think that the prejudice of the earlier Christian writers has given them a far worse character than was really their due. For their other name of "Assassins," which has come to be a term of infamy in Europe, we presume our readers are aware that it was derived from the eastern drug *hashish,* a vile preparation of hemp used by devotees in the East to this day—and in which no doubt the followers of the "Old Man of the Mountain" (as their chief was called) indulged when about to undertake any desperate enterprise. The Crusaders who suffered from the daring attacks of this tribe, naturally ascribed every crime to the hated "*hashisheen,*" and the word has come down to our time as the most degrading epithet which can be applied to man.

The Druses of Mount Lebanon are the undoubted descendants of this tribe of Ismaelites. All travellers agree that these people have preserved a strict morality and a sober and decent deportment. The religious doctrine which they profess appears to be a pure unitarianism. Even at the present day are found traces of an association similar to those which doubtless existed amongst their ancestors in the time of the Crusaders. There is preserved by this singular people an institution which has many similar points to the Masonic Order (excepting that we are told both sexes are admissible); it requires a probation of twelve months previous to the admission of a member; in the second year he assumes the distinguishing mark of the white turban; and afterwards, by degrees, is allowed to participate in the whole of the mysteries. Simplicity of attire, self-denial, temperance, and irreproachable moral conduct are essential to admission to the Order.

To return to the subject more immediately before us. We have shown that the early Freemasons were the architects of all structures above the hovels of the peasantry; and we have endeavoured to trace to Masonic influence the eminence attained in structural science by the various knightly Orders. Though the original object of these institutions was the protection and assistance of the Christian pilgrims whose piety had led them to the Holy Land, there is no doubt that, with increasing power and influence, the views of the Knights became much changed and extended. In our opinion there is little room to doubt that the practice of Masonry soon became a prominent feature of the Order, and that Masonic secrets alone were the far-famed mysteries of the Templars. As it is evident that these pursuits would not in the eyes of the world appear to further the original objects of the chivalric Orders, we cannot be surprised that the Knights made no profession of their Masonic studies; perhaps, even at that remote period, there was a well-grounded fear of the animosity which has been since so fearfully developed in the Church of Rome against all secret societies. That power has ever trembled at the progress of liberality and science, knowing full well that in proportion as the intellect of man is strengthened by freedom of thought, her influence, founded upon blind superstition and puerile credulity, must gradually disappear from the earth. In illustration of the alarm of the papal Church at societies of this kind, we will refer, though not strictly belonging to our subject, to the Academy of Secrets, established in Italy in the sixteenth century by Baptista Porta, for the advancement of science. This association was called *I Secreti,* and was accessible only to such as had made some new discovery (real or supposed) in physical science. Porta did not content himself with this private means of instruction and education; he also to the utmost of his power promoted public academies, wherein were taught the then recondite sciences of chemistry, optics, and natural history. His voluminous works extended his fame, and he was visited by the learned from all parts of Europe. Such a man, in that age, could not escape the notice and pressing attentions of Holy Church. Writing, of course, much that was perfectly incomprehensible to the ignorant priests of the time, he was summoned to Rome to answer for his conduct and opinions, the charge of magic being brought against him, as was the established rule at that time when any thing scientific passed the understanding of the spiritual gentry. Eventually Porta was released, but his society was suppressed. Numerous absurdities may be traced in his works, owing to the imperfect light which fell to his lot; he was, nevertheless, a philosopher, and a man of practice as well as theory. To him we owe the camera obscura, and a variety of optical, chemical, and other valuable experiments instituted by him have in later ages produced fruitful results.

And here we may pause to notice the wonderful results which were produced, directly and indirectly, by the institutions of chivalry. That society ultimately benefited by them there can be no doubt. The rise of independent corporate bodies, even, may in some degree be traced to this source. The great feudal chiefs, anxious in many instances to join in the glories and spiritual benefits of the Crusades, in order to raise supplies of men and money, sold their seignorial rights to their vassals, and many towns and cities, which had been previously under the protection of some mighty lord, were compelled to combine for mutual defence. Hence arose free cities, charters, and franchises, institutions to which England and Europe owe whatever they possess of national liberty. The influence of a religious feeling, immediately before and during the period of the Crusades, upon the progress of architectural science is admirably displayed by *Michaud* in the following remarks:—

"In the tenth century, architecture consisted in the construction of towers, ramparts, and fortresses. In the habitations of the great every thing was sacrificed to the necessity of providing defences against an enemy; nothing could be afforded to comfort or magnificence. The dwellings of the people, even in cities, scarcely protected them from the injuries of weather or the intemperance of the seasons. The only architectural monuments were those which devotion raised to ancestors. Before magnificent palaces for princes, or convenient houses for the rich were thought of, edifices consecrated to religion were constructed. It is scarcely possible to enumerate the churches and monasteries built in the eleventh and twelfth centuries. According to the opinion of the time, the most certain mode of expiating sins was to build a church or a monastery. Thus architectural monuments arose at the voice of repentance, and religious inspirations revived, in some sort, the prodigies which fabulous antiquity attributed to the lyre of Amphion.

"In every city, in every town, the inhabitants made it their pride to ornament their cathedral, and the altars at which they invoked the saint whom the parish had chosen for its patron. It may be said that there was something like patriotism in this pious zeal; for the basilica, or paternal church, was then the most noble and the most sensible image of the country.

"At the commencement of the Crusades there existed a religious confraternity composed of men practised in the labours of building; they travelled about the world, offering their services to the faithful to build or repair churches. Another confraternity was formed with the useful design of constructing bridges for pilgrims and travellers. A chapel or an oratory reminded passengers that the bridge they were crossing was the work of charity.

"The clergy, who were rich, and could only display their opulence in buildings, made it their glory to erect churches. To complete their work they called in the aid of painting and sculpture, which, like architecture, owed their first encouragement to piety, and whose earliest masterpieces were consecrated to the ornamenting of the altars of the Christian religion.

"Nothing was more common than to see noble Crusaders, on their departure for Palestine, or on their return to the West, found a monastery or a church. Several pilgrims are named, who, on coming back from Jerusalem, employed their treasures in constructing churches, the form of which might offer them an image of the holy sepulchre they had visited. The treasures conquered from the infidels were often appropriated to such buildings."

The origin and progress of the pointed arch has been rendered one of the most complicated problems in the history of architecture. It was during the twelfth and thirteenth centuries this innovation upon the long monotony of the circular arch appeared and was perfected. This style, which bears the name of Gothic, is by writers of eminence assumed to be of oriental growth, and by Wren's theory, that the Freemasons were its inventors. Its earliest adoption was undoubtedly in England, and we have abundant evidence that the splendid specimens of Gothic architecture that cover our own land and adorn many Continental cities were built by Freemasons.

Numerous indeed have been the conjectures, and various the writers, upon the interesting subject of the secret associations and practices of the early Crusaders. Some of these authors have brought to bear upon the subject much learning and archæological knowledge, whilst others are more distinguished for the enthusiastic views they hold upon the subject, than for any great value that can be attached to their real or supposed discoveries. Prejudice and ignorance have of course been frequently busy in detraction of these Orders, as being more or less connected with the essence of Masonry; we have, however, the satisfaction of knowing that, while those writers who have attacked the Templars are gradually sinking into well-deserved obscurity, there is on the other hand a brilliant galaxy of advocates of the Masonic and general virtues of the Knights. A somewhat peculiar theory as to the Masonic customs of the Knights was held by Hutchinson, who in his "Spirit of Masonry" (a work which claims for our Institution a far more exalted origin than the mere practice of building) has the following remarkable observations:—

"No sooner was Christianity fully developed in this land (England), than all Europe was inflamed with the cry and madness of an enthusiastic monk, Peter the Hermit, who prompted the zealots in religion to the holy war; in which, for the purpose of recovering the holy city and Judea out of the hands of the infidels, armed legions of saints, devotees, and enthusiasts, in tens of thousands, poured forth from every state of Europe, to waste their blood and treasure in a purpose as barren and unprofitable as it was impolitic.

"It was deemed necessary that those who took up the ensign of the cross in this enterprise should form themselves into such societies as might secure them from spies and treacheries; and that each might know his companion and brother as well in the dark as by day. As it was with Jephtha's army at the passes of the Jordan, so also was it requisite in these expeditions that certain signs, signals, watchwords, or passwords, should be known amongst them; for the armies consisted of various nations and divers languages. No project or device could answer the purposes of the Crusaders better than those of Masonry:—the maxims and ceremonials attending the Master's Order had been previously established, and were materially necessary on that expedition; for as the Mohammedans were also worshippers of the Deity, and as the enterprisers were seeking a country where the Masons were in the time of Solomon called into an association, and where some remains would certainly be found of the mysteries and wisdom of the ancients and of our predecessors, such degrees of Masonry as extended only to the acknowledgment of their being servants of the God of nature would not have distinguished them from those they had to encounter, had they not assumed the symbols of the Christian faith.

"All the learning of Europe in those times, as in the ages of antiquity, was possessed by the religious (priesthood); they had acquired the wisdom of the ancients, and the original knowledge which was in the beginning, and now is *the truth;* many of them had been initiated into the mysteries of Masonry; they were the projectors of this enterprise, and as Solomon at the building of the Temple introduced orders and regulations for the conduct of the work, which his wisdom had been enriched with from the learning of the sages of antiquity, so that no confusion should happen during its progress, and so that the rank and office of each fellow-labourer might be distinguished and ascertained beyond the possibility of deceit,—in like manner, the priests projecting the Crusades, being possessed of the mysteries of Masonry, the knowledge of the ancients, and of the universal language which survived the confusion of Shinar, revived the orders and regulations of Solomon, and initiated the legions therein who followed them to the Holy Land: hence that secrecy which attended the Crusaders.

"Amongst other evidence which authorizes me in the conjecture that Masons went to the holy wars, is the doctrine of that Order of Masons called the Higher Order[1]. I am induced to believe that Order was of Scottish extraction; separate nations might be distinguished by some separate Order as they were by peculiar ensigns; but be that as it may, it fully proves to me that Masons were Crusaders."

But supposing the mysteries of the Templars might not have been wholly connected with those of Freemasonry, still there can be little doubt that many of the Templar Order were Freemasons,

[1] Masonry, as practised at that time, included all of what are now termed the Higher Degrees, but as one order or degree.

and initiated into the secrets of occult philosophy or the Rosicrucian Order.

Having endeavoured thus far to trace the peculiarities of the Order of Templars, we will for the present leave that most interesting subject—upon which very much more might be said—and will draw the reader's attention to the fact that secret societies of a totally different kind existed in this country and on the Continent long before the era of the Crusades. These were in fact associations by which men were enabled to gain subsistence for themselves and fellows. The accounts handed down to us by the earliest Anglo-Saxon writers whose works have been preserved, and which are amply corroborated by Stow, Fitzstephen, and others, describe these associations very fully, under the name of *gilds* or *guilds,* as bodies maintaining certain secrets for the benefit of their own Order. They were ecclesiastical and secular; the former for the practice of alms-deeds, the latter both for trade and alms; both were distinguished for their religious observances, and partook much of the nature of monastic institutions. The trading guilds have survived (of course in a modified form) to the present day; and, as our readers may have noticed, an effort has not been unsuccessfully made within the last few years, by a certain party in the Church of England, to revive the *religious* guilds, which are again flourishing under the names of divers saints, as "The Guild of St. Francis," "The Holy Guild of Poor Brethren of St. Cuthbert," &c. The great and important Livery Companies of the city of London are derived from these trading guilds.

The word *guild, gild, geld,* or *gelt,* as it is variously written, has many significations among the earlier writers. It is used to signify, primarily, a payment, mulct, composition, or amercement; it also denoted an enfranchised district (otherwise called *soke,* as in the wards of the city of London), and moreover was used for the free customs and privileges of such guild or soke; in later times its most usual acceptation was in the sense of an associated brotherhood or body, which might be a whole town, or only a minor incorporation—of such, every member was a *gildar*, i.e. a contributor to the support of the general body. The learned Johnson defines the word as meaning "fraternities originally contributing sums to a common stock; the word is to be found in various tongues,—in old French, Teutonic, and Icelandic,—*gilde, convivium, symposium;* a society, a fraternity or company, combined by orders and laws made amongst themselves, and by their prince's licence. Hence the word *guild* proceeds, being a fraternity or commonalty of men gathered together in one combination, supporting their common charges by mutual contribution."

Very great antiquity can be claimed for these and similar societies. They may even be traced to classical times, in which it is well known that artificers and traders were formed into companies like those of later days, and even occupied particular localities, to which they gave name. To this Fitzstephen has alluded in his description of London (A.D. 1180):—"This citie, even as Roma, is divided into wardes, and alle the sellers of wares, and alle the workemen for hyre, are distinguished everie morninge, each in his place, and everie one in his own streete."

The Anglo-Saxon guilds were an undoubted element in the origin of some of the most valuable points of our constitution, and sprang from the Saxon custom of frank-pledge. That the members of the guilds might the better identify each other, as well as ascertain whether any man was absent on unlawful business, it was their custom to assemble at stated periods, when they ate and drank together. The guilds devoted to religious or to trading objects, which afterwards arose, copied not only the convivialities but also most of the customs of their predecessors. These ecclesiastical guilds are mentioned so early as the *Capitula* of Carloman (A.D. 770), and the records of our Anglo-Saxon synods mention that both laymen and priests were members of these confraternities.

A custom prevailed in those early times of dividing whole towns into guilds, the government of which consisted of a triple estate—the chief or president, the council, and the members or associates. A favourite number of the council, including the chief, was thirteen—alluding to our Lord and the twelve Apostles. To such a source may be traced the origin of "Portsoken" Ward in the city of London. "In the days of King Edgar, more than six hundred years since," says old Stow, "there were thirteen knights, or soldiers, well beloved of the king and the realme (for service done by them), which requested to have a certain portion of land on the east part of the citie, left desolate and forsaken by the inhabitants by reason of too much servitude. They besought the king to have this land, with the liberty of a guilde, for ever: the king granted their request, with conditions following, that is to say, that each of them should victoriously accomplish three combates, one above ground, one under ground, and the third in the water; and after this, on a certain day, in East Smithfield, they should run with spears against comers; all which was gloriously performed: and the same day the king named it knighten guilde." To this fraternity a charter was granted by Edward the Confessor, and it continued to flourish for several centuries. In 1145, however, Queen Maud founded the priory of the Holy Trinity, which she endowed by the transfer of the lands of the "knighten guilde;" the other rights and privileges of that ancient corporation being transferred to certain burgesses of the city of London, who had the right to be a guild or trade corporation reserved to them. A curious anomaly arose in consequence; the prior of the Holy Trinity became the territorial lord and alderman of Portsoken Ward. It is said that a memorial of the ancient "knighten guilde" has descended to our own days in the corrupted name of "*Nightingale*-lane."

These several associations of Anglo-Saxon origin had each its secrets; and the same principle of union united them, assimilated in a great degree to that sacred bond of brotherhood which has ever characterized the institution of Freemasonry. We may observe that ecclesiastics identified themselves both with the peaceful guilds and with those devoted to the profession of arms, and we have ample proof that they were fostered and patronized by the Church of Rome, until the period when the wealth of some of the chivalric Orders having attracted the envy of both prince and pontiff, they first fell a sacrifice, and the policy of the Church ever afterwards denounced all secret associations as irreligious and heretical. The associations of trading guilds, however, continued to flourish in England, and especially in the city of London, all the great Companies of which, till within a recent period, kept up a show of preserving the customs and secrets of the ancient guilds. In these guilds all the more important and essential processes of their crafts were concealed as mysteries in the true sense of the term. During the earlier periods, the hereditary character of the handicraft must have greatly assisted in preventing the profane from withdrawing the veil: other means were practised for the purpose of keeping the secrets of the trades, and defending their monopoly, including many awe-inspiring ceremonies and initiations—sometimes terrific, sometimes painful or ludicrous. Here the candidate trembled beneath the arch of steel, with swords suspended over his head; there, unless his agility preserved him, the incipient workman enjoyed the full application of the lash of the whip. The aspirant admitted into the Worshipful Company of Cooks, binds himself under a heavy penalty not to reveal to any stranger the secret of raising puff paste!

The most celebrated and enduring of these ancient guilds on the Continent was the League of the Hanseatic Towns. This far-famed commercial confederacy was established during the rule, if not by the direct influence, of the Order of Teutonic Knights. The name is derived from the ancient German word "Hanse," signifying an association for mutual support and defence[2]. The Hanseatic League maintained ships and soldiers at their joint expense, to protect their commerce from pirates and enemies. In 1428 they had a fleet of 248 ships, and maintained a force of 20,000 soldiers. This extraordinary association and the great Order of Teutonic Knights flourished at the same period; during the 200 years from 1250 to 1450 they were perhaps at their highest power, and in the most perfect organization. The Teutonic Order eventually became absorbed into the Electorate of Bradenburg; the Hanse Towns existed as free republics until the year 1810, when they were crushed by the despotic rule established over Europe by the first Napoleon.

The illustrious Order of the Temple has, through many vicissitudes, survived to our times; and, indeed, of late years a great, and we may say an astonishing, influence has been exercised in the Masonic Craft by this brotherhood in England, on the continent of Europe, and in the United States. Notwithstanding the persecution the Order was subjected to, consequent upon the machinations of Philip le Bel and Pope Clement, it continued to exist, if not to flourish. Jaques de Molay, the martyred Grand Master, in anticipation of his fate, appointed his successor to rule the Fraternity, and from that time to the present there has been an uninterrupted succession of Grand Masters. It is true, that as years passed on, and clouds arose still more ominous to the existence of the society, the Templars (we believe there is no doubt) amalgamated their body with that of their ancient brothers in arms, the Knights of St. John, or, as they were afterwards called (from the island that became their head-quarters), the Knights of Malta. In the Preceptories of the Order which remained in England the secrets imparted to the newly installed brother of the Temple included, for many years, the degrees known as Knight of St. John and Knight of

[2] The term has been adopted in our own tongue, and is found in two ancient charters granted by King John to the city of York, and the town of Dunwich, in Suffolk.

Malta. With these were also conferred the "Rose-Croix of Heredom," one of the higher degrees, which, it is said, was originally brought into this country from Scotland (where, as well as in Ireland, many interesting, curious, and even valuable Masonic rites are preserved, which are generally unknown to the younger English Masons), and the "Kadosh," or *ne plus ultra* of Masonry. Of the Kadosh there are said to be six degrees, and, however worked, we are at liberty to say that there is little doubt that they are intimately connected with the ancient ceremonies of the Order of the Temple.

We have spoken of the wide-spread influence of the Templar Order at the present day; the fact is, however, not perhaps known to the generality of our readers, that the vows of this degree were embraced to as great, if not to a greater extent, in proportion to the Masonic population of Great Britain a century ago, than at the present time. Great, and we fear not to say unpardonable, neglect has been manifested with regard to the records of the Order at that period, and the documents which have been preserved are meagre in the extreme.

The influence of this noble Order has been widely exercised on the Continent. In France and Italy chapters of the chivalric degrees have always been held, and latterly under the sanction of the Church. At Sonnenberg, in Germany, there was a Grand Encampment of the Knights of St. John early in the present century, where several German princes were elevated to the privileges of the Order, amongst whom were Leopold of Saxe-Coburg, the present sovereign of Belgium, and Michaud, the historian of the Crusades. In Prussia the military Orders flourish, and there is good ground for tracing their preservation up to the Teutonic Order, the Knights of which were the original founders of the power of the Prussian monarchy. It is not unreasonable to conclude that a portion of the persecuted brotherhood of the Temple sought refuge with their more prosperous fellow-soldiers of the Teutonic Order, and that their secrets and ceremonies may have been thus perpetuated in the north of Europe, while the Knights of St. John preserved them in the south.

The sovereigns of Prussia have always been patrons of Masonry in every form. Their descent from the illustrious Grand Master of the Teutonic Order may, it is not improbable, have influenced their predilections; be that as it may, it is well known that they have always, and more particularly since the time of Frederick the Great, manifested the warmest interest in the affairs of the Craft. The active part taken by that illustrious prince in Masonry is indeed surprising, when we consider the magnitude and importance of his military and political transactions. He is known to have attained to the greatest proficiency in what are known as the higher degrees in Freemasonry, and established in Prussia the Supreme Council of Grand Inspectors General, in order to preserve to his successors the Masonic privileges which he possessed as the acknowledged head of that rite.

The Templar Degree derived its origin in this country from two sources—France and Germany: the *Cross of Christ Encampment*, held at Clerkenwell, was of French origin; the *Observance* was from Germany, and presided over by Brother Burckhardt.

The Knights Templar Degree is highly valued in all countries, and its ritual is, we believe, identical. The candidate for its honours, in England, must be a Royal Arch Mason, and as such he presents himself at the Encampment—as the meetings are called—in the character and garb of a pilgrim, or palmer, as they were designated in the Holy Land; he figuratively undergoes seven years' travel, and then seven years' warfare, when, having conducted himself courageously through his trials, he is finally admitted into the Order. It need hardly be said that this is entirely a Christian degree, and into it none but such as are professors of Christianity can be admitted. There is not a vestige of Freemasonry, as such, in the degree, save the absolute necessity of candidates having been admitted into the Royal Arch. The New Testament is, except one slight extract, exclusively used for illustration; and the three great lights represent Peter, James, and John. The object of this degree is similar to that of the Rose-Croix Knight, but whereas that deals with the event of man's redemption in an allegory, this celebrates the fact. The obligation of a Masonic Knight Templar is not unlike that taken by the Soldier Monk, and he becomes by his vow a Soldier of the Cross.

The officers of Grand Conclave are, Most Eminent and Supreme Grand Master, Sir Knight William Stuart, of Aldenham Abbey, Herts; Very Eminent Deputy Grand Master, Sir Knight Colonel George Augustus Vernon; Grand Seneschal, Sir Knight Right Hon. the Earl of Carnarvon. The other officers appointed annually are, Grand Prior and Sub-Prior, Grand Prelate, First and Second Grand Captains, Grand Chancellor and Vice Chancellor, Grand Registrar, Grand Treasurer, Grand Chamberlain, Grand Hospitaller, Grand Constable or Mareschal, Grand Provost, First and Second Grand Experts, First and Second Grand Standard-bearers, Grand Almoner, Grand Director of Ceremonies, First and Second Grand Aidede-Camp, First and Second Grand Captain of Lines, Grand Sword-bearer, Two Grand Heralds, Grand Superintendent of Works, Grand Organist, Grand Banner-bearer, and two Grand Equerries.

No Encampment can install a knight into the Order for a less sum than three guineas (except in case of a serving brother, for which a dispensation is necessary).

The costume of the degree is as follows:—*Badge*, a white kid skin with a border of black watered ribbon—the ribbon to be four inches broad; in the centre of the badge a red cross patee in velvet or embroidery. A belt of black silk velvet, five inches broad in front, is worn attached to the badge; the belt has on the front the emblems of mortality in a triangle in silver. Grand officers are distinguished by the black ribbon being intersected by three white stripes. A sash of black watered ribbon, four inches wide, is worn over the right shoulder. Commanders are distinguished by having gold fringe and button at the ends. Grand officers' sashes have three white stripes.

The members of Grand Conclave are all Present and Past Grand Officers, all Present and Past Commanders, and the Present Captains, of private Encampments.

The Grand Conclave is held on the second Friday in the month of May, at Freemasons' Hall, London.

Every Encampment must be constituted by a warrant or patent with the great seal of the Order affixed, and under the sign manual of the Grand Master, and witnessed by the Deputy Grand Master and the Grand Chancellor.

The form of petition for a warrant for opening a new Encampment is as follows:—

To the Grand Conclave of the Royal Exalted and Military Order of Knights Templar in England and Wales, and the Colonial Dependencies of the British Crown.

We the undersigned being regularly registered members of Encampments mentioned against our respective names, having the prosperity of the Order at heart, are anxious to exert our best endeavours to promote and diffuse the genuine principles of the Ancient Order of Masonic Knights Templar; and for the greater convenience of our brethren, and other good reasons, are desirous of establishing a new Encampment, to be named the Encampment, and pray for a Warrant of Constitution empowering us to meet as a regular Encampment at on the day of the months of in every year, and there to discharge our duties in a constitutional manner according to the Statutes of the Royal Exalted and Military

Order of Masonic Knights Templar in England and Wales, and have nominated and do recommend Sir Knight as First Eminent Commander, and Sir Knights as First and Second Captains of the said Encampment.

The prayer of the petitioners being granted, we promise strict obedience to the commands of the Most Eminent and Supreme Grand Master and the Laws and Statutes of the Grand Conclave.

To be signed by seven Knights of the Order.

The fee for a warrant is five guineas, which must be remitted to the Vice-Chancellor with the petition.

Every Encampment must consist of an Eminent Commander, a Prelate, two Captains, a Registrar (who acts as Secretary), a Treasurer, an Almoner, an Expert, two Standard-bearers, a Captain of the Lines, two Heralds, and an Equerry.

The ritual, from its solemnity, is most impressive. The Encampment is opened by a prayer to the Redeemer, so to direct the suppliants' labours that they may be inspired with love to Him, affection to their companions, protection to the distressed, and obedience to the Order. It is closed with this prayer:—

"O Merciful Lord, grant thy holy protection and salutary blessing to this Encampment; enlighten its rulers with the rays of thy brightness, that they may always see the just ways of our Heavenly Captain, and may by their example induce the companions committed to their charge so to follow them through this wilderness of temptation, that, having overcome the enemies of thy holy Name, they may arrive at the Heavenly Jerusalem, armed with the shield of faith and the breastplate of righteousness, through Jesus Christ our Saviour."

In the ceremony of installing a knight, he is invested with the armour, while the Prelate reads from St. Paul's Epistle to the Ephesians, chap. vi. ver. 10—17:—

"Finally, my brethren, be strong in the Lord, and in the power of his might. Put on the whole armour of God, that ye may be able to stand against the wiles of the devil. For we wrestle not against flesh and blood, but against principalities, against powers, against the rulers of the darkness of this world, against spiritual wickedness in high places. Wherefore take unto you the whole armour of God, that ye may be able to withstand in the evil day, and having done all, to stand. Stand therefore, having your loins girt about with truth, and having on the breastplate of righteousness; and your feet shod with the preparation of the gospel of peace; above all, taking the shield of faith, wherewith ye shall be able to quench all the fiery darts of the wicked. And take the helmet of salvation, and the sword of the Spirit, which is the word of God."

The novitiate is then thus addressed: "Pilgrim, now a novice of the Order, the ceremonies in which you are now engaged are calculated deeply to impress your mind, and we trust will have a long and happy effect on your future character. You were first, as a trial of your faith and humility, enjoined to perform a seven years' pilgrimage, which represented the pilgrimage of life through which we are all passing; we are all weary pilgrims looking forward to the asylum where we shall rest from our labours and be at rest for ever. You were then directed, as a trial of your courage and constancy, to perform seven years of warfare; it represented the constant warfare with the living vanities and deceits of this world, in which it is necessary for us to be always engaged. You are now called upon to perform one year of humility, and it is also a trial of the faith which will conduct you safe over the dark gulf of everlasting death, and land your enfranchised spirit in the peaceful abode of the blessed. Let the emblems of life and death now before you remind you of the uncertainty of human life, and lead you to be prepared for the closing hour of existence. And rest assured that a firm faith in the truths revealed to us will afford you consolation in the gloomy hour of dissolution, and ensure ineffable and eternal bliss in the world to come."

After the novitiate has undergone his trials of fortitude and courage,—during which is read the First Epistle of Peter, chap. ii. ver. 1—17:

"Wherefore laying aside all malice, and all guile, and hypocrisies, and envies, and all evil speakings, as newborn babes, desire the sincere milk of the word, that ye may grow thereby: if so be ye have tasted that the Lord is gracious. To whom coming, as unto a living stone, disallowed indeed of men, but chosen of God and precious, ye also, as lively stones, are built up a spiritual house, an holy priesthood, to offer up spiritual sacrifices, acceptable to God by Jesus Christ. Wherefore also it is contained in the scripture, Behold, I lay in Sion a chief corner stone, elect, precious: and he that believeth on him shall not be confounded. Unto you therefore which believe he is precious: but unto them which be disobedient, the stone which the builders disallowed, the same is made the head of the corner, and a stone of stumbling, and a rock of offence, even to them which stumble at the word, being disobedient: whereunto also they were appointed. But ye are a chosen generation, a royal priesthood, an holy nation, a peculiar people; that ye should show forth the praises of him who hath called you out of darkness into his marvellous light. Which in time past were not a people, but are now the people of God: which had not obtained mercy, but now have obtained mercy. Dearly beloved, I beseech you as strangers and pilgrims, abstain from fleshly lusts, which war against the soul; having your conversation honest among the Gentiles: that, whereas they speak against you as evildoers, they may by your good works, which they shall behold, glorify God in the day of visitation. Submit yourselves to every ordinance of man for the Lord's sake: whether it be to the king, as supreme; or unto governors, as unto them that are sent by him for the punishment of evildoers, and for the praise of them that do well. For so is the will of God, that with well doing ye may put to silence the ignorance of foolish men: as free, and not using your liberty for a cloke of maliciousness, but as the servants of God. Honour all men. Love the brotherhood. Fear God. Honour the King:" —a small cube of marble is presented to him, in illustration of which is read from Revelation, chap. ii. ver. 17:—

"He that hath an ear, let him hear what the Spirit saith unto the churches; To him that overcometh will I give to eat of the hidden manna, and will give him a white stone, and in the stone a new name written, which no man knoweth saving he that receiveth it."

The sacred emblems of the Order are the Lamb, the Dove, and the Cock. The first is emblematic of the Paschal Lamb, slain from the foundation of the world; the Dove, of the Almighty Comforter which descended in a bodily shape on Jesus Christ at his baptism, when his Divine mission was indicated to John the Baptist; the Cock, the monitor of the Order—for his crowing heralds the morn—especially calls to our remembrance our duties as Knights Templar, and reminds us to ask thus early for assistance to perform them throughout the coming day. May we ever welcome the sound as a friendly caution, and not have reason to fear it as the periodical memorial of a broken vow.

The installation of the Eminent Commander has reference to an event in the Holy Wars. At the time when the Crusaders were led by Godfrey de Bouillon to Jerusalem, he being anxious to have a first sight of the Holy City, pushed forward with a few followers, and being in advance, on arriving at an elevated point near to a village, distant threescore furlongs from Jerusalem, he saw the towers and pinnacles of the city shining bright with the morning sun; he turned round to his companions in arms, and made known their near approach, as had been agreed, by informing them they were at Emmaus.

The emblem of Knights of the Order is a cross patée; Commanders and Past Commanders wear the patriarchal cross, which is suspended by a white watered, or in some cases by a Syrian ribbon. The Grand Master is distinguished by the triple cross of Salem. The star of the Order is of silver, with seven points; it has a passion cross in the centre, around which is the motto, *In hoc signo vinces*. The cloak or mantle is of white camlet, with a cape or hood; on the left shoulder is the cross to which the wearer is entitled, in red silk.

ROLL OF ENCAMPMENTS REGISTERED UNDER THE GRAND CONCLAVE OF ENGLAND AND WALES, 1861.

Abbey Chapter, Assembly Rooms, Low Pavement, Nottingham.
Albert, Littleborough, near Rochdale.
All Souls, Masonic Hall, Weymouth.
Almeric de St. Maur, Queen's Arms Hotel, Bolton.
Ascalon, Poona, East Indies.
Beauseant, New Inn, Handsworth, Staffordshire.
Bermuda, Hamilton, Bermuda.
Bladud, 3, Westgate Buildings, Bath.
Calpe, General Lodge Rooms, Gibraltar.
Cœur de Lion, Masonic Hall, Oxford.
Cornubian, or Conclave of the Holy City, Masonic Hall, Falmouth.
De Furnival, Sheffield.
Edmund Plantagenet, New Inn, Openshaw.
Excelsior, In H.M. 21st Foot, Royal North British Fusilier, Barbadoes.
Faith, Bradford, Yorkshire.
Faith, Horse Shoe Inn, Pendleton, Lancashire.
Faith and Fidelity, or Early Grand Encampment of England, Freemasons' Tavern, Great Queen Street, London.
Fearnley, Masonic Hall, Dewsbury West, Yorkshire.
Frederick of Unity, London Tavern, Bishopsgate Street.

Godefroi de Bouillon, Hamilton, Canada West.
Godefroi de Bouillon, Wheatsheaf Inn, Stoke-upon-Trent, Staffordshire.
Geoffrey de St. Omer, Palestine Hotel, Manchester.
Geoffrey de St. Aldemar, Masonic Hall, Toronto, Canada West.
Holy Cross, George Hotel, Axminster.
Holy Trinity, Grapes Inn, New Street, Whitehaven.
Hope, Freemasons' Hall, Fitzwilliam Street, Huddersfield.
Howe, Masonic Rooms, Newhall Street, Birmingham.
Hugh de Payens, Masonic Hall, Kingston, Canada West.
Hugh de Payens, Old Bull Hotel, Blackburn.
Jaques de Molay, Masonic Temple, 22, Hope Street, Liverpool.
Jaques de Molay, Sandhurst, Victoria, Australia.
Jerusalem, Masonic Lodge Rooms, Cross Street, Manchester.
Joppa, Sunderland.
Kemeys-Tynte, Masonic Hall, William Street, Woolwich, Kent.
Loyal Ashton-under-Lyne Encampment of Volunteers, Swan Inn, Stamford Street, Ashton-under-Lyne.
Loyal Brunswick, St. George's Hall, Stonehouse, Plymouth.
Love and Friendship, Vernon Arms, Stockport.
Melita, Valetta, Malta.
Mount Calvary, Ship and Turtle, Leadenhall Street.
Mount Carmel, London Tavern, Bishopsgate Street.
Mount Zion, Bombay, East Indies.
Nova Scotia, Freemasons' Hall, Halifax, Nova Scotia.
Observance, Thatched House, St. James's Street.
Observance, Masonic Temple of the Lodge of Perfect Unanimity, Madras.
Pembroke, Tattersall's Hotel, Melbourne, Australia.
Plains of Mamre, Cross Keys, Burnley.
Plains of Rama, in the Room of the Royal Yorkshire Lodge, Keighley.

Prince Edward, Station House, Bottom's Stanfield, Todmorden.
Prudence, Great White Horse Hotel, Ipswich.
Richard Cœur de Lion, London, Canada West.
Richard de Vernon, Dudley Arms Hotel, Dudley, Worcester.
Royal Edward, Astley Arms Inn, Dukinfield.
Royal Gloucester, Freemasons' Hall, Southampton.
Royal Kent, Freemasons' Hall, Bell Court, Newgate Street, Newcastle-on-Tyne.
Royal Kent, Calcutta, East Indies.
Royal Naval, Phœnix Lodge Rooms, High Street, Portsmouth.
Royal Sussex, Freemasons' Hall, Tiverton.
Royal Veteran, Golden Fleece Inn, East Street, Plymouth.
Salamanca, 2, West Gate, Halifax, York.
Sepulchre, Bengal, East Indies.
St. Augustine, Lahore, Punjaub.
St. George [formerly *Cross of Christ*], Radley's Hotel, Bridge Street, Blackfriars, London.
St. George's, Angel Inn, Oldham.
St. James of Jerusalem, alternately at the Rising Sun, Three Tuns, and the Legs of Man, Bolton.
St. John of Jerusalem, Queen's Hotel, Todmorden.
St. John, Simlah, East Indies.
St. Joseph, Masonic Rooms, Cross Street, Manchester.
St. Michael, Masons' Arms, Newchurch, Lancashire.
St. Michael and St. George, Corfu.
St. Salem, Dog and Partridge Inn, Stockport.
Stuart, Freemasons' Hall, Watford.
Temple Cresing, George Hotel, Colchester.
Trinity in Unity, Assembly Rooms, Barnstaple.
Tynte Encampment of Redemption through Christ, Taunton, Somersetshire.
Union, or Rougemont, Masonic Hall, Exeter.

William de la More the Martyr, Quebec.
William de la More, Queen's Hotel, Manchester.
The King Baldwin, Belleville, Canada West.

With regard to the present government of the Order, we must acknowledge that serious anomalies have arisen, which we would gladly see reconciled. According to the constitutions of the Order, it is clear that there can be but one Supreme Grand Master, whose authority all Preceptories (or, as they are now termed, Encampments) are bound to acknowledge. The subordinate heads of the brotherhood in the various parts of Christendom are properly designated Masters, or Grand Priors. If then the succession of Grand Masters is allowed to have continued unbroken in France, it is clear that to the Grand Master of the Temple in Paris belongs the right of appointment of the heads of all subordinate Preceptories or Encampments. If, on the other hand, this authority be disavowed, to whom of right belongs the rule of the Order, and what becomes of its ancient customs, traditions, and landmarks? When the late Duke of Sussex was in the zenith of his power as Grand Master of Masons in England, he wished to obtain also the supreme authority in the higher degrees, as well in Craft as Royal Arch Masonry; and to this end, carrying out the wishes of the majority of the brethren in this country, he applied to the Emperor Alexander of Russia, as the nominal head of the Knights of Malta, for authority to rule the chivalric orders established in this country, and received from that potentate the title of Grand Prior of England, uniting under his control the three degrees of Knights Templar, Knights of St. John, and Knights of Malta. At the Duke's death the supreme authority in England was conferred upon that very worthy and highly-esteemed Mason, the late Colonel Kemeys Tynte, who was styled "Grand Master" of the Knights Templar,—an innovation which caused considerable discontent at the time, and in some measure tended to results to be regretted. Brother William Stuart, of Aldenham Abbey, Herts, eldest son of the late Archbishop of Armagh, is the present Grand Master of the Order.

Under the Ancient and Accepted Rite reference is made to the Templar, and the other degrees connected with it, which were conferred by the certificate; the author having received the Templar Degree under the old constitution, can affirm that in the ritual then practised no reference was made to those other degrees. On the settlement by the Supreme Council and the Grand Conclave, as already mentioned, in the year 1851 the degrees of Knight of Malta or Knight of St. John, the Prince Rose-Croix, and also the Kadosh, were separated from the Templar Degree, a severance which caused at the time much dissatisfaction, and the heart-burnings arising from which can hardly yet be said to have subsided.

The appointment of the Duke of Sussex himself, as derived from the Emperor Alexander, is liable to the following objections: the Knights Templar, it is acknowledged, were incorporated with the Knights of St. John, or Knights of Malta, who, after their expulsion from that island, elected, undoubtedly, as their Grand Master, the Emperor Paul of Russia. But the title of Grand Master, assumed by his son and successor, Alexander, was never conferred by the votes of the Order; on the contrary, after the assassination of Paul, they elected the Prince Caraccioli. After the removal of the Order from Malta in 1800, the chief seat was transferred to Catania in Sicily, whence, in 1826, it was removed by the Pope's authority to Ferrara.

Having shown that the title of the Duke of Sussex, as derived from the Emperor of Russia, was, to say the least, unsatisfactory, are we not justified in taking another and very different view of the subject? The Order having in the course of time fallen into decay abroad, and infirmity having been displayed in its government and management, the English knights, whose Encampments had been in a healthy condition for many years, were fully entitled to take the steps necessary for their own good government; and this course, we fully believe, would have been followed by the ancient brethren of the Order, had indecision or weakness manifested themselves at the fountain-head. Viewed from this point, the rule of the Duke of Sussex, accepted though not elected by the knights in England, seems perfectly satisfactory, nor can we see that any really important objection can be made to the assumption of the title of "Grand Master," if the Order think fit to confer it upon their head.

There are several Encampments in England claiming great antiquity. It is asserted that the Encampment of Baldwin was established at Bristol by the Templars who returned from Palestine with Richard I.; it is still one of the most flourishing in England, and has preserved the ancient costume and ceremonial of the Order. This, with another at Bath, and a third at York, constitute the three original Preceptories of this kingdom. It must be confessed, however, that though there is no reason to doubt their authenticity, our information is derived only from the traditions current in these Encampments. It would be more satisfactory if the members would communicate any facts corroborative of the statement. We cannot but think that in their archives is concealed much matter of interest to the Order in general, and which would prove of value in any future regulations for the government of the Fraternity, though at present they do not work in connexion with the Grand Conclave.

We hope that the time is not far distant when the different systems of our Masonic institution, in the higher as well as in the Craft degrees, will be brought under one government; and we trust that an attempt will also be made to assimilate the workings in this country with that pursued under the sanction of the Grand Lodges of Scotland and Ireland, a consummation which would be welcomed by every true brother of the Craft.

It will be seen from the numerous list of Encampments, that the Templar institution is popular with English Masons; and although the Ancient and Accepted Rite appears to be in some measure antagonistic, yet with the rise and progress of the latter Templarism continues to increase, and among its members are ranked some of the most distinguished Masons in the realm.

In Scotland the Templars have an organization different from our own and from that existing in any part of the world where this ancient Order is to be found.

"The Religious and Military Order of the Temple" in Scotland consists of two classes, 1. Novice or Esquire; 2. Knight Templar. The Knights consist of three grades, 1. Knights created by Priories; 2. Knights Commanders, elected from the Knights on memorial to the Grand Master and Council, supported by the recommendation of the Priories to which they belong; 3. Knights Grand Crosses, to be nominated by the Grand Master.

The supreme legislative authority of the Order is the Grand Conclave, which consists of the Grand Officers, the Knights Grand Crosses, the Knights Commanders, and the Prior of each priory. Four Chapters are held annually. At the meeting in March the Grand Officers are elected. The Grand Master is elected triennially.

The subordinate Chapters are designated Priories, and are equivalent to our Encampments.

CHAPTER XX.

THE RITES OF FREEMASONRY.

"What I understand I find to be excellent; and, therefore, believe that to be of equal value which I cannot understand."—SOCRATES.

IT is not, perhaps, generally known to English Masons, and more particularly to the younger members of the Craft, that in modern times numerous modifications have been introduced, or rather interpolated, in the glorious fabric of Freemasonry, embodying a variety of degrees, the ceremonials of which greatly resemble one another, and have similar designations. These have nearly all originated on the continent of Europe, and have been concocted, some for political, and some for religious, influence; and to all of them is affixed the solemn appellation of "Rite." We believe we are correct in saying, that in all these the three ancient degrees and their essentials were preserved. Most of these novelties originated in the vanity of their contrivers, ambitious of making themselves a name; some fell into oblivion in the inventor's lifetime, others died out with their authors, and nearly all are now extinct.

At the present time the Masonic family in England may be considered as divided into four distinct bodies, in which we have four several constitutions acknowledged, viz.:—The United Grand Lodge, the Supreme Council of the Ancient and Accepted Rite, the Grand Conclave of Knights Templar, and the Grand Lodge of Mark Masters; besides the schism, if we may so term it, of the Baldwin Encampment of Templars, claiming the same prerogatives as the Supreme Council and Grand Conclave.

Seeing the position of Masonry in this island, it does appear surprising that we can number little more than forty of these varieties of Masonic government on the great continent of Europe. We believe that a brother who has been admitted into a degree of any rite, is always received and acknowledged in a degree of like name or rank in any Lodge or assembly practising under the constitution of another rite.

YORK RITE.

The *York Rite,* the most ancient, has existed from time immemorial, and originated in the city of York, where the first Grand Lodge of England was held A.D. 926. In this, the parent Lodge of pure Masonry, it is said only the three primitive degrees of ancient Craft Masonry were in the first instance acknowledged. To them, in modern times, have been added four other degrees, viz.:—Mark Master, Past Master, Most Excellent Master, and the Supreme Degree of the Holy Royal Arch. Thus this rite consists of seven degrees; but in some parts of the United States, where it is still practised, two have been annexed in addition—those of Royal, and Select Master. But, as mentioned in the account of the Ancient and Accepted Rite, the Ancient York Masons in England in the last century practised other degrees. This rite is not at present practised in this country; but as the most ancient Masonic Institution in the British Isles, and, it appears, of all those we are about to describe, it is entitled to priority. From this arose—

THE ENGLISH RITE.

The *English Rite,* or that adopted by the United Grand Lodge of England and Wales. The solemn act of union in 1813 declared and pronounced that pure ancient Masonry consists of three degrees and no more, viz., those of the Entered

Apprentice, the Fellow-Craft, and the Master Mason, including the Supreme Degree of the Holy Royal Arch. Notwithstanding this, we consider the Masonic fabric really to consist of nine degrees, which are these:—1. Entered Apprentice; 2. Fellow-Craft; 3. Master Mason; 4. Royal Arch; 5. Installed Master or Past Master; 6. Joshua, or Third Principal; 7. Haggai, or Second Principal; 8. Zerubbabel, or First Principal; 9. Past Principal. Now, if the word "degree" be correctly defined by Johnson and other lexicographers, to be "a step, or preparation for another step, a high state, station, rank," it is worthy of remark, that to qualify a brother for permanent admission to membership of the Grand Lodge and Grand Chapter, each and all the steps above enumerated must be taken; and, as to each is attached distinct signs and secrets, they must, in the common acceptation of the word, be "degrees." Hence, although our nomenclature may differ from that adopted by our transatlantic brethren in the York Rite—in the number of degrees (nine) they correspond.

ANCIENT AND ACCEPTED RITE.

The history of the *Ancient and Accepted Rite* has already been so fully treated upon, that no further explanation is needed. The exact date at which it was formed is uncertain, but as it is the most extensively diffused of those rites in which the historical and chivalric degrees are embodied, we give it the next place in rank.

CHAPTER OF CLERMONT.

In the year 1753, in the Jesuit College of the city of Clermont in France, in defiance of the bull of Pope Clement XII., as well as the denunciation of the King of France, the brethren of that College founded a Masonic Lodge, to which they gave the name of the *Chapter of Clermont.* All that is distinctly known of this society or its teaching is, that, besides the three ancient symbolic degrees, there were introduced some of the higher ones; all the allegories and symbols of which, *Fessler* asserts, pointed to the establishment of an universal dominion, the desired end and aim of the Jesuit institution. Into this Chapter the famous Baron Hunde, though a member of the Protestant faith, contrived to gain admission, and upon the Masonic instruction he there received, and the ritual of the new degrees, was formed the nucleus of the system which he introduced into Germany.

STRICT OBSERVANCE.

The *Rite of Strict Observance* was founded in Germany by the Baron Hunde, in 1754; and, according to *Clavel,* is based on the Order of the Knights Templar. It comprises seven degrees, viz.:—Entered Apprentice, Fellow-Craft, Master Mason, Scotch Master, Novice, Templar, and Professed Knight. The legend of the rite thus narrates its origin. On the murder of Jaques de Molay, the Grand Master of the Templars, Pierre d'Aumont, Grand Prior of Auvergne, with two Commanders and five Knights, escaped from France, and sought safety in Scotland, under the disguise of operative Masons. Soon after their arrival they were so fortunate as to discover one George Harris, a Grand Commander, with some other Templars; a Chapter of all the Knights was held on St. John's day, 1313, and Pierre d'Aumont was elected Grand Master. To avoid the persecution which still pursued their own body, they met as a Lodge of Freemasons, that Order being tolerated at the period of the Templar persecution. In 1361 the chief seat of the Order was established at Old Aberdeen; and, under the veil of Masonry, in this rite the Templar Order was diffused from Scotland to various parts of the Continent. Some of the degrees embody the practice of alchemy, magic, and other now obsolete pseudoscientific delusions. We have no knowledge of this rite being now any where practised. The rite nevertheless attained considerable influence at one period; proof of which is found in the schism that was created among its members, and resulted in an Order called the *Clerks of Relaxed Observance,* which offset claimed pre-eminence, not only over the parent rite, but over the whole brotherhood of Masons. For admission into this association it was imperative that the candidate should be a member of the Catholic Church of Rome, and that he should have taken all the degrees of the Rite of Strict Observance. The new rite had ten degrees:—Apprentice, Fellow-Craft, Master Mason, African Brother, Knight of St. Andrew, Knight of the Eagle, Scotch Master, Sovereign Magus, Provincial Master of the Red Cross, and Knight of Light: the last degree was divided into five sections, and it required seven years for completion. Alchemy and magic were the objects of this rite. *Clavel* says its members boasted that they had possession of the true philosopher's stone, the elixir of life, the command of spirits, and a method of discovering the hidden treasures of the Temple.

RITE OF PERFECTION.

The *Rite of Perfection.* We have already referred to the rite denominated "Chapter of Clermont." The Chevalier de Bonneville is said to have taken a prominent part in its establishment, about the year 1753-56, to do honour to Louis of Bourbon, Prince of Clermont, who was at that period the Grand Master of the Freemasons of France. The leading principle in this rite is to establish the connexion of the Knights Templar with Freemasonry. It bore also the name of the *Rite of Heredom,* and consisted of twenty-five degrees, most of them being the same as those of the Ancient and Accepted Rite—1. Entered Apprentice; 2. Fellow-Craft; 3. Master Mason; 4. Secret Master; 5. Perfect Master; 6. Intimate Secretary; 7. Intendant of Buildings; 8. Provost and Judge; 9. Elect of Nine; 10. Elect of Fifteen; 11. Illustrious Elect; 12. Chief of the Twelve

Tribes; 13. Royal Arch; 14. Grand Elect Perfect Ancient Master; 15. Knight of the Sword; 16. Prince of Jerusalem; 17. Knight of the East and West; 18. Rose-Croix Knight; 19. Grand Pontiff; 20. Grand Patriarch; 21. Grand Master of the Key of Masonry; 22. Prince of Libanus; 23. Sovereign Prince Adept, Chief of the Grand Consistory; 24. Illustrious Knight Commander of the Black and White Eagle; 25. Most Illustrious Sovereign Prince of Masonry, Grand Knight, Sublime Commander of the Royal Secret. This rite was in practice a few years since in Paris, and possibly is still in existence. It will be seen that the names of some of the degrees which differ from the first formation of the Ancient and Accepted Rite are the same as those adopted by the Supreme Council in England. The *Primitive Scotch Rite* was founded on the Rite of Perfection by Marchot, an advocate at Namur, and is said still to be practised in that city, but we cannot learn that it was adopted in any other place. There are thirty-three degrees in this rite, and they are similar to the Scotch Rite; but in this the Rose-Croix is the twenty-second, and the Kadosh the twenty-eighth degree.

In the historical part of the lecture in this rite we are told that the Masons who were employed in constructing the first Temple acquired immortal honour; and the world-wide fame of that stately edifice caused the Order to become more uniformly established and regulated than before. Their scrupulousness in admitting new members into the Order brought it to a high degree of respect—merit alone being regarded in the admission of candidates. With these principles instilled into their minds, many of the Grand Elect left the Temple after its dedication, and dispersed themselves among the neighbouring kingdoms, instructing all who applied and were found worthy in the sublime degrees of ancient Craft Masonry.

FRENCH RITE.

The *French or Modern Rite* was established by the Grand

Orient of France about the year 1786, to preserve the high degrees; and for the purpose of simplifying the system, the number was reduced to seven, viz., Entered Apprentice, Fellow-Craft, Master Mason, Elect, or First Order of Rose-Croix, Scotch Order, or Second Order of Rose-Croix, Knight of the East, or Third Order of Rose-Croix, and the Rose-Croix, or *ne plus ultra.* The peculiar signs and secrets of the two first symbolical degrees under this rite are in reverse of those adopted by the Grand Lodge, or Supreme Council of the Ancient and Accepted Rite, of France, in which the practice is the same as in our own Grand Lodge. In the Third Degree the Lodge has a very solemn appearance, being hung with black drapery, and displaying many sombre and awe-inspiring emblems. The Master is designated *Très Respectable* (Very Worshipful), and the members Venerable Masters; all the brethren appear covered. In the Fourth Degree there are three chambers—the Room of Preparation, the Council Chamber, and the Cavern. The lesson inculcated in this degree is intended forcibly to imprint on the mind of its recipient the certainty with which punishment will follow crime. The Fifth Degree requires also three chambers, the second of which is most elaborately furnished and decorated with various Masonic attributes; in the east is a triangular pedestal, on which is placed the cubical stone; in the centre of the chamber is a column, and by it a table, having upon it the corn, wine, and oil; and in the north is a sacrificial altar. The Lodge is illuminated by twenty-seven lights, in three groups of nine each; it represents the Temple completed, and its whole appearance is most gorgeous. The Lodge is denominated Sublime; the presiding officer is *Très Grand* (Very Great), and the brethren are Sublime Masters. In this degree the passwords correspond with those of our Royal Arch installation. The Sixth Degree also requires three chambers; the second, which is called the Hall of the East, represents the council of Cyrus at Babylon, and is described—in somewhat inconsistent terms—as being composed of that prince, seven principal officers, and other *knights*. The decoration is green, and requires many lights. Behind the throne is a transparency, representing the vision of Cyrus, in which he received the injunction, "Restore liberty to the captives." The candidate, in passing from the second to the third chamber, has to cross a bridge of timber over a stream choked with corpses and rubbish; and having at length arrived at the last, or western chamber, he perceives the Masons reposing among the ruins of Jerusalem. The room is hung with red, and illuminated by ten groups of candles of seven each. In the centre is the representation of the ruined Temple. The Sovereign Master represents Cyrus; the chief Officer, Daniel the Prophet. The badge is of white satin, bordered with green; the sash, of water green, is worn from left to right; the jewel is the triple triangle, crossed by two swords. The Seventh Degree is precisely our own Eighteenth Degree[1].

A rite, slightly differing from the preceding, and called the *Ancient Reformed Rite,* we are told, is now practised in Holland and Belgium.

ELECTED COHENS.

The *Rite of Elected Cohens,* or *Priests,* was founded some time between 1754 and 1760 by Martinez Paschalis, by whom it was introduced into the Lodges of Bordeaux, Marseilles, and Toulouse. Of its principles very little is known, but it is said to have been divided into two classes; in the first of which was represented the fall of man from virtue and happiness, and in the second his final restoration. It consisted of nine degrees:—Entered Apprentice, Fellow-Craft, Master Mason, Grand Elect, Apprentice Cohen, Fellow-Craft Cohen, Master Cohen, Grand

[1] Ragon, in his "Cours Philosophique," says the symbolism of this rite is entirely astronomical. This is erroneous, as the first six degrees have all reference to the Old Testament history; the Rose-Croix being identical with the Ancient and Accepted Rite.

Architect, and Knight Commander. Clavel tells us this rite was rather popular among the *littérateurs* of Paris for a short time, but it has now ceased to exist.

MARTINISM.

The *Rite of St. Martin,* or *Martinism,* was instituted by the Marquis de St. Martin, a disciple of Paschalis, some time after—of whose system it was said to be a reform. There were in this novelty two classes, embodying ten degrees; after the three first degrees followed the First Temple, as it was termed by De St. Martin, comprising those of Ancient Master, Elect, Grand Architect, and Master of the Secret. The degrees of the Second Temple were Prince of Jerusalem, Knight of Palestine, and Knight Kadosh. It was first brought out at Lyons, but in time extended to the principal cities of France and Germany. This rite most likely perished when all the Continental Lodges were closed, during the panic produced by the French Revolution.

COUNCIL OF EMPERORS OF THE EAST AND WEST.

Under this pompous name was established, about 1758, in Paris, an authoritative body, the members of which at first assumed the titles of "Sovereign Prince Masters, Substitutes General of the Royal Art, Grand Superintendents and Officers of the Grand and Sovereign Lodge of St. John of Jerusalem." Ragon, in his "*Orthodoxie Maçonnique,*" asserts that this is the parent of the Ancient and Accepted Rite, which was established by Frederick II. at Berlin in the same year. This rite had twenty-five degrees, the first nineteen being the same as the Ancient and Accepted Rite, the others being—Grand Patriarch, Noachite, Key of Masonry, Prince of Lebanon, Knight of the Sun, Kadosh, and Prince of the Royal Secret. In the year in which it was formed, the degrees and their ritual were adopted by the Grand Lodge of the Three Globes in Berlin.

The Ancient and Accepted Rite has superseded the practice of this rite in France and Germany.

ELECT OF TRUTH.

Elect of Truth, or *Lodge of Perfect Union,* was the name given to a rite adopted in a Lodge at Rennes in France, and for a time extended to other cities. It was divided into three classes, which contained fourteen degrees; the first class comprising the Entered Apprentice, Fellow-Craft, Master, and Perfect Master; the second, the Elect of Nine, Elect of Fifteen, Master Elect, Minor Architect, Second Architect, Grand Architect, Knight of the East, Rose-Croix; and the third class, the Knight Adept and Elect of Truth. This rite has ceased to exist.

PHILOSOPHIC SCOTCH RITE.

The *Philosophic Scotch Rite* was established in Paris, and adopted by the Grand Lodge in 1776. Some few years previously a Mason named Pernetti founded a rite, to which he gave the name of "*Hermetic,* or *Sublime Masters of the Luminous Ring,*" the object of the contriver being to instruct his disciples, not only in the higher degrees of Masonry, but also in the art of transmuting metals and preparing the elixir of life. Pernetti had for a pupil a physician named Boileau, who did away with the alchemy, and made it more purely Masonic, and then gave this reformed rite the name above affixed to it. This rite, which Clavel says is still practised in France, has twelve degrees, the three degrees of ancient Craft Masonry being necessary pre-requisites, though they do not form a part of the rite. The degrees are—1, 2, and 3. Knight of the Black Eagle or Rose-Croix, divided into three parts; 4. Knight of the Phœnix; 5. Knight of the Sun; 6. Knight of Iris; 7. Freemason; 8. Knight of the Argonauts; 9. Knight of the Golden Fleece; 10. Grand Inspector, Perfect Initiate; 11. Grand Inspector,

Grand Scotch Mason; 12. Sublime Master of the Luminous Ring. The doctrine taught in this rite was, that Freemasonry was founded by Pythagoras; and the lectures consisted of an explanation of the philosophy and peculiar doctrines of the Samian sage, asserting, for instance, that the symbols he adopted in his secret instruction were chiefly derived from geometry; thus, the right angle was an emblem of morality and justice; the equilateral triangle was a symbol of God, the essence of light and truth; the square referred to the Divine mind; the cube was the symbol of the mind of man after it had been purified by acts of piety and devotion, and thus prepared for mingling with the celestial beings. The point within a circle, and the dodecahedron or figure of twelve sides, were symbols of the universe; the triple triangle was an emblem of health; and the letter Y a representation of the course of human life, in which there were two diverging paths, the one of virtue leading to happiness, and the other of vice conducting to misery. Pythagoras, in pursuit of knowledge, travelled into Chaldea and Egypt, and is said to have been instructed in the sacred lore of the Hebrews, either by the Prophet Ezekiel or Daniel. Dr. Oliver asserts that he was initiated into the Jewish system of Freemasonry, and that "his mysteries were the most perfect approximation to the original science of Freemasonry which could be accomplished by a philosopher bereft of the aid of revelation." Jamblicus relates, as evidence of their brotherly love and of their means of mutual recognition, the following incident:—A Pythagorean travelling in a distant country, fell sick and died at a public inn. Previously, however, to his death, being unable to compensate the landlord for the kindness and attention with which he had been treated, he directed a tablet, on which he had traced some enigmatical characters, to be exposed on the public road. Some time after another disciple of Pythagoras passed that way, perceived the tablet, and learning from the inscription that a brother had been there sick and in distress, and that he had been treated with kindness, he stopped and reimbursed the innkeeper for his trouble and expense.

AFRICAN ARCHITECTS.

The Order of *African Architects* was established by a Prussian named Baucherren, with the sanction of Frederick II. It was divided into two temples, having eleven degrees. The first temple contained the three symbolic degrees; in the second temple were—Apprentice of Egyptian Secrets, Initiate in the Egyptian Secrets, Cosmopolitan Brother, Christian Philosopher, Master of Egyptian Secrets, Esquire, Soldier, Knight. The object of the institution was historical research, and the ritual was not confined to Masonry, but contained allusions to the mysteries of Christianity, and to the pursuits of alchemy and chivalry. Ragon tells us that the society possessed a large mansion for the Grand Chapter of the Order; this had an extensive library, a museum of natural history, and a perfect chemical laboratory. In their assemblies they read essays and communicated the results of their researches. They emulated the philosophers of Greece in their simple and decorous banquets, at which instructive discourses were delivered; and much affected sententious apothegms, whose meaning was sublime but concealed. The society for some years annually decreed a gold medal, with the sum of fifty ducats, for the best memoir on the history of Masonry; many of these documents have been published, and some are of value.

RITE OF PHILALETHES.

The *Rite of the Philalethes,* or *Searchers after truth,* which was a compound of the reveries of Swedenborg and Paschalis, is said to have been invented by Salvalette de Langes, keeper of the royal treasury, and was first adopted in the Lodge of *Amis Réunis* at Paris, about the year 1775. It consisted of twelve degrees, viz.:—Apprentice, Fellow-Craft, Master, Elect, Scotch Master, Knight of the East, Rose-Croix, Knight of the Temple, Unknown Philosopher, Sublime Philosopher, Initiated, and Philalethes, or Searcher after Truth. At the death of the founder of the rite, the Lodge of *Amis Réunis* was dissolved; and the rite, not having extended further, ceased to exist. An attempt to revive a rite bearing this name was recently made in London.

ILLUMINATI OF AVIGNON.

The *Illuminati of Avignon* was a species of Masonry intermingled with the reveries of Swedenborg, somewhere about the year 1760, by Pernetti (who was a Benedictine monk), and the Baron Gabrianca, a Polish nobleman. Very little is known of the institution, and it might have been forgotten but for the Marquis de Thomé, in 1783, taking up the system that had been adopted in the Avignon Lodge, and from it framing what is now known as—

SWEDENBORG'S RITE.

The *Rite of Swedenborg* had the six grades of Apprentice, Fellow-Craft, Master Theosophite, Illuminated Theosophite, Blue Brother, and Red Brother. It is said that this rite is still practised in some Lodges in Sweden. Rosetti, in his "Essay on the Anti-papal Spirit of Secret Societies," asserts that an expert Mason would find much of the institution of Freemasonry in the writings of Swedenborg; but excepting some principles general to Christians as well as Masons, we ourselves have not been able to discover any thing to show that Swedenborg was a Freemason. Swedenborg, for fifty-eight years of his life, devoted himself to the cultivation of science, and produced a great number of works, in which he broached some novel and ingenious theories, one of which consists in applying positive science to all; for instance, one of his rather incomprehensible rules runs thus:

—"The beginning of nature is the same as the beginning of geometry: thus natural particles arise from mathematical points, precisely as the lines and forms of geometry; and this, because every thing in nature is geometric." His scientific labours are forgotten, but his theological labours, which occupied the latter part of his life, resulted in the establishment of a sect, or new church, designated by his name, in England, the United States, Sweden, and Germany. He was a most methodical man, and laid down these rules for the guidance of his life:—1. Often to read and meditate upon the Word of God. 2. To submit every thing to the will of Divine Providence. 3. To observe in every thing a propriety of behaviour, and always to keep the conscience clear. 4. To discharge with fidelity the functions of his employment, and the duties of his office, and to render himself in all things useful to society. The tenets inculcated in his writings and adopted by his followers are—1. There is one God: that there is in Him a Divine Trinity, and that He is the Lord and Saviour Jesus Christ. 2. That having faith consists in believing in Him. 3. That evil actions ought not to be done, because they are of the devil and from the devil. 4. That good actions ought to be done, because they are of God and from God. 5. And that they should be done by man himself, as of himself; nevertheless, under the belief that they are from the Lord, operating in him and by him. This is all very good; but we are led to suppose that it was Swedenborg's reveries concerning angels and celestial visions that were transformed into the rites we have alluded to—and with these Masonry can have no connexion.

RITE OF ZINNENDORFF.

The *Rite of Zinnendorff* was a modification of the Illuminism of Avignon, with additions from the Swedenborgian, and combining also several selections from the Scotch and other rites. Its promulgator, Count Zinnendorff, was the chief physician to the Emperor Charles VI. The system consisted of seven degrees, divided into three sections, the first of which is entitled St. John's Masonry, and comprises, 1. Entered Apprentice; 2. Fellow-Craft; 3. Master Mason. The second section, or Red Masonry, contains the Scotch Apprentice, and Fellow-Craft, and the Scotch Master; while the third, called Capitular Masonry, embraces the Favourite of St. John, and Elected Brother.

REFORMED RITE.

The *Reformed Rite* was an emendation of the "Rite of Strict Observance," rejecting the connexion which the latter rite had with the Knights Templar; and was established by an assembly of Masons who met at Wilhelmsbad, under Ferdinand, Duke of Brunswick, in the year 1782, assuming in the first instance the title of the "Order of Charitable Knights of the Holy City." M. de St. Martin's system was merged in this; and Clavel says, the Lodges that had adopted Martinism, adopted the Reformed Rite. Novelties charm the gay and versatile French, and the rite soon spread over the country. Clavel further states it to be in practice in France and Switzerland. The rite had what were called five degrees, but as the last had three sections, there were really seven in all: Apprentice, Fellow-Craft, Master, Scotch Master, Charitable Knight of the Holy City; the three sections of the last were named—Novice, Professed Brother, and Knight.

REFORMED HELVETIC RITE.

The *Reformed Helvetic Rite* was the name given to the preceding rite, when introduced into Poland in 1784, by Brother Glayre, of Lausanne (minister of state to Stanislaus, King of Poland), who had been the Provincial Grand Master of this rite in Switzerland. Clavel says, that several alterations were made in the rite, and hence the addition to its name. The Grand Orient of Poland adopted it.

TRUE MASONS.

The *Order of the True Masons,* which was an offshoot of the "Hermetic Rite" of Pernetti, was formed at Montpelier, in France, in 1778, by Pernetti's pupil, Boileau. This rite had six degrees beyond the three symbolic degrees of ancient Craft Masonry, which were essential for admission, but not practised. The degrees were—The True Mason; The True Mason in the Right Way; Knight of the Golden Key; Knight of the Rainbow; Knight of the Argonauts; and Knight of the Golden Fleece.

ADONIRAMITE.

Adoniramite Masonry was a rite established in France shortly before the Revolution. The exact date of its rise, and the name of its founder, we are unable to learn. It consisted of twelve degrees, of which, four—the sixth, seventh, eighth, and ninth—are peculiar to this rite; the others correspond with those of the same name in the Ancient and Accepted Rite. The degrees are—Entered Apprentice, Fellow-Craft, Master Mason, Perfect Master, Elect of Nine, Elect of Perignan, Minor Architect or Scotch Apprentice, Grand Architect or Scotch Fellow-Craft, Scotch Master, Knight of the East, Rose-Croix Knight, and Prussian Knight.

FESSLER'S RITE.

It is well known that during the panic created by the French Revolution, Masonry, as well as most other beneficent institutions, declined, and the Lodges were generally closed, and only met occasionally under circumstances of great difficulty; but so soon as order was restored and Masonry began to revive, Professor Fessler, Grand Master of the Grand Lodge "Royal York of Friendship," at Berlin, revised the statutes and regulated the proceedings of the Lodges under his jurisdiction. He also created, or perhaps more properly speaking, selected, nine degrees for this rite; they were—Entered Apprentice, Fellow-Craft, Master, Holy of Holies, Justification, Celebration, Knight of the Passage, Fatherland, and Perfection. The ritual was drawn from the "Golden Rose-Croix," the "Strict Observance," and the "Chapter of Clermont." Clavel says, it was the most abstrusely learned and philosophical of all the degrees in Masonry. It was abandoned with the intention of bringing the Ancient York Rite into unison with the Constitutions of England. We may here remark, that degrees in Prussia are not passed through with the same rapidity as in some other countries—twelve months at least being requisite between each of the symbolic degrees.

RITE OF MIZRAIM.

The *Rite of Mizraim* was first promulgated in Italy, we believe at Milan, in 1805, and was said to have been brought from Egypt by a learned philosopher of that country, named Ananiah. It is said that its founders were some Masons who had been refused admission into the Supreme Council of the Scotch Rite then organized in Milan. It was established in France in 1814, and is continued in some Lodges in Paris at the present time, but the Grand Orient of France has never recognized it. It consists of ninety degrees, which are divided into four series—symbolic, philosophic, mystical, and cabalistic; and in each series are seventeen classes. The names of the degrees, in this more than any other of the rites, prove that the founders must have sorely tested their inventive faculties. They appear indeed to have been driven to their wit's end, for the forty-ninth and fiftieth bear the very expressive titles of "Chaos the First and Second," while the fifty-second rejoices in the somewhat profane designation of "Supreme Commander of the Stars!" At the fifty-fifth and fifty-sixth the comic element predominates; they are the "Washer and Bellows-blower!" Many of the degrees pretend to be founded upon and borrowed from the rites of ancient Egypt, but allowing that the rite may have in many degrees an eminently philosophical character, it is altogether too complicated and diffused ever to be practised. One of its chiefs, Marc Bedarride, in 1835 published an elaborate work, exponent of its principles, under the title of "De l'Ordre Maçonnique de Mizraim," from which we learn that the legend of the Third Degree is abolished in this rite. H. A. B. is said to have returned to his family, after the completion of the Temple, and to have passed the remainder of his days in peace and opulence. The legend substituted for that admitted by all the other rites, is carried back to the days of Lamech, whose son Jubal, under the name of Hario-Jubal-Abi, is reported to have been slain by three traitors, Hagava, Hakima, and Haremda!!

GRAND LODGE OF BERLIN.

The *Rite of the Grand Lodge of the Three Globes of Berlin.* In his "Historical Landmarks," Brother Oliver says, "At this time, (about 1775,) the increasing innovations," as our account of these varied rites shows, "covered pure Masonry with disgrace; and with a view of applying a remedy, Lord Petre, the English Grand Master (from 1772 to 1777), entered into a negotiation with the Prince of Hesse Darmstadt, Grand Master of Germany, which resulted in a mutual compact being formed, which confirmed to the Grand Lodge at Berlin the sole authority in Germany; thus annihilating the 'Strict Observance' of Baron Hunde. This compact was further confirmed by the King of Prussia, who erected the Grand Lodge at Berlin into a body corporate." The three ancient symbolic degrees are under the control of the Grand Lodge, but the higher degrees— seven only being practised—are governed by the Internal Supreme Orient, which council is appointed by the Grand Lodge. This rite is not exclusively practised in Prussia, but also to a very great extent throughout Germany.

PERSIAN RITE.

The *Persian Philosophic Rite* was formed in France about the year 1819. It was not much encouraged, and has now ceased to exist. Little is known of its ritual, and whether the three symbolic degrees were essential to its members, or whether they are included in the fanciful names of the degrees adopted, we are unable to learn. It consisted of the seven degrees that follow:—1. Listening Apprentice; 2. Fellow-Craft Adept, Esquire of Benevolence; 3. Master, Knight of the Sun; 4. Architect of all Rites, Knight of the Philosophy of the Heart; 5. Knight of Eclecticism and of Truth; 6. Master, Good Shepherd; 7. Venerable Grand Elect.

THE TEMPLE.

At what period the rite of the *Order of the Temple* was formed, Clavel, from whom we gather our account, does not say, but it appears that its members claim for the institution a regular descent from the Knights Templar. The degrees are evidently borrowed from the Scotch Rite, and were originally as follow:—Apprentice, Fellow-Craft Master, Master of the East, Master of the Black Eagle of St. John, and Perfect Master of the Pelican. But in 1808, as our author says (endeavouring to disguise its evident Masonic origin), it was re-organized, and the degrees, eight in number, were thus named: 1. Initiate (this is E.A.); 2. Initiate of the Interior (this is the F.C.); 3. Adept (this is the Master); 4. Adept of the East (the Illustrious Elected of Fifteen of the Scotch Rite); 5. Grand Adept of the Black Eagle of St. John (the Elected Knight of Nine)—these they call the House of Initiation. 6. Postulant of the Orders (Perfect Adept of the Pelican)—this is called the House of Postulance, and is the Rose-Croix of the Scotch Rite. 7. Esquire; 8. Knight or Levite of the Interior Guard—these last degrees are called the Covenant, and are the same as the Knight K.H. of the Scotch Rite.

ORDER OF CHARLES XII.

Although, properly, it does not directly bear upon the subject we have in hand, still, as a solitary instance of the honours paid to distinguished Masons by a sovereign in modern times, we must notice the *Order of Charles XII.*—an order of knighthood instituted by the King of Sweden in 1811, which he intended to be conferred only on the principal dignitaries of the Masonic institution in his dominions. In the manifesto establishing the Order, the King decrees:—"To give to this (the Masonic) society a proof of our gracious sentiments towards it, we will and ordain, that its first dignitaries, to the number which we may determine, shall, in future, be decorated with the most intimate proof of our confidence, and which shall be for them a distinctive mark of the highest dignity." The number of Knights in the Order is twenty-seven, all Masons, and the King of Sweden is the perpetual Grand Master.

RITE OF MEMPHIS.

The *Rite of Memphis* was established in Paris, in 1839, by Brothers J. A. Marconis and E. A. Moutet, and extended itself to Marseilles and Brussels. It is said to have been a variation of the Rite of Mizraim, and was composed of ninety-one degrees.

THE MOPSES.

The *Mopses,* which name, from the German "*mops,*" signifies a young mastiff, is intended to indicate the mutual fidelity and attachment of the brethren—those virtues being characteristic of the noble animal. This Order originated in the following manner. In 1738, Pope Clement XII. issued a bull, condemning and forbidding the practice of the rites of Masonry. Several brethren in the Catholic States of Germany, unwilling to renounce the Order, yet fearful of offending the ecclesiastical authority, formed, in 1740, under the above name, what was pretended to be a new institution, devoted to the papal hierarchy, but which was, in truth, nothing else than Freemasonry under a less offensive appellation. It was patronized by the most illustrious persons in Germany, and many of the princes of the empire were its Grand Masters.

THE ROYAL ORDER OF HEREDOM AND ROSY CROSS,

said to have been founded by King Robert Bruce at Kilwinning. After the battle of Bannockburn, on the 24th of June, 1314, the King created the Order of St. Andrew of the Thistle, to which was afterwards united that of Heredom, for the sake of the Masons who formed a part of his troops. The King established the Royal Grand Lodge of Heredom at Kilwinning, reserving to himself and his successors the office of Grand Master. This Order is, we believe, entirely confined to Scotland, and is given only to those who, by exaltation or affiliation, are registered in the books of the Grand Chapter of Royal Arch Masons. The historical tradition relates, that after the dissolution of the Templar Order, several of the Knights placed themselves under the protection of Bruce, and greatly contributed to gain the victory of Bannockburn; these were the Masons, it is said, for whom he instituted the Order of Heredom. All Masonry declined during the sixteenth and seventeenth centuries, and this Order was in abeyance until the middle of the last century, when its functions were resumed at Edinburgh. In order to preserve a marked distinction between the Royal Order and Craft Masonry, which had formed a Grand Lodge in that city in 1736, the former confined itself entirely to the two degrees of Heredom and Rosy Cross. Dr. Oliver says, the Heredom was not originally Masonic, but appears to have been connected with some ceremonies of the early Christians, which are believed to have been introduced by the Culdees, whose principal seat was at I-Colm-Kill, during the second and third centuries of the Christian era. The Rosy Cross, which in French was termed the *Grade de la Tour,* is honorary, the tradition being that it was an order of knighthood first conferred on the field of Bannockburn.

The *Swedish Rite,* or that practised by the sanction of the

Grand Lodge of Sweden, consists of twelve degrees, the fifth of which, we are told, confers upon its possessor the rank of nobility in the state. The degrees are—Apprentice; Fellow-Craft; Master; Apprentice and Fellow-Craft of St. Andrew; Master of St. Andrew; Brother Stuart; Favourite Brother of Solomon; Favourite Brother of St. John, or White Ribbon; Favourite Brother of St. Andrew, or Violet Ribbon; Member of the Chapter; Dignitary of the Chapter; and Reigning Grand Master.

SCHRÖEDER'S RITE,

which is said to be still practised at Hamburgh, was invented by a person of that name, and besides the three degrees of ancient Craft Masonry, had many others containing a mixture of alchemy, magic, and theosophy. It was first practised in a Lodge at Sarreburg.

THE PRIMITIVE RITE OF NARBONNE

was established in that city in 1780. The degrees were selected from other rites, and were chiefly of a philosophical character, assuming as their object the reformation of intellectual man, and his restoration to his primitive rank of purity and perfection.

The *Frères Pontives* were a community of operative and speculative Masons, who, as a religious house of brotherhood, established themselves at Avignon, at the close of the twelfth century; they devoted themselves, as the name denotes, to the construction and repair of stone bridges. It is on record, that the community existed as late as 1590; John de Medicis, who was Master in 1560, may perhaps have been a son of Cosmo, Duke of Florence, who died 1562, and was made a cardinal shortly before.

THE ORDER OF MUSTARD SEED,

or "The Fraternity of Moravian Brothers of the Order of Religious Freemasons," was instituted in Germany in 1739. Its mysteries were founded on the parable in St. Mark's gospel, where our Lord said, "Whereunto shall we liken the kingdom of God;

or with what comparison shall we compare it? It is like a grain of mustard seed, which, when it is sown in the earth, is less than all the seeds that be in the earth: but when it is sown, it groweth up, and becometh greater than all herbs, and shooteth out great branches: so that the fowls of the air may lodge under the shadow of it." The description which our Lord has given of the mustard tree occasioned much conjecture, and Lightfoot cites a passage from the Talmud, in which a mustard tree is said to have been possessed of branches sufficiently large to cover a tent, while Scheuchzer describes and represents a species of the plant several feet high, and possessing a tree-like appearance. The jewel of the order, suspended from a green ribbon, was a cross of gold surmounted by a mustard plant, with the words, "What was it before? Nothing!" The brethren wore a ring on which was inscribed, "No one lives for himself."

KNIGHT OF MALTA,

as a Masonic grade, was an appendant to that of the Knights Templar, and in this country never existed as a separate degree. It is now disused.

COUNCIL OF THE TRINITY.

It is said in Mackay's Lexicon to be an independent Masonic jurisdiction, in which are conferred the degrees, I. of Knight of the Christian Mark and Guard of the Conclave; II. Knight of the Holy Sepulchre; and III. The Holy and Thrice Illustrious Order of the Holy Cross. They are, as it will be readily seen, all Christian degrees, and conferred only on Knights Templar. I. This degree is said to have been organized by Pope Alexander IV. (who authorized the distinguishing attire of the Knights to be a red tunic with a white cross), for the defence of his person, selecting for the purpose a body of Knights of St. John. The officers are an Invincible Knight, Senior and Junior Knights, Recorder, Treasurer, Conductor, and Guard. The ritual is composed from passages in the books of Ezekiel and Jeremiah. The jewel is a triangular plate of gold, with the letter G within a five-pointed star. II. This degree was instituted by St. Helena, the mother of Constantine, A.D. 326, when, on her visit to Jerusalem, she is said to have discovered the true cross. During the war of the Crusades, the Knights of the Holy Sepulchre were eminent for their valour. Upon the loss of the Holy Land they took refuge in Perugia, and afterwards were incorporated with the Knights of Rhodes. Curzon, in his "Visits to the Mountains in the Levant," says, "The order is still continued in Jerusalem, but conferred only on Roman Catholics of noble birth, by the superior of the Franciscan College, and that the accolade is bestowed with the sword of Godfrey de Bouillon, which, with his spurs, is preserved in the sacristy of the Church of the Holy Sepulchre." The presiding officer in America is called the Right Reverend Prelate. The whole ceremonial has reference to death. III. This, we presume, is the governing council.

Order of High Priesthood. In the old ceremonial of the Royal Arch in England, the government was vested in the *Three Chiefs,*—High Priest, King, and Prophet,—and this form is preserved in the United States. An honorary degree was conferred on the retiring first officer, as we now confer one on the Past First Principal. When the ritual was performed in ample form, the presence of nine High Priests was required.

ROSAIC RITE

was the name given by its institutor, M. Rosa, a Lutheran minister in Germany. It was for a short time highly patronized and exceedingly popular, but was superseded by the Rite of Strict Observance. We have no information as to the ritual or practice.

BAHRDT'S RITE.

At the close of the last century Bahrdt opened a Lodge at Halle in Saxony, under the name of the "German Union," and succeeded in securing the protection of the Prince of Anhaldt-Bernburg, and the co-operation of twenty persons of rank. The rite had six degrees, viz., the Youth, the Man, the Old Man, the Mesopolyte, the Diocesan, and the Superior. The Grand Lodge of the State, however, dissolved the fraternity.

KNIGHTS AND LADIES OF THE DOVE.

In the year 1784 a secret society of both sexes was framed on the model of Freemasonry; its meetings were held at Versailles under the title of *Chevaliers et Chevalières de la Colombe.* Its existence, we believe, was of brief duration.

The Baron de Knigge, in 1783, established at Frankfort an order or rite which he called *Eclectic Masonry,* having for its object the abolition of the high grades or philosophical degrees. Hence Eclectic Masonry only acknowledged the three symbolic degrees, but permitted any Lodge to select at its option any of the higher degrees, provided they did not interfere with the uniformity of the first three. It is clear the Baron did not succeed in his endeavours, as the degrees he reprobated are in high estimation, and nothing is heard now of his system.

GRAND CHAPTER OF HARODIM,

an institution revived (it is supposed, by Brother Preston) in 1787. He says, "Though this order is of ancient date, and had been patronized in different parts of Europe, there appears not on record, previously to this period, the regular establishment of such an association in England. For some years it was faintly encouraged, but after its merit had been further investigated, it received the patronage of several exalted Masonic characters. The Grand Chapter is governed by a Grand Patron, two Vice-Patrons, a Chief Ruler or Harod, and two Assistants, with a Council of Twelve Companions. It was a school of instruction, organized upon a peculiar plan, and the lectures were divided into sections, and the sections into clauses. Its teaching embodied the whole art of Masonry."

KNIGHT OF THE RED CROSS.

A Masonic degree so named is continued in the United States of America. No record of its existence in England can be traced, and if it ever was conferred in this country, it was no doubt one of the many degrees united under that of the Knights Templar. The legend is similar to that of the Fifteenth Degree of the Ancient and Accepted Rite.

KNIGHT OF THE MEDITERRANEAN PASS

was an honorary degree conferred on Knights Templar as Knights of Malta, under the old constitution. The degree is said to have originated from the following circumstance. In an excursion of the Knights of Malta into the kingdom of Naples, while crossing the river Offanto (the ancient Aufidus), they were attacked by a very superior force of Turks. However, notwithstanding the disparity of numbers, the Knights succeeded in obtaining a complete victory, the Moslems being entirely routed, and the river dyed with their blood. As a reward for the valour displayed by these Knights, they had granted to them free permission to pass and repass at every port in the Mediterranean in possession of the Christians. The legend of the degree relates that this event occurred in 1367, nearly 200 years before the Knights of St. John, or Rhodes as then called, obtained Malta. At this period the Knights, headed by the Grand Master Raymond Berenger, with a large naval force attacked the Ottoman corsairs in the Mediterranean and chased them into the port of Alexandria, but were compelled at last to retire before the superior force of the Sultan of Egypt.

KNIGHT OF CONSTANTINOPLE

is a side degree invented in America. We are told it can be conferred by any Master Mason who is possessed of its secrets on another, but there is a ritual for the full performance of the degree, though seldom used.

KNIGHTS AND NYMPHS OF THE ROSE

was an order of Adoptive or Androgynous Masonry, invented towards the close of the eighteenth century by M. de Chaumont, the Masonic Secretary to the Duc de Chartres. The only establishment known was in Paris; the place of meeting was called the Temple of Love. It was ornamented with garlands of flowers, and hung round with escutcheons, on which were painted various devices and scenes of gallantry. There were two presiding officers, the man being styled the Hierophant, the female the High Priestess. The former initiated men, the latter women. The Conductor Assistant of the men was called Sentiment, that of the women Discretion. The Knights wore a crown of myrtle, the Nymphs a crown of roses. The Hierophant and High Priestess wore in addition a rose-coloured scarf, on which were embroidered two devices within a myrtle wreath. One dull taper was the only light during the initiation; at the closing business the hall was illuminated by numerous wax candles. When a candidate was to be initiated, he or she was taken in charge by Sentiment or Discretion, divested of all weapons, jewels, or money, hoodwinked, and loaded with chains, and conducted to the door of the Temple of Love, where admission was demanded by two knocks. When admitted and presented, the candidate was asked his or her name, country, condition in society, and having answered these questions was asked, "What are you now seeking?" to this the answer was, "Happiness." The interrogatory then proceeds a little further, "What is your age?" and the candidate has, if a male, to reply, "The age to love;" the female, "The age to please and to be loved." The candidate's feelings and opinions on matters of gallantry are further probed, and all being satisfactory, the chains are removed and replaced by garlands of flowers, which are called "the chains of love." After some other probationary exercises of a like character, the O B is administered: "I promise and swear by the Grand Master of the Universe never to reveal the secrets of the Order of the Rose, and should I fail in this my vow, may the mysteries I shall receive add nothing to my pleasures, and instead of the roses of happiness may I find nothing but thorns of repentance." The candidates were then conducted to the mysterious groves in the neighbourhood of the Temple of Love, and during the time there spent, slow and delicious music in march style is played. These trials ended, the novice is next conducted to the altar of mystery, placed at the foot of the Hierophant's throne, and there incense is offered to Venus and her son Cupid: a brief space spent there, and after some more ceremonies of a like character, the bandage is removed from the novitiate's eyes, and with delicious music and in a brilliantly lighted apartment, the signs and secrets are communicated.

All the information here given is gathered from Clavel, "Maçonnique Picturesque."

ROMAN EAGLE.

A LATIN LODGE was in 1784 organized by Dr. John Brown, of Edinburgh, under the title of the *Roman Eagle Lodge,* the whole ritual being in Latin. It had a brief existence.

ADOPTIVE MASONRY.

The Masonry of Adoption is the term used in France for a system of Masonry for Women. It would appear that the perfection of character which their husbands had reached, excited a desire in the breasts of some of the other sex to obtain a knowledge of the foundation of Freemasonry.

Those who are admitted bear the appellation of Sisters. The Order contains five grades, which are the Apprentice, Companion, and Mistress; these are obligatory;—the others are called high grades, High Mistress and Sublime Scottish.

As we might expect, the garden of Paradise, with our first parents and the tempter, are prominent illustrations, and the dreadful punishment our mother Eve inflicted on her posterity by giving way to curiosity is the first lesson. EVE is the password throughout, and BALBA (Babel), which signifies confusion, is not inappropriate to this mixture of brothers and sisters. The third degree embraces a vast portion of Scripture History, the whole of the events recorded in the book of Genesis, after the subsidence of the waters of the deluge, being brought to view. The prominent vices of both sexes are dilated on, even to a reference to the crimes which drew down the vengeance of the Most High on Sodom, Lot's wife not being forgotten, of course to read another lesson to the ladies on the evils of curiosity. Joseph's adventures are related in the examination, but the part played by Potiphar's wife appears unaccountably to be omitted, we suppose because it tells unfavourably to the ladies. Balls and banquets are inseparable from these associations, and they are no doubt the real design of the organization, the ceremonies being merely a pretext.

We are told that, when first organized in France, the institution was acknowledged by the Masonic authorities of the kingdom. The first Lodge, "La Candeur," was opened in Paris on the 11th of March, 1785, a Marquis being the President, and a Duchess acting as Grand Mistress: in the same year the Duchess of Bourbon was installed as Grand Mistress. The Revolution of course checked this as well as other associations, but in 1805 there was a revival, and the Empress Josephine presided over the "Lodge Impériale d'Adoption des Francs Chevaliers," at Strasburg.

ARK DEGREES.

Ark and Dove, and *Ark Mariners,* were degrees in some practice in London during the present century. Their names imply that they have a reference to the salvation of Noah and his family from the deluge. They bore much similitude to the Noachite in the Ancient and Accepted Rite.

MASONIC BAPTISM.

Although we have rites and ceremonies sufficient to task the powers of memory in the best constructed brain, our continental brethren are ever at work to contrive some novelty for the Masonic institution. In France has been instituted an order for the Baptism of the sons of Masons, which has been also adopted by the *Foyer Maçonnique* Lodge in New Orleans, and the first opening of the proceedings occurred in

1859. The proceedings do not appear to have any very remarkable characteristic. The Sponsors make promises of good order and moral conduct, and the neophyte's left hand is dipped into the water by the W.M. To the mother is given a gold alliance ring with this injunction, "May this ring recall to you, as to us, your future steps in the Masonic temple; always remember what you have seen and heard. Henceforth Masonry can have no secrets for you; you know her laws and obligations; be then satisfied, dear sister, for this name, which it gives us pleasure to bestow on you, makes us feel that there cannot exist true fraternity and happiness unless accompanied by the presence of woman."

THE ILLUMINATI.

About the year 1775 or 1776, Adam Weishaupt, a professor of canon law in the University of Ingolstadt, in Bavaria, in conjunction with a few other men of high position and intellectual attainments, formed a secret society of a more extraordinary character than modern times had ever known. Of this association the most extraordinary accounts have been given at various periods, in which the romantic element has combined with malicious exaggeration to distort the few facts which are really known concerning it. We are told that the design of the institution was to accomplish the overthrow of all civil and religious government—the throne and the altar were equally destined to annihilation, and society was to have been completely disorganized. Weishaupt himself is said, by the opponents of his system, to have been an extreme political reformer, and an infidel. But little is known of this person; the meagre accounts that we have of him have been written under the influence of strong prejudice; and there is great reason to doubt whether he or the society which he established deserved the bad character which has been attached to them.

Freemasonry has been frequently accused of a connexion with the much dreaded, but little known institution of the

Illuminati: and the world at large has been led to believe that the French Revolution, and all the horrors that followed, were, in a great degree, the result of conspiracies hatched under their united auspices.

The idea of connecting his institution with Freemasonry did not exist in Weishaupt's mind at its formation, for it will be seen that the first steps have no Masonic bearing whatever; but it seems that imagining that union with an ancient and honoured institution would be favourable to the promulgation of his scheme, he became a member of a Lodge in Munich, and in a short time his persuasive arguments induced many Masons to enlist into the new Order. He then contrived to interweave the three ancient symbolic degrees with Illuminism, the better by their means to get over the scruples of the more enlightened of those who became his followers. By his adversaries it is said that, as soon as the Masons witnessed the development of his "high degrees," they saw their error, and one and all retreated; while some, who had left the society in disgust at witnessing the disloyal and infidel precepts that were broached, betrayed its principles.

Upon learning the political tenets taught in its assemblies, the Elector of Bavaria ordered a judicial examination into the charges made against the Order, and the result was that the meetings were forbidden, and the society extinguished in his dominions. It, however, spread into other parts of Germany, and was introduced into France in 1787; the state of the public feeling in France at this period was favourable to the tenets of an institution like Illuminism, and it made rapid progress.

Although Professor Robison and others have endeavoured to connect the Illuminati with Freemasonry, certainly no where has it been established that there was ever any specific union or connexion with our noble Order. Events which occurred in France during the fever of the French Revolution cannot be received in evidence, all society and order having been overturned in that convulsion. It is clear that the institution had but a very brief existence in the country of its birth, and that throughout Germany the Masonic Lodges were closed against its founder; indeed several dissolved themselves, as it was said Lodges might by possibility harbour conspirators, and therefore they must remain closed till quieter times.

Weishaupt himself, in recommending his scheme, speaks disparagingly of all Masonry, but says he has contrived a system, "inviting to Christians of every communion, which gradually frees them from all religious prejudices, and which animates them by a great, a feasible, and speedy prospect of universal happiness, in a state of liberty, free from the obstacles which society, rank, and riches continually throw in our way." Certainly Freemasonry teaches nothing of this sort. Doctrines even more alarming to the minds of those who reverence "the right divine for kings to govern wrong," were promulgated in France, and the causes of the Revolution may at this day be traced, not to such institutions as the Illuminati, but to the deplorable corruption of the national morals, and the exhaustion of its resources.

The wasteful wars of Louis XIV., his stupendous public works, the splendid edifices erected by him, and the pomp of his magnificent court, although supported by the most oppressive taxation, had at least the effect of flattering the national vanity; but the wanton prodigality of Louis XV. produced a different result upon the national mind. The habit of lavishing the public money in profligate expenditure was firmly fixed in the court, and the corrupt system of government too deeply rooted to be easily eradicated, and when Louis XVI. ascended the throne he succeeded to an empty treasury and a debt of four millions of livres. The young king's virtuous attempts at reform were opposed by the clergy and noblesse, and at the period of which we are treating, the smouldering fire of public indignation was ready to break into flame.

Accounts of an institution holding tenets like those attributed to the *Illuminés* would naturally increase the alarm of the upper classes, who saw on every hand signs that their days of public plunder were approaching to an end. A work entitled *Essai sur la Secte des Illuminés,* which was published anonymously, but has since been ascertained to have been the production of the Marquis de Luchet, made its appearance in the year 1788; and the pretended disclosures which were therein made increased the prevailing excitement.

The Illuminati, says our author, began by excluding the New Testament, and every reference to Christianity, altogether from their Lodges; no part of their system, however, from his account, appears to bear the slightest resemblance to symbolic Masonry. The sect had two classes, which were subdivided into lesser degrees, their first class containing the following:—Novices; Illuminatus Minor; Illuminatus Major. In the second class were attained the mysteries; this was divided into two degrees, lesser and greater: the lesser comprehended the degrees styled "Priests" and "Regents, or Princes;" in the greater are comprehended those of "Magus" and "Rex." Between these two classes were afterwards interwoven the three symbolic degrees of Masonry, with those of Scotch Novice and Scotch Knight. From the last class were chosen the "elect," who were the supreme council, and the "Areopagites." The operations of the sect depended in every degree on the tact of one single brother, designated the Brother Inquisitor, whose office was to make proselytes, and to prepare the minds of the newly initiated for the part they were intended to act.

It has been said that Illuminism found its way into Britain, but the statement is without foundation, and there is no record of any one of our countrymen having embraced its principles. As all we know of the institution is derived from hostile writers, it is quite possible that Illuminism is wrongly judged.

CHAPTER XXI.

SOLOMON'S TEMPLE; OR, THE HOUSE OF GOD WHICH SOLOMON BUILT AT JERUSALEM.

"Behold the Temple
In undisturbed and lone serenity,
Finding itself a solemn sanctuary
In the profound of heaven! It stands before us
A mount of snow fretted with golden pinnacles!
The very sun, as though he worshipped there,
Lingers upon the gilded cedar roofs;
And down the long and branching porticoes,
On every flowery-sculptured capital,
Glitters the homage of his parting beams."

MILMAN.

OUR traditional history ascribes the foundation of Freemasonry to the building of King Solomon's Temple, or, as it is called in Scripture, "the palace of Jehovah," a designation intended to intimate that its splendour and magnificence were not intended to reflect honour on those engaged in its construction, but only that it should be rendered a fit dwelling for Him who is the "King of kings, and Lord of lords." As the ceremonies and lectures have many allusions to the Temple, a description of the building and its situation is essential to obtaining even a general notion of this remarkable structure. The following account is drawn from the historical books of the Old Testament and other trustworthy sources.

Temple, the house of God, the sanctuary, the tabernacle of the Lord, the palace of the Most High, are terms often used synonymously in Scripture, though, strictly speaking, they import very distinct things. The sanctuary was but one part of the tabernacle, or temple; neither does the word temple describe the tabernacle; nor tabernacle the temple. The Hebrews, before Solomon, could not properly be said to have had a temple, yet they did not scruple by the word temple to describe the tabernacle; as, on the contrary, they sometimes, by the tabernacle of the Lord, expressed the temple built by Solomon.

After the Lord had instructed David that Jerusalem was the place He had chosen, in which to fix his dwelling, that prince began to realize his design of preparing a temple for the Lord, that might be something worthy of his divine majesty. He opened his mind on this subject to the prophet Nathan, but the Lord did not think fit that he should execute his purpose, however laudable. The honour was reserved for Solomon, his son and successor, who was to be a peaceable prince, and not like David, who had shed much blood in war. David, however, applied himself to collect great quantities of gold, silver, brass, iron, and other materials for this undertaking.

When David thought of the temple, his country was at rest, and the ascendancy he had gained greatly favoured the arts of peace and the blessings of civilized society. He looked to his neighbours, the Tyrians, for aid, as a people in possession, not only of architectural skill, but also men capable of constructing buildings. The flourishing state of the Phœnicians at the time of David indicates the growth of ages. In the book of Joshua, 600 years before Solomon's time, Tyre is called "the great city." The Old Testament in many places refers to the extent of their commerce and the wealth of their cities. They traded in timber, iron, copper, tin, glass, and especially in that brilliant dye and those rich fabrics of art which gave them their name, and awakened the songs of poets as they gazed on the sumptuous beauty of court dresses, and the dazzling decorations of thrones. Of this people, in the time of David, Hiram was king.

The two sovereigns formed an alliance on the basis of mutual advantage, and as soon as Hiram heard that Solomon had been anointed king in the room of his father, he sent him an embassy of congratulation. We learn that Solomon sent to Huram (in Kings he is called Hiram, in Chronicles Huram), saying, "As thou didst deal with David my father, and didst send him cedars to build him an house to dwell therein, even so deal with me." (2 Chron. ii. 3.) Solomon agrees to give him corn, wine, and oil in exchange for the services of his men, and the materials he required. At this period there lived at the court of Tyre an artificer of great celebrity, and whose name was the same as that of his royal master, and whom we are accustomed to designate Hiram Abif (an appellative said to mean his counsellor or head workman). This Hiram was a widow's son, his mother being of the tribe of Dan, or, according to some accounts, of Napthali; his father, it is supposed, being a native of Tyre. The preliminary arrangements which Solomon made to carry out the great undertaking on which he had set his heart, appear in his message to the King of Tyre, and in the answer of Hiram, one of the oldest letters on record in the world, in which he assents to Solomon's request.

"Behold, I build an house to the name of the Lord my God, to dedicate it to him, and to burn before him sweet incense, and for the continual shewbread, and for the burnt offerings morning and evening, on the sabbaths, and on the new moons, and on the solemn feasts of the Lord our God. This is an ordinance for ever to Israel. And the house which I build is great: for great is our God above all gods. But who is able to build him an house, seeing the heaven and heaven of heavens cannot contain him? who am I then, that I should build him an house, save only to burn sacrifice before him? Send me now therefore a man cunning to work in gold, and in silver, and in brass, and in iron, and in purple, and crimson, and blue, and that can skill to grave with the cunning men that are with me in Judah and in

Jerusalem, whom David my father did provide. Send me also cedar trees, fir trees, and algum trees, out of Lebanon: for I know that thy servants can skill to cut timber in Lebanon; and, behold, my servants shall be with thy servants, even to prepare me timber in abundance: for the house which I am about to build shall be wonderful great. And, behold, I will give to thy servants, the hewers that cut timber, twenty thousand measures of beaten wheat, and twenty thousand measures of barley, and twenty thousand baths of wine, and twenty thousand baths of oil.

"Then Huram the king of Tyre answered in writing, which he sent to Solomon, Because the Lord hath loved his people, he hath made thee king over them. Huram said moreover, Blessed be the Lord God of Israel, that made heaven and earth, who hath given to David the king a wise son, endued with prudence and understanding, that might build an house for the Lord, and an house for his kingdom. And now I have sent a cunning man, endued with understanding, of Huram my father's, the son of a woman of the daughters of Dan, and his father was a man of Tyre, skilful to work in gold, and in silver, in brass, in iron, in stone, and in timber, in purple, in blue, and in fine linen, and in crimson; also to grave any manner of graving, and to find out every device which shall be put to him, with thy cunning men, and with the cunning men of my lord David thy father. Now therefore the wheat, and the barley, the oil, and the wine, which my lord hath spoken of, let him send unto his servants: and we will cut wood out of Lebanon, as much as thou shalt need: and we will bring it to thee in flotes by sea to Joppa; and thou shalt carry it up to Jerusalem."

The result soon appears. Tens of thousands are busy in the mountains of Lebanon. Stones are hewed, and cedar trees are felled. Ancient Joppa is in motion, for the Tyrian fleet and rafts have passed the Phœnician coast, and rounded the promontory of Carmel; and artisans and cunning workmen of all needful crafts, and the materials on which they will employ their skill, will soon be tossing amid the surf that here rolls violently in from the great sea, and should they land safely after a journey of nearly forty miles, they will find themselves and their burdens near the hallowed spot where they will be employed to aid a more sublime object than Phœnician ever thought of; and in the neighbouring territory Tyrians shall hear the voice of Him to whom Baal and Astarte are an insult and an abomination.

Eastern empires, with all their magnificent resources, have at this time—about a thousand years before Christ—temples, altars, and idols, but the true and living God has no place, save among the Israelites, in the religions and worship of the world.

The place chosen for erecting this magnificent structure was Mount Moriah, the summit of which, originally, was unequal and its sides irregular, but it was an object of ambition with the Jews to level and extend it. This they effected, and during the second temple, it formed a square of 500 cubits, or 304 yards on each side, allowing, as is commonly done, 21.888 inches to the cubit. Almost the whole of this space was arched underground, to prevent the possibility of pollution from secret graves; and it was surrounded by a wall of excellent stone 25 cubits, or 47 feet 7 inches high; without which lay a considerable extent of flat and gently sloping ground, which was occupied by the buildings of the tower of Antonia, gardens, and public walks.

The plan and the whole model of this structure was laid by the same Divine Architect as that of the tabernacle, viz., God Himself; and it was built much in the same form as the tabernacle, but was of much larger dimensions. The utensils for the sacred service were also the same as those used in the tabernacle, only several of them were larger, in proportion to the more spacious edifice to which they belonged. The foundations of this magnificent edifice were laid by Solomon in the year of the world 2992, and it was finished A.M. 3000, having occupied seven years and six months in the building. It was dedicated A.M. 3001, with peculiar solemnity, to the worship of Jehovah, who condescended to make it the place for the special manifestation of his glory. (2 Chron. v. vi. vii.) The front or entrance to the temple was on the eastern side, and consequently facing the Mount of Olives, which commanded a noble prospect of the building; the holy of holies, therefore, stood towards the west. The temple itself, strictly so called, which comprised the portico, the sanctuary, and the holy of holies, formed only a small part of the sacred edifice, these being surrounded by spacious courts, chambers, and other apartments, which were much more extensive than the temple itself.

From the descriptions which are handed down to us of the temple of Solomon, it is utterly impossible to obtain so accurate an idea of its relative parts and their respective proportions, as to furnish such an account as may be deemed satisfactory to the reader. Hence we find no two writers agreeing in their descriptions. The following account may be sufficient to give us a general idea of the building:—

The temple itself was 70 cubits long; the porch being 10 cubits (1 Kings vi. 3), the holy place 40 cubits (ver. 17), and the most holy place 20 cubits (2 Chron. iii. 8). The width of the porch, holy, and most holy places, was 20 cubits (2 Chron. iii. 3), and the height over the holy and most holy places was 30 cubits (1 Kings vi. 2), but the height of the porch was much greater, being no less than 120 cubits (2 Chron. iii. 4), or four times the height of the rest of the building. To the north and south sides, and the west end of the holy and most holy places, or all around the edifice, from the back of the porch on the one side, to the back of the porch on the other side, certain buildings were attached. These were called side chambers, and consisted of three stories, each 5 cubits high (1 Kings vi. 10), and joined to the wall of the temple without. But what may seem singular is, that the lowest of these stories was 5 cubits broad on the floor, the second 6 cubits, and the third 7 cubits, and yet the outer wall of them all was upright (ver. 6). The reason of this was, that the wall of the temple, against which they leaned, had always a scarcement of a cubit at the height of every 5 cubits, to prevent the joists of these side chambers from being fixed in it. Thus the three stories of side chambers, when taken together, were 15 cubits high, and consequently reached exactly to half the height of the side walls, and end of the temple, so that there was abundance of space, above these, for the windows which gave light to the temple (ver. 4). Josephus differs very materially from this in his description, for which we know not how to account, but by supposing that he has confounded the Scripture account of Solomon's temple with that of the temple after the captivity and of Herod.

In noticing the several courts of the temple, we naturally begin with the outer one, which was called *the court of the Gentiles,* and into which persons of all nations were permitted to enter. The most natural approach to this was by the east gate, which was the principal gate of the temple. It was by far the largest of all the courts pertaining to the sacred building, and comprised a space of 188,991 superficial cubits, or 14 English acres, 1 rood, 29 poles, and 13 yards, of which above two-thirds lay to the south of the temple. It was separated from the court of the women by a wall three cubits high, of lattice work, so that persons walking here might see through it, as well as over it. This wall, however, was not on a level with the court of which we are speaking, but was cut out of the rock 6 cubits above it, the ascent to which was by 12 steps. On pillars placed at equal distances in this wall were inscriptions in Greek and Latin, to warn strangers, and such as were unclean, not to proceed further on pain of death. It was from this court that our Saviour drove the persons who had established a cattle-market, for the purpose of supplying those with sacrifices who came from a distance (Matt. xxi. 12, 13).

We must not overlook the beautiful pavement of variegated marble, and the piazzas, or covered walks, with which this court was surrounded. Those on the east, west, and north sides were of the same dimensions, but that on the south was much larger. The porch called *Solomon's* (John x. 23. Acts iii. 11) was on the east side or front of the temple, and was so called because it was built by this prince, upon a high wall of 400 cubits from the valley of Kedron.

The court of the women, called in Scripture *the new court* (2 Chron. xx. 5), *and the outer court* (Ezek. xlvi. 21), was so designated by the Jews, not because none but women were permitted to enter it, but because it was their appointed place of worship, beyond which they might not go, unless when they brought a sacrifice, in which case they went forward to the court of Israel. The gate which led into this court, from that of the Gentiles, was *the beautiful gate* of the temple, mentioned Acts iii. 2, so called, because the folding-doors, lintel, and sideposts, were all overlaid with Corinthian brass. The court itself was 135 cubits square, having four gates, one on each side, and on three of its sides were piazzas, with galleries above them, whence could be seen what was passing in the great court. At the four corners of this court were four rooms, appropriated to different purposes (Ezek. xlvi. 21—24). In the *first* the lepers purified themselves after they were healed; in the *second* the wood for the sacrifices was laid up; the Nazarites prepared their oblations, and shaved their heads, in the *third;* and in the *fourth* the wine and oil for the sacrifices were kept. There were also two rooms more, where the Levites' musical instruments were laid up, and also thirteen treasure chests, two of which were for the half-shekel, which was paid yearly by every Israelite, and the rest for the money for the purchase of sacrifices and other oblations. It was in this court of the women, called the treasury, that our Saviour delivered his striking discourse to the Jews, related in John viii. 1—20. It was into this court, also, that the Pharisee and publican went to pray (Luke xviii. 10—13), and into which the lame man followed Peter and John after he was cured, the court of the women being the ordinary place of worship for those who brought no sacrifice (Acts iii. 8). From thence, after prayers, he went back with them, through the *beautiful gate* of the temple, where he had been lying, and through the sacred fence, into the court of the Gentiles, where, under the eastern piazza, or *Solomon's porch,* Peter delivered that sermon which converted five thousand. It was in the same court of the women that the Jews laid hold of Paul, when they judged him a violator of the temple, by taking Gentiles within the sacred fence (Acts xxi. 26, &c.). In this court the high priest, at the fast of Expiation, read a portion of the law. Here also the king, on the sabbatical year, did the same at the feast of Tabernacles.

The court of Israel was separated from the court of the women by a wall 32½ cubits high on that side, but on the other only 25. The reason of which difference was, that as the rock on which the temple stood always became higher on advancing westward, the several courts naturally became elevated in proportion. The ascent into the court was by a flight of 15 steps, of a semicircular form, on which it is by some thought that the Levites stood and sung the "Psalms of degrees" (cxx.—cxxxiv.), at the feast of Tabernacles. This gate is spoken of under several appellations in the Old Testament, but in the time of our Saviour it was known as the gate Nicanor. It was here the leper stood, to have his atonement made, and his cleansing completed. It was here they tried the suspected wife, by making her drink of the bitter water; and it was here likewise that women appeared after childbirth, for purification. The whole length of the court from east to west was 187 cubits, and the breadth from north to south, 135 cubits. This was divided into two parts; one of which was the court of the Israelites, and the other the court of the priests. The former was a kind of a piazza surrounding the latter, under which the Israelites stood while their sacrifices were burning in the court of the priests. It had 13 gates, with chambers above them, each of which had its particular name and use. The space which was comprised in the court of the priests was 165 cubits long, and 119 cubits wide, and was raised 2½ cubits above the surrounding court, from which it was separated by the pillars which supported the piazza, and the railing which was placed between them (2 Kings xi. 8. 10). Within this court stood the brazen altar on which the sacrifices were consumed, the molten sea, in which the priests washed, and the ten brazen lavers, for washing the sacrifices, also the various utensils and instruments for sacrificing, which are enumerated in 2 Chron. iv.

It is necessary to observe here, that although the court of the priests was not accessible to all Israelites, as that of Israel was to all the priests, yet they might enter it on three several occasions, viz., to lay their hands on the animals which they offered, or to kill them, or to waive some part of them. And then their entrance was not by the east gate, and through the place where the priests stood; but ordinarily by the north or south side of the court, according as the sacrifices were to be slain on the north or south sides of the altar. In general, it was a rule, that they never returned from this court by the same door that they entered (Exod. xlvi. 9). From the court of the priests the ascent to the temple was by a flight of 12 steps, each half a cubit in height, which led into the sacred porch. Of the dimensions of this, as also of the sanctuary and holy of holies, we have already spoken. We shall therefore only observe here, that it was within the door of the porch, and in the sight of those who stood in the courts immediately before it, that the two pillars, *Jachin* and *Boaz,* were placed (2 Chron. iii. 17. Ezek. xl. 49).

The consummate art displayed in the fabrication and enrichment of these remarkable pillars especially demands our notice.

The compiler of the books of Kings says that Hiram, who was "filled with wisdom and understanding to work all works of brass," cast for Solomon "two pillars of brass eighteen cubits high apiece" (1 Kings vii. 15), while the writer of the Chronicles says that "he made two pillars of thirty-five cubits high" (2 Chron. iii. 15). The explanation here is not very doubtful. The Chronicles speak of both the pillars, while the two of 18 cubits each mentioned in the former book would be together 36 cubits: the difference of half a cubit in a column of that height might be swallowed up in the chapiter or base. The whole height, adding the capital of five cubits, according to different authorities, would be 35 or 40 feet. They were adorned with a considerable depth of lily work, and on the projecting part of the capital there were, in several rows, two hundred pomegranates, which, with other beautiful ornaments, crowned the head of each pillar as it rose in majesty before this holy house.

These pillars Solomon ordered to be placed in the porch of the temple; and "he set up the right pillar, and called the name thereof *Jachin;* and he set up the left pillar, and called the name thereof *Boaz."* Although these names have occasioned much dispute, *stability* is the fundamental idea they embody; the two names together form a kind of sentence, as the marginal interpretation reads; or it may be otherwise rendered—*Jachin,* it shall stand,—*Boaz,* in strength. There have been various mystical speculations about these pillars and their names, which it is not necessary here to enter into.

The walls of the temple were covered with fir and cedar; the latter, however, predominating to such a degree that the whole was said to be covered with it. "All was cedar, there was no stone seen" (1 Kings vi. 18). Carvings of plants and flowers beautified the woodwork. A partition separated the oracle from the holy place; it had doors of olive-tree, offering to the eye carvings of cherubims, palm-trees, and open flowers (ver. 32); a curtain suspended by gold rings and chains veiled the interior from the gaze of mortal, and over the central point of its mysterious depth the wings of cherubims met, indicating the care with which the heavenly powers watch over God's covenant and law. In Exod. xxv. we find the command given that two were to be made of pure gold, and overshadow the mercy-seat. The two belonging to the temple were of olive-wood. They were as colossal as some of the Assyrian figures, and there was a squareness about them, each covering a space of 10 cubits, in height and length. The two thus rising either 15 or 17½ feet, having their fore and hind wings extending over an equal portion of the breadth of the chamber, meeting and filling it from side to side (ver. 27), must have had a very imposing appearance. The small engravings we are accustomed to see deceive us in this matter. We must strive to paint it on the mind's eye in order to conceive of it correctly, and spread a canvas of the appropriate size before the imagination.

Near the entrance of the oracle was placed the altar of incense, often called the golden altar. Here also, as in the tabernacle, were the golden candlesticks with seven branches, and the table of shewbread. The light of the holy place was wholly, or mainly, derived from the seventy lights; for it appears there were ten of them made "according to their form," which must mean that given in Exod. xxv., and therefore having three branches on each side of the shaft, thus making with the central light the number we have named. Five of these were placed on the right, and five on the left, before the oracle.

The whole temple of which we have been treating was overlaid with gold in a style of extraordinary magnificence. The accounts given in the history baffle all conception. When the reader has occupied himself with only a small part of the details, he finds himself bewildered with their richness and variety. Nor, in view of the statement that Solomon made gold and silver at Jerusalem as plentiful as stones (2 Chron. i. 15), can we, as some seem disposed to do, suspect the writers of exaggeration.

It is worthy of remark that the building of King Solomon's temple was begun on the 2nd day of the month of Zif, corresponding with the 21st day of April, in the year of the world 2992, or 1012 years before the Christian era, and was completed in little more than seven years, on the 8th day of the month of Bul, or the 23rd of October in the year 2999, during which period no sound of axe, hammer, or other metallic tool was heard, every thing having been cut and framed in the quarries or on Mount Lebanon, and brought, properly carved, marked, and numbered, to Jerusalem, where they were fitted in by means of wooden mauls. So of Freemasonry it has always been the boast, that its members perfect the work of edification by quiet and orderly methods, "without the hammer of contention, the axe of division, or any tool of mischief." The excellency of the craft in the days of our Grand Master Hiram was so great, that although the materials were prepared so far off, when they were put together at Jerusalem each piece fitted with such exactness, that it appeared more like the work of the Great Architect of the universe than of human hands.

The temple thus described retained its pristine splendour but thirty-three years, when it was plundered by Shishak, king of Egypt (1 Kings xiv. 25, 26. 2 Chron. xii. 9). After this period it underwent sundry profanations and pillages, and was at length utterly destroyed by Nebuchadnezzar, king of Babylon, A.M. 3416, B.C. 588, after having stood, according to Usher, four hundred and twenty-four years, three months, and eight days.

CHAPTER XXII.

THE NAME.—THE SACRED ELEMENTS OF CONSECRATION.—THE ARMORIAL BEARINGS OF THE ORDER.—THE SYMBOLIC COLOURS OF FREEMASONRY.—THE DATES OF MASONRY.

"Discover not a secret to another, lest he that heareth it put thee to shame."—PROV. xxv. 9.

ON THE NAME.

"FATHER OF ALL, in every age,
In every clime adored,
By saint, by savage, and by sage,
JEHOVAH, JOVE, or LORD."

THE English version of the Old Testament Scriptures invariably translates the name of God as THE LORD, although in the Hebrew it assumes different forms; the more usual is Jehovah; thus it appears in the Prophets Isaiah and Jeremiah, and also in many instances in the Psalms. From the time when God first announced his name to Moses at the burning bush, and said, "This is my name for ever, and this is my memorial unto all generations" (Exod. iii. 15), it was the only name by which He was known to the Israelites. Although God had thus declared his Name, it was considered unlawful to pronounce it except on the great day of atonement, when it was only uttered by the High Priest in the Holy of Holies, amid the sound of trumpets and cymbals, which prevented the people from hearing it. This custom is supposed to have arisen originally from a wish to prevent its becoming known to the surrounding nations, and being by them blasphemously applied to their idols.

In consequence of the people thus abstaining from its utterance, the true pronunciation was lost. It will be readily seen that as the Hebrew alphabet consists entirely of consonants, the vowel sounds having to be supplied by the reader, if not previously made acquainted with the correct pronunciation, he was of course unable to pronounce the word.

In this way it was that during the captivity the word was lost.

The fundamental principle of Masonry is the knowledge of the True and Living God; hence his Name in varied form, as symbolic of his attributes, appears in the entire system.

JEHOVAH is his ineffable and mysterious Name. "I appeared," says the Almighty, "unto Abraham, unto Isaac, and unto Jacob, by the name of God Almighty (*Al-Shaddai*), but by my Name JEHOVAH was I not known to them" (Exod. vi. 3). SHADDAI signifies the self-sufficient (or all-bountiful); JEHOVAH signifies the Self-existent, He who gives being and existence to others. There has been much written on this passage, which, as it stands in our translation, is taken to be a direct contradiction to several instances in which this Name appears to have been *known* long before Moses, and applied to the Supreme object of worship. The first woman, Eve, when she had "got" her son Cain, appears to have designated the Deity by the Name JEHOVAH; and in the same chapter (Gen. iv. 26) Seth called his son Enos—then the Lord was invoked under his Name JEHOVAH. In what sense, then, could God assert to Moses that his ancestors had not *known* Him by his Name JEHOVAH? Mr. Charles Taylor, in his English edition of Calmet's Dictionary, offers an elucidation which certainly clears away the difficulty. The word used in the original is נודעתי (*nodati*), the root of which is ידע, *to know;* but knowledge has various degrees, and he cites several instances of the different degrees of strength the verb and its accessories obtain in the Old Testament, as *aware, full perception, appropriate,* the latter meaning being that most frequently employed; and he suggests that the proper rendering is, "but by my name JEHOVAH was I not *appropriate* to them." It is to be observed that when in our translation the word LORD occurs in capital letters, it stands for the JEHOVAH of the original: this substitution has the sanction of the Septuagint (the Greek translation, made at Alexandria in the third century), which commonly renders it by Κύριος, or "Lord," whence it has been inferred that the translators were not accustomed to pronounce the Name; to which we may add, that they were probably unwilling to communicate what they knew of it to strangers. It is certain that the Jews associated much mystery with the Name; their respect for it led them to abstain from pronouncing it after the captivity, until *ultimately they forgot the true pronunciation. Origen, Jerome,* and other early fathers of the Christian Church, mention that in their time the Jews wrote the Name in their copies of the Scriptures in Samaritan characters, in order to veil it from the profane inspection of strangers. *Josephus,* in his account of the portion of Scripture history referred to, says, "that Moses entreated God to tell him his Name, that he might know how to invoke Him properly when he offered sacrifice; whereupon God declared to him his Name, which had never before been revealed to man, and concerning which it is not lawful for me to say more."

It must be borne in mind also that the book of Genesis was written after God had revealed his Name to Moses, who may have used it by anticipation.

Some learned Jews even doubt whether Jehovah be the true name of God, which they consider to have been irrecoverably lost; and they say that this is one of the mysteries that will be revealed only at the coming of the Messiah. They attribute this loss to the sinful habit of applying the Masoretic points to so sacred a name, in consequence of which the true vowels were lost. They even relate the legend of a celebrated Hebrew scholar whom God permitted to be burnt by a Roman emperor, because he had been heard to pronounce the Holy Name with these points (*Oliver*).

The pronunciation of the Name, it is said, was preserved and transmitted by the Essenes, who always communicated it to each other in a whisper, and in such a form, that while its component parts were known, its connected whole still remained a mystery.

The modern Jews say it was engraved on the rod of Moses, and enabled him to perform his miracles; and they attribute all the wonderful works of Jesus Christ to the potency of this incommunicable Name, which they say He stole out of the Temple and wore about Him.

Josephus calls the Tetragrammaton, or four-lettered name (יהוה), "the sacred letters—the shuddering Name of God;" and *Caligula,* in *Philo,* swears to him and his associates by "the God who was to them of unpronounceable Name."

The very heathen seem to have had some knowledge of this great ineffable Name; we have an oath in Pythagoras's golden verses, "By Him who has the four letters;" and *Eusebius* (A.D. 320) says that on the frontispiece of a temple at Delphi was inscribed, "Thou art;" on one of the Egyptian temples was inscribed, "I AM."

The heathen had names of their gods which they did not dare to pronounce. *Cicero* produces an example in his catalogue of deities (De Natura Deorum, lib. iii.), and *Lucan* says the earth would have trembled had any one pronounced them. The disciples of Mohammed use the name Hu or Hou, which has almost the same signification as Jehovah, that is, *He who is.*

Without further remarks on the incommunicable Name, it

may not be amiss to remind the reader that, although it signifies the state of being, yet it forms no verb, it never assumes a plural form, it does not admit an article or take an affix, neither is it placed in a state of construction with other words—though other words may be in construction with it. It seems to be a compound of יה, *the essence,* and הוה, *existing,* that is, *always existing;* whence the word *Eternal* appears to express its import; or, as it is well rendered in Rev. i. 4; xi. 17,—"He who is, and who was, and who is to come." It is abbreviated in the form of יה, *Jah,* which also enters into the formation of many Hebrew appellations, as Adonijah, Hallelujah:—God is my Lord, praise the Lord, &c.

ELOHI, ELOHA, ELOHIM, or Alëhim, is another form of the Name of the Supreme Being, and would seem to be second in dignity only to the Name JEHOVAH; as that Name imports the essential *being* of the Divinity, so Elohim seems to import the *power* inherent in Deity, or the *manifestation of that power* on its relative subjects. It is in this form the Name appears in the Mosaic account of the creation of the world; and wherever the messages of the prophets or other commissioned ambassadors of the Most High appear, they are delivered in the Name of JEHOVAH or ELOHIM; no where is it said, EL SHADDAI spake. We are told (Gen. xxxiii. 20) when Jacob came to Shalem from Padan-aram, "he erected there an altar, and called it El-elohe-Israel"—that is, the God of Israel.

EL SHADDAI is generally translated God Almighty; it is said to be derived from שדא, *to ascend,* or *sit in the highest place;* and in this view it is synonymous with (עליון) *Most High.* Job more frequently uses it than any other of the sacred writers.

ADONAI (*Lord*). This word is by the Jews substituted for that of Jehovah, which they never pronounce. *Lanci* gives the signification of *Adon,* the Lord, the Dominator, and *Adonai,* the Lord, the most firm or most strong. Hence it may be assumed to express *most powerful.* When the Jews first adopted this form it is difficult to ascertain; but as it has a Greek resemblance, it is presumed to have been used among strangers. In the Greek mythology, Adonis was the son of Cinyras, by his daughter Myrrha, and his beauty captivated Venus. He was fond of hunting, and in the chase was mortally wounded by a wild boar. The goddess of beauty, after shedding many tears for his death, changed him into the flower called anemone. *R. Payne Knight* says, "Adonis or Adonai was an oriental title of the sun signifying Lord." Adonis was the same deity with the Syrian *Tammuz,* whose festival was celebrated by the Jews when they degenerated into idolatry (see Ezekiel viii. 14). The fable originated with the Phœnicians, was carried to Egypt, and there identified in Osiris, from whence it was transferred to Greece.

Urquhart mentions one name of God among the Hebrews as EL GIBAL, *the Master-builder.* This is curious, as it proves that the men of Gebal were beyond all others famed for their skill, or the name was given to their city as a token of their pre-eminence in architecture.

JAH is the Syriac form of the name of Jehovah; it appears but once in the Sacred Scriptures, in that noble Psalm (68th) which begins with the well-known exordium on the removal of the ark; it is concluded it was composed by David in order to be sung in the procession of the ark from the house of Obededom to Mount Zion;—"Sing unto God, sing praises to his name; extol him that rideth upon the heavens by his name JAH, and rejoice before him." It is supposed that this form was well known among the Gentile nations as the tri-literal Name of God; for, although bi-literal among the Hebrews, it assumed among the Greeks the tri-literal form, as IAΩ. *Macrobius* (A.D. 400) says this was the sacred Name of the Supreme Deity; and the Clavian Oracle, being asked which of the gods was IAΩ, replied, "The initiated are bound to conceal the mysterious secrets. Learn then that IAΩ is the Great God Supreme, who ruleth over all."

BELUS was the name by which the Deity was known to the Assyrians and Babylonians; in Chaldee it assumes the form BEL. It appears frequently in the Old Testament, in allusion to the idolatrous worship into which the Israelites fell when they came into contact with surrounding nations.

Baal or Bel, signifying governor, ruler, Lord, was the name of the God worshipped by the Phœnicians and Chaldeans. Some have supposed it was the same as the Saturn of Greece and Rome, others that it was the Tyrian Hercules; but it is most generally agreed that it was the Sun as the symbol of creative power, that great luminary being adored all over the East. Philo Biblius, from Sanchoniatho, says the Phœnicians called the sun Beel-samun, which in their language signifies the *Lord of Heaven.* Herodian says that some call the same deity Apollo which others call Belin. The worship of Bel, Belus, or Belinius was general throughout the British Islands, and notwithstanding the spread and establishment of Christianity through so many ages, some traces of it still remain in the fires lighted on the 1st of May in the north of England, and in Ireland on the 24th of June. An ancient memorial of this god of the heathens is retained in the name of our great fish-market, *Belins-gate.*

ON was the Name by which Jehovah was worshipped by the Egyptians. *Plato,* in *Timœus,* says, "Tell me of the God ON, which IS and never knew beginning." Thus ON may be considered as the equivalent for JEHOVAH among the Egyptians, as JAH was among the Syrians, and BEL among the Chaldees.

The ineffable degrees record a great variety of the names of God; in fact the whole system may be properly said to be a science of the name of the Most High. It is to be observed that the same awe and reverence for the unutterable Name is to be found in the doctrines and ceremonies of other nations as well as the Jews[1].

Sir William Jones says, "The name of God forms a mystical word which never escapes from the lips of a pious Hindoo. He meditates on it in silence." The institutes of Menu refer to its peculiar efficacy as an omnific word,—"All rites in the Veda, oblations to fire, and solemn sacrifices, pass away; but that which passes not away is the syllable AUM, thence called *aishara,* since it is the symbol of God, the Lord of created beings." In the Brahminical rites the name was bestowed in this triliteral form on the aspirant at the completion of his initiation, by whispering it in his ear. The Mohammedans have a science called *Ism Allah,* or the science of the name of God; and *Niebuhr,* speaking of it, says, "They pretend that God is the lock of this science, and Mohammed the key: that consequently none but Mohammedans can attain it; that it discovers what passes in different countries; that it familiarizes the possessors with the genii who are at the command of the initiated, and who instruct them; and that it places the winds and seasons at their disposal."

THE SACRED ELEMENTS OF CONSECRATION.

"Therefore, brethren, stand fast, and hold the traditions which ye have been taught, whether by word, or our epistle."—ST. PAUL TO THE THESSALONIANS.

The Rev. Brother Thaddeus Mason Harris, in a discourse delivered in aid of a charitable institution, says, "Wherefore, my brethren, do you carry *corn, wine,* and *oil* in your processions, but to remind you that, in the pilgrimage of human life, you are to

[1] "All pure beings, past, present, and to come, were created by the *word,* and that *word* is I AM."—ZENDA VESTA.

impart a portion of your *bread* to feed the hungry, to send a cup of your *wine* to cheer the sorrowful, and to pour the healing *oil* of your consolation into the wounds which sickness has made in the bodies, or affliction rent in the hearts of your fellow-travellers?"

CORN, WINE, and OIL are the Masonic elements of consecration, and their adoption is supported by the highest antiquity. Being all the most important productions of eastern countries, as constituting the wealth of the people, they were necessarily esteemed as the supports of life and the means of refreshment. From the earliest ages, in devoting any place or thing to religious purposes, the anointing with *oil* was considered a necessary part of the ceremony: a custom which has descended to our own times.

By God's express command to Moses, the Tabernacle in the wilderness and all its holy vessels were consecrated with "an holy anointing oil;" for the preparation of which specific directions were given (Exod. xxx. 23). Aaron and his two sons were anointed and consecrated to the priesthood. Kings and prophets of the Hebrew nation were all alike consecrated. The sovereigns of our own land at their coronation are consecrated with an holy oil. Freemasons' Lodges, and Royal Arch Chapters, which are emblems of the Ark and Temples dedicated to the Most High, are solemnly consecrated to the sacred purposes of the institution; and the Tracing Board, symbolically termed *the Lodge,* as representing the Holy Ark of the Covenant, is strewed with corn, wine, and oil. For these purposes, properly the corn is carried in a cornucopia (or horn of plenty), or a golden dish, the wine and oil in silver ewers.

David, in that most magnificent composition, the 104th Psalm, which demonstrates the wisdom, beauty, and variety of God's works, as also his providential care, in the enumeration of his blessings, mentions "wine that maketh glad the heart of man, oil to make his face shine, and bread which strengtheneth man's heart." They may be characterized as emblems of health, plenty, and peace, essential blessings to the happiness of a Lodge.

THE ARMORIAL BEARINGS OF THE ORDER.

The banners of the twelve tribes which adorn the Royal Arch Chapter, are as follow:—

Judah, scarlet, a lion couchant.

Issachar, blue, an ass crouching beneath its burden.

Zebulun, purple, a ship.

Reuben, red, a man.

Simeon, yellow, a sword.

Gad, white, a troop of horsemen.

Ephraim, green, an ox.

Manasseh, flesh-coloured, a vine by the side of a wall.

Benjamin, green, a wolf.

Dan, green, an eagle.

Asher, purple, a cup.

Naphtali, blue, a hind.

When the twelve tribes marched through the wilderness, they were gathered in four divisions, and when encamped round about the Tabernacle, three tribes were under the standard of Judah, which was a lion, and placed on the east; on the west were three tribes under the standard of Ephraim, an ox; on the south were three tribes under the standard of Reuben, a man; and on the north, three tribes under the standard of Dan, an eagle (Numbers ii.); and whence were framed the hieroglyphics of the cherubim and seraphim to represent the people of Israel. Therefore God chose to sit upon cherubims bearing the forms of the four animals, to signify that He was the leader and king of the cohorts of the Israelites. (*Traditions of the Hebrews.*)

These four standards compose the banner or armorial bearings of the Order of Freemasonry, and although only in use as attached to the Royal Arch Degree, they belong to the whole craft, and are intended to denote the origin of the institution from Solomon, who was the last king under whom all the twelve tribes were united. The armorial bearings of the Order may be thus described:—

The shield is divided into eight compartments. On the dexter side the arms of the London Guild of Masons are thus heraldically described: *sable,* on a chevron between three castles *argent,* a pair of compasses of the first crest, a castle of the second. This society was incorporated in the year 1410 by the name and style of the Society of Freemasons, and William Hankstow, Clarencieux King at Arms, granted them the above coat. It is generally believed that this company is a branch of the ancient fraternity; and in former times no one could take up his freedom in it unless he had been first initiated in some lawful Lodge of Free and Accepted Masons. On the sinister side, in the first quarter is a golden lion on a field of blue; on the second, a black ox on a field of gold; on the third, a man on a field of gold; and on the fourth, a golden eagle on a blue ground. The crest is the ark of the covenant, the motto being "*Audi, vidi, tace.*" The supporters are two cherubims. The Arms of the Grand Chapter are without the Craft Masons' Bearings; and the motto is "*Holiness to the Lord.*"

MASONIC COLOURS. BLUE is the appropriate colour of the first three degrees or Ancient Craft Masonry, and is emblematic of universal friendship and benevolence, instructing us, that in the mind of a Mason those virtues should be as extensive as the blue arch of Heaven itself. DARK, or, as it is generally called, GARTER BLUE, is the distinguishing colour of the Grand Lodge.

PURPLE is a Royal Arch colour and an emblem of union, because it is produced by the combination of *blue* and *scarlet,* the former being the characteristic colour of the symbolic degrees, and the latter the chief colour of the Royal Arch.

SCARLET, the peculiar emblematic colour of the Royal Arch. and significant of the zeal and ardour which should inspire its possessors.

Blue, purple, scarlet, and white or fine linen, are the colours with which the veils of the Tabernacle were interwoven. The robes of the Principals of a Royal Arch Chapter are of these colours, Joshua wearing blue, Haggai purple, and Zerubbabel scarlet; the scribes wearing white. *Josephus* informs us that the Jews gave to the veils an astronomical signification, and supposed them to represent the four elements. Fine white linen was a symbol of the earth, because it was made out of flax, a production of the earth; the blue, as the colour of the sky, was a symbol of the air; the purple, of the sea, because it derived its colour from the murex, a shell-fish that inhabits the sea; and the scarlet was the natural symbol of fire.

DATES OF MASONRY.

In affixing dates to official documents Freemasons never make use of the common calendar or vulgar era, but with different rites have peculiar modes of computation; thus: in Craft Masonry they date from the creation of the world, A.L. Anno Lucis, the year of light; thus 1860 is A.L. 5860. Royal Arch Masonry dates from the building of the second Temple, which being 530 years before Christ, makes our 1860 A.I., Anno Inventionis, 2390. The Knight Templars' era dates from the organization of their Order, 1118; thus A.O., Anno Ordinis, in 1860 would be 742.

CHAPTER XXIII.

WISDOM, STRENGTH, AND BEAUTY,

A LECTURE DELIVERED BY THE EDITOR IN THE BERKHAMPSTEAD LODGE, NO. 742, JANUARY 2, 1861.

"The Universe is the temple of that Deity whom we serve, and from whom all goodness emanates. WISDOM, STRENGTH, and BEAUTY are about his throne as pillars of his work; his Wisdom is infinite, his Strength omnipotent, and his Beauty shines forth throughout the whole of Creation in symmetry and order."—*Lectures.*

WISDOM.

IN our symbolic language the three great pillars which support the Lodge are called Wisdom, Strength, and Beauty. They emblematically represent the three Grand Masters who presided at the building of the house of God at Jerusalem:—Solomon, the King of Israel, as a semblance of his *wisdom* in building and dedicating the Temple to God's service; Hiram, King of Tyre, of his *strength* in supporting Solomon with men and materials; and Hiram, the widow's son, who by his masterly workmanship in adorning the structure, rendered it marvellous for *beauty.* These pillars, which are essential parts of the furniture of a Lodge now, are three architectural columns, examples of the Ionic, Doric, and Corinthian orders;—the Ionic representing *wisdom;* the Doric, *strength;* and the Corinthian, *beauty.* These pillars have, however, more important significations:—*Wisdom,* by our moral teaching, we require to conduct us in all our undertakings; *Strength,* we need for supporting us under all our difficulties; and *Beauty,* of holiness to adorn our mind and manner. As a further illustration:—the universe is the temple of that Deity whom we serve, and from whom all goodness emanates. *Wisdom, strength,* and *beauty* are about his throne as pillars of his work; his wisdom is infinite, his strength omnipotent, and his beauty shines forth throughout the whole of Creation in symmetry and order. Having thus briefly noticed these symbols in combination, let us treat their characteristics separately. WISDOM is represented by the Ionic column and the Worshipful Master, because the Ionic wisely combines strength without the massiveness of the Doric, with the grace without the exuberance of ornament in the Corinthian, and because it is the duty of the W.M. to superintend, instruct, and enlighten the Craft by his superior wisdom.

WISDOM is personified in King Solomon as the column of wisdom that supported the Temple; and David's choice in naming his successor on the throne of Israel emanated from Divine dictation. Soon after his accession he went to Gibeon, and "a thousand burnt offerings did he offer upon that altar." In Gibeon the Lord appeared to him in a dream by night, saying, "Ask what I shall give thee." He replied, "Give thy servant an understanding heart to judge thy people, that I may discern between good and bad: for who is able to judge this thy so great a people?" "And God said unto him, Because thou hast asked this thing, and hast not asked riches for thyself, nor asked the life of thy enemies; but hast asked for thyself understanding to discern judgment; behold, I have done according to thy word: lo, I have given thee a *wise and understanding heart;* so there was none like thee before thee, neither after thee shall any arise like unto thee." And in process of time we are told in the sacred volume, "God gave Solomon wisdom and understanding exceeding much, and largeness of heart, even as the sand that is on the sea shore. And Solomon's wisdom excelled the wisdom of all the children of the east country, and all the wisdom of Egypt." From this it appears that among the Hebrews, as well as among the Greeks, the Egyptians were justly famous for their wisdom—that is, their knowledge in science and art. Egypt was deemed the fountain of the arts and sciences, and the Gentile philosophers were wont to go thither to fertilize their minds by the dew of Egyptian wisdom. This did Pythagoras, Anaxagoras, Herodotus, Plato, and others. Solomon enjoyed a profound peace throughout his dominions. "Judah and Israel dwelt safely, every man under his vine and under his fig-tree;" and his neighbours either paid him tribute or were his allies. He ruled over all the countries from the Euphrates to the Nile. He exceeded the Orientals and the Egyptians in wisdom and prudence; and his reputation as the wisest of mankind spread through all nations. He extended the commerce of his country, and imported largely of foreign produce. He fitted out a fleet at Ezion-geber and at Elath on the Red Sea, and in conjunction with Hiram of Tyre, who furnished him with mariners, traded to Ophir for ivory, ebony, precious woods, peacocks, &c. All this peace and prosperity was the result of Solomon's judicious government. That he was the wisest man of all times must be allowed. We have the warrant for this in God's promise made to him in his dream at Gibeon; and we must remember that his wisdom was a supernatural gift from Jehovah, whereas all other men have been obliged to acquire knowledge by the slow and difficult processes of study and experience.

While Solomon was at the height of his prosperity, he received a visit from the Queen of Sheba, or Saba, in Ethiopia, who had heard of his wisdom, and came to prove it with hard questions; to which Solomon gave such answers that she confessed that half of his wisdom had not been told her.

But, alas! prosperity was at length too much for even Solomon: among his magnificent establishments he had a large harem, composed, in direct opposition to the Divine command, of women from the idolatrous nations of Canaan, who seduced him into idolatry. Hence pleasure became the great object of his pursuit; but as the cup of which he drank was not prepared for him by the Divine hand, the result was disappointment, pain, and misery. God threatened to divide his kingdom after his death, and during his lifetime there were signs of the coming calamity in the rebellions of Hadad, Rezon, and Jeroboam. This threat of the Most High had the effect of recovering him from his idolatry, and he has recorded his confession of the vanity of worldly wisdom, riches, and honours.

Besides the records in the sacred historical books, we have the testimony in the same holy volume of the wisdom of this great monarch, as displayed in the books that bear his name, Proverbs and Ecclesiastes. Although the Book of Proverbs has always been ascribed to Solomon, some doubts have been expressed as to his being the author of the whole. The first nine chapters seem to form a kind of introduction, and it has been suggested were proverbs in use before the time of Solomon; and from the tenth chapter to the twenty-fourth are the monarch's own production. The rest are supposed to have been collected after his time, and form an appendix to the whole. We do not assent to this explanation, but suggest that the book is a collection of the proverbs of Solomon compiled by several hands. We cannot conclude from hence it is not the work of Solomon, as we have it stated (1 Kings iv. 32) "he composed three thousand proverbs." The title, Proverbs of Solomon, rather shows the author than the compiler.

In those periods of remote antiquity, which may with the utmost propriety be styled the infancy of societies and nations, the usual, if not the only, mode of instruction was by detached aphorisms and proverbs. Those who by genius and reflection—

exercised in the school of experience—had accumulated a stock of knowledge, were desirous of rendering it into the most compendious form, and comprised in a few maxims those observations which they apprehended most essential to human happiness. This manner of instruction, which with other nations prevailed only during the first periods of civilization, with the Hebrews continued to be a favourite style to the latest ages of their literature. Of this didactic poetry there are still extant many specimens in the writings of that people, and among them the first rank must be assigned to the Proverbs of Solomon; who has himself explained the principal excellences of this form of composition, exhibiting at once a complete definition of a proverb or parable, and a very happy specimen of what he describes—

"Apples of gold in a network of silver
Is a word seasonably spoken."

Thus he insinuates that grave and profound sentiments are to be set off by a smooth and well-turned phraseology, as the appearance of the most beautiful and exquisitely coloured fruit is improved by the circumstance of shining, as through a veil, through the reticulations of a silver vessel exquisitely wrought. And further, that it is not only a neat and polished diction which must recommend them, but that truth itself acquires additional beauty when partially discovered through the veil of elegant fiction and imagery. We select three other examples which are deserving our attention for their propriety and elegance:—

"Clouds and wind without rain
Is a man who glories in a fallacious gift."
"Gold and abundance of rubies,
And precious ornaments, are the lips of knowledge."
"Hate stirreth up strifes;
But love covereth all transgressions."

In the ritual of the Royal Arch we have adopted a selection from the first portion of the Proverbs, as a means of urging the necessity of acquiring knowledge. This first portion, Bishop Lowth says, "is varied, elegant, sublime, and truly poetical. It is embellished with many beautiful descriptions and personifications, the diction is polished and abounds with all the ornaments of poetry, insomuch that it scarcely yields in elegance and splendour to any of the sacred writings." This portion of the book is chiefly confined to the conduct of early life, before a permanent condition is made choice of; and all the formidable dangers to which this season of life is exposed, and the sins which most easily beset it, are painted with the hand of a master. And while the progress and issues of vice are exhibited, under a variety of the most striking delineations and metaphors, in their utmost deformity and horror, all the beauties of language, and all the force and eloquence, are poured forth to win the ingenuous youth to virtue and piety, and to fix him in the steady pursuit of his duties toward God and toward man.

The Book of Ecclesiastes has in all ages been ascribed to Solomon; the tradition of the Jews states that he composed this book in his old age, after he had repented of his former vicious practices, and had become by sad experience convinced of the vanity of every thing terrestrial, except *piety* and *wisdom*. The acknowledgment of the numerous follies and delusions implies that it was composed after the author had apostatized from Jehovah, and had subsequently repented of his past misconduct. The frequent assertion of the emptiness of earthly greatness; the declaration that human enjoyments are unsatisfactory; the enumeration of gardens, edifices, and possessions, requiring a long life for their completion; the deep condemnation of former pursuits; the expression of satiety and disgust at past pleasures; and the tone of cool and philosophical reflection which pervades the whole, are strikingly characteristic of an advanced period of life.

The general opinion of the design and scope of the Book of

Ecclesiastes regards it as an inquiry into the chief good. The inquiry after the chief good, the *summum bonum,* was much practised by the old pagan philosophers; but it is ever to be remembered, that they only sought to know in what lay the prime happiness of the present life; whereas the sovereign good, as understood by *the Preacher,* is that which is ultimately good; that which, in all its bearings and relations, is conducive to the best interests of man. This is the object of the Preacher's inquiry; and after discussing various erroneous opinions, he finally determines that it consists in TRUE WISDOM. The scope of the whole argument therefore is, the praise and recommendation of wisdom, as the supreme good to creatures responsible for their actions. But in this wisdom there is nothing worldly or carnal: it is the wisdom from above,—holy, spiritual, and undefiled,—and which, in the writings of Solomon, is but another name for religion.

Some commentators object to the style as of a very inferior character to that of Proverbs, but we suggest that it contains numerous precepts for conduct applicable to all ages. All will acknowledge the truth of this aphorism, "A good name is better than precious ointment." Content, the only happiness on earth, is exhibited in this sentence, "Better is a handful with quietness, than both hands full with travail and vexation of spirit:" and how truly Masonic is the counsel—"Cast thy bread upon the waters, and thou shalt find it after many days." This must be regarded as enforcing the great and distinguished liberality of doing good to those from whom no return can be expected, and on whom the benefaction may seem as much thrown away, as if a man were to sow his seed in the sea; but with the promise annexed, that it shall not be thrown away, but in the end receive its due recompense.

Freemasonry affords a striking instance of the faithfulness of this aphorism in the case of Brother Ruspini, the founder of the Freemasons' School for Female Children. At the period of its formation Ruspini was possessed of a good income, and could have had no idea of his family requiring the aid of charity. The property he had accumulated was wasted by his successor, and when his remains were slumbering in the tomb, two of his grandchildren became the recipients of the benefits of the noble institution their ancestor had originated.

But the crowning portion of the Book of Ecclesiastes is the twelfth chapter, which, after admonishing his reader, "Remember now thy Creator in the days of thy youth," gives a highly figurative and poetical representation of old age, in which the various infirmities and imbecilities of that period of life are pourtrayed in a great variety of images in themselves unconnected, yet mutually tending to identify their prototype.

In this allegory, which is contained in the first seven verses, Solomon, after the manner of the Oriental philosophers, meant to put to trial the acuteness of his readers. It has, on this account, afforded much exercise to the ingenuity of the learned, and it has consequently had many different explanations. As this celebrated passage is introduced by our transatlantic brethren in the ceremonial of the Third Degree, the Rev. G. Holden's "Attempt to illustrate the Book of Ecclesiastes" offers the best elucidation.

"Remember now thy Creator in the days of thy youth, while the evil days come not, nor the years draw nigh, when thou shalt say, I have no pleasure in them: while the sun, or the light, or the moon, or the stars, be not darkened, nor the clouds return after the rain."

This figurative beginning, intended as a general statement of the pains and miseries of age, serves as an introduction to the more specific details which follow. Remarking that as clouds and rain do not appear during the summer in Judea, we may understand this image to be taken from the winter season, denoting the succession of pains and infirmities which so often attend the winter of life.

"In the day when the keepers of the house shall tremble, and the strong men shall bow themselves."

By the "keepers of the house," the arms and hands are intended, as being to the body what guards and keepers are to a palace; or rather, perhaps, they are so called, as providing for the sustenance of the house or body: how they "tremble" in old age is well known. "The strong men bow themselves" may allude to the lower limbs, which bow and totter beneath the aged.

"And the grinders cease because they are few, and those that look out of the windows shall be darkened."

The allusion to the "grinders" is derived from the Eastern custom of females, who daily grind the corn required; and thus denotes the teeth, which masticate and grind down the food for the stomach. The eyes, which become dimmed or "darkened," are indicated by the windows.

"And the doors shall be shut in the streets, when the sound of the grinding is low, and he shall rise up at the voice of the bird, and all the daughters of music shall be brought low."

In consequence of the loss of teeth, the act of eating is usually performed by aged persons with closed lips; and then also the gums with their smooth surfaces are obliged to perform the office of the teeth, masticating the food with slow and silent labour, which is probably what the Preacher meant by the low sound of the grinding. The word rendered "bird" (*tzippon*) denotes a sparrow or any small bird, and hence we shall then have the sense that the aged sleep so unsoundly that the twittering of the smallest birds will suffice to rouse them. When the aged Barzillai (2 Sam. xix. 35) was invited by David to accompany him to Jerusalem, he replied, "I am this day fourscore years old: . . . can thy servant taste what I eat or what I drink? can I hear any more the voice of singing men or singing women?" He here describes deafness as one of the infirmities of age; but it may allude also to the decay of the organs employed in the production and enjoyment of music.

"And when they shall be afraid of that which is high, and fears shall be in the way, and the almond-tree shall flourish, and the grasshopper shall be a burden, and desire shall fail; because man goeth to his long home, and the mourners go about the streets."

The elucidation of this passage is apparent; it alludes to the difficulty which the aged find in ascending high places, as well as to the timidity which the consciousness of their infirm condition leads them to exhibit, when they venture to walk out in the public ways; and which, in the narrow streets of the East, is necessarily more marked than with us. The almond-tree having white blossoms refers to the white hair of aged persons. By the word rendered *grasshopper* a species of locust is alluded to; and Parkhurst says in explanation, "The dry, shrunk, crumbling, scraggy old man—his backbone sticking out, his knees projecting forward, his arms backward, his head downward, and the apophyses, or bunching parts of the bones, in general enlarged—is very aptly described by that insect. And from this exact likeness, without all doubt, arose the fable of Tithonus, that, *living to an extreme old age,* he was turned into a grasshopper." This idea was familiar to the classical ancients, for we find engraved gems in which an emaciated old man is represented by a locust walking erect on its hind legs, and in which all the characteristics enumerated above, are brought out with truly singular effect. All that precedes refers to the decay of man. We now reach another class of circumstances, descriptive of what attends and denotes death itself. "Man going to his long home," and "the mourners going about the streets," require no explanation.

"Or ever the silver cord be loosed, or the golden bowl be broken, or the pitcher be broken at the fountain, or the wheel broken at the cistern. Then shall the dust return to the earth as it was; and the spirit shall return unto God who gave it."

The *silver cord* signifies that resplendent white cord—the spinal marrow which passes through the entire length of the backbone, and which is very liable to be relaxed and weakened in old age, or a part thereof altogether broken in its functions, producing the various paralytic complaints, the tremors and debilities to which the aged are so frequently subject. By the *golden bowl* is understood the skull, and the epithet golden we conclude to be a term of excellence, denoting the importance of the skull and its valuable contents. The *pitcher* denotes the large canals which issue from the heart, and receive the blood therefrom as from a fountain; the *fountain* is the right ventricle of the heart, and the *cistern* the left ventricle. The *wheel* is the aorta, the great vessel from which all the arteries of the body which carry red blood derive their origin. This explanation, we must allow, suggests that Solomon was acquainted with some idea of the circulation of the blood, a discovery of comparatively modern date. Another suggestion has been offered, that, in their literal import, the series of images is evidently suggested by some hydraulic process for raising water from wells and cisterns, such methods being extensively in use in the East. (*Holden.*)

The *Preacher* thus sums up his discourse:—

"Let us hear the conclusion of the whole matter: Fear God, and keep his commandments: for this is the whole duty of man."

This we must acknowledge to be a truly Masonic charge, and hence, when the subject of Divine wisdom is considered, deserves our especial notice.

There are two things in general that perfect a good man; the one a clear and distinct knowledge of his duty, the other a conscientious practice of it, both being equally necessary. It has pleased God, who is the Governor of the universe and will be the righteous Judge of all, to prescribe laws for the regulation of our actions, so that we may know what we ought to do, and what to avoid. The volume of the Sacred Law is the statute book of God's kingdom; therein is comprised the whole body of the heavenly laws, the perfect rules of a holy life, and the sure promises of a glorious immortality. The Decalogue, or Ten Commandments, is a summary of those laws written by the finger of God!

Looking to the brevity of the expressions and the copiousness and variety of the matter contained in them, we must acknowledge the wisdom of their Divine Author in reducing the whole duty of man to so small a compendium. These Commandments were delivered 2500 years after the creation of the world, according to the Mosaic history. The manner in which God appeared to pronounce his law was terrible—in thunder and lightning, fire and clouds of darkness—intended, no doubt, to put the people in mind that if He was thus terrible in delivering his law, how much more so will He appear, when He shall come to judge the transgressors of it.

The tables of the law are two: the first, comprehending four enactments, contains our duties to God; the other, comprising six enactments, contains our duties to our neighbour, and by Divine authority "on these hang all the law and the prophets." These objects are the beginning and end of Freemasonry, and hence it is not necessary in this place to urge the practice of them.

WISDOM, the main pillar that supports the Lodge, is the Master, who represents King Solomon—the wisest man of all time—and it is practically represented in the moral government of those who are sworn to obey him, who, by a knowledge of the laws and the rites and ceremonies of the institution, is enabled to preserve due order, and maintain peace and unity among the brethren under his charge. It is the bounden duty of every brother to follow the bright example of a worthy Master, and while he commemorates the wisdom of King

Solomon, let him act as a disciple of wisdom; and remembering that the interests of Masonry are in the hands of every individual brother, be careful not to blend it with his weaknesses nor stain it with his vices, but to "walk in wisdom towards them that are without."

The Royal Psalmist says, "The fear of God is the beginning of wisdom; a good understanding have all they that do thereafter." (Ps. cxi. 10.) So also in the ninetieth Psalm, which is generally ascribed to Moses, and is doubtless the most sublime prayer in the Sacred Volume, the great lawgiver beseeches Jehovah, "So teach us to number our days, that we may apply our hearts unto wisdom."

To conclude,—

"Whatsoever thy hand findeth to do,
Do it with thy might;
For there is no work, nor device,
Nor knowledge, nor wisdom,
In the empire of shadows
Where thou goest."

STRENGTH.

Previously to attempting an elucidation of the other supports of a Mason's Lodge, a few remarks upon the adopted form, a suggestion for their improvement, may be properly advanced: as upon examination every one must allow that there is in our traditional legend, and in our uses and explanations as given in the lecture, some incongruity as well as anachronism. Intimately connected as they are with our rites, they deserve to have their form, as described 1 Kings vii., preserved with integrity. The Lodge figuratively represents the Temple of Solomon, the Master personifying, as we have said, the mighty monarch, and his principal officers (by name) the two remarkable pillars wrought by Hiram the widow's son. These pillars, to keep the representation consistent, ought to be placed side by side; that is, one at the south-west, and the other at the north-west of the Lodge. They should be wrought strictly in conformity with the description in the Sacred Volume.

"And King Solomon sent and fetched Hiram out of Tyre. He was a widow's son of the tribe of Naphtali, and his father was a man of Tyre, a worker in brass: and he was filled with wisdom, and understanding, and cunning to work all works in brass. And he came to King Solomon, and wrought all his work. For he cast two pillars of brass, of eighteen cubits high apiece: and a line of twelve cubits did compass either of them about. And he made two chapiters of molten brass, to set upon the tops of the pillars: the height of the one chapiter was five cubits, and the height of the other chapiter was five cubits: and nets of checker work, and wreaths of chain work, for the chapiters which were upon the top of the pillars; seven for the one chapiter, and seven for the other chapiter. And he made the pillar, and two rows round about upon the one network, to cover the chapiters that were upon the top, with pomegranates: and so did he for the other chapiter. And the chapiters that were upon the top of the pillars were of lily work in the porch, four cubits. And the chapiters upon the two pillars had pomegranates also above, over against the belly which was by the network: and the pomegranates were two hundred in rows round about upon the other chapiter. And he set up the pillars in the porch of the temple: and he set up the right pillar, and called the name thereof Jachin: and he set up the left pillar, and called the name thereof Boaz. And upon the top of the pillars was lily work: so was the work of the pillars finished." (1 Kings vii. 13—22.)

How the Greek and Italian orders of architecture came to be introduced into the Masonry of the old covenant, it is difficult for us to divine; but if to preserve the teaching of the lectures it is necessary we should still have the Ionic, the Doric, and Corinthian capitals, let the three lights, as is generally the case, yet keep these ornaments for the purpose of illustration; but as representations of the three Grand Masters who presided at the building of the Temple they are decidedly incorrect. Boaz and Jachin doubtless in ancient Masonry were the two columns; their curious beauty, enriched with network, lily work, and pomegranates, claims their restoration, and our reverential respect for the great Master of our art demands their presence in a perfect Masons' Lodge. There can be no difficulty in their construction, and it will violate no law to adopt the suggestion now made. In a Grand Lodge especially, the situation of the Wardens and the form of their columns are decidedly objectionable, and out of keeping with the ritual.

The *pommels,* that are mentioned 2 Chron. iv. as being on the top of the pillars, were merely rounded knobs or balls for finish, and these, most improperly in some instances, are now represented as the celestial and terrestrial globes; a very palpable anachronism, as at the period alluded to, the theory of the rotundity of the earth was unknown. The word rendered *pommels* in the English Authorized Version, has been by some critics translated *bowls;* but as the Hebrew original does not mention these appendages further, we must conclude they were merely completing ornaments.

Holy Writ tells us that David, having been a man of blood, was not allowed to build a house to God; but the Most High reserved that honour for David's son and successor, Solomon. Hiram, King of Tyre, on the accession of Solomon, sent to him a message of congratulation, and the latter on his reply announced the intention to build a house to God's Holy Name, and desired Hiram to command cedar-trees out of Lebanon to be hewed for that purpose, for "there is not among us any that can skill to hew timber like unto the Sidonians." And Hiram gave Solomon cedar and fir trees, as he desired. For this service Solomon paid Hiram in wheat and oil. A treaty of alliance and friendship was made by the two sovereigns, by which the King of Israel was to send thirty thousand to labour in hewing the materials he required of the King of Tyre, and over these men was Adoniram. There were also fourscore thousand hewers in the mountains, with overseers to superintend their work; these, we presume, must have been the King of Tyre's subjects. For the foundation they brought great, costly, and hewed stones, which were prepared by the stone-squarers or Gebalites.

In the treaty with Hiram no mention is made of stone. The timber was from Lebanon; and wherever the stone was obtained, it was quarried and hewn with the help of the Phœnicians. In Lebanon and throughout Syria the stone is all of the same character, a kind of freestone, and still used for building.

Josephus describes the stone with which Solomon's Temple was built as "white stone." In the ancient structures of Syria, the stones were of an astonishingly large size. The sub-basement of the great temple of Baalbeck, which belonged to an earlier structure, has one stone that measures sixty-six feet in length and twelve feet in breadth and thickness; and *Wood* measured one lying in the quarry ready for removal larger still, which is calculated to weigh above 1100 tons!

Tyre and Sidon were the chief cities of Phœnicia, the people of which country appear to have been in advance of all others in the arts of commerce and ship-building; and in the fine arts rivalled the Egyptians. Sidon was termed "great" in the time of Joshua. Homer tells us that the Queen of Troy

"kept
Her mantles of all hues, accomplished works
Of fair Sidonians;"

and describes a silver goblet—

"earth
Owned not its like for elegance of form.
Skilful Sidonians had around
Embellished it."

Many other passages might be quoted to prove the repute in which they were held by the Greeks. The superiority in manufactures and commerce does not, however, form the only distinction of the Phœnicians, for they were great adepts in all the sciences of their time, particularly astronomy and arithmetical calculation.

Herein, we must consider, lay the *strength* of King Hiram. It was by the power of art and science he was enabled to aid Solomon in the raising that glorious house of God.

The Phœnicians were a branch of the Shemitic family of nations, and originated on the borders of the Red Sea; but it is not known at what period they migrated to the Mediterranean. There was constant commercial intercourse between them and the Israelites; and Tyre is repeatedly mentioned by the Hebrew prophets, who speak of its strength, wealth, beauty, and flourishing commerce. The country suffered in many wars, and its cities were despoiled by different conquerors; by Assyrian, Babylonian, Greek, Persian, and Roman; and in the Holy Wars Tyre suffered many sieges. Its fortifications were entirely razed when the Christians were expelled from the Holy Land. The Phœnicians extended their trading over all the known world. We have tolerably good evidence that they came to Cornwall for tin five centuries before our present era. Looking back through the dim vista of past ages, we can find no parallel nations with our own so fit as the Phœnicians. Their progress amid surrounding barbarism was marvellous, for until the reign of Solomon the Israelites were incessantly at war; and the Holy Scriptures tell us something of their neighbours' habits. When Abraham came from Mesopotamia to dwell in the land, it was then inhabited by the Canaanites, descendants of Canaan, the son of Ham, whose eldest son Sidon was the first governor of that part of the country bordering the seacoast, where were founded the cities of Tyre and Sidon. The whole of the land of Canaan, save this portion, was subjugated by

Joshua. We find this district called first Phœnicia by the Greeks, from Φοῖνιξ, "palm-tree[1]," which abounded in this country. Here the spies sent by Moses found a people called Anakim, who were distinguished for their strength. The invention of letters, or rather the art of writing, is attributed to Cadmus, King of the Phœnicians, B.C. 1550; and, as the formation and order of the Greek alphabet bear a close resemblance to those of the alphabets which belonged to the Shemitic race, or more especially the Phœnicians,—for these and the Jews until the time of Cyrus used the same characters,—we think with good evidence. We acknowledge there exists diversity of opinion upon this subject; it is, however, not denied that Cadmus did visit Greece, and it is said he merely introduced more convenient and suitable materials for writing; and that from the Pelasgi, an early race of their own country, they derived the knowledge of letters. Now tradition also assigns to the Pelasgi various monuments of architecture, and especially the ancient walls known by the name of Cyclopean. There are two kinds of these ancient walls; the first constructed of rude and irregular rocks of stone, laid together without mortar, and the second formed of stones regularly cut and squared. The former are denominated Cyclopean, and the latter Pelasgic. The Pelasgi, it is generally assumed, were the aborigines of Greece; and if the visit of the Phœnicians is allowed, may we not conclude that the first rude structures were the work of the natives, and the more perfect, that of the *stone-squaring* Phœnicians, the *Gebalites?* While noticing this people, it is worthy of remark, that Gebal, although it makes a very mean figure at present, was in ancient times a city and seaport of some note, and there is still remaining a ridge running into the sea, composed of huge square stones which once formed a mole.

[1] The date-tree, or palm-tree of Scripture, was emblematic of *Judea,* as we see on coins with the inscription of *Judea capta.*

There are also the ruins of a noble theatre, the semicircle of which is 100 yards across: the outside wall is nearly four yards thick, and built of very large and firm stones; which great strength has preserved it thus long from the ravages of time, and from that general ruin the Turks bring to all places where they come.

The Gebalites were, like the Sidonians, far advanced in the arts and sciences in the earliest ages of the world, and their knowledge was, in their commercial intercourse, carried to other countries. As a people the Phœnicians are dispersed and lost. In investigating the history of Zoroaster and the mysteries of the ancient Magi, we find that some acute commentators consider the Chaldeans (as the Magi were called) a foreign race in Assyria, and that they were a Shemitic people. All the ancient writers say their acquaintance with astronomy exceeded that of all others, and that their skill in all the sciences was very great. In another place we have endeavoured to show that Zoroaster, the great reformer of the Magi religion, was the Prophet Daniel, and now venture to claim for these Gebalites the foundation of the science of astronomy. In modern times the followers of the ancient religion of the Magi have been known by the appellation of *Gebers,* the derivation of which is unknown. The Gebalites were worshippers of Apollo, whom they symbolized by *fire.* Through all time, from the Magi of Chaldea down to the remnant now in the mountains of Guzerat, and as Parsees in Bombay, the Deity is symbolized in fire. Rosetti endeavours to show that Freemasons are the descendants of the Manichæans and Albigenses, who all held the same tenets. This investigation does not, however, belong to our present subject.

Strength, as the second principal support of Masonry, is physically and personally represented by the Doric column and the Senior Warden, because it is considered the strongest of the orders of architecture, and because it is the duty of the Senior

Warden to aid the Master in his duties, and to *strengthen* and support his authority. Of the Doric, our lectures thus instruct us;—It is the most ancient of all the orders, and hence is plain and natural. Its column is eight times its diameter in height, and originally had no ornaments on its capital or base. The solid composition of this Order gives it a preference where *strength* is the chief quality desired. The gigantic remains of this style in Sicily are the wonder of travellers, some of the columns being of one block of marble sixty feet high. The Parthenon was of this Order, and some of its ponderous blocks are in the British Museum.

With regard to the Senior Warden as the representative of *strength* in his Lodge, it is to be observed that by our laws the Master and Wardens govern the Lodge, and in case of the death or absence of the Master the Senior Warden summons the Lodge. It is of the utmost importance the Warden should be well skilled in the Craft, and it was intended by the United Grand Lodge, when the Constitutions were framed in 1813, the better to prepare the Master for his office, that a twelvemonth's service as Warden was essential to his election; and, although the law does not demand it, it is desirable a brother should have served a year as Junior Warden ere he attains the Senior's column, that he may be said to be in *strength* to be established in all our mysteries.

BEAUTY.

BEAUTY is symbolized by the Corinthian column, because that Order is the most beautiful and highly finished of all. This is committed to the care of the Junior Warden, because his situation in the Lodge enables him better to observe that bright luminary which at its meridian height is the beauty and glory of the day. But as representing the column of *Beauty* which supported the Temple of Solomon, we must first bestow a few remarks on Hiram the widow's son. Before we proceed farther, it is to be remarked, that in Freemasonry the number three is the most important and universal in its application of all the mystic numbers, and we find it pervading our whole ritual. There are three degrees of Ancient Craft Masonry; and there are three supports and three principal officers to a Lodge; three working tools to each degree; three greater and three lesser lights; with many other instances of the consecration of this number, besides there being three Ancient Grand Masters, of whom the last, but not the least in importance, was Hiram the widow's son.

Among the workmen sent by Hiram of Tyre to aid Solomon in raising the House of God was one whom he styles "a cunning man endued with understanding, a widow's son of the tribe of Naphtali, and his father had been a man of Tyre, a worker in brass." This was Hiram, who, it is to be noticed, although resident among the Phœnicians, and a subject of the King of Tyre, was an Israelite by parentage, his mother being one of the daughters of Dan. The narratives of the building, as related in the Books of Kings and Chronicles, somewhat differ. Hiram in the former is not mentioned until the decoration commences, while in the latter he appears in the outset, and sent with the King of Tyre's letter, which describes him "skilful to work in gold and in silver, in brass, in iron, and in stone, and in timber, in purple, in blue, and in fine linen, and in crimson; also to grave any manner of graving, and to find out every device which shall be put to him." By this and what follows, Solomon was indebted to Hiram for all the ornament; and we are disposed to conclude he was the architect of the building. It is clear that the King of Israel had no subject capable of undertaking the construction of the House he purposed to raise, and it was to the skilful men of Tyre he had recourse. From the description we must conclude the structure was of timber; "it was ceiled with fir-tree, which he overlaid with gold, and set thereon palm-trees." The beams, walls, and doors were overlaid with gold. The capitals of the pillars were carved with figures of pomegranates. In both accounts mention is made of the ornamental palm-trees which were carved in the wood with which the sanctuary was lined, and these were afterwards overlaid with gold. These palm-trees were doubtless pilasters, as that would be the form in which the palm-tree would be exhibited to most advantage.

We are not now called upon to describe the building of the Temple (as that is done in another place), but notice the peculiarities of ornament by which Hiram rendered the structure marvellous for *beauty*. It has been remarked that wherever a style of architecture originated, the imitated vegetable forms (if any) are those which nature *there* offered; but where it is borrowed, the fact is attested by the foreign character of the vegetable forms imitated or represented. The palm-tree and pomegranate were natives of Palestine, and the use of the latter as an ornament appears in none of the varied styles of architecture, and hence it must have been the distinguishing feature of the Jewish style; and with reference to the palm-tree, Sir James Hall, in his Essay on the Origin of Gothic Architecture, ingeniously refers us to interlaced wickerwork as the undoubted type of the Gothic style in all its leading forms, its arched and grained roofs, its clustered pillars, its windows and their fanciful tracery. Sir James does not mention the palm, but his drawings show how peculiarly adapted to the purpose is that graceful and elegant tree. This strengthens the theory given in another place in support of Wren's statement, that the Gothic style originated with the Freemasons on their return from the holy wars. We are warranted in believing, that on first seeing the palms some ingenious artisan must have noticed their adaptation for constructing a building where height and lightness were requisite; and it is quite probable that when the Holy City was gained, the first inquiry would be, where was Solomon's Temple placed? and next, what kind of building was it? No traces even of the third Temple remained, and the Sacred Volume was referred to. We have heard that many models in wood were wrought and brought into Europe, and some years since we read a statement of such a model being in existence at Dresden. The description in the Old Testament, combined with the growing palms, suggested the idea for the style of ecclesiastical architecture, which is unrivalled for its adaptation to the Christian Church.

The decoration of the Temple, which undoubtedly was entirely under Hiram's direction, rendered it *marvellous for beauty.* At the entrance of the sanctuary were the two remarkable, and we may say Masonic, pillars, which were of brass, hollow within, to contain the rolls of the Sacred Law: they were profusely ornamented with representations of leaves and pomegranates, lilies and network. From this a door of olive wood, and ornamented with figures of the cherubim, palms, and flowers of carved work, led into the sanctuary; this door was covered with gold, and turned on hinges of the same metal. A similar door from the sanctuary led to the Holy of Holies; and both doors were covered with a veil of linen richly embroidered. It was distinguished from all other temples of remote antiquity by the sumptuousness of detail. All this was the work of our Grand Master Hiram.

The word *beauty,* it has been observed, was first applied to objects perceptible by the sight; and by an easy transition it has been extended to objects perceptible by the hearing, as when we speak of beautiful music, a beautiful voice, &c. Therefore we may say *beauty* is that quality in visible objects in consequence of which their forms and colours are agreeable to the human mind.

With regard to works of constructive art which belongs to our present purpose, it is an essential feature of *beauty* that the adaptation of means to the end is observable, and that there is a similar correspondence in the constituent parts.

Every part of a building has therefore its peculiar form and *beauty,* dependent on its destination. For this reason all ornament in architecture should be subordinate to use, and should grow out of and be suggested by it; whence professed architects, with whom the idea of decoration is predominant, often fail in their attempts to produce *beauty,* and in many cases seem rather to adapt the building to the ornament, than the ornament to the building. Accordingly it has been observed that civil engineers, whose attention is solely directed to the *use* of that which they plan, often construct more *beautiful* buildings than persons with whom *beauty* is the chief consideration. And generally it may be observed that all ornament, if accumulated to an excessive degree, either from a love of gaudy magnificence, or for the sake of ostentation, is devoid of beauty;—

"'Tis use alone that sanctifies expense,
And splendour borrows all its rays from sense."

The *Corinthian Order,* to which the column of *Beauty* belongs, is one of the three ancient Greek Orders of architecture; its shaft is taller in its proportion than that of either of the others, and its capital is profusely ornamented. Without entering into a detailed description, the very pretty story, which Vitruvius tells us, of its origin will sufficiently explain the style of the capital. Callimachus accidentally passing the tomb of a young lady, perceived a basket of toys which had been left there by her nurse—perhaps as a votive offering of affection—covered with a tile, and placed over an acanthus root; as the branches grew they encompassed the basket, till, arriving at the tile, they met with an obstruction, and turned downwards. Callimachus was struck with the object, and he made a drawing of it; the base of the capital he made to represent the basket, the abacus the tile, and the volutes the bended leaves. Vitruvius is the only architect of the ancients whose writings have come down to us; he flourished during the reign of Augustus, about the birth of Christ.

As *wisdom* is practically represented by the Master, so *strength* and *beauty,* the pillars that complete the triform supports of a Mason's Lodge, are exhibited by the Wardens as representatives of the two Hirams by whose power and talent Solomon was enabled to construct and beautify the house of God, and *in strength to establish it.* The union of these two qualities in his holy tabernacle is proclaimed by David in the Psalms, "*Strength and beauty* are in his sanctuary;" and 1 Chron. xvi., in the psalm of thanksgiving which he composed for Asaph on the Ark being placed in the tabernacle, he calls on the people to "seek the Lord in his *strength,*" and he tells them that "glory and honour are in his presence; *strength* and gladness in his place." "God is our refuge and *strength.*" (Ps. xlvi.) In Ps. lxxxiv., which is expressive of confidence, "Blessed is the man whose *strength* is in thee." The *strength* which is referred to with commendation or praise in the Sacred Volume is Godlike majesty and puissance; for mere brute force is set at nought, in Ps. xxxiii.—"There is no king saved by the multitude of an host: a mighty man is not delivered by much *strength.* An horse is a vain thing for safety: neither shall he deliver any by his great *strength.*"

Wisdom, strength, and beauty of Nature. From the form of vegetables we have some of the choicest of our ornaments, and have taken some of the most useful hints in architecture. Smeaton, who first succeeded in fixing upon the dangerous rock of the Eddystone a lighthouse that has resisted for a hundred years the violence of the sea, and, as far as human calculation may venture to surmise, will endure many centuries, moulded its contour from the bole of an oak that had withstood the tempests of ages.

To conclude:—The Hebrew word נוה, *naveh,* which signifies *beauty* in some places, refers to a dwelling or the tabernacle.

Singers were appointed by Jehoshaphat to "praise the Lord in the *beauty* of holiness;" and David also says, "Worship the Lord in the *beauty* of holiness"—which by the marginal explanation is "in his holy sanctuary." From these passages, and many more might be selected, the designations our Masonic supports received from our ancient brethren, are proofs of the diligent use they made of the Sacred Volume of God's Law; and thus a study of our Institution and its teaching must infallibly require a frequent and careful perusal of the Book of Life. There we are instructed that the fear of the Lord is the beginning of *wisdom,* and happy is the man that findeth it. Let us in *strength* be clothed in the armour of righteousness, and endeavour to grow more and more into the likeness of God; and to whatever station the providence of God may please to call us, let us adorn it with the *beauty* of holiness. If thus, to use the language of David, *"we set God always before us"* (Ps. xvi.), like him we shall not be moved. The apprehension of his omnipresence will be the guard of our conduct and the support of our steps here; and the enjoyment of that presence our exceeding great reward hereafter.

CHAPTER XXIV.

FAITH, HOPE, AND CHARITY.

THE three great principles upon which our Order is founded, are Brotherly Love, Relief, and Truth, and their importance is inculcated in our Lectures. The first renders us affectionate and kind, the second generous, and the third just.

In Craft Masonry the supporting pillars of the Lodge, as already described, are the three architectural columns denominated Wisdom, Strength, and Beauty; these, in the Ancient and Accepted Rite, are displayed by three others of triangular form, and representing the virtues of *Faith, Hope,* and *Charity.*

In his second Epistle, St. Peter exhorts his readers to the practice of what we are accustomed to call the cardinal virtues: "add to your faith virtue; to virtue knowledge; to knowledge temperance; to temperance patience; to patience godliness; to godliness brotherly kindness; and to brotherly kindness charity."

These virtues are enforced in various parts of the rituals, and enlarged upon in the first lecture of Craft Masonry. A more wide extension is, however, given to them in those degrees that have especial reference to Christianity (the degrees being not antagonistic to the Craft Degrees, but in reality an expansion of them). The great duties of man to God, his neighbour, and himself, are the precepts most strongly enforced; hence the points to direct the steps of the aspirant to higher honours are Faith, Hope, and Charity.

FAITH.

FAITH is the basis of all Christian virtues, and is defined to be a disposition of mind by which we hold for certain the matter affirmed. The Faith that produces good works gives life to a righteous man. It may be considered, either as proceeding from God, who reveals his truths to man, or from man, who assents to and obeys the truths of God. Faith is taken also for a firm confidence in God, by which, relying on his promises, we address ourselves without hesitation to Him, whether for pardon or other blessings. Faith is a reliance on testimony: if it be human testimony, in reference to human things, it is not entitled to reception until after examination and confirmation. Human testimony, in reference to divine things, must also be scrupulously investigated before it be received and acted upon, since the grossest of all deceptions have been imposed on mankind in the Name of God. Nor is testimony assuming to be Divine, entitled to our adherence, or affection, or obedience, until its character is proved to be genuine and really from Heaven. The more genuine it is, the more readily it will undergo and sustain the trial, and the more clearly will its character appear. But after a testimony, a maxim, or a command is proved to be Divine, it does not become a creature so ignorant and so feeble as man, to doubt its possibility, to dispute the obedience to which it is entitled, or to question the beneficial consequences attached to it, though not immediately apparent to human discernment.

Faith is the full assurance or personal conviction of the reality of things not seen; it looks backward to past ages as well as forward to futurity. By Faith we believe that the world was originally created by God; though we can form no conception of, much less can we see, the matter out of which it was composed. By Faith we believe in the existence of ancient cities, as Jerusalem, Babylon, &c.; also of distant places, as Egypt, &c.; also of persons formerly living, as Abraham, David,

Jesus Christ, &c. Faith anticipates things never seen as yet: so Noah by Faith built the ark, although no general deluge had ever then been witnessed; so Moses, actuated by Faith in the descent of the Messiah from Israel, quitted the honours and pleasures of Egypt; and so every pious man, believing what God has promised He is able to perform, looks forward with realizing belief in the existence of heaven and hell; of rewards and punishments beyond the grave, not such as are restricted to this world, but such as coincide with the immortality of the soul, and with the power and wisdom of the Supreme and Universal Judge.

St. Paul's words in the original are, "Faith is the firm and assured expectation of things hoped for, the evidence of things not seen." Those things not seen by sense, and yet made manifest, are the being of God, and the rewards of the life to come. Faith is that firm conviction of the promises and threatenings of God, and the certain reality of the rewards and punishments of the life to come, which enables a man in spite of all temptations to obey his Creator in expectation of an invisible reward hereafter.

"Faith, like a simple unsuspecting child,
Securely resting on its mother's arm,
Reposing every care upon her God,
Sleeps on his bosom, and expects no harm:

"Receives with joy the promises He makes,
Nor questions of his purpose or his power;
And does not doubting ask 'Can this be so?'
The Lord has said it, and there needs no more.

"However deep be the mysterious word,
However dark, she disbelieves it not:
Where reason would examine, Faith obeys,
And 'It is written,' answers every doubt.

"As evening's pale and solitary star
But brightens while the darkness gathers round,
So Faith, unmoved amidst surrounding storms,
Is fairest seen in darkness most profound."

HOPE.

Hope is distinguished from Faith by its desire of good only, and by its reference to futurity. Faith contemplates evil as well as good, and refers to things past as well as to things future; but this is not the case with Hope. We are therefore said to be "saved by hope," by the hope, or conviction, or desire, of unseen things; and we read of the "full assurance of hope," which may be taken as synonymous with cheerful and earnest expectation. In the New Testament it is generally taken for hope in the Messiah, hope of eternal blessings, hope of a future resurrection. "Experience produceth hope, and hope maketh not ashamed."

Hope,—which is a confident expectation of future good,—like all other graces, admits of degrees; it is sometimes feeble, but when it is the result of experience, it is confident and proof against shame or hesitation; it is sometimes limited to things near or to things likely; but it also extends beyond this world, to possessions laid up in heaven, to glory, immortality, and eternal life. It is repeatedly connected with patience, with waiting, with expectation, with rejoicing, and with reason; for the hope of a pious man, however it may refer to Divine things, or be founded on Divine promises, or be derived from, or promoted by, the Sacred Spirit, is yet a reasonable hope, and combines purity of heart and life, that is, obedience, with devout and firm reliance on the promises and perfections of God.

The hope of Israel was, the end of the Babylonish Captivity, the Coming of the Messiah, and the happiness of Heaven. The prisoners of hope (Zech. ix. 12) are the Israelites who were in captivity, but in hopes of deliverance. The Lord is the Hope of the righteous, "their hope shall not be confounded;" "the hope of the ungodly shall perish," it shall be without effect, or they shall live and die without hope.

The poet Young is eloquent in its commendation:—

"Hope, of all passions, most befriends us here;
Passions of prouder name befriend us less.
Joy has her tears, and Transport has her death:
Hope, like a cordial, innocent though strong,
Man's heart at once inspirits and serenes,
Nor makes him pay his wisdom for his joys.
'Tis all our present state can safely bear;
Health to the frame, and vigour to the mind,
A joy attempered, a chastised delight,
Like the fair summer evening, mild and sweet.
'Tis man's full cup, his Paradise below."

The Greek fable is too instructive to be omitted:—

"In the house of Epimetheus there was a large box which an oracle had forbidden to be opened. Pandora, full of curiosity, lifted the fatal lid, and immediately all evils issued forth, and spread themselves over the earth. The terrified female at length regained sufficient presence of mind to close the lid, and Hope on this was alone secured. There is a curious analogy between this more ancient tradition and the account of the fall of our first parents, as detailed by the inspired penman. Prometheus, *forethought,* may denote the purity and wisdom of our early progenitor before he yielded to temptation; Epimetheus, *afterthought,* indicates his change of resolution, and his yielding to the arguments of Eve; which the poet expresses by saying, that Epimetheus received Pandora, after he had been cautioned by Prometheus not to do it. The curiosity of Pandora violates the injunction of the oracle, as our first parent Eve disregarded the commands of her Maker. Pandora, moreover, the author of all human woes, is the author likewise of their chief and, in fact, only solace; for she closed the lid of the fatal box before Hope could escape; and this she did, according to Hesiod, *in compliance with the will of Jove.* May not Hope thus secured be that hope and expectation of a Redeemer, which has been traditional from the earliest ages of the world? Even so our first parents commit the fatal sin of disobedience; but from the seed of the woman, the first to offend, was to spring One who should be the hope and only solace of our race." (Barker's Lempriere.)

CHARITY.

Our Grand Master Moses, in stating the law for the institution of the Jubilee, or Year of Liberty, which was to take place every fiftieth year, gives us the earliest injunction in the law of Charity and beneficence. "If thy brother be waxen poor and fallen into decay with thee, thou shalt relieve him; yea, though he be a stranger or sojourner, that he may live with thee."

Thus under the Mosaic dispensation there was an express exhortation to the practice of the law of Charity; and St. Peter, in a regular and artificial gradation, has connected all the several virtues that form the life and complete the character of a good man under the new covenant: "Add to your *faith virtue;* and to virtue *knowledge;* and to knowledge *temperance;* and to temperance *patience;* and to patience *godliness;* and to godliness *brotherly kindness;* and to brotherly kindness CHARITY." Charity, or universal benevolence, is added as a supplement to brotherly love, and closes the catalogue of the cardinal virtues. Charity, in this sense, comprehends all the social virtues which depend upon our relation to one another as men, connected by various ties in life, as relations, friends, and neighbours. But so general is the law of good-will towards men, that it extends to our very enemies. St. Paul best shows the nature and extent of this virtue: "Charity suffereth long, and is kind; charity envieth not; charity vaunteth not itself, is not puffed up, doth not behave itself unseemly, seeketh not her own, is not easily provoked; thinketh no evil; rejoiceth not in iniquity, but rejoiceth in the truth; beareth all things; believeth all things; hopeth all things; endureth all things."

How extensive is this virtue, and how fruitful of blessing to mankind! It cuts up by the root all the causes of contention and mischief. It drives from the heart of man pride, hatred, and envy, impatience and anger, animosity, suspicion, and jealousy. It plants in room of them, the love of truth and justice, integrity, equity, kindness and forbearance, a courteous and obliging bearing. By the comprehensive virtue of Charity we may secure good order, peace, and happiness in this world, whilst it opens to us the prospect of a better.

Now St. Paul has determined that "though they bestow all their goods to feed the poor," yet if they have not the charity to act in other respects as they ought, "it will profit them nothing." But still, although almsgiving is by no means the whole of beneficence, yet it is an essential part in those whom God hath qualified for it. And He hath given them all things richly and in plenty, not merely for themselves to enjoy in a vulgar sense, but that others may enjoy a due share of them; and they the pleasure of imparting it,—the worthiest and highest enjoyment of wealth that can be.

In general, both our charity and our generosity should bear some decent and liberal proportion to our abilities; for if we are deficient, the poor widow with her two mites will far outdo us in that very virtue by which our Maker justly expects we should be distinguished. Nor is it sufficient to give plentifully according to our means; but we should do it on every needful occasion, speedily, and not stay till the circumstances of the poor applicant are beyond recovery. Our Grand Master Solomon says, "Say not unto thy neighbour, Go, and come again to-morrow, and I will give." (Prov. iii. 28.)

By the practice of these virtues, we shall feel how delightful it is to think, that by our means the miseries of God's creation are lessened.

Charity, the most lovely of virtues, represents others as lovely as possible. It does not merely let us see an object as it is; it is a kind of sunshine, which brightens what it lets us see: whereas ill-nature passes over all the shining parts of a man's character, and dwells entirely on the dark side of it, as a painter of low rank throws those beauties into darkness and shade which his eye cannot endure to behold, because his mind cannot reach them.

It is no unusual thing to hear some men complaining that their abilities to do good, and to abound in works of charity, are cramped within a narrow sphere, though their inclinations are very large and extensive. Now if these men are in earnest, there is one kind of charity which will not be expensive to themselves, and yet endear them to their fellow-creatures. Their worldly circumstances may not enable them to cherish merit by their generosity, and to relieve distress by almsgiving, but this charitable office is daily in their power,—to cast in shade their neighbour's misconduct, and to set out in the most advantageous point of view their good qualities; to extenuate their failings, and to do justice to their virtues; to draw an obscure character into the light, and to rescue an injured one from obloquy! Silver or gold they may have little or none, but such as they have they may give, namely, what is better than silver and gold, a good name and reputation to their neighbours.

The truly Masonic virtues of Beneficence and Charity are enforced in the most impressive manner on our first admission to the light of Masonry, and at every meeting the charitable institutions of the Order are prominently brought before the Fraternity; and although many pens have in powerful language enforced these virtues, we can find none more eloquently than the poet *Prior*.

"CHARITY, decent, modest, easy, kind,
Softens the high and rears the abject mind:
Knows with just reins and gentle hand to guide
Betwixt vile shame and arbitrary pride.
Not soon provoked, she easily forgives,
And much she suffers, as she much believes;
Soft peace she brings wherever she arrives,
She builds our quiet, as she forms our lives,
Lays the rough paths of peevish nature even,
And opens in each heart a little heaven.
Each other gift which God or man bestows,
His proper bound and due restriction knows;
To one fixt purpose dedicates its power,
And finishing its act exists no more.
Thus, in obedience to what Heaven decrees,
Knowledge shall fail, and prophecy shall cease:
But lasting Charity's more ample sway,
Nor bound by time, nor subject to decay,
An happy triumph shall for ever live,
And endless good diffuse, and endless praise receive."

INDEX.

THE END.

www.ingramcontent.com/pod-product-compliance
Lightning Source LLC
LaVergne TN
LVHW020519100826
845148LV00010B/1277

* 9 7 8 1 6 0 5 3 2 0 5 2 6 *